FREEDOM AND AUTHORITY

By GERALD R. CRAGG

FREEDOM
AND
AUTHORITY

A Study of English Thought
in the Early Seventeenth Century

THE WESTMINSTER PRESS
Philadelphia

Book Design by Dorothy Alden Smith

Published by The Westminster Press®
Philadelphia, Pennsylvania

PRINTED IN THE UNITED STATES OF AMERICA

Library of Congress Cataloging in Publication Data

Cragg, Gerald Robertson.
    Freedom and authority.

    Bibliography: p.
    1. Authority (Religion)—History. 2. Liberty—History. 3. England—Intellectual life—17th century. 4. Catholics in England. 5. Religious thought—England. I. Title.
BR757.C85   209'.42   75-4946
ISBN 0-664-20738-3

CONTENTS

PREFACE

FREEDOM AND AUTHORITY do not exhaust the intellectual concerns of the seventeenth century. They certainly embrace a large proportion of them. The problems connected with both these concepts are very old; at the beginning of the seventeenth century they began to assume the forms in which we have been familiar with them ever since. In political theory the prerogatives of sovereignty were challenged in the name of the liberties of the people. Intellectually the prestige of old assumptions was called in question by the insights and methods of the new science. Traditional ways of interpreting the universe were reexamined, but they still retained their hold on men's minds. Often old and new patterns of thought persisted side by side. A great deal of time and attention was devoted to religious issues. Catholics and Protestants, Arminians and Calvinists, Anglicans and Puritans bitterly assailed one another, and many of the subjects on which they differed were closely related to the nature of authority or the scope of freedom.

Freedom and authority are persistent issues. Seldom have they demanded so much attention or appeared in so many forms as they do today. In many respects our problems have a closer affinity with those of the seventeenth century than with those of the nineteenth. Many of the areas in which the issues became acute three centuries ago are those in which authority is now requiring closer examination and more careful definition. The seventeenth century was a revolutionary age; so is ours. Today freedom and authority are interrelated in ways that often parallel the experience of our seventeenth-century predecessors. Political and social liberties were limited then, as they are now, by restrictions from which the men of the nineteenth century were largely free. Enterprise is subject to regulation in a wide variety of ways that the subjects of the early Stuarts would have found familiar but that our Victorian ancestors believed they had left behind them forever. It is generally conceded that freedom operates within a context of responsibility which both simplifies and complicates the task of interpretation. Too much emphasis on

7

resemblances can, of course, distort the picture. The men of the seventeenth century faced their problems, not ours, and there is no simple way of applying their solutions to our situation. But history can possibly help us to see the issues of our age in clearer perspective.

I have concentrated attention on the first forty years of the seventeenth century. This period possesses a large degree of unity. After 1640 the situation changes radically; the revolutionary tendencies latent in the first part of the century find explosive expression. For the most part, therefore, I have restricted myself to works published during the first forty years of the century, but I have not hesitated to trace in the Elizabethan period the antecedents of trends that found full expression under the early Stuarts. Occasionally I have ventured into the decades between 1640 and 1660 in order to show how tendencies at work in the earlier years reached more complete development when certain restraints were lifted. My references are almost entirely to works by seventeenth-century authors. I have, of course, learned a great deal from many recent writers; if I do not quote from them more often, it is not due to any lack of appreciation but to a fear lest my pages be overburdened with authorities.

It is a privilege to thank those who have helped me in this task. Much of the initial research was completed during a sabbatical leave, for which I am grateful to the trustees of Andover Newton Theological School. Librarians have assisted me at every turn. In particular I wish to thank the staffs of the British Museum, the Cambridge University Library, the libraries of Trinity and Emmanuel Colleges, Cambridge, Dr. Williams Library, and the Houghton Library of Harvard University. As always my wife has helped me in innumerable ways: by gathering material, by typing the early drafts of the manuscript, by criticizing the work at every stage, and by constant encouragement.

G.R.C.

I

THE INTELLECTUAL BACKGROUND OF THE AGE

THE PROBLEM of authority is as old as human society. So is the correlative problem of freedom. Thomas Hobbes was satisfied that any discussion of the commonwealth must begin with "the rights of sovereigns"; only then could it usefully proceed to "the liberty of subjects." The reason for this seemed obvious. "The final cause, end or design of men (who naturally love liberty and dominion over others) in the introduction of that restraint upon themselves (in which we see them live in commonwealths) is the foresight of their own preservation, and of a more contented life thereby." [1] So "for attaining of peace and conservation of themselves thereby," they created "an artificial man, which we call commonwealth," and they found that they had inevitably circumscribed their freedom. [2]

Hobbes's purpose was to explore the theory of the state. Political authority had become a subject of absorbing concern. When he wrote his *Leviathan,* the civil war was a very recent experience. The structure of government had been shaken to its foundations. To prevent the recurrence of such disasters, Hobbes felt compelled to define as sharply as possible the rights of sovereignty, and then to buttress them against the danger of renewed infringement. He stated his position with great cogency; he won few converts. He violated the theological and ecclesiastical susceptibilities of most of his fellow countrymen. He related authority to the possession of power, and consequently he antagonized the defeated royalists. Many Englishmen were intent on defining the measure of freedom that the citizen could claim. The radicals of the Interregnum insisted that the ordinary man must be freed from the shackles of an ancient servitude. By the middle of the seventeenth century, political authority and civil freedom had been pushed to the forefront of national debate. The civil war, so far from solving the problems involved in these

[1] Thomas Hobbes, *Leviathan,* Pt. II, Ch. XVIII.
[2] *Ibid.*, Pt. II, Ch. XXI.

9

questions, had intensified them. But the constitutional issues did not stand alone, nor were they entirely the result of the struggles of the early part of the century. The ineptitude of James I and Charles I undoubtedly aggravated them, and they gained added gravity because freedom and authority were topics canvassed in other areas as well, but in various forms the issues had been present throughout the sixteenth century. The great Tudors were vigorous monarchs, with a strong feeling for authority. They were not despots. The Elizabethans believed that they enjoyed a reasonable measure of freedom, but they knew that the queen's will was a formidable factor which they would be foolish to ignore. Their liberties were not circumscribed merely by political considerations. Freedom of every kind was effective only within a social context, and was therefore governed by forces that were partly traditional, partly pragmatic. Many of the most hotly debated political problems of the age had religious, even theological, overtones. Men were beginning to ask awkward questions about conscience, though as yet the current answers were often determined by the prevailing view of social obligation. The freedom a person could claim was defined by the duties he had to accept. The citizen was a churchman; the converse was equally true. "There is not any man of the Church of England," wrote Richard Hooker, "but the same is a member of the commonwealth, nor any member of the commonwealth which is not also of the Church of England." [3] Divisions among churchmen threatened to become conflicts between citizens. Since uniformity in the church meant unity in the state, dissent was dangerous. Catholics were persecuted because their loyalty was suspect. The Puritans, whose loyalty was effusive, were harried because they challenged the polity of the church— and to the Elizabethans that suggested dangerous possibilities. It might be argued that neither the Puritans nor the Catholics were advocates of any comprehensive measure of religious freedom. Both were committed to doctrines which severely restricted the number that could be saved; both felt they had good grounds for believing that they were the special recipients of divine favor. Queen Elizabeth, who was impatient of dogmatism in others and who never revealed any intense doctrinal convictions of her own, at least maintained authority and freedom in some kind of equipoise. She demanded obedience, but she was determined "to open no windows into men's souls." Any degree of toleration presupposed a balance between contending forces and beliefs. Elizabeth compelled her countrymen to take some account of the difficulties involved in maintaining sovereignty and yet preserving freedom.

With Elizabeth's death one age ended and another began. Contemporaries felt as much and freely said so. She bequeathed her problems to her successor, and James had his own way of complicating the relations of freedom and authority. Charles aggravated existing tensions to such a

[3] Richard Hooker, *Of the Laws of Ecclesiastical Polity*, Bk. VIII, Ch. i, 2.

degree that men despaired of finding a solution less drastic than civil war. Thus in the political realm the crisis of authority reached violent proportions. In other areas it had implications that were equally revolutionary. In the course of the seventeenth century the modern intellectual outlook began to emerge. The change from the old to the new cannot, of course, be dated with precision. We can measure the magnitude of the transformation that was taking place if we compare the works published late in the century with those that appeared at the beginning. The cool detachment of the Marquis of Halifax belongs to a different world of thought and feeling from the dogmatic confidence of King James I. Locke and Hooker appeal to different concepts and express them in very different ways. But there are parallels as well as contrasts. The earlier writers not only reflect the old era, they also anticipate the new. Hooker relies heavily on Aquinas, but he uses him to establish positions akin to those of Locke and even of Burke. On the threshold of one of the most revolutionary periods in intellectual history, the old and the new jostled each other in uneasy proximity. This explains the sense of crisis that oppressed many of the greatest figures in the early part of the seventeenth century. It accounts for many of the problems inseparable from the discussion of both freedom and authority.

Shakespeare, Ralegh, Donne, and their contemporaries lived in an age when the old world was far from dead and the new world was struggling to be born. The intellectual background of these men was often compounded of seemingly incongruous combinations of the ancient and the modern. Even the greatest authors were often strangely traditional in outlook. They thought and wrote in a context molded by centuries of Christian theology. Sin and salvation, man's fall and redemption, the beginning of all things in creation and the consummation of human destiny in heaven or hell—these formed the background of everybody's thought. Other ingredients were already clamoring for recognition, but the established intellectual patterns were surprisingly persistent. Some of Ralegh's contemporaries accused him of atheistic tendencies, but the Puritans of the next generation found his writings uniquely edifying and congenial. They hailed him as an author whose interpretation of the created world confirmed their deepest convictions.

> In the glorious light of heaven we perceive a shadow of [God's] divine countenance; in his merciful provision for all that live his manifold goodness; and lastly, in creating and making existent the world universal, by the absolute art of his own Word, his power and almightiness; which power, light, virtue, wisdom and goodness, being all but attributes of one simple essence and one God, we in all admire and in part discern *per speculum creaturarum*, that is, in the disposition, order and variety of celestial and terrestrial bodies; the terrestrial in strange and manifold diversi-

ties; the celestial in their beauty and magnitude, which in their continual and contrary motions are neither repugnant, intermixed, nor confounded. By these potent effects we approach to the knowledge of the omnipotent cause, and by those motions their almighty mover.[4]

If the universe was created by wisdom, it was assuredly controlled by order. The intense and unremitting preoccupation with order was not due simply to a preference for cosmic tidiness. The threat of chaos was near and always terrifying. The memory of the barons' wars was still fresh, and men realized how unstable and precarious was the balance of social forces. The fabric of society might easily crumble and all the bulwarks of security collapse.

> 'Tis all in pieces, all coherence gone;
> All just supply, and all relation:
> Prince, subject, father, son, are things forgot.[5]

The confusion that threatened the inner world of the human spirit found its counterpart in the tempests that disrupted the outer world of nature. The storm on the heath in *King Lear* owed its harrowing impact in part to the demonstration that order both in man and in his environment could be engulfed by confusion, but far more terrifying was the implicit threat of cosmic dissolution. The mind quailed at the thought that Providence itself might fail. Thus order was all the more precious because it seemed to be precarious. In Ulysses' famous speech on "degree" he emphasized the disastrous consequences that follow when the essential elements of balance and priority—in nature or in society—are disrupted.

> . . . when the planets
> In evil mixture to disorder wander,
> What plagues and what portents, what mutiny,
> What raging of the sea, shaking of earth,
> Commotion in the winds, frights, changes, horrors,
> Divert and crack, rend and deracinate
> The unity and married calm of states
> Quite from their fixture! O, when degree is shaked,
> Which is the ladder to all high designs,
> The enterprise is sick! How could communities,
> Degrees in schools and brotherhoods in cities,
> Peaceful commerce from dividable shores,
> The primogenitive and due of birth,
> Prerogative of age, crown, sceptres, laurels,
> But by degree, stand in authentic place?

---

[4] Sir Walter Ralegh, *The History of the World*, Bk. I, Ch. I.
[5] John Donne, "An Anatomie of the World," lines 213–215, *The Poems of John Donne*, p. 214.

> Take but degree away, untune that string,
> And, hark, what discord follows! [6]

The order that underlies all things manifests itself in a variety of forms. Hooker detected it in the system of laws that controls phenomena at different levels and preserves inviolate the consistency of the universe. "So that no certain end could ever be attained unless the actions whereby it is attained were regular; that is to say, made suitable, fit and correspondent unto their end, by some canon, rule or law. Which thing doth first take place in the works even of God himself." [7]

Order manifests itself in harmony. The smooth and perfect functioning of the universe finds glorious expression in the music of the spheres,[8] but it is reflected in other and humbler ways. "For there is a music," said Sir Thomas Browne, "wherever there is a harmony, order or proportion; and thus far we may maintain the music of the spheres: for those well-ordered motions, and regular paces, though they give no sound unto the ear, yet to the understanding they strike a note most full of harmony." [9] Proportion led from harmony to symmetry, and here the order in the world around man found fullest expression within man himself. "Man is all symmetry," said George Herbert.[10]

But before examining in detail the prevailing interpretation of man's role, we must note how fully the image of the chain of being gathered up many of the most popular concepts of the age. It was sufficiently comprehensive to provide a safe shelter for many of the traditional ideas that man's intellectual progress had already placed in jeopardy. Donne, who was well abreast of new scientific developments, referred in his sermons not merely to the celestial sphere but to the characteristic medieval interpretation of the elements that constitute the earth.[11] George Jenney, an intelligent layman, described how God, having created the four elements, assigned to them their distinctive "forms," and established a proper and necessary balance between them.[12] In preaching on obedience, Francis Holyoke laid the foundation for his social theory by describing the way the elements function. Some rise to a higher plane, others sink to a lower one; in just the same way there are superiors and inferiors among men. "For in the order of the universal," he continued,

> all creatures are subordinate unto their superiors, until they
> come to the highest supreme power. Among the elements the
> earth is under the water, the water the air, the air the element of

---

[6] William Shakespeare, *Troilus and Cressida,* Act I, Sc. iii.
[7] Hooker, *Laws of Ecclesiastical Polity,* Bk. I, Ch. ii, 1.
[8] Cf. Shakespeare, *The Merchant of Venice,* Act V, Sc. i.
[9] Sir Thomas Browne, *Religio Medici,* Pt. II, §8. Cf. John Milton, "At a Solemn Music."
[10] George Herbert, "Man," *The Poems of George Herbert.*
[11] Donne, *The Sermons of John Donne,* VII, 71.
[12] George Jenney, *A Catholike Conference,* p. 57.

fire, and that to the orb of the moon, and every planet with their orbs one under another, and all the celestial bodies differ one from another in glory and dignity, which order the superior bodies by their influences and the elements by their alterations do not only bring perfection unto the whole, but is the preservation of the whole.[13]

The elements in nature were parallel to the humors in man. The subjects of James I were fascinated by the grandeur and misery of man, and many (perhaps most) of them found that they could explore the human dilemma with greatest profit if they remembered man's place in the hierarchy of being. "What a piece of work is a man!" cried Hamlet, and forthwith assigned him his proper place in the chain of being. Man is "like an angel"; he is "the paragon of animals." [14] He resembles the creatures immediately above him and he shares the existence of the order just below. He partakes of the nature of both, but remains distinctively himself. In *The Tempest*, Prospero, for all his mastery of the spirit world, is still a man, while Caliban, in spite of his outward form, finally falls on the wrong side of the frontier that divides the human from the bestial.

The great dramatists and the serious moralists of the age were intensely aware of man's place in the hierarchy of being. But how, they asked, does his mind function? To what extent does he reflect the nature of the wider world of which he forms a tiny part? It was natural that a whole series of handbooks on psychology should make their appearance, but it could hardly be anticipated that they would culminate in Burton's *The Anatomy of Melancholy*—according to Sir William Osler, the most remarkable medical work ever written by a layman.[15] Man, it was often noted, constituted the link that joined together the worlds of matter and spirit. He is

a little world made cunningly
Of Elements, and an angelic sprite.[16]

"We are only that amphibious piece between a corporeal and spiritual essence, that middle form that links those two together, and makes good the method of God and nature, that jumps not from extremes, but unites the incompatible distances by some middle and participating natures; . . . thus is man that great and true amphibium whose nature is disposed to live not only like other creatures in diverse elements, but in divided and distinguished worlds." [17] From this it was a short step to that favorite

---

[13] Francis Holyoke, *A Sermon of Obedience*, pp. 3–4.
[14] Shakespeare, *Hamlet*, Act II, Sc. ii. Cf. Hooker, *Laws of Ecclesiastical Polity*, Bk. I, Ch. vi, 1–3.
[15] Cf. *Oxford Bibliographical Society Proceedings and Papers*, Vol. I, Pt. III. Far less recondite testimony to the interest in melancholy and in violent passion is provided by *Hamlet* or *The Duchess of Malfi*.
[16] Donne, "Holy Sonnets, V," *Poems*, p. 296.
[17] T. Browne, *Religio Medici*, Pt. I, §34.

thought of man as the microcosm of the world. In small compass he epitomizes what the universe manifests on a much grander scale.[18] Ralegh pointed out that the distinguishable parts of man's physique correspond to the physical structure of the world—our flesh to dust, our bones to rocks, our blood to brooks and rivers, "the beauty of our youth to the flowers of the spring." The passion for correspondences found endless scope in such comparisons. "The seven ages of man resemble the seven planets, whereof our infancy is compared to the moon . . . ; the second age to Mercury, wherein we are taught and instructed; our third age to Venus, the days of love, desire and vanity; the fourth to the sun, the strong, flourishing and beautiful age of man's life; the fifth to Mars." [19]

The familiar patterns of thought, it is clear, were governed by metaphors rather than fashioned as concepts. Favorite images are not only traditional but persistent, and even in the middle years of the seventeenth century we find Sir Thomas Browne elaborating in *The Garden of Cyrus* the significance of the quincunx, "artificially, naturally, mystically considered." Much of the imagery popular at the time is clearly related to medieval ways of understanding the world. But meanwhile the new was insistently pressing in, taking its place beside the old, challenging and gradually displacing it. On the eve of the seventeenth century, John Case published a commentary on Aristotle's physics that might appropriately have been written two centuries earlier,[20] yet at the same time Bacon was pondering his "Great Instauration." In *The Advancement of Learning,* Bacon not only surveyed the obstacles that traditional patterns of thought erected in the path of progress, but boldly set forth a program that would revolutionize human knowledge. The tensions created by this clash of ideas can easily be imagined. In Donne's familiar words, "and new philosophy calls all in doubt." [21] Men clung to old ideas and only diffidently began to venture into unfamiliar but exciting regions. The varied and often incongruous strands of thought in Lord Herbert of Cherbury's *De Veritate* reflect the confusion and perplexity that were so rife in the early seventeenth century. The Puritans held unquestioningly to an Augustinian interpretation of life, but they were also unusually receptive to new scientific theories. They preferred the new logic of Ramus to the old system of Aristotle. They were interested in new discoveries and in the experimental method which might lead to them. They proposed that at

---

[18] Robert Burton, *The Anatomy of Melancholy,* Pt. I, Sec. I, Mem. I, Subs. I. Even in poetry the comparison between the world and man is worked out: e.g., Phineas Fletcher, "The Purple Island." Francis Bacon was critical of the concept: *The Advancement of Learning,* Bk. II, II. But note Samuel Purchas, in *Purchas his Pilgrim,* pp. 25–26: "This body is a microcosm and created after the rest, as an epitome of the whole universe and truest map of the world, a summary and compendious other world."

[19] Ralegh, *The History of the World,* Bk. I, Ch. II, 5.

[20] John Case, *Lapsis philosophicum* (1599).

[21] Donne, "An Anatomie of the World," line 205, *Poems,* p. 213.

the universities the traditional medieval disciplines should give way to a drastically revised pattern of studies—one looking to the future, not to the past.[22] But their writings illustrate how stubbornly they clung to the old. John Preston was not only a great Puritan preacher, but for a time he was a powerful influence in the circle of Charles I and the Duke of Buckingham. He was preacher to Lincoln's Inn and master of Emmanuel College, Cambridge. He was well aware of the trends in intellectual circles, yet his illustrations are often purely medieval. "The meteors have matter enough in the vapours themselves to carry them above the earth, but not enough to unite to the element of fire; therefore they fall and return to their first principles."[23] Thomas Adams, another distinguished Puritan preacher, claimed that "the cause of the megrim is the ascending of many vaporous humours, hot and cold, by the arteries."[24] Perhaps a preacher's illustrations should be treated with reserve; after all, his chief concern is to help his hearers grasp a moral or spiritual truth with the aid of a fact so familiar that its meaning need not be labored. The case is surely different with John Bastwick, a physician of Puritan sympathies and a progressive outlook. He was an intelligent and well-educated man, but he was quite prepared to enforce an argument by citing the treatment by music of those stung "by the tarantula in Apulia"; not every kind of music will neutralize the poison, and by experiment the physician must discover what harmonies will serve his ends.[25] How seriously did he regard his own illustration? Bacon pointed out that it would be "a strange conclusion if a man should use a similitude for ornament or illustration sake, borrowed from nature or history according to vulgar conceit, as of a basilisk, an unicorn, a centaur, a Briareus, an hydra, or the like, that therefore he must needs be thought to affirm the matter thereof positively to be true."[26] It is necessary to bear this in mind when we read Donne or Browne or Milton, but many of the lesser figures did not write as if they were consciously using images that they knew did not correspond to reality. Some of these men simply belonged to a departed age. "The stately elephant," wrote Dr. John Stoughton in 1640, "hath no joints they say, and yet hath been taught to stoop and take up his ruler."[27] But many reflected an uneasy consciousness that they were trying to live in a divided world.

The sense of strain, the consequence of civil war in the mind, must have been intense. Doubt and ambiguity assailed the thoughtful man, but the

[22] Note John Webster's appeal that experimental science be substituted for classical studies in the universities: Webster, *Academiarum Examen,* esp. Ch. III. Cf. also John Hall, *An Humble Motion to the Parliament of England concerning the Advancement of Learning.*

[23] John Preston, *The Golden Scepter,* pp. 131–132.

[24] Thomas Adams, *The Sermons of Thomas Adams* (ed. John Brown), p. 216.

[25] John Bastwick, *The Answer of John Bastwick,* p. 2.

[26] Bacon, *The Advancement of Learning,* Bk. II, XXV, 16.

[27] John Stoughton, *The Magistrates Commission,* p. 34.

conflict, because so personal, is often difficult to trace. But in the wider world of public debate, the clash between the old and the new was one of the conspicuous features of the age. The authority of the ancient world often stood as a major obstacle in the path of intellectual progress. The Renaissance had turned back to the classical world in search of patterns of thought and modes of expression that would free the human mind from the dead hand of Scholasticism. Aristotle was liberated from the interpretation that the Middle Ages had imposed upon his works; he still remained the undisputed arbiter of knowledge. The Reformation also had turned back to the past—in this case to the New Testament world. As the seventeenth century opened, the challenge of new ways faced the weight of traditional authorities. In logic the disciples of Ramus disputed the predominance of Aristotle's system. Copernicus had shown that the Ptolemaic vision of the heavens was wrong; Tycho Brahe, Kepler, and Galileo were pressing further the new understanding of the universe, but the new interpretation made slow progress against the accepted beliefs. The evidence of the senses, as well as the teaching of the Bible, of Aristotle, and of tradition all seemed to favor the older view. Far into the century an enlightened conservative like Sir Thomas Browne could maintain a cautiously noncommittal attitude to the Copernican system.[28] In his *Pseudodoxia Epidemica* he attacked many popular errors, but he perpetuated many others. An age still conditioned by the belief that truth needs to be supported by quotation hankered after the assurance provided by ancient authorities. Even some of the boldest innovations in politics and religion were accomplished in the name of some distinguished precedent supplied by classical antiquity or primitive Christianity. As Milton convincingly demonstrates, originality of ideas was often inextricably interwoven with the appeal to ancient authority. Yet in various ways the prestige of the traditional patterns was visibly waning. The ancient classics were less exclusively the intellectual fare of men. Latin was less often used than formerly. Robert Burton apologized for publishing his *Anatomy* in English, but he explained that he had no choice in the matter: the "mercenary stationers" were prepared to publish "any scurrile pamphlet" in English, but would not touch a serious treatise written in the language of international learning.[29]

The struggle between old authorities and a new approach was apparent in almost every sphere of human thought. In geography, men were gradually assimilating the implications of recent explorations. On the eve of the civil war an old-fashioned preacher could declaim on the vanity and inhospitality of this world, and dismiss it as "this same dirty prison earth." [30] More characteristic of the new day were Samuel Purchas'

---

[28] T. Browne, *The Works of Sir Thomas Browne*, I, 111; II, 318; III, 47, 76.
[29] R. Burton, *The Anatomy of Melancholy*, Democritus to the Reader.
[30] E. Sparke, *The Christians Map of the World*, p. 5.

strange and chaotic folios. He proposed to provide a historical geography combined with an account of the rise and development of the major religions. The task was difficult; there were no precedents, and the scope was vast. "The newness also makes it more difficult, being an enterprise never yet (to my knowledge) attempted in any language." The new venture demanded an immense amount of scholarly insurance, and Purchas pointed to the "seven hundred authors" whose opinions he quoted.[31] Meanwhile, serious work was being done in mathematics and in navigation, and a growing literature on travel kindled interest in geography. John Wilkins provides a good example of the way men's minds were moving. He is usually remembered for his ability to prosper even amid the mercurial fluctuations of fortune; he was related to Cromwell, yet he became a Restoration bishop and a moving spirit in the Royal Society. But before the outbreak of war he made a significant contribution to thought about man's home in space. His *A Discourse concerning a new World* is ostensibly a discussion of the possibility of life on the moon, but it is also an important examination of the place of authority in shaping our thought on scientific matters. At the very outset he lays down the conditions that govern every successful intellectual quest. Wilkins insists that if the reader is to get any benefit from the work, he must "come unto it with an equal mind, not swayed by prejudice, but indifferently resolved to assent unto that truth which upon deliberation shall seem most profitable unto [his] reason." [32] In any scientific undertaking it is "a preposterous course to begin at the testimony and opinion of others and then afterwards to descend unto the reasons that may be drawn from the nature and essence of the things themselves." [33] Aristotle may have been a great authority in his day, but even he had conceded that he might be wrong. When you quote him, you pit the prestige of the ancients against the claim of modern men to intellectual freedom. "In such learning as may be increased by fresh experiments and new discoveries, 'tis we are the Fathers and of more time than they had, and truth (we say) is the daughter of time." [34] So in judging of new discoveries, it is not the multitude of references that counts. After all, we know much more about our world than the Greeks, and most of the ancient fathers were very ignorant concerning scientific matters.[35]

The clash, of course, was not merely between the ancient and the modern, between the authority of the past and the claims of the new day. The emerging disciplines were contending for men's allegiance with the old forms of science. Contrary to reasonable expectation, the pseudo

[31] Purchas, *Purchas his Pilgrimage,* Ep. Ded. In later editions his "700 authors" nearly doubled in number.
[32] John Wilkins, *A Discourse concerning a new World,* To the Reader.
[33] *Ibid.,* p. 2.
[34] *Ibid.,* p. 7.
[35] *Ibid.,* pp. 8, 10–11.

sciences had recently experienced a surprising renascence. The sixteenth century was a golden age for astrology in England. Elizabeth appointed a court astrologer and consulted him. The subject had a recognized place in the academic curriculum. It was regarded as a valuable adjunct to the practice of medicine. Astrology rested on the theory that every feature of the universe is reflected in its counterpart; what happened in the heavens therefore affects what takes place on earth. Many able scholars were prepared to accept this assumption. John Dee, a famous mathematician, wrote about astrology with enthusiasm. Joseph Mede, a distinguished fellow of Christ's College, Cambridge, "spent no small pains (in his younger years) in sounding the depths of astrology and much paper he blotted in calculating the nativities of his near relations and fellow students, having to this art (he would say) above all other studies a natural propension." [36] William Gilbert, whose work on magnetism is one of the notable scientific achievements of the early seventeenth century, believed in animism and in judicial astrology. Henry Coley illustrates the way a man could cling to the old patterns of thought, even though he held the key to many of the new scientific advances. In John Aubrey's words, "he hath great practise in astrology and teacheth mathematics." [37] But protests against the popularity of astrology were increasing. Many of the earlier attacks concentrated on its incompatibility with the principal doctrines of Christian theology. John Chamber made the argument even more accessible to the popular mind when he insisted that there were two chief reasons for repudiating astrology: it denied man's free will, and it encouraged intercourse with devils.[38] Bacon denounced both astrology and alchemy as obstacles to the progress of true science.[39]

Various other strains mingled in the confused intellectual heritage of the early seventeenth century. Stoicism, a persistent though often an unacknowledged strain in European ethics, is clearly present in men like Drummond. Platonic and Neoplatonic influences are encountered on every hand. Thomas Jackson, the Arminian president of Corpus Christi College, Oxford, constantly appeals to Plato, while the Neoplatonists had a pronounced effect on the later poetry of Donne and on George Herbert. More exotic influences are represented by Hermetic philosophy, introduced into England by the works of Marsiglio Ficino and the Florentine Platonists. Late in the fifteenth century Ficino translated into Latin the formidable bulk of the Hermetic writings; by the middle of the seventeenth century, twenty-two editions had been published. In Ralegh's circle—the "School of Night"—the Hermetic theories were studied with fascinated interest, and later in the century Elias Ashmole reflects their

[36] *The Life of Joseph Mede*, pp. viii ff.
[37] John Aubrey, *Brief Lives, Chiefly of Contemporaries*, I, 182.
[38] John Chamber, *A Treatise against Judicial Astrologie* (1601).
[39] Bacon, *The Advancement of Learning*, Bk. I, IV, 11.

continuing appeal. Even more esoteric in quality were the cabalistic works, which claimed descent from the Hebrew prophets, but which, in the course of their long transmission, had been mixed with Stoic, Neoplatonic, and other equally incongruous elements. Robert Burton and Sir Thomas Browne were familiar with this material; it had a marked effect on the poetry of Spenser, Donne, and Henry Vaughan. Nor can we ignore the influence of Paracelsus, especially on those who were trying to penetrate the secrets of the physical universe. Central to his system was a belief in the fundamental unity between man and the whole of nature. His aim was to discover the ultimate secret of unity; his followers concentrated their search in three areas: they sought the elixir of life, the philosopher's stone, and the means of accomplishing the transmutation of metals. As the seventeenth century progressed the influence of Paracelsus became one of the strongest solvents of traditional authority.

The appeal of these various strains of thought is intelligible. Many of them had a long ancestry; but to a culture that was beginning to find the conventional orthodoxies oppressive, they offered the excitement of novel and intriguing alternatives. They are often found in curious combinations in the work of a single individual. James Maxwell acknowledged his debt to "Plato, Hermes Trismegistus, Franciscus and Johannes Picus Mirandula, Marsilius Ficinus, Franciscus Patricius." [40] Here was a man clearly reacting against the Aristotelian tradition, but he had chosen with a less Catholic taste than Ralegh, who, while still at Oxford, had jettisoned the old philosophy. Ralegh's new sources were Machiavelli, Plato and Neoplatonism, the Hermetic writings and the evidence of science.[41] With the passage of time the Aristotelian system had been fashioned into a comprehensive synthesis. This was its strength; it had originally been its appeal. Latterly it had become its weakness; it had hardened into inflexibility and men reacted against its deadening influence. But the new ingredients were not fused into a comparably cohesive system. Fragments of different types of thought often coexisted in the same mind. This was stimulating; it could be puzzling, and sometimes the diversity of systems almost drove men to despair. Some fled for reassurance to the familiar patterns of thought and belief. Others found that their confusion led to skepticism.

Certain types of ancient irrationality survived into the seventeenth century. To most people, witchcraft was an undisputed fact. It awakened not incredulity but an intense and horrified fascination. As the sixteenth century closed, there appeared in rapid succession a number of works recounting the activities of witches.[42] "This realm is known by common experience to be troubled with witches, sorcerers and other such wise men

---

[40] James Maxwell, *A New Eightfold Probation,* Ep. Ded.
[41] Cf. Pierre Lafrance, *Sir Walter Raleigh Ecrivain.*
[42] H. S. Bennett, *English Books and Readers, 1558–1603,* p. 243.

and women"—so it seemed appropriate to take an interest in this characteristically English phenomenon.[43] Many of these works were popular and unsophisticated in character, but serious dissertations were also devoted to the subject. King James I showed much more than a passing interest in witches. When certain old women of North Berwick were accused of practicing the black arts to hinder his return from Denmark, he presided at their trial, and urged one of the accused to play him the devil's tune to which all witches were supposed to dance.[44] Among his works there is a solemn treatise on witchcraft. With a flourish of erudition and with considerable intelligence perversely applied, the royal author examines the occult arts.[45] The Rev. George Gifford of Malden published a work in which he "laid open how craftily the devil deceiveth not only the witches, but many others, and so leadeth them into many great errors."[46] Thomas Tuke denounced witchcraft as a sin "which is very sacrilegious and altogether derogatory to the glory of God." It was the assumption of a Satanic alliance that caused such dismay. "Every witch is at a league with the devil, open or secret, and doth wittingly and willingly use his help."[47]

Throughout the seventeenth century, belief in the occult stubbornly resisted erosion by new knowledge. This was not the mark merely of the credulous and the ignorant. Cudworth and More, the Cambridge Platonists, regarded witchcraft as a manifestation of spirit forces—sinister ones, admittedly—and consequently a useful bulwark against the materialism of writers like Hobbes. Joseph Glanvill was a member of the Royal Society and one of its ablest apologists, yet he argued just as persuasively for belief in witches as for the acceptance of the new science. It is a well-known fact that Sir Thomas Browne appeared as an expert witness on witchcraft at a trial over which Sir Matthew Hale presided; seldom have two men so humane and so enlightened been involved in so benighted a cause. Though the ancient belief yielded ground reluctantly, it was under steady pressure. Even in the early years of the century, the critical spirit had begun to challenge the disposition to make confused and demented old women the scapegoats for the mysteries and misfortunes that abounded in daily life. In his later years King James showed considerable ingenuity in exposing fraudulent claims to the possession of occult powers. There is no evidence that he abandoned his belief in witchcraft, but he became extremely skeptical about all who claimed to be or who were regarded as witches or wise women.[48] Donne often referred to witchcraft; in his sermons he usually used the prevalent belief to illustrate an argument, but

[43] Anne Brigges, *The Disclosing of a late counterfeyted possession by the devyl*, Sign. A2.
[44] Cf. *Cal. S. P. Scottish, 1589–93*, pp. 307, 311, 359, 420, 453, 522–525.
[45] James I, *Daemonology*, in *The Workes of the Most High and Mightie Prince, James* (1616).
[46] George Gifford, *A Dialogue concerning Witches and Witchcraftes*.
[47] Thomas Tuke, *A Treatise against Painting and Tincturing of Men and Women*, pp. 50–54.
[48] D. H. Willson, *King James VI and I*, pp. 310–311.

in doing so he subtly insinuated a doubt concerning the reality of the phenomenon.[49] During the closing years of Elizabeth's reign, a famous exorcist named John Darrel published a series of works in which he justified his belief in witches. For his pains he drew down upon himself a vigorous onslaught by Samuel Harsnet, a future archbishop of York.[50] Particularly interesting are Richard Bernard's comments on the subject. It is sometimes assumed that the Puritans, being Biblical literalists, were particularly vulnerable to such aberrations as belief in witchcraft. Bernard shows that some of them were clearly ahead of most of their contemporaries. He published his *A Guide to Grand Jury Men* because he was disturbed by recent developments. Five members of a certain family had "lately [been] condemned and executed for witches"; the one surviving member was "now in danger to be questioned again." [51] Bernard had no wish "to prevent justice or hinder legal proceedings," but he was convinced that popular phobias, combined with outmoded legal procedures, were depriving harmless people of their elementary rights. He strongly appealed for a new approach to the whole question; until witchcraft could be examined in a dispassionate and scientific spirit, people who offended merely by being peculiar would continue to run the gravest risks. Bernard did not challenge the fact of witchcraft; "there are witches," he declared roundly, and he believed that those who dabbled in such wicked practices had been seduced by the devil.[52] But he also insisted that many of the phenomena popularly ascribed to occult powers were susceptible of perfectly simple and natural explanations.[53] In his very popular allegorical work, *The Isle of Man*, Bernard described the assizes which had just been held in his imaginary country. "There should have been," he said, ". . . the arraignment of certain suspected witches; but this was prevented, because the grand-jury gentlemen could not agree to bring in their *billa vera;* for that they made question of divers points, whereof they could not be resolved at that present." Thereupon Bernard set down five questions that seriously perplexed the members of the grand jury and made it impossible for them to proceed against the accused. The case against belief in witchcraft had seldom been presented with such brevity and cogency. As the book passed through edition after edition it must perceptibly have modified prevailing beliefs.[54]

[49] Donne, *Sermons*, I, 159–160; IX, 323.

[50] Samuel Harsnet, *A Discoverie of the fraudulent practises of John Darrel* (1599).

[51] Richard Bernard, *The Isle of Man*, Ep. to the Reader. In the epistle to this book, Bernard relates the circumstances that prompted him to write his previous work on witches and their treatment.

[52] Bernard, *A Guide to Grand Jury Men*, pp. 87–121.

[53] *Ibid.*, pp. 11–53. When Bernard comes to his critical study of the phenomena connected with witchcraft (pp. 155–267), he shows that he is still very much a child of his age.

[54] Since the case is stated in the Epistle to the Reader, even those who read only the first few pages would be exposed to Bernard's argument. The book was published in 1626; by 1635 it had reached its tenth edition.

In medicine the old methods appealed to the authority of the Greeks but often relied on folklore or superstition; a new approach, scientific and forward-looking, was clearly emerging. Harvey's discovery of the circulation of the blood was one of the major achievements of the age. On a much less sophisticated plane, an interest in the problems of health was growing, and a new kind of literature appeared to satisfy the demand for reliable information. William Vaughan's guides to good health met with an immediate response, and rapidly passed through several editions.[55] Books were written on the benefits or dangers of "taking the fume of tobacco." [56] Edward Jorden published *A brief discourse of a disease called the suffocation of the mother,* in which he proved that the malady was wrongly attributed to "possession of an evil spirit" and described the wholly natural causes that were responsible for it. But curiosity was often content to dwell on the bizarre and the exotic. Monstrous births were regularly reported, often by the local rector. In 1640 there appeared a "relation of the hog-faced gentlewoman . . . who was bewitched in her mother's womb in the year 1618, . . . and can never recover her true shape till she be married."

In even the most critical minds ancient assumptions persisted side by side with modern insights. This accounts for much seeming incongruity. It is responsible for the tensions so visible in some of the greatest works of the period. It explains the way in which apparently incompatible strains of thought struggle inconclusively for mastery. Both pessimism and optimism had a strong appeal. Some believed in the fatal decay of nature; others looked for its imminent renewal. Doubt and atheism on the one hand, assurance and faith on the other, marked the mood of the age. These conflicting elements appear in many periods; in the early seventeenth century they are not only encountered in the same circle, they often existed in the same mind.

The mood of the Jacobean period has sometimes been contrasted with that of the Elizabethan age. It is assumed that after the brilliance of the great queen's reign a chilling gloom descended on the minds of Englishmen. This is temptingly easy; clearly it is not true. The last decade of Elizabeth's life had lost the verve and excitement of an earlier period. The war with Spain dragged on; political and economic problems multiplied. Uncertainty about the succession created a mood of apprehension. But with James on the throne and a promising heir in Prince Henry, some of the fears about the future were dispelled. Peace was achieved—without glory, it is true, but without disgrace. In any case, the prevalence of confidence or apprehension did not depend entirely upon the reigning dynasty. They coexisted under both Elizabeth and James.

---

[55] William Vaughan, *Natural and artificial directions for health; idem, Approved directions for health.*

[56] Cf. Tobias Venner, *A brief and accurate treatise.* James I wrote an angry blast against smoking.

There seemed to be sufficient grounds for either hope or fear. Jeremiads were common; often they merely reflected the tendency of moral critics to present a gloomy picture of their own times. Thomas Proctor sadly noted that "most men, laying the commandments of God aside, do live their lives in disobedience to God's commandments." The need of the hour was the exposition of the Decalogue, but he had little expectation that his contemporaries would listen to its injunctions, "for such rooting in men hath the pleasure of sin taken, that it is almost unexpectable that they should leave to sin those sins by which their laughter, heart's joy and firmest bond of fellowship is commonly occasioned." [57] The problems of human behavior were compounded, according to Paul Bayne, by "these evil times wherein darkness and lusts of ignorance abound." [58]

Everyone agreed that disasters could hardly be avoided; man's fallen nature gave too hospitable a welcome to the destructive forces of the age. His frail constitution provided little protection: "how weakly is he fenced about with these thin walls of clay that every ague shakes, every dropsy drowns, every fever fires, every danger batters!" [59] Sorrow is entailed on man from his birth. "What is the first song that he singeth at his coming into the world, but only weepings and wailings?" Even the advantages of kings are their undoing. "The abundance of honours and pleasures that princes enjoy serveth as a bait to induce them to evil and are the very matches to give fire to vice." [60] Repeatedly we detect traces of the pessimism that was one aspect of the legacy of the Renaissance. Honor and riches, said Ralegh, are no protection against the inexorable fate that awaits us all, "but by what crooked path soever we walk, the same leadeth on directly to the house of death, whose doors lie open at all hours and to all persons. For this tide of man's life, after it once turneth and declineth, ever runneth with a perpetual ebb and falling stream, but never floweth again. Our leaf once fallen springeth no more, neither doth the sun nor the summer adorn us again with the garments of new leaves and flowers." [61] Misery is the distinguishing feature of human life. "You may as soon separate weight from lead, heat from fire, moistness from water, brightness from the sun, as misery, discontent, care, calamity, danger from a man." [62]

With some Jacobeans melancholy was a mood. With others it may have been a pose. In Burton's case it was an absorbing and lifelong interest. For Godfrey Goodman it was a conviction carefully elaborated in one of the classics of late Renaissance pessimism. He was entirely orthodox in finding the origin of our miseries in the Fall. "The greatness of our woe

[57] Thomas Proctor, *The Righteous mans way,* Ep. to the Reader.
[58] Paul Bayne, *Christian Letters,* p. 202. Cf. also p. 317.
[59] E. Sparke, *op. cit.,* p. 11.
[60] *The Pilgrimage of Man,* pp. 727, 816.
[61] Ralegh, *The History of the World,* Bk. I, Ch. II, 5.
[62] R. Burton, *The Anatomy of Melancholy,* Pt. I, Sec. II, Mem. III, Subs. X.

shows the large extent of our sin: this world which we inhabit is but a vale of misery, the happiness of the world is only a painted misery." [63] Nature itself cannot escape involvement in man's corruption. "She is more plentiful and abounding in evil than in good." Health is one, diseases various; "the truth is single, falsehoods many." [64] Every part of man's life is invaded by misery. His body is diseased. His mind is disturbed. He is tormented by the memory of past shame and by the anticipation of future sorrows.[65] In all this the wisdom of God is revealed, "that whereas blessing and happiness could not contain man within the bounds of obedience, that therefore man being forced into a vale of misery, his own sorrow might enforce him to cry for succour and release." [66] Goodman finds a partial mitigation of our unhappy state in the marvelous benefits of tobacco, which are able to remedy "the rawness of the stomach, to extenuate and exhale the ill humours, to help the undigested food." [67] But this is small consolation when man is involved in a process of universal and irreversible decay. Men today are but a shadow of their ancestors. Formerly the human body was more vigorous than now. The ancients were less subject to disease and "more apt to engender." Their intelligence was keener (which explains their success in laying bare the secret of all knowledge), and their lives were longer. Now everything participates in a universal decline. Fish are less plentiful in the seas, and crops are less abundant on land. There is less honey, and grapes do not ripen as once they did. Scarcity is responsible for high prices. Even coins are fewer and lighter than in the past.[68]

Viewed simply in the light of reason, all things are hastening to their end. Death provides a merciful release for the individual; the final consummation promises a climax to the slow process of universal decline. "To let pass many strong presumptions of our divines concerning the approach of that day, these three proofs, drawn from natural reason, as easily induce me to believe it. First, looking to the general decay of this world, which argues the approach of this judgement. Secondly, to the great preparation for fire which must then serve for the execution of God's wrath. Thirdly, the fit occasions seeming to hasten this judgement." [69] All things are moving inexorably to their end. What Goodman stated with earnest but pedestrian fervor early in this period, Sir Thomas Browne repeated, with his unique and solemn eloquence, at its close. " 'Tis too late to be ambitious. The great mutations of the world are acted, or time may be too short for our designs." [70]

[63] Godfrey Goodman, *The Fall of Man*, Ep. Ded.
[64] *Ibid.*, p. 14.
[65] *Ibid.*, pp. 26, 67 ff., 107 ff., 129 ff., 153 ff.
[66] *Ibid.*, p. 182.
[67] *Ibid.*, p. 353.
[68] *Ibid.*, pp. 353–373.
[69] *Ibid.*, p. 383.
[70] T. Browne, *Hydriotaphia: Urne-burial*, Ch. V (*Works*, III, 138).

Unrelieved pessimism was relatively rare. In Tourneur and Marston and some of the other Jacobean dramatists a bitter and vicious mood is all-pervasive, but this is the exception rather than the rule. Goodman admits that so long as you judge human life simply by the canons of reason, you see only the signs of unrelieved decay, but in sifting the evidence he comes at last to the convictions that tip the balance on the side of hope. Revelation offers what the course of nature cannot provide: grounds for believing that pessimism does not have the final word. The Christian doctrine of redemption was familiar to a generation with a passion for sermons and an insatiable appetite for theological literature. Thus pessimism was usually a passing mood rather than a settled conviction. In his sermons Donne often struck a somber note, but essentially he was a preacher of hope. He might revert, with a kind of fascinated horror, to death and man's dissolution, but he always drew himself hand over hand out of that pit of despair into an assured confidence, and he did so by dwelling on the doctrines that are the ground of hope. Hooker's robust confidence sprang from the same source. "And because there is not in the world anything whereby another may not someway be made the perfecter, therefore all things that are, are good." [71] On slightly different grounds Bacon also rebuked the spirit of discouragement. The myth of the superior intelligence and capacity of the ancients rested on false assumptions. There was no evidence that nature had decayed, or that man's mental powers had in any way declined from the level that prevailed in classical times. Thus mere hallucinations buttressed the belief in the inherent inferiority of modern man and his achievements. From a rebirth of learning and science, Bacon anticipated a vast extension of human capacity and a comparable increase in human happiness. [72]

Scattered comments were clearly not a sufficient refutation of the dispirited temper that was undermining confidence in the possibility of progress. The times demanded an ampler statement of the general grounds of hope. George Hakewill provided it in his massive *An Apologie or Declaration of the power and providence of God in the government of the world.* He dismissed as absurd the assumption that the ancients possessed an inherent advantage over their successors.

> I think that the wits of these latter ages, being manured by industry, directed by precepts, regulated by method, tempered by diet, refreshed by exercise and encouraged by rewards may be as capable of deep speculations and produce as masculine and lasting births as any of the ancienter times have done. But if we conceive them to be giants and ourselves dwarves, if we imagine all sciences already to have received their utmost perfection, so as we need not but to translate and comment upon that which they

[71] Hooker, *Laws of Ecclesiastical Polity,* Bk. I, Ch. v, 1.
[72] Bacon, *The Advancement of Learning,* Bk. I, V, 2.

have done, if we so admire and dote upon antiquity as we emulate and envy, nay scorn and trample underfoot whatsoever the present age affords, . . . surely there is little hope that we should ever come near them much less match them.[73]

But a new attitude, confirmed by a new approach to the problem and issuing in a new method of dealing with it, would radically transform the situation. As his first step, Hakewill attacked the doctrine of a general decay of nature. The theory was so widely disseminated that many people accepted it without scrutiny. But all the evidence pointed to a wholly different conclusion. The results seemed equally conclusive when he turned to "the pretended decay of the heavens and the elements." [74] So, far from degenerating, man had steadily improved. This was true of his physique; it was no less true of his knowledge, and this was a far more significant fact. In one discipline after another Hakewill pointed to the unquestioned progress that man had made. Technical advances had kept pace with theoretical gains. Admittedly morals were bad—so bad that some men predicted the imminent destruction of the world—but beyond any question they had been far worse in ancient times.[75] The advent of Christianity had vastly raised the level of religious insight; the recent reformation had consolidated earlier gains. Laws, too, had been purified. "As religion is the hinge upon which the government of the political state depends and moves, so next after it good and wholesome laws serve much for the bettering of a commonwealth in matters of manners." [76] But the expectation of the final cataclysm does not necessarily imply a steady deterioration of all things until that consummation is fulfilled. The last day will be dramatic and the final judgment decisive, but we need neither despair of the present nor be unduly apprehensive about the future.[77] The scale of Hakewill's book reflects his estimate of the seriousness of the crisis of confidence. At stake was the possibility of a revitalized and expanding intellectual enterprise. His success was considerable. Few authors did more to lift from men's minds the paralyzing grip of the past. By reducing to reasonable proportions the authority of the ancients, he helped his contemporaries face the intellectual challenge of the new era.

An age susceptible to pessimism was naturally beset by skepticism. A critical temper implied that nothing could be regarded as certain or established. This was one aspect of the rising challenge to authority of every kind. In all areas—in theology and politics, in philosophy and science—the old certainties were being undermined by a variety of corrosive forces. Some of these were familiar—the age-old problems that

[73] George Hakewill, *An Apologie,* Ep. Ded.
[74] *Ibid.,* p. 52.
[75] *Ibid.,* pp. 154 ff.
[76] *Ibid.,* p. 308.
[77] *Ibid.,* p. 310.

have always beset human life—but rendered far more irksome by the prospect of modifying our situation. Some were the result of the impact of new intellectual influences. Of recent writers Montaigne was one of the principal disseminators of a skeptical outlook. Shakespeare and Bacon had certainly read his *Essays*. Most Englishmen recoiled from Machiavelli; they saw him as a cynical advocate of treachery and murder. Ralegh read him with appreciation. But the contemporaries of Shakespeare did not simply assimilate the outlook of their predecessors. They were primarily concerned to rethink their own problems in the light of the ancient questions that had once more been raised. In many areas the concept of infallible authority was being challenged. This posed in an acute form the issue of creative responsibility. Shakespeare agonized over issues that Montaigne could handle with a deft, ironic touch. *Hamlet* raises in inescapable terms the problem of intellectual uncertainty and failure. A prince, of whom vigorous action is demanded, is paralyzed by indecision. He does not think too much; he merely thinks to no useful purpose. The soul without conviction drifts impotently toward disaster. God and man, life and death, heaven and hell have all lost their clear definition. Skepticism mingles with credulity. "So have I heard," says Horatio about the behavior of ghosts, "and do in part believe." With these problems Donne also was concerned; as poet and as priest he constantly recurred to the issues of certainty and doubt.

The spirit of skepticism assumed many forms. It might simply be the cynical appraisal of claims usually uncritically accepted, as in Selden's comment that exorcists only cast out what they first put in, and do nothing that ordinary skill cannot accomplish.[78] For Ralegh, skepticism was perhaps a refuge from ardent but frustrated intellectual ambition. "The sceptic doth neither affirm, neither deny any position; but doubteth of it, and opposeth his reasons against that which is affirmed or denied, to justify his not consenting."[79] This suspension of judgment seemed to many of his contemporaries to suggest the noncommittal attitude which is the very essence of skepticism. According to John Earle, "a sceptic in religion is one that hangs in the balance with all sorts of opinions, whereof not one but stirs him and none sways him. . . . He finds reason in all opinions, truth in none."[80] Conduct was often regarded as more important than creeds. "We profess that we know God," wrote Ralegh, "but by works we deny him. For beatitude doth not consist in the knowledge of divine things, but in a divine life."[81] The reluctance to submit to the claims of a single dogmatic system was perfectly compatible with a firm religious faith. Sincere Christians sometimes believed that

[78] John Selden, *Table Talk*, p. 40.
[79] Ralegh, *Works*, VIII, 548.
[80] John Earle, *Micro-cosmographie*, 48.
[81] Ralegh, *Works*, VIII, 551.

ecclesiastics were exclusively preoccupied with questions of marginal importance. This was one variant of the reaction against too arrogant an appeal to authority. It found persuasive expression in the works of William Chillingworth and his friends. In due course the Cambridge Platonists provided it with its most ample exposition.

Both John Donne and Sir Thomas Browne showed that a persistent strain of skepticism could coexist with complete acceptance of the truth of the Christian faith. In Donne we repeatedly encounter the spirit of restless inquiry, probing the causes of doubt, searching for the grounds of certainty. He was acutely conscious of the challenge of a world disjointed and fragmented by the impact of discordant insights. He knew that the Fall was responsible for man's present plight, but he also realized that at many points the new science was calling accepted convictions in question. Intellectual confusion, as he pointed out in "The Progresse of the Soule," is symptomatic of man's basic ignorance, and it is doubtful whether this can ever be completely overcome.

> Forget this rotten world; and unto thee
> Let thine own times as an old story be.
> Be not concern'd: study not why, nor when;
> Do not so much as not believe a man.[82]

The same question arises in his sermons. "And how imperfect is all our knowledge? What one thing do we know perfectly? All knowledge is rather like a child that is embalmed to make mummy than that is nursed to make man." [83] In Donne we can detect most of the tendencies that combine to constitute the mood of early seventeenth-century skepticism. There is doubt concerning the validity of knowledge, though Donne believed that the future life would make good what the present life could not achieve. He was aware of the challenge of doubt, but he was satisfied that it could have a useful and constructive function. Doubt indeed might serve to crystallize belief.[84] Since belief was not above challenge, faith could not risk subsiding into complacency. Donne was convinced that there can be no escape from the strange and paradoxical character of life. Since this is the nature of our experience as human beings, it is necessarily the mark of both Christian faith and Christian conduct. He was vividly conscious of the staggering paradox of the incarnation.[85] He believed that anyone who trusted in the Word made flesh would find his experience compounded of seemingly irreconcilable ingredients.

In Browne, as in Donne, skepticism and belief were held in delicate balance. He conceded that at many points he passed beyond the frontiers

---

[82] Donne, "The Progresse of the Soule," lines 49–53, *Poems,* p. 228.
[83] Donne, *Sermons,* VII, 260.
[84] *Ibid.,* IX, 371–372.
[85] Cf. Donne, "Divine Poems: Annunciation," *Poems,* p. 290.

of his knowledge. He was ready to admit that he could not pierce to the secret of the unknown, and he was content to marvel at God's mysteries when he could not comprehend his ways. "I know he is wise in all, wonderful in what we conceive, but far more in what we comprehend not." [86] A humble patience is often our best wisdom. "When there is an obscurity too deep for our reason, 'tis good to sit down with a description, periphrasis or adumbration." [87] He freely acknowledged that doubts often assailed him, but they fell into proper place in the perspective of a faith that was assured though not omniscient. Where doubt was teachable it could play a useful, even a constructive role. When it forgot the lessons of humility it became an erratic and destructive force.

> And as credulity is the cause of error, so incredulity oftentimes of not enjoying truth; and that not only an obstinate incredulity, whereby we will not acknowledge assent unto what is reasonably inferred, but any academical reservation in matters of easy truth, or rather sceptical infidelity against the evidence of reason and sense. For these are conceptions befalling wise men, as absurd as the apprehensions of fools and the credulity of the people which promiscuously swallow anything. For this is not only derogatory unto the wisdom of God, who hath proposed the world unto our knowledge, and thereby the notion of himself; but also detractory unto the intellect and sense of man expressly disposed for that inquisition.[88]

In Browne, the element of paradox is even more pronounced than in Donne. He not merely accepts it, he exults in it. "Some truths seem almost falsehoods; and some falsehoods almost truths." The surface of his work appears to be littered with unreconciled antipathies; essentially he resolves them into an amazingly harmonious microcosm of the age. His contemporaries were acutely aware of a whole range of tensions—body and soul, faith and reason, dry rationalism and irrational enthusiasm. From within these paradoxes he discovered the means of achieving the union of apparent opposites. This was especially true of the dichotomy that most deeply disturbed his contemporaries. The impact of new thought had thrown into sharp relief the dualism of faith and reason. Ralegh seemed to acquiesce in a "double truth": "we have sense and feeling of corporal things, and of eternal things but by revelation." Bacon rigorously separated the truths of science and the insights of faith, though in the last resort he defined the relation between them with considerably less precision than he promised. Donne, who was acutely aware of the problem, saw that faith can transform reason and give it a discernment far

[86] T. Browne, *Religio Medici*, Pt. I, §13.
[87] *Ibid.*, §10.
[88] T. Browne, *Pseudodoxia Epidemica*, Bk. I, Ch. V.

beyond its normal reach. For Browne even skepticism could lead to conviction; rationalism is by no means the only avenue to the truth, and we sometimes reach our destination by unexpected byways. "I have therefore always endeavoured to compose those feuds and angry dissensions between affection, faith and reason. . . . There is, as in philosophy, so in divinity, sturdy doubts and boisterous objections, wherewith the unhappiness of our knowledge too nearly acquainteth us. More of these no man knoweth than myself, which I confess I conquered, not in a martial posture, but on my knees." [89]

Not every skeptic could resolve the conflict between faith and reason into the creative tension of paradox. In some cases disbelief hardened into atheism. The early seventeenth century harbored an intense distrust of atheists. Those "who think there is no day of account or live as if there were none" posed a threat to the order and stability of society.[90] Its sources were usually traced to intellectual pride or to an attempt to achieve and maintain a pose of complete neutrality. Sometimes it was due to the flippancy that ridicules sacred things. "For every witty or rather indeed witless brain, will be devising and belching out the scum of their wit, in jesting and scoffing at God's works, or with God's Word, or other holy writing agreeable to the Word and consecrated to the worship of God." [91] Thomas Jackson attributed its rapid growth in modern times to a preoccupation with secular values, caused by an undue concentration on scientific and technical progress.[92] Thomas Nashe distinguished between the "inward atheist" who "devours widows' houses under pretence of long prayers" and the "outward atheist" who "establisheth reason as his god, and will not be persuaded that God (the true God) is, except he make him privy to all the secrecies of his beginning and government." [93] The best efforts of the best minds—so Nashe suggested—are necessary to overcome this menace. The term "atheism" was, however, often used with little precision, and in these cases it cloaked a general uneasiness about the new trends in thought. Ralegh, as we have noticed, was commonly regarded as an atheist. It is clear that though he was not an orthodox Christian, he was certainly not an unbeliever in any sense that the modern world associates with the word. The preoccupation with the subject was a by-product of the crisis of authority. Men were not sure which certainties stood firm; in their perplexities they branded with a term of infamy anyone who threatened the traditional convictions. When menaced by so extreme a form of skepticism, some took refuge in a faith no less dogmatic. Fideism is always one kind of retort to atheism.

Life ends in death. To the men of the seventeenth century this seemed

[89] T. Browne, *Religio Medici*, Pt. I, §19.
[90] Robert Horn, *The Christian governour*, p. 81.
[91] John Smyth, *Works*, I, 147.
[92] Thomas Jackson, *Works*, IV, 37–65.
[93] Thomas Nashe, *Works*, II, 114 ff.

the most bitter paradox of all. Was it tolerable, they asked, that the vividness of human experience and the excitement of man's quest for the truth should find their culmination in a handful of dust? Our most somber and our most magnificent meditations on the theme of death come to us from this period. Browne explored with imaginative care the parallels and contrasts between life and death.[94] Shakespeare returned repeatedly to the subject and probed it sometimes from the perspective of hope, sometimes from that of despair. Donne was often aware of the arrogance of death, and he found it hard to forget its horror; but as a preacher he kept steadily before his hearers' minds the fact that death lacked the finality usually attributed to it. The charnel house had a morbid fascination for many of the contemporaries of Shakespeare. The eyeless skull, the stench of putrefaction might inspire Hamlet to whimsical speculations about the fate of dead men's dust, but death, said Shakespeare, remains a fearful thing:

> to die, and go we know not where;
> To lie in cold obstruction and to rot.[95]

The inevitability of death robs man of any avenue of escape; he helplessly awaits his doom, and trembles at the prospect of it. "O death, which dost astonish man with thy sight, how fearful is thy blow!" [96] This is the consequence of the Fall, and human ingenuity can find no way to lift the menace. "Everyone fears death and dreads it. O death, how bitter is thy mention and memory. Ask nature and call to philosophy, and see if they can afford any aid." [97]

Death, however, has its dignity as well as its horror: "man is a noble animal, splendid in ashes and pompous in the grave." [98] Death brings us to the self-knowledge which in our folly we avoid, and inexorably demolishes the pretenses behind which we try to hide from reality. This is the theme of the greatest of all apostrophes to death.

> It is therefore death alone that can suddenly make man to know himself. He tells the proud and insolent that they are but subjects and humbles them at the instant and makes them cry, complain and repent, yea, even to hate their fore-passed happiness. He takes the account of the rich and proves him a beggar, a naked beggar, which hath interest in nothing but in the gravel that fills his mouth. He holds a glass before the eyes of the most beautiful and makes them see therein their deformity

---

[94] Cf. especially the twin studies on the theme in *Urne-burial* and *The Garden of Cyrus.*

[95] Shakespeare, *Measure for Measure,* Act III, Sc. i. In Marston and Tourneur we have unrelieved horror. Cf. also Donne, *Sermons,* III, 92.

[96] Goodman, *The Fall of Man,* p. 339.

[97] Samuel Ward, *A Collection of such sermons,* No. 2, p. 2.

[98] T. Browne, *Hydriotaphia: Urne-burial,* Ch. V (*Works,* III, 142).

and rottenness, and they acknowledge it. O eloquent, just and mighty death! whom none could advise, thou hast persuaded; what none have dared thou hast done; and whom all the world hath flattered thou only hast cast out of the world and despised. Thou hast drawn together all the far-stretched greatness, all the pride, cruelty and ambition of man, and covered it all over with these two narrow words, *Hic jacet.*[99]

But this is not the only lesson that death teaches the living. The fear it inspires ought to prove a spur to repentance, and so "a profitable means to keep us from eternal death."[100] Funeral sermons were more than a routine part of the obsequies for the deceased. They were in such demand that printers pirated them to satisfy the public clamor.[101] The purpose of this kind of literature was to resolve the paradox of life ending in death by demonstrating that death actually issues in fuller life. "So then this death is a sleep, as it delivers us to a present rest; and then lastly it is so also as it promises a future waiting in a glorious resurrection."[102] Armed with this confidence, men could look fearlessly at death. "Death, be not proud. . . ."

> One short sleep past, we wake eternally,
> And death shall be no more; death, thou shalt die.[103]

Donne is a particularly illuminating figure; in his early work he reflected the growing awareness that the cohesion of the familiar intellectual world was threatened if not already shattered. By resorting to paradox he held in tension elements that were in danger of appearing as stark opposites—confidence and pessimism, body and soul, skepticism and faith, worldliness and otherworldliness, humanism and antihumanism. With Donne the effort was successful because it reflected an achievement progressively realized within himself—the reconciliation of seemingly incompatible elements. His restless and insatiable thirst for truth was finally balanced by the humble acceptance of human limitations. In his later poems and in his sermons he showed that he had discovered the secret of holding in one the very factors that had once threatened to disrupt his intellectual world. His sermons thus provide an unusually revealing clue to the forces shaping the thought of his period. Nowhere else do we find so clearly reflected the concepts that occupied the minds of his more thoughtful contemporaries. No one appreciated more fully the tensions that these disparate tendencies created. No one provided a comparably powerful resolution of the inward stresses of the age.

[99] Ralegh, *The History of the World,* Bk. V, Ch. VI, 12.
[100] Tuke, *A discourse of death,* To the Reader.
[101] Robert Harrice [Harris], *Samuels Funerall,* Ep. Ded.
[102] Donne, *Sermons,* VIII, 191.
[103] Donne, "Holy Sonnets, X," *Poems,* p. 297.

Donne was an exceptional man, and his sermons occupy a unique position. What he did with rare power and perception many others attempted in much more pedestrian ways. It is difficult to follow the trends of seventeenth-century thought if we ignore the place occupied by the pulpit.[104] For many people the sermon was their only contact with literature of any kind. It was the sole medium through which they learned of the issues of the day. Only a small minority of the sermons preached ever appeared in print, yet they account for a high proportion of the output of the presses.[105] Many of these sermons do not excite the admiration of the modern reader. It is a mistake to overlook them. They were published because the booksellers anticipated a sale, and the numbers that appeared reveal a great deal about the appetite that clamored to be satisfied. The readers were taught how to understand the authority of the Bible and the church, but they also heard about the claims of reason and tradition. They learned about political theory and the obedience that the sovereign could rightfully demand. The arguments heard from the pulpit were repeated in many other places. As Sir William Holdsworth pointed out, "the public law of the whole of the seventeenth century, and more especially of the first half of that century, is dominated by religious quite as much as political questions. Religion occupies quite as large a space in the debates of parliament as politics." [106] Of even greater importance than the explicit teaching delivered from the pulpit were the assumptions silently built up, week after week, by the preachers. A certain view of life was steadily inculcated. Man was a creature, fallen indeed, but still bearing traces of the fact that he was made in the image of God. Sin was a mighty force, but it was less powerful and less decisive than righteousness. The great events of the drama of redemption were recounted again and again for the delight and edification of the hearers. A gracious purpose and an exacting will confronted man, demanding of him ceaseless effort, assuring him continual support, promising him blessing and fulfillment. Salvation was both a present experience and an eternal destiny. These themes were repeated in innumerable sermons; they were reinforced by participation in the liturgy and by listening to the Scriptures. But the reading of the Bible was not restricted to the services of worship in the parish churches. Judged by its far-reaching effects, the publication of the Authorized Version of the Bible was certainly one of the most important events of the early seventeenth century.

Certain major intellectual interests preempted a great deal of attention. Certain methods (such as preaching) helped to disseminate the ideas that were silently shaping the pervasive patterns of thought. It is also necessary

[104] Cf. Walter Yonge, *The Diary of Walter Yonge*, pp. 85–86.
[105] Cf. Bennett, *op. cit.*, p. 148, on the number of sermons published in Elizabeth's reign. Under the early Stuarts the output certainly increased.
[106] Sir William Holdsworth, *A History of English Law*, VI, 19.

to remember the wide range of miscellaneous works that reflect an expanding range of interests. Specialization had not yet begun to limit intellectual curiosity. James Ussher was a classical scholar of great eminence, but he corresponded on mathematical questions with Henry Briggs and Dr. Bambridge, and on scientific matters with William Gilbert.[107] Interest in geography was expanding. Helps to better navigation were required if exploration was to be safe as well as exciting. Mathematics attracted the attention of large numbers of intelligent people. Works of popular science were increasing in numbers. Newsletters recounted the trend of events in Scandinavia, Germany, France, and various other countries. The immense popularity of Ralegh's *The History of the World* showed that the interpretation of the past was a matter of intense concern to men and women eager to understand the background of contemporary developments. The variety of materials offered to the public had an important bearing on the doctrines commended to the people. Because of the diversity of emphasis the claims of authority were scrutinized with greater care. Freedom—personal, political, intellectual, religious—was certain to be conceived in more inclusive ways. Traditional patterns of authority could not escape the challenge of new kinds of liberty. In an atmosphere strangely compounded of the old and the new, Englishmen began to examine with a new intensity the perplexing interrelations of freedom and authority.

[107] Richard Parr (ed.), *A Collection of Three Hundred Letters*, pp. 35, 370, 492.

II

BACON
AND THE NEW SCIENCE

THE SEVENTEENTH CENTURY witnessed a major revolution in the intellectual outlook of western Europe. Few areas of thought remained untouched; in none was the change so dramatic as in the world of science, and nowhere was the transformation more remarkable than in England. In the latter part of the sixteenth century, English scientists had lagged behind their Continental colleagues. By the end of the seventeenth century they had swept their country into the forefront of scientific progress.

So drastic a change inevitably involved a reassessment of many accepted beliefs and a challenge to many long-established authorities. In most spheres of endeavor the towering prestige of the ancients had become a fatal obstacle to progress. This is hardly surprising. The full recovery by the Renaissance of the heritage of the classical world had provided exciting and satisfying sources of knowledge. The very old seemed so much better than the more recent that men tended to rest content with what they had regained. The veneration with which scholars and scientists regarded the past discouraged new discoveries. This was apparent in every field. Even in medicine men did not experiment or even observe. It was enough, they felt, to rearrange the legacy of Hippocrates and Galen; a man who had never examined a patient could, it was assumed, write a perfectly satisfactory textbook provided he had diligently studied the Greek sources of medical knowledge.[1] Moreover, the limited state of knowledge about the universe encouraged the elaboration of various systems, all based on speculation, none tested by experiment. This was feasible as long as men believed that the classical ages provided all the necessary materials. Different interpretations of the universe could be provided by appealing to one authority rather than to another or by combining in new ways the elements contributed by the classical heritage.

But this approach could no longer be maintained. By the beginning of

---

[1] Cf. R. F. Jones, *Ancients and Moderns*, pp. 5–6.

the seventeenth century it was obvious that the traditional systems were beginning to collapse. The Schoolmen had accepted whatever Aristotle told them; out of the materials that he provided they had erected an elaborate intellectual structure. Now the situation had changed; in some fields men knew as much as Aristotle, in others they knew a great deal more. Indeed, it was clear that the greatest of the ancients had often been wrong. "It may be thought a strange and harsh thing," said Bacon, "that we should at once and with one blow set aside all sciences and all authors; and that, too, without calling in any ancients to our aid and support, but relying on our own strength." [2]

Moreover, the attack on the authority of the ancients could be sustained even by materials that the ancients themselves supplied. The classical heritage was by no means uniform. The assured confidence of Aristotle was matched by the strain of philosophical skepticism in Pyrrho and Sextus Empiricus. The antirationalist tradition was appropriated and transmitted by the medieval nominalists. It was used for apologetic purposes by Renaissance scholars like Cornelius Agrippa and Francisco Sanchez. It was given wide diffusion by Montaigne; his *Essays* were popular reading in Elizabethan England. Men learned to question much that authority had bidden them accept. "They say miracles are past," wrote Shakespeare, "and we have our philosophical persons, to make modern and familiar, things supernatural and causeless." [3] Men were encouraged to doubt; they asked new questions in many areas—in government, in religion, and (naturally enough) in science. So the challenge to old authorities arose in part from a new intellectual confidence, in part from an ancient but persistent strain of doubt.

New methods and new instruments encouraged results that had hitherto eluded man's powers. Scientists began to count and weigh and measure where previously they had been content to classify. Rapid development of the various branches of mathematics made it possible to replace surmise and speculation with careful reasoning and exact investigation. The new cosmology depended on mathematical calculations, and in England the men who accepted the Copernican system were those able to follow the reasoning on which it rested. Elizabethan England had been rather backward in mathematics. The universities had ignored the subject. Intellectuals were largely unaware of its importance. But though lethargy reigned in some circles, in others a new spirit was stirring. London was filling the vacuum created by indifference at Oxford and Cambridge. Gresham College fostered the study of mathematics and the sciences; it even encouraged in the general public an interest in modern subjects.

---

[2] Bacon, *Novum Organum*, Bk. I, li. Cf. the opening words of the Preface to his *De Augmentis Scientarium*: "The philosophy we principally received from the Greeks must be acknowledged puerile, or rather talkative than generative—as being fruitful in controversies but barren of effects."

[3] Shakespeare, *All's Well That Ends Well*, Act II, Sc. iii.

Craftsmen and mechanics did what scholars and intellectuals failed to do: they made promising contributions to the scientific resources of the new day.[4] The new geographical discoveries not only opened vast areas about which the ancients knew nothing but made the kind of knowledge that is useful in navigation a matter of great practical relevance.

The new outlook found expression in a new vocabulary. The figures of speech that gained currency both challenged old authorities and suggested exciting new possibilities. The structure of the universe, it seemed, could be illuminated if compared with a vast and intricate piece of machinery. The idea was new but reasonable; it promised to be fruitful and rewarding. Clockwork provided the favorite analogy. The idea of physical law acquired new meaning when the concept of the universe as a machine was used to expound it. The analogy, it was claimed, enabled men to see the regularities of nature as a disclosure both of the way God had constructed the machine and of how he intended it to function. Latent in the figure of speech was an invitation to scientists to search out those laws which would lay bare the meaning as well as the structure of the universe.

Certain influences were compelling thoughtful men to claim a new freedom in investigating natural phenomena. But other factors were at work to retard any revolutionary changes. Before the seventeenth century was over, the genuine sciences, especially astronomy and cosmology, would transform the outlook of man, but at the beginning of this period the pseudo sciences, such as alchemy and astrology, still had a powerful appeal. Late in the Elizabethan age they had actually experienced a perceptible revival. Alchemy rested on the hypothesis that an integrating unity underlies all natural phenomena; if man could only discover that secret, he could seize the power to work those transmutations which must surely be implied by the divine oneness of creation.[5] The Paracelsians, also, while initiating genuine and important advances in medicine and chemistry, represented a mystical theosophy which effectively challenged old authorities but did not easily coalesce with the new sciences. The influence of these rather erratic tendencies was obviously strong in literature and in popular thought. Donne, more receptive than most of his contemporaries to new scientific truths and much better informed about them, could write poetry hardly intelligible to a reader unfamiliar with alchemical imagery.[6] In one of his later sermons he used the bezoar stone as an illustration; he cited an interesting scientific fact, but his interpretation of its medicinal qualities bordered on pure folklore.[7] Jeanes, citing

[4] Cf. Christopher Hill, *Intellectual Origins of the English Revolution*, Ch. II.

[5] The immense impact of Newton's theory of gravitation was due to his having established exactly the kind of unity that the pseudo sciences had promised but had never produced.

[6] Prof. Douglas Bush cites as an example Donne's "Nocturnal upon S. Lucie's Day" as a good example. H. H. Rhys (ed.), *Seventeenth Century Science and the Arts*, p. 35.

[7] Donne, *Sermons*, X, 148.

Holerius as his authority, tells us that "an Italian . . . by his often smelling the herb basile, had a scorpion engendered in his head." [8] John Swan, the author of *Speculum Mundi*, a popular and edifying work, was familiar with the astronomical theories of Tycho Brahe and Kepler, but he believed that the stars are elemental compounds "glued together and firmly concreted into a durable lump," and any vagaries in their motion could be attributed to defective composition.[9] Daniel Featley, a man of some erudition, mentioned the crocodiles "which besiege the banks of Nilus and waylay those who travel into Egypt," and insisted that "if they be rubbed or but pricked with the quill of the ibis, are so weakened and stupified thereby that they cannot stir." [10] At the end of this period, Henry More, a correspondent of Descartes, could assert that quinces, being downy, are an effective remedy for falling hair.[11] In 1638, Milton "visited the famous Galileo, grown old, a prisoner to the Inquisition, for thinking in astronomy otherwise than the Franciscan and Dominican licencers thought," [12] but the cosmology of *Paradise Lost* is distinctly different from anything that Galileo would have taught him. Even in the most hospitable minds, the new sciences made slow headway against the old authorities.

The obstacles in the way of a new outlook were many, and progress was painfully slow. But by the beginning of the seventeenth century there were signs that pointed to a better day. As we have already noted, much useful exploratory work was being done by artisans and craftsmen. As the seventeenth century opened, William Gilbert's *De Magnete* (1600) represented a scientific achievement of the first importance. Unlike so many of his contemporaries, he turned his eyes from the past and gazed steadily at the phenomena around him. Intellectual freedom, he believed, presupposed emancipation from antiquity: "it is permitted to us to philosophize freely and with the same liberty which the Egyptians, Greeks and Latins formerly used in publishing their dogmas; whereof very many errors have been handed down in turn to later authors, and in which smatterers still persist, and wander as though in perpetual darkness." [13] The tyranny of book learning, he contended, had blocked the way to genuine knowledge. Folklore had been solemnly transmitted as though it were truth. "Why the sucking fish Echineis or the Remora should stay ships has been variously treated by philosophers, who are often accustomed to fit this fable (as many others) to their theories, before they find out whether the

---

[8] Henry Jeanes, *A Treatise concerning a Christians carefull abstinence from all appearance of evill*, p. 114. John Stoughton (*The Magistrates Commission*), though writing fifteen years after Bacon's death, draws his scientific illustrations from medieval lore.

[9] John Swan, *Speculum Mundi*, Bk. VII, ii.

[10] Daniel Featley, *Clavis Mystica*, Ep. Ded.

[11] Henry More, *Antidote Against Atheism*, Bk. II, Ch. VI.

[12] Milton, *Areopagitica*, in *Works* (Columbia ed.), IV, 330.

[13] William Gilbert, *De Magnete*, Preface.

thing is so in nature." [14] From this morass of canonized ignorance there was only one avenue of escape: "clearer proofs, in the discovery of secrets and in the investigation of the hidden causes of things, being afforded by trustworthy experiments and by demonstrated arguments, than by probable guesses and opinions of the ordinary professors of philosophy," men must turn to new ways of discovering the truth.[15] William Harvey, like Gilbert, contributed a notable example of a piece of patient and highly skilled research. His discovery of the circulation of the blood permanently altered man's understanding of his own physical structure. These achievements were important, but it was clear that the great need of the moment was not a little progress at this point or that, but a radical change in the "climate of opinion." But neither Gilbert nor Harvey could drastically alter man's outlook on the world. This much more difficult task was reserved for Francis Bacon.

It has been debated whether Bacon was a great scientist; unquestionably he was a very great advocate of a new scientific outlook. His anomalous position is reflected in his relationship with his distinguished scientific colleagues. He and Gilbert were both members of Queen Elizabeth's court, and they must have known each other. Bacon had a modest opinion of Gilbert's work, and evidently failed to grasp its scientific importance. Harvey was Bacon's physician, and saw him at close quarters. Bacon, he said, wrote science like a lord chancellor—one of those tributes most damning because so discreetly ambiguous.

The immediate effect of Bacon's contribution to science was certainly heightened by his versatility. In an age that delighted in lavish display, he was a flamboyant figure with the Elizabethan flair for magnificence and ostentation.[16] He was a brilliant writer, a distinguished lawyer, a political theorist with experience in politics. In spite of discouragements, he had carved out for himself a great career in public affairs. His multifarious activities inevitably deflected him from his true vocation as the herald of a new outlook. The debts into which his extravagance plunged him tempted him, as lord chancellor, to accept gifts that had every appearance of being bribes and that brought him to disgrace and ruin. But even in his time of humiliation, he insisted that he had sought position and power only to secure the resources with which to pursue his primary objective: to discover a new method of scientific investigation in order that he might unfold the truth about nature.

Bacon was never hampered by diffidence. Early in his career he informed his uncle, Lord Burghley, of the intended scope of his investiga-

---

[14] *Ibid.* In *Pseudodoxia Epidemica* (1646), Sir Thomas Browne dealt wittily and with scientific precision with a vast array of popular fables. The book played a valuable and necessary role—nearly half a century after Gilbert's work.

[15] Gilbert, *op. cit.*, Preface.

[16] In connection with Bacon's prodigality, see L. Stone's *The Crisis of the Aristocracy, 1558–1641,* Ch. X.

tions. "I have," he said, with a characteristic touch of arrogance, "I have taken all knowledge to be my province." [17] In Bacon there survived more than a trace of the *hubris* of the age of the Renaissance. We can detect it in his zest for life, in his inordinate scientific ambition, in his eagerness to organize and to reform, in his disdain of tradition and in his Utopian projects. He saw himself as the *buccinator novi temporis*, the herald whose trumpet blast announced the dawning of a new day. It was his task, he said, "to ring a bell to call other wits together." [18] His distinctive mission presupposed appropriate methods. As a first step he had to arrest men's attention and persuade them to heed what he had to say. He could not use the subdued tone and the dispassionate language which have seemed suitable to later scientists. He expected opposition; he met it both from the champions of antiquity and from the custodians of academic tradition. He had to convert the reluctant. He knew that the task was immense, and he feared that the time available might be brief. This explains the feverish urgency of his proposals and the impractical character of many of his programs. He had to popularize a new understanding of science, a fresh approach to its problems and possibilities. "It would be an unsound fancy and self-contradictory," he wrote, "to expect that things which have never yet been done can be done except by means which have never yet been tried." [19] He hoped to determine the scope of the new science, to establish its methods, to work out in detail its programs. Though he admitted that he was a herald, he actually claimed for himself a much more extensive role. He proposed to establish science anew. What he called "the Great Instauration" was nothing less than the restoration of knowledge. His design was to "raise or rebuild the sciences, arts and all human knowledge from a firm and solid basis." He would provide a frame of reference within which all that men knew about the natural world could fruitfully be displayed. He realized that as matters stood, man's knowledge was of little benefit to him. "The knowledge whereof the world is now possessed, especially that of nature, extendeth not to magnitude and certainty of works." [20] Man had once enjoyed sovereignty over nature; he had forfeited it. There had once been a free and creative commerce between man's mind and the world about him; now there was only an ineffective dabbling in phenomena. The immediate task, therefore, was to restore the proper relationship between man and nature. This would be the first step in reestablishing the *regnum hominis,* the kingdom of man. [21] It would even be a means of reversing the disastrous consequences of Adam's Fall and of restoring to man the powers that he forfeited in Eden. [22]

[17] Bacon, Letter to Lord Burghley, *Works,* V, 205.
[18] Bacon, Letter to Dr. Playfere, *Works,* V, 289.
[19] Bacon, *Novum Organum,* Bk. I, vi.
[20] Bacon, *Instaurationis Magnae,* Pars V (*Scala Intellectus, sive Filum Labyrinthi*), *Works,* IX, 92.
[21] Bacon, *Novum Organum,* Bk. I, lxviii.
[22] Bacon, *The Great Instauration,* Preface.

The results of this restoration would be both spiritual and material: on the one hand a deep and abiding satisfaction, on the other a harvest of immediate benefits. "Is there any such happiness," Bacon asked,

> as for a man's mind to be raised above the confusion of things, where he may have the prospect of the order of nature and error of man? But is this a view of delight only and not of discovery? of contentment and not of benefit? Shall he not as well discern the riches of nature's warehouse as the beauty of her shop? Is truth ever barren? Shall he not be able to produce worthy effects and to endow the life of man with indefinite commodities? [23]

The advantages that Bacon anticipated from the Great Instauration would appreciably raise the level of man's life. The utilitarian note is highly characteristic of Bacon's program. Nature, he said, is our teacher; the knowledge it imparts is the secret of power—power over nature itself. Abstract ideas might be interesting; Bacon dismissed them as of little value to mankind. The true aim of science, he believed, was "to extend more widely the limits of the power and greatness of man." [24] In his work of restoration it was naturally Bacon's purpose "to lay the foundation not of any sect or doctrine but of human ability and power." [25] If mankind would allow itself to be guided by his "experimental philosophy," [26] it would achieve an immense increase in power and material progress. Utility, so far from being an alternative to truth, was its most accurate measure. "Fruits and works are as it were sponsors and sureties for the truth of philosophies. . . . Truth therefore and utility are here the very same thing: and works themselves are of greater value as pledges of truth than as contributing to the comforts of life." [27] Bacon, it is clear, was not merely a technologist, intent on harnessing knowledge to man's material advantage. Though he despised learning that was purely speculative and consequently fruitless, he had no patience with those who proposed to subordinate truth to utility. As "the beholding of light," he said, "is itself a more excellent and a fairer thing than all the uses of it, so the very contemplation of things as they are, without superstition and imposture. . . . We must from experience of every kind first endeavour to discover true causes and axioms, and seek for experiments of light, not experiments of fruit." [28] The pragmatic results, therefore, do not so much justify the search for truth as validate the results of the endeavor. Both the abstract theorists and the doctrinaire utilitarians are wrong. The pure rationalists

[23] Bacon, *Letters and Life* (ed. J. Spedding), I, 123.
[24] Bacon, *Novum Organum*, Bk. I, cxvi.
[25] Bacon, *The Great Instauration*, Preface.
[26] It must be remembered that in seventeenth-century usage "philosophy" embraced what we would call "science."
[27] Bacon, *Novum Organum*, Bk. I, lxxiii and cxxiv.
[28] *Ibid.*, Bk. I, lxxi, lxx.

are like spiders: out of their own entrails they spin beautiful but
unsubstantial webs. The mere empiricists are like ants that collect raw
materials without discrimination and store them up without modifying
them in any significant way. The true scientist must combine the search
for truth with an appreciation of utility; he must imitate the bee, which
gathers nectar from every flower and by its own activity reduces to pure
honey all it has collected.[29]

Utility, so important a consideration with Bacon, does not take
precedence over truth, nor can it be entirely equated with material
advantage. The benefits that Bacon anticipated from the pursuit of
science had social and even humanitarian implications. Once science was
liberated from dependence upon speculative thought, men with relatively
little formal education could share in its endeavors. The artisan and the
farmer could gather facts and verify hypotheses. For centuries, craftsmen
rather than scholars had provided information about the material world,
and any significant expansion of knowledge presupposed their cooperation. Not only would the humble contribute to the program, they would
benefit from it as well.[30]

The new age could not begin, of course, until the old era had definitely
ended. The first stage in Bacon's program was the destruction of the
obstacles to progress which the discredited authorities had erected. The
old schools of philosophy would have to be swept away. The Platonists
had woven words and ideas into elaborate patterns that had no contact
with reality. The Aristotelians had tried to interpret the whole of nature
by methods suitable only for dealing with man. Bacon knew that the
representatives of traditional authority, even in natural philosophy, would
oppose him; so false had been the presuppositions of what had passed for
science that its practitioners would inevitably resist his new method. "I
descry in the condition of the times," he said, "the decline and fall of the
science and learning which is now in use," [31] and this confirmed his belief
that the old barriers would have to go.

An even more serious obstacle had to be surmounted. There was a
widespread belief that such an enterprise as Bacon proposed was not only
misguided but positively wrong. God did not intend man to know
everything. Some things—so ran the argument—were better left untouched; to try to penetrate their mystery was a symptom of demonic
pride. There was a genuine fear of the Faustian element in learning. The
attempt to penetrate forbidden knowledge had caused the Fall; too curious
a probing of nature was surely a symptom of sin.

> Man, dream no more of curious mysteries,
> As what was here before the world was made,

[29] *Ibid.*, Bk. I, xcv.
[30] Bacon, *The New Atlantis.*
[31] Bacon, *De Interpretatione Naturae.*

The first man's life, the state of paradise,
Where heaven is, or hell's eternal shade,
    For God's works are like him, all infinite;
    And curious search but crafty sin's delight.[32]

It was best for man to be content with his restricted knowledge; pride, even in learning, always goes before a fall.[33] Entrenched authority and diffident piety both counseled acquiescence in things as they were. They were fortified by a pessimistic view of the prospects of the world. The universe was old and tottering on the verge of dissolution. At creation it had come fresh from the hand of God; since then decay had inexorably eroded its beauty and its vigor. Men were now living in "the dog days of the world's declining age," [34] and the end could not long be delayed. This theme is developed with great power in Donne's *First Anniversary,* and with a wealth of dreary exposition in Godfrey Goodman's *The Fall of Man.*[35] "By far the greatest obstacle to the advancement of natural philosophy and the undertaking of anything new," said Bacon, "is to be found in men's *despair* and the idea of impossibility." Bacon, therefore, constituted himself as the spokesman for the spirit of hope. He rebuked the attitude that questioned the legitimacy of inquiry. "It was not," he remarked, "the pure knowledge of nature and universality, a knowledge by the light whereof man did give names unto other creatures in Paradise, as they were brought before him, according to their properties, which gave that occasion to the Fall." [36] The inquirer after truth should not allow himself to be intimidated by the fainthearted. Bacon believed that his approach to science could dispel the shadow of pessimism which had fallen across the human spirit. With an expanded kingdom of knowledge man's mind would experience a new freedom. Even the titles of Bacon's early work are instinct with a confidence inspired by an immense hope. This was not merely the reflection of a buoyant temperament. Bacon laid under contribution a view of history that looked toward a triumphant fulfillment, not toward an ignominious collapse.[37] The present was moving to a glorious culmination, to which the new science would significantly contribute. Bacon's optimistic outlook was sustained by advances registered in the recent past, and he suggested that these "may plant also great expectation of the further proficiencies and augmentation of the sciences." [38] Certain achievements

[32] Fulke Greville, *Caelica,* 88.
[33] Sir John Davies' very popular poem, *Nosce Teipsum,* opens with a very pessimistic picture of the state of human knowledge since the Fall.
[34] John Wood, *Practicae Medicinae Liber,* Ad Lectorem.
[35] See Marjorie H. Nicolson, *The Breaking of the Circle,* p. 65, where she points out that Donne's two *Anniversaries* together form one of the great religious poems of the seventeenth century.
[36] Bacon, *The Advancement of Learning,* Bk. I, I, 3.
[37] Cf. C. E. Raven, *Natural Religion and Christian Theology,* I, 100.
[38] Bacon, *De Dignitate et Augmentis Scientiarum,* Bk. II, Ch. X.

were already revolutionizing the lives of men. In particular, Bacon pointed to the invention of printing, of gunpowder, and of the magnet, which, he claimed, had "changed the whole face and condition of the world—the first in literature, the second in warfare, the third in navigation." Who need despair when so much had already been achieved?

Thus far Bacon had described only the first tentative steps in sweeping away the impediments to a new science. The next stage was to identify certain persistent obstacles to truth and to warn men of their presence. Truth gets mixed with error; fact becomes entangled with fable and fiction. Men cling to erroneous ways of looking at nature because they accept false notions of things. These distortions are not restricted to a given period. They recur in every age, and Bacon believed that learning could advance only if men were constantly on guard against what he called the *idola*, the prejudices or limitations to which the mind is subject.[39] There are, he suggested, four kinds of "idols"—of the tribe, the cave, the marketplace, the theater. Of these the first two are innate; we must guard against their effects, but we cannot hope to eradicate them. The third creeps insensibly into the mind, and is almost as difficult to eliminate as the first two. The fourth kind is imposed from without.

The "idols of the tribe" are the fallacies to which the race in general is exposed. We accept certain presuppositions without question; we support preconceived ideas with a few affirmative instances and tacitly ignore the negative evidence which weighs against them. We attribute to nature a far greater measure of uniformity than it actually possesses. We allow our hopes, our fears, our pride to influence our understanding. Even the defects of our senses impede the operation of our minds; we cannot even see the world of nature as it really is.

By the "idols of the cave" Bacon indicated the errors to which the individual is liable because of his distinctive mental and physical characteristics. Our environment and our education foster prejudices which we mistake for eternal truths. Our predilection either for what is old or for what is new warps our judgment and determines our response, for "everyone has a cave or den of his own which refracts and discolours the light of nature." [40] Since each of us has his characteristic foibles and misconceptions, these idols are innumerable, but Bacon suggested a principle for limiting their effect. "In general let every student of nature take this as a rule, that whatsoever his mind seizes and dwells upon with particular satisfaction is to be held in suspicion." [41]

The "idols of the marketplace" are the misconceptions due to the

---

[39] This is one of Bacon's favorite themes. It occurs in a number of his earlier works; its most complete exposition is in the *Novum Organum*, Bk. I, xxxix–lxvi.

[40] *Ibid.*, Bk. I, xlvii.

[41] *Ibid.*, Bk. I, lviii.

tendency of words themselves to confuse and distort men's thinking. Here, said Bacon, we are confronted with one of the most pernicious kinds of error, and in philosophy its effects have been particularly serious. Words can engender a wholly false way of regarding reality. Once a thing is designated by a word, we assume—though often with insufficient reason— that the thing actually exists. Often a word is coined after the examination of a limited and unrepresentative number of cases, and it is then stretched to embrace objects to which it can be applied only if meaning is seriously distorted. Thus language often hinders the mind from grasping the true nature of material reality. It actually fills it with fantastic misconceptions.

Finally there are the "idols of the theater," the products of a slavish attachment to fallacious systems of philosophy or of dependence upon erroneous methods of demonstration. Bacon pointed to three types of philosophy as illustrations of the dangers of this kind of error. As an example of the "sophistical school" he cited Aristotle, who forced nature into the molds provided by his abstract patterns of thought and who apparently believed that phenomena could be explained by definitions. The "empirical school" was guilty of a different error: on the basis of a few experiments, usually far too restricted in scope, its members immediately leaped to the most sweeping general conclusions. The "superstitious school" corrupted the disciplines of exact thought by infusing into them irrelevant poetic or theological materials. Plato represented many of its most dangerous tendencies, but its errors could equally well be studied in those who proposed to construct a cosmology out of the first chapter of Genesis or the book of Job.

Having removed the obstacles to progress, Bacon felt able to proceed to his basic enterprise. He could show how the next era might be inaugurated. He was ready to expound his distinctive scientific method. At no point did he place a higher valuation on his special contribution. Like many of his contemporaries he believed that right method was the key to progress, and he felt that here he was helping men to use their intellectual freedom to constructive purpose. It was not enough to break out of the prison house of ancient authority; men had to be taught how to achieve the knowledge that would make them masters of the material world. Bacon believed that "natural philosophy" was the archetype of all exact knowledge; it was primarily to this area that his new method ought to be applied. His mind was too capacious to isolate science from other intellectual pursuits; only when seen in proper perspective could the distinctive character of natural philosophy be appreciated. As a necessary preliminary, therefore, Bacon provided a relief map of the intellectual terrain.[42] There are three major areas, he pointed out, which correspond to the three principal activities of the mind. Memory stores up facts;

[42] Cf. Bacon, *The Advancement of Learning,* Bk. II, I, 2 to XXIII, 49.

history is the exposition of the information thus accumulated. Imagination takes the materials provided by our faculties and rearranges them according to its own pleasure; the result is "poesy" or feigned history. Reason accepts what is offered to it by the senses and deals with it as nature itself directs, and so we have philosophy. This third discipline is further divided into three divisions: natural theology deals with God, human philosophy with man, natural science with the material world. Bacon pushed still further the refining of his distinctions. Natural science embraces physics (which examines the efficient and material causes of things) and metaphysics (which is concerned with formal and final causes). Bacon, of course, assigned to "metaphysics" a meaning very different from that which it normally bears. For him the "metaphysics of forms" was an empirical science and corresponded to the theoretical physics of the microscopic world.[43] The study of "forms" was the point where physics and metaphysics most closely converged.

Bacon believed that the pursuit of science ultimately resolves itself into the study of "forms." "Of a given nature to discover the form or true specific difference, or nature engendering nature or source of emanation (for these are the terms which are nearest to a description of the thing), is the work of human knowledge." [44] Bacon offered a number of other interpretations of his meaning, but his explanations are far from clear, and he did not improve matters by the Aristotelian terminology which he deliberately used: it seemed best, he remarked, "to keep way with antiquity *usque ad aras,* and therefore to retain the ancient terms, though I sometimes alter the uses and definitions." [45] Aristotle's forms were merely "figments of the mind"; those of Bacon referred to the essential nature or cause of a phenomenon. They are the laws that constitute and control any simple nature, and "the invention of forms is of all other parts of knowledge the worthiest to be sought, if it be possible to be found." [46] If we wish to discover the form of a simple nature, we must "find a nature which is convertible with the given nature, present wherever the given nature is present, absent wherever it is absent, and is, at the same time a specification of a more generic nature." [47] As an illustration, Bacon used whiteness. To find the form of whiteness, we must isolate what it is that is always present when we have whiteness, and invariably absent when we do not. We must also discover what it is that determines some character more specific than itself. Once we have found what we were seeking, we know how to reproduce whiteness without limitation, so long as the requisite conditions obtain. At times it seems that Bacon was equating forms with natural forces. "When I speak of forms," he said, "I mean

[43] Cf. C. D. Broad, *Ethics and the History of Philosophy,* p. 132.
[44] Bacon, *Novum Organum,* Bk. II, i.
[45] Bacon, *The Advancement of Learning,* Bk. II, VII, 2.
[46] *Ibid.,* Bk. II, VII, 4.
[47] Bacon, *Novum Organum,* Bk. II, iv.

nothing more than those laws and determinations of absolute actuality which govern and constitute any simple nature, as heat, light, weight, in every kind of matter and subject that is susceptible of them. Thus the form of heat or the form of light is the same thing as the law of heat or the law of light." [48] We have already noted Bacon's insistence that knowledge is power. If we understand nature more fully, we shall be able to release its potentialities more completely. The knowledge of forms is an essential step in that understanding without which there can be no mastery of nature. Consequently, the method which unlocks for us that knowledge is a long step, and a very practical one, toward the enrichment of man's life through the effective control of his environment.

Bacon did not define his forms with much precision, but even if he had achieved far greater clarity, it is obvious that thus far he had barely begun the exposition of his revolutionary scientific method. He had, however, established a number of important principles. He had made it clear that in dealing with the determinative elements in phenomena we are discussing not intellectual abstractions but highly general physical properties. This was an important advance toward acknowledging the physical character of natural principles. He had also prepared the way for the enunciation of a conviction that permeates his whole treatment of the sciences. His predecessors had been content to treat each division of knowledge as an autonomous kingdom, sufficient unto itself and governed by its own laws. To Bacon this was a disastrous fragmentation of truth; he regarded it "as a great impediment towards the advancement and further invention of knowledge." [49] His ideal was a single unified science, embracing the entire field of intellectual achievement. All partial truths, he believed, were a part of one essential truth, and each subject should consequently be studied in relation to every other subject.

If all knowledge is one, the artificial barriers, so laboriously erected in the past and so sedulously maintained even in his own day, had to be demolished. Beneath the diversity of phenomena and the variety of disciplines devoted to their study, Bacon recognized a primary philosophy. On this foundation he could convincingly set forth the unity of nature by incorporating in one body of truth all those principles which, so far from being restricted to a single subject, applied to the whole field of science. To help others appropriate what he had seen so clearly, Bacon proposed to demonstrate the interrelations of the various departments of knowledge. He would provide a map. This was an indispensable preliminary to further progress, and at the outset there would be innumerable blank spaces where exploration had not yet revealed the details of the intellectual terrain. Without delay a complete compendium of the materials of knowledge had to be compiled. All available information had

[48] *Ibid.,* Bk. II, xvii.
[49] Bacon, *Valerius Terminus, Works,* III, 228–229.

to be coordinated into "a single systematic treatise, a Natural History such as may supply an orderly foundation for philosophy and include material reliable, abundant and well arranged for the task of interpretation." [50] He regarded natural history as indispensable to the rejuvenation of science; it would be "the main foundation of a true and active philosophy." [51] In the elaborate program which at the outset he drew up for the Great Instauration he originally assigned it a place far down on his list of priorities, but he soon realized that it was too vital to the success of his enterprise to be postponed for so long. If a natural history were not available, the entire project might as well be abandoned.

> What we have said on many occasions must be especially repeated, that if all the wits of all the ages had concurred or shall hereafter concur, or if the whole human species had applied or shall hereafter apply itself to philosophy, and the whole earth had been or shall be nothing but academics and colleges and schools of learned men; still, without such a natural and experimental history as we are going to prescribe, no advance worthy of the human race could have been made or can be made in philosophy and the sciences. Whereas on the other hand, once such a history is collected and arranged, with the addition of such auxiliary and light-bearing experiments as will occur or be elicited in the course of interpretation, the investigation of nature and of the science will be the work of a few years. This therefore must be done or the business abandoned. [52]

Bacon envisioned a mighty cooperative effort. All the "wits," assembled by the ringing of his bell, would penetrate nature's secrets and bring in the harvest of their endeavors. [53] In his buoyant but unrealistic optimism, he grossly underestimated the magnitude of the undertaking. A few years of this joint effort would suffice, he felt, to finish the task. His own frustrations should have shown him his miscalculation. As he quickly discovered, the utmost that he could do was to set forth the governing principles that would guide the project. Since he could not even inaugurate the kind of natural history that the scheme demanded, he had to be content with listing the areas that ought to be explored—a kind of agenda for future scientific endeavors. [54] Bacon's program was unrealistic, and his actual achievements in this area were slight, but his ideal was beyond reproach:

> If there be any love of truth, hatred of darkness and desire for purification of the understanding, men must be implored again

[50] Bacon, *Parasceve ad Historiam Naturalem et Experimentalem*, Praef. Cf. *Novum Organum*, Bk. II, x.

[51] Bacon, Letter to King James I, when presenting his *Novum Organum*, 12 Oct. 1620.

[52] Bacon, *Parasceve*, Praef.

[53] Cf. Bacon, *Works*, II, 63–65; VIII, 353–355.

[54] It is in this light that the founders of the Royal Society regarded his work.

and again . . . to draw near with reverence and humility in order to unroll the volume of creation, to linger and reflect upon it, and, washed clean from prejudices, to meditate on it disinterestedly and with integrity.[55]

Accumulating data was a necessary step, but it involved its own characteristic hazards. Reflection convinced him that it was a stage in the projected advance which could not be avoided. Generalization on an insufficient basis had been responsible, he contended, for the sterility and emptiness of the Aristotelian system. It was therefore necessary to go back to facts, to facts in much greater abundance than had ever been available before. So facts had to be collected, classified, and tabulated; only when *all* the facts had been assembled could valid deductions be drawn from them. But accumulating data might prove to be as sterile as making generalizations. This was the danger to which Bacon's proposal was exposed. He has been accused of failing in the same way as Aristotle, though at a different point. Bacon, however, did not regard the gathering of data as an isolated activity. In his mind it was closely related to the conducting of experiments. And experiments were expected to fulfill a certain purpose. The man who carried out the experiment would naturally be interested in discovering what happened under certain circumstances, but this was not his essential aim. He designed his experiment in order to get an answer to a question posed by the nature of his material. The results that he obtained constituted a further fact in the expanding area of our grasp of the phenomena under investigation. Bacon has often been criticized for divorcing experimentation from the accumulation of data. The strict division of labor proposed in *The New Atlantis* has been denounced as artificial and stultifying. In no scientific discipline would it now be tolerated as a governing principle. But the history of science shows that the generalization which synthesizes a great mass of material has often been made on the basis of facts accumulated by many investigators over a period of many years.[56] Where Bacon was unquestionably vulnerable to criticism was in his failure to distinguish between the process of discovery and the demonstration of discovery. Nor did he recognize that judgment is as deeply involved in the effective collecting of facts as in their imaginative use. Sometimes Bacon's proposals seem naïve—which is hardly surprising since he was a pioneer in an area where only wide experience can give insight.

Bacon's aim throughout was to provide a new method of investigation. Science, as he constantly affirmed, had to be freed from the shackles of an authoritative but purely theoretical approach to knowledge. The application of his new method had to wait upon the assembling of the facts that it would interpret, but Bacon believed that once "a natural and experimen-

---

[55] Bacon, *Historia Naturalis et Experimentalis ad Condendam Philosophiam,* Auctoris monitum.
[56] A. R. Hall, *The Scientific Revolution, 1500–1800,* p. 164.

tal history, sufficient and good" [57] had been provided, it would be possible to move forward. A prolonged course of observation and experiment would lead up to the confirmation of scientific laws by means of a process of induction. Induction would be "the key of interpretation," "the thread of the labyrinth," a "machine" capable of controlling and directing the capacities of man. It seemed clear to Bacon that once the facts had been collected a new kind of logic was needed to deal with them. "There are two ways," he said,

> and can only be two, of seeking and finding truth. The one from sense and reason, takes flight to the most general axioms, and from these principles and their truth, settled once for all, invents and judges of all intermediate axioms. The other method collects axioms from sense and particulars, ascending continuously and by degrees so that in the end it arrives at the most general axioms. This latter is the only true one, but never hitherto tried.[58]

Bacon dismissed the old logic because it was merely a form of intellectual gymnastics. The type of induction with which he proposed to supplant it was to be an instrument to assist the mind in the process of discovery. Induction, indeed, was designed to guide the development of knowledge from its beginnings in sense experience to its fulfillment in reasoned interpretation. It begins, he argued, with the development of natural history; it progresses through the controlled observation of phenomena; it reaches its completion in the formulation of general axioms. Scientific knowledge has its origin in the response of the senses to individual objects, but its contents consist, not of impressions received directly from things but of "abstract notions derived from these impressions." It is induction that enables the mind to proceed from phenomena to theory. As Bacon pointed out, knowledge begins with "whatever has been the occurrence of individual objects collected and digested by the mind into general notions." [59] Induction had the great advantage that it combined empiricism and rationalism in a unified method capable of obtaining illuminating results from individual phenomena.

Induction was a necessary part of Bacon's scientific revolution, but, as frequently happens, Bacon was imparting a new meaning to an old term. Induction had been a part of the Aristotelian system. The classical type of logic proceeded, at a single bound, from the particulars supplied by experience to the most general theoretical propositions; then, by means of middle terms, it descended to intermediate axioms.[60] The vitiating error of

---

[57] Bacon, *Novum Organum*, Bk. I, x.
[58] *Ibid.*, Bk. I, xix.
[59] Bacon, *Descriptio Globi Intellectualis*, Ch. I, *Works*, Vol. IX.
[60] Bacon, *Novum Organum*, Bk. I, lxix.

the old approach was that it allowed reason to prescribe to things; the benefit of the new method was that reason followed and obeyed nature, discovering her secrets by obedience and submission to rule. Bacon's system of induction recognized that the senses, when unassisted, provide unreliable information; it therefore began by supplying the necessary aid and direction. The formulation of axioms came as the climax of a carefully graduated progression. "Then and only then may we hope well of the sciences, when in a just scale of ascent and by successive steps, not interrupted or broken, we rise from particulars to lesser axioms; and then to middle axioms, one above the other; and last of all to the most general." [61] Thus the whole process of inductive reasoning has assumed an entirely new guise. "The induction which is to be available for the discovery of sciences and arts must analyze nature by proper rejections and exclusions; and then, after a sufficient number of negatives, come to a conclusion on the affirmative instances, which has not yet been done, or even attempted, save only by Plato. . . . And this induction must be used not only to discover axioms, but also in the formation of notions." [62]

The method of induction occupied a crucial position in Bacon's program for the Great Instauration, but it was not intended to stand alone. On the one hand, it was intimately related to the theory of forms: the theory explained the method, the method fulfilled the theory. On the other hand, Bacon believed that induction, as he expounded it, would remain imperfect unless supplemented by certain further developments. He still had to elaborate a means of dealing with what he called latent processes and latent schematisms. In outlining his program he indicated their place and even suggested their significance. He never found time to develop this phase of his project. It should have formed the concluding section of the *Novum Organum*, but Bacon was shorthanded and sorely pressed for time. So he turned from the second to the third division of his sixfold scheme for the renovation of knowledge. In attempting to provide directions for fashioning a natural history he left unfinished his exposition of the inductive method. This was an unhappy necessity; Bacon still believed that the Great Instauration ultimately depended on the efficacy of induction: his new method would promote knowledge of and effective control over nature, and thus it would inaugurate an era of incalculable enrichment for all mankind.

Bacon rigorously separated science and theology. The relations between the two raised in a particularly acute form the authority exercised by traditional disciplines and the freedom claimed by the new types of investigation. The division that Bacon made created for him certain theoretical problems, and actually his position is not as clear and simple as initially it seems to be. He insisted on the essential unity of the intellectual

[61] *Ibid.,* Bk. I, civ.
[62] *Ibid.,* Bk. I, cv.

world. He proposed to construct a map that would include all that man can know about his life and his environment. He insisted that his method was applicable to all fields of endeavor. Then he sharply divided the interests of science from the concerns of theology.

The separation was not original; it had often been made before. It has been suggested that the freedom of science was still precarious and that Bacon had no desire to court the hazards of churchly censure. But in England a man of Bacon's standing ran little risk of persecution on account of heresy. When Milton was in Italy he found that England was considered a haven of intellectual liberty; Continental scholars accounted him "happy to be born in such a place of philosophic freedom as they supposed England was." [63] Possibly Bacon forfeited some support in high places because his views were considered inimical to faith, but this is largely surmise. He adopted his position on this matter because it seemed likely to safeguard the intellectual interests he most deeply cherished.

Bacon accepted the view, widely held in certain quarters, that it was wisest to isolate incompatible types of knowledge. Whatever we can discover about the world around us must be gleaned by methods entirely different from those appropriate to theology. Religion and science ought not to be "commixed together," since the one is "grounded only upon the Word and Oracle of God," the other "upon the light of nature." [64] Bacon believed that certain results would probably follow from any blurring of the frontiers; he found that they have consistently appeared. Ever since the days of Plato, science has been confused and misguided whenever it has become entangled with theology. The objectives and the methods of the two disciplines are completely incompatible. Theology is concerned with purpose and ends, and Bacon could find no place for teleology in experimental science. We should not ask why certain things happen in the physical world; it is a fruitless question and deflects us from the kind of investigation that will probably bring useful results. Final causes cannot profitably be investigated in physics: research into such questions, Bacon remarked, "like a virgin dedicated to God, is barren and produces nothing." [65] At this point, however, it is important to notice what Bacon actually said. He conceded that teleology may properly have a place in the study of nature, provided it is restricted to the division of "metaphysics" and excluded from that of physics. It is a legitimate subject for research, but it has its own methods and its distinctive limitations. For example, its conclusions can never have the kind of practical application to which the study of physics so often leads. But that the pursuit of natural theology can produce valid and significant (though perhaps limited) results he did not doubt. He believed that the investigation of nature

[63] Milton, *Areopagitica, in Works* (Columbia ed.), IV, 330.
[64] Bacon, *The Advancement of Learning,* Bk. II, VI, 1, and XXV, 3.
[65] Cf. Bacon, *De Augmentis Scientarium,* Bk. III, Ch. IV.

conclusively proves the existence of God. It even establishes certain of his attributes. "And concerning divine philosophy or natural theology," he wrote, "it is that knowledge or rudiment of knowledge concerning God which may be obtained by the contemplation of his creatures: which knowledge may be termed divine in respect of the knowledge, and natural in respect of the light. The bounds of this knowledge are that it sufficeth to convince atheism but not to inform religion." [66]

Bacon's separation of religion and science was rigid only up to a certain point; it was not inspired by a denial of the legitimacy of theology, so long as theology was restricted to its proper sphere. The realms of nature and of grace should normally be kept apart in order to protect each against the other. Hooker had advocated the same separation in the interests of religion; Bacon clearly had at heart the well-being of science. He did not believe that the knowledge of nature could be used to undermine the foundations of faith, but he was very apprehensive lest the dogmatism so often associated with religious belief might restrict the inquiries of science. He foresaw the danger that Biblical statements might be invoked to refute the conclusions dictated by research into natural phenomena. The Bible should not be used as evidence on scientific questions because, said Bacon, it is too sacred a book to serve such mundane ends. It must therefore be reserved for supernatural purposes alone.

Bacon evidently did not find it easy to reduce to perfect consistency his treatment of scientific knowledge and of two kinds of religious truth. An emphatically rationalist strain runs through his scientific exposition. In his discussion of religion the role of reason is studiously minimized. How, then, did he conceive of the relation of faith and reason? We might expect that in dealing with religious questions he would stress the duty of unquestioning acceptance of authority and thus restrict the free exercise of our minds. He frankly admitted that difficulties, even dangers, beset the problem, but he insisted that within proper limits we ought to use our reason even in dealing with revelation. He suggested that there are two ways in which we can legitimately do so. We can try to understand the meaning of what God has revealed. We must not expect to make dramatic progress: we have no better right to expect that he will commend his ways to our minds than that he will adjust his commands to our wishes.[67] Actually it would be unreasonable to hope for too much intelligibility in revelation; in that case religion would be reduced to little more than common sense, while faith would become our acceptance of an argument, not our submission to a person. "For if we believed only what is agreeable to our sense, we give consent to the matter and not to the author; which is no more than we would do towards a suspected and discredited witness." [68]

[66] Bacon, *The Advancement of Learning*, Bk. II, VI, 1.
[67] Cf. *ibid.*, Bk. II, XXV, 1.
[68] *Ibid.*

This is a part of the paradox of faith. "A Christian is one who believes things his reason cannot comprehend; he hopes for things which neither he nor any man alive ever saw; he labours for that which he knoweth he shall never obtain; yet in the issue, his belief appears not to be false; his hope makes him not ashamed; his labour is not in vain." [69] It must be understood, of course, that when God unfolds his mysteries, he stoops to man's capacities; he applies his inspiration to open man's understanding, "as the form of the key to the ward of the lock." [70] Yet this does not drag down the content of revelation to the level at which our minds normally function. "So as we ought not to attempt to draw down or to submit the mysteries of God to our reason; but contrariwise to raise and advance our reason to the divine truth." [71] There is, as Bacon pointed out, a second way in which our minds can deal with what God has disclosed. We may take the revealed nature and commands of God as fixed premises. They may appear arbitrary to us, but so do the rules of chess, which are laid down and which it is entirely pointless to discuss. In the latter case, we "direct our play thereupon with best advantage to win the game," and we do not waste time in arguing about things which cannot be altered.[72] So with the purposes of God: we can employ our reason to deduce from his laws certain inferences, implications or consequences, but we can do nothing to change those laws.

Bacon believed that reason has a place in the life of faith, but he carefully restricted its sphere. He urged that religion be studied with greater care, but his directions often did more to confuse the question than to clarify it. His map of human learning presupposed some place for natural theology, and accordingly he found room for it, but he did little to explore its significance. He permitted the reasonable examination of revelation, but he did not really encourage it. In his works, faith and reason have a minimal connection. Rational knowledge deals with matters about which faith is not concerned. Natural theology was supposed to link these two divided areas, but in his system the bridge was feebly built and little used. The effect of Bacon's thought was to encourage the doctrine of twofold truth. He wished to safeguard science against interference by theology. In this he had considerable success. His influence certainly increased the freedom that scientific investigation enjoyed and in the process gave it a much more secular quality. By the same token he diminished the authority of all traditional types of knowledge and hastened the exclusion of theology from areas where it had long reigned supreme.

What, it may be asked, was Bacon's motive in separating religion and

[69] Bacon, *Christian Paradoxes* (*The Character of a Believing Christian*, §1), *Works*, II, 478.
[70] Bacon, *The Advancement of Learning*, Bk. II, XXV, 5.
[71] *Ibid.*, Bk. II, VI, 1.
[72] *Ibid.*, Bk. II, XXV, 5.

science? The most diverse opinions have been advanced. Some have regarded him as a sincere and orthodox Christian. Others have seen him as a hypocrite who cloaked his lack of conviction behind a fulsome commendation of religious faith. Still others have detected in him a cryptoatheist, invoking religion as a shelter behind which he could pursue an essentially subversive aim. In view of the prevailing atmosphere in the seventeenth century and the engrossing interest of the age in religious issues the latter interpretation hardly seems convincing. The prayers that he composed do not impress the reader as a studied exercise in hypocrisy, nor do they suggest profound religious insight. Probably he was an Anglican of the Erastian type, genuine in his acceptance of a somewhat formal faith and persuaded of the social utility of the Church of England.

On the wider issue of his contribution to the revolution of his age opinions have been even more fiercely divided. He has been reviled as a "magnificent charlatan." He has been extolled as the inaugurator of a new age. In the latter part of the seventeenth century his popularity was immense and probably unparalleled. His theories were popularized, and his contribution was praised by English, French, German, and Italian authors. In the eighteenth century the French Encyclopedists hailed him as the great defender of freedom against obscurantist authority; to d'Alembert he was "le plus grand, le plus universal, et le plus éloquent des philosophes." [73] Coleridge placed him among the four greatest Englishmen. Macaulay's famous essay was typical of the chorus of uncritical nineteenth-century praise. But it has also been asserted that he really contributed little to science and that much of his influence has been bad.

Bacon may have failed magnificently, but there is no doubt that at many points he failed. He planned more than he could finish—more, indeed, than any man could accomplish in a single lifetime. He lacked concentration; he allowed himself to be distracted by ambitions incompatible with his professed objectives. He proposed to inaugurate the new age of science, but he made no significant discoveries. He laid down rules to govern scientific procedures; he himself broke them repeatedly, and few have even tried to follow them. His method, it has been claimed, was logically defective; it was able to answer certain questions, but not those which Bacon particularly hoped to solve. He had no skill in mathematics; he was not even aware that it provided the real key to that scientific progress in which he longed to play a part. His defects at this point are responsible for his striking failure to appreciate the great achievements of men like Gilbert, Kepler, and Galileo. It cannot be claimed that in any significant respect science has followed the course which Bacon charted for it. To a surprising extent his own thought was governed by medieval presuppositions. This was probably inevitable. The effects of a millennium of thought are not dissipated in a generation. If Bacon clung to

[73] d'Alembert, *L'Encyclopédie*, Disc. prelim.

outmoded conceptions, so did Harvey (who, like Bacon, believed in vital spirits in the blood) and Boyle (who described inanimate objects as having aspirations and dispositions). In his method Bacon often looked to the past; in his aims he anticipated the future.

An awareness of the prevailing intellectual outlook sets Bacon's achievement in a different light. In his mistakes he was often the victim of the existing state of scientific knowledge. His failures were many because he proposed a completely comprehensive scheme for disciplines that had barely begun to march forward into the modern age. Part of his importance in the intellectual revolution lay in his perception that a better system of scientific explanation was needed and that it could be found. His "Great Instauration" provided his contemporaries with a clear and comprehensive outline of the tasks they had to undertake. His success in this was not affected by the fact that he was not a creative scientist. He was sensitive to the intellectual atmosphere which engendered the new science, and he performed the inestimable service of systematizing thought. What he provided might be called the Declaration of Rights of the new scientific disciplines. We must remember, of course, that Bacon's proposals awaken in a modern reader a response very different from that which they aroused in his own contemporaries. To us, his comments and proposals may seem pedestrian and even flat; in the seventeenth century they had the novelty and excitement of a revolutionary program. The important issue is not how much he discovered, or how exactly his successors followed his guidance. The task that he accepted and that he discharged with magnificent effect was somewhat different. It was his mission, he believed, to liberate mankind from the errors and illusions of the past. He was intent on destroying the prejudices which were too uncritically accepted by his contemporaries. His very limitations contributed to his success. He set little store by the heritage of the past. He lacked the historical insight necessary to appreciate what had been achieved by his predecessors. He was an innovator, with many of the shortcomings that are typical of the breed. But he also had the distinguishing mark of the true revolutionary: he was intensely aware that he was inaugurating a new age. This accounts for his immense impact on his contemporaries. They responded to him because they saw in him the herald of the new day.

Bacon himself defined his role. "I am but a trumpeter," he said, "not a combatant." [74] As a herald he was without a peer. With an incomparable eloquence he defined the task, and summoned his contemporaries to undertake it. His performance may have been meager and his actual achievements of slight account, but as a propagandist for science he was beyond compare. He recognized the conditions that would determine scientific progress, and he proclaimed them with unrivaled persuasiveness

[74] Raven, *Natural Religion*, I, 100.

and power. He created a new mentality, and when, later in the seventeenth century, the Royal Society of London was founded, its members hailed Bacon as the forerunner who had anticipated what they had now achieved. In Cowley's famous tribute he was depicted as the Moses who had led his countrymen to the frontier of the promised land, even though he himself only saw it from afar.

> Bacon, like Moses, led us forth at last,
> The barren wilderness he past,
> Did on the very border stand
> Of the bles'd promis'd land,
> And from the mountain top of his exalted wit,
> Saw it himself, and shew'd us it.
> But life did never to one man allow
> Time to discover worlds, and conquer too.[75]

[75] Abraham Cowley, *Verses to the Royal Society.*

III

POLITICAL THOUGHT:
THE AUTHORITY OF THE PRINCE
AND THE LIBERTIES OF THE PEOPLE

In POLITICAL THEORY the sixteenth century often framed the questions; the seventeenth century usually tried to answer them. Old patterns of authority had crumbled. The supranational empire had dwindled to approximate equality with other states, and in the political maneuvers of a new day its honorary precedence proved a hindrance as often as a help. The unity of the universal church had been shattered, but the pope had not relinquished his ancient claim to make and unmake kings. Had his pretensions, it was asked, any bearing on the question of authority? As soon as men challenged the claims of St. Peter's successor, they began to raise other issues which also demanded answers. How was sovereignty constituted? What was the measure of obedience appropriate to a subject? When (if ever) might a nation throw off the yoke of oppression? Was unfaltering submission the only permissible response to kingly tyranny? What were the prerogatives of royalty, and what were the liberties of the people?

I

In England seventeenth-century political theorists examined such problems in the light of certain presuppositions, and these had largely been fashioned either by the experience of the Tudor period or by the debates in France prompted by the Wars of Religion.

The great Tudor rulers were not seriously concerned about developing political theory; they were primarily intent on creating a strong national state and an effective system of government. Because the turmoil of the baronial wars was a recent and painful memory, few challenged the need either for a powerful prince or for an obedient people. All subjects, declared the Elizabethan homily, "are bounden to obey their magistrates"; they should "all therefore fear that he that resisteth (or withstandeth) common authority resisteth (or withstandeth) God and his ordinance." [1] It was clear that "a rebel is worse than the worst prince, and rebellion worse than the worst government of the worst prince that hitherto hath been." [2] Here iniquity appears in its most comprehensive form. "How horrible a sin against God and man rebellion is, cannot possibly be expressed according unto the greatness thereof. For he that nameth rebellion nameth not a singular or one only sin, as is theft, robbery, murder, and such like; but he nameth the whole puddle and sink of all sins against God and man; against his prince, against all men universally; all sins, I say, against God and all men heaped together nameth he that nameth rebellion." [3]

This was a practical matter, and one of considerable urgency. National survival demanded a strong government; a strong government presupposed complete submission. An effective doctrine of obedience had to enlist religious constraint. So the people must be reminded that "rebellion is as the sin of witchcraft" (I Sam. 15:23). Was not the warning of the apostle perfectly explicit? "The powers that be are ordained of God. Whosoever therefore resisteth the power, resisteth the ordinance of God: and they that resist shall receive to themselves damnation." (Rom. 13:1–2.) It was assumed that every constituted authority could invoke a divine sanction. The father and the landlord, no less than the magistrate and the prince, derived their claim from God. Consequently, to submit to authority was both a religious duty and a civil obligation. Arguments like this had a medieval lineage and so a wide familiarity. The Tudors did not need a new theory of kingship; they required an interpretation that their subjects could easily understand and that, because of its religious appeal, they would readily accept.

The views that were gaining ground embraced medieval concepts but they assumed a form dictated by Reformation experience. They exalted absolute national sovereignty, but they insisted on its religious implications. They saw both church and state as correlative parts of a single commonwealth. To invoke an ancient heritage and yet to invest the modern state with religious authority invited a clash with papal claims. The likelihood of such a conflict did not deter the Tudors. Medieval theorists like William of Ockham and Marsiglio of Padua had challenged the pope's supremacy. Englishmen had seldom understood the claims of Rome and had always disliked what little they understood. Admittedly the Catholic and conservative traditions of the country dictated that changes should come slowly. Even in the seventeenth century the pope's

---

[1] "An Exhortation to the Good Order and Obedience to Rulers and Magistrates," *Certain Sermons or Homilies*, pp. 118, 119.

[2] "An Homily Against Disobedience and Wilful Rebellion," *ibid.*, p. 594.

[3] *Ibid.*, p. 609. The homilies treat disobedience at far greater length than any other subject. They prove its futility as well as its iniquity (e.g., p. 621), and the relevance of the teaching is underlined by the prayer that concludes the sixth part of the homily against disobedience: "A Thanksgiving for the suppression of the last rebellion" (pp. 641–642).

right to intervene could provoke a violent controversy. But gradually the implications of the Tudor revolution became apparent. When the Thirty-nine Articles insisted that "the chief power in this realm of England . . . is not, nor ought to be, subject to any foreign jurisdiction," they struck at papal pretensions: "the bishop of Rome hath no jurisdiction in this realm of England." [4] The royal prerogative, it is clear, was not yet a matter of dispute between prince and people. Political debate was almost exclusively concerned with ecclesiastical issues and their implications.

Until Hobbes appeared, political theory in England was largely preoccupied with the problem of church and state, but it was apparent that the nature of authority was increasingly demanding attention. What, it was asked, is the source of sovereignty? Where does it actually reside, and what does it entail? Kingship itself was discussed in a new spirit. It was assumed that monarchy is the "natural" form of government, and therefore peculiarly acceptable to God. But a further question began to take shape: can any limits be set to royal authority? At this point French experience and theories based upon it proved of particular interest to Englishmen.

In the latter part of the sixteenth century, the French were compelled to treat political theory with the utmost seriousness. This is not surprising. So long as security prevails, speculation about constitutional questions seems superfluous. The threat of chaos compels men to reexamine the principles which undergird social order. In the bitter civil strife that convulsed France, religious loyalties were loudly invoked, but they did not play an exclusive—perhaps they did not even play a predominant—part. The form in which any theory was cast was usually religious; the presence of other factors is proved by the remarkable extent to which controversialists could reverse their positions. Originally the Huguenots claimed that resistance to authority was sometimes legitimate; the Catholics insisted that it was always wrong. But once it became clear that Henry of Navarre would gain the throne, the Catholic League began to justify rebellion and the Huguenots contended for absolute submission. Moreover, experience proved that more than one political program might be deduced from a given religious position. Before 1572—the year of the massacre of St. Bartholomew—all royalists argued that civil order is God's good gift and that rebellion destroys it. They assumed that an unquestioning submission to authority was the only safeguard against anarchy, and this defense presupposed uniformity of belief. But after 1572 Catholic opinion pursued divergent lines. The members of the League still insisted that without an agreed faith there could be no peace. The Politiques, on the other hand, claimed that the ideal of a nation united in doctrine had ceased to be a realistic goal. Persecution was ineffective and therefore pointless; the

[4] Article XXXVII.

toleration of heretics had become the precondition of social order. The futility of civil strife had shaken confidence in the intransigent religious claims that both sides usually advanced.[5]

The issues in the great constitutional debate were relatively clear. The basic problem concerned the nature of sovereignty. Central to this were the relations between the king and his people. The controversy in France raised in an acute form the right of the subject to resist the ruler. As the sixteenth century neared its end, certain convictions could claim fairly wide acceptance. In the first place, it was agreed that a single will must be recognized as endowed with the unchallenged power to fashion laws. Secondly, it was generally admitted that this sovereign authority, so essential to the well-being of society, was instituted by God. The religious emphasis was natural: political theory was still largely a theological exercise.

The increasing stress laid on the sovereignty of the king sharpened the question of the role of the people. The Huguenots admitted that authority is instituted by God, and that normally rebellion is resistance to his will. But they also insisted that the power committed to magistrates is not unlimited. Rulers, they argued, are established by the consent of their subjects. These doctrines, expounded by a number of pamphleteers,[6] received their most complete and influential exposition in a very celebrated work, the *Vindiciae Contra Tyrannos*. In any given instance, said the author, the prince actually receives his power from the people. But the authority attached to his office comes from God, and so submission to kingship is a divine command. Obedience, however, is not an absolute requirement: God has committed authority to the king for the benefit of the people, and once the ruler contravenes the terms of this contract, his subjects may deprive him of his office.[7] He is answerable to them for the justice and legality of his rule, and they in turn are bound by inescapable constraints. They can resist tyranny, not as individuals impatient of oppression but only as a community safeguarding its essential rights. The *Vindiciae* advances a position peculiarly relevant to the political problems of Stuart England. The translation of the work found a much wider public in England than the French and Latin editions had reached in the author's own country.

The suggestion that political power stems from the people prompted an

[5] Early in the seventeenth century, an exiled English Jesuit cited the Politiques to illustrate the tension between conscience and "reasons of state." The folly of the Politiques, he said, showed their ingratitude to God and the insufficiency of man's unaided intelligence to cope with the problems of government. Thomas Fitzherbert, *The First Part of a Treatise concerning Policy and Religion*, pp. 35–36, 38, 42–44, 49.

[6] See especially R. Hotman, *Franco-Gallia;* S. Goulart (ed.), *Mémoires de l'estat de France sous Charles Neufiesme.*

[7] The *Vindiciae* presupposes a twofold contract: between God and king-and-people, and between people and king. The idea of contract emphasizes reciprocal obligation, especially on the part of the prince.

immediate retort. A particular divinity, it was argued, invests royal authority: God himself regards it with special favor. This view had ancient antecedents. As it developed during the sixteenth century it did not initially imply a preference for absolutism rather than constitutional government, but absolute sovereignty, when vested in the ruler, was seen as a particularly effective defense against political chaos. The French civil wars had exposed the dangers lurking in a clash between religious parties; royal power provided the only dependable barrier against the disasters that threatened the nation. As developed by Pierre de Belloy,[8] the theory insisted that real authority derives from God alone. The people may be able to delegate a limited amount of power, but the right to demand obedience is a divine endowment. Subjects cannot require anyone to bow to their collective demands. They have no authority; God grants that to whomsoever he will, and (so the theory insisted) he has chosen to entrust it to kings. Why to kings? The theory did not offer a philosophical explanation: being miraculous, the king's authority needs no logical defense. God has chosen kingship as the proper pattern of sovereignty among men; he has also decided that it must be transmitted from father to son. Like kingship itself, primogeniture has the mysterious but inescapable constraint of a law of nature: it may not be understood, but it must not be defied. The analogy of a parent's authority may illuminate the divine right of kings; logic alone cannot establish it.[9]

By the end of the sixteenth century, French political thought had thus developed a theory that asserted the king's indefeasible right to his throne. The doctrine found the source of royal authority in God; it believed that authority could be transmitted only by inheritance, and it insisted that the people had no right to challenge that sovereignty. Passive obedience was the corollary of divine right; though the subject might not agree with the king, he was forbidden to resist. To explore the significance of sovereignty was the notable achievement of Jean Bodin. To the claims of royalty he yielded unqualified assent. He regarded kingship as the one power capable of restraining chaos and creating order. His *De la république* (1576) profoundly influenced the course of English political thought in the closing years of Queen Elizabeth's reign. The pattern of English ideas closely followed French precedents; the evidence of French influence is inescapable.[10] A steady stream of French books appeared in English translations. Arguments that had been first evolved in France did service in English constitutional debates. The champions of Stuart kingship repeated the arguments of French royalists and accused their opponents of borrowing the subversive doctrines of French enemies of absolute monarchy.

---

[8] In Pierre de Belloy, *De l'Authorité du roi*(1587).

[9] William Barclay's *De Regno et Regali Potestate* (1600) summarized previous discussion and set it forth in the most elaborate form.

[10] See J. H. M. Salmon, *The French Religious Wars in English Political Thought*.

French ideas, so readily admitted to England, found an even warmer welcome in Scotland. It was by this route, indeed, that one of the political theories most fiercely debated in seventeenth-century England reached the country. The vigor of Tudor government had made monarchy by divine right a superfluous doctrine; in Scotland circumstances made it particularly gratifying to the king. The Stuarts had long been harried by the turbulent nobles of their land. James VI had been hectored and berated by Calvinistic churchmen perfectly familiar with one of the theories most often invoked on the continent to challenge royal prerogative. With understandable enthusiasm James appropriated a doctrine that lifted his authority above contradiction. In "Basilikon Doron" and *The Trew Law of Free Monarchies* he gave the first full and explicit exposition attempted in Britain of the divine right of kings. He took the doctrine with him when he moved to England; there he elaborated it in his speeches and proclamations. He bequeathed it, a very dangerous legacy, to the members of his house. The fact that when he came to England it was so readily adopted in certain quarters suggests that a considerable section of the nation was already predisposed in favor of such a theory.

James VI and I was exceptional among kings, not in holding an exalted view of his office but in giving it explicit literary expression. His efforts were not received with unqualified approval. "If a king will needs write," argued the critics, "let him write like a king, every line a law, every word a precept, every letter a mandate." [11] Both at the time and subsequently, however, James did not lack admirers. He was often likened to Solomon, and it was implied that he survived the comparison with credit.[12] Bishop Barlow hailed him as "a universal scholar, acute in arguing, subtle in distinguishing, logical in discussing, powerful in persuading, admirable in discoursing." [13] James engaged in theological and political controversy with manifest relish. Modern historians concede that he had many of the skills essential to a debater: an argumentative disposition, a restless curiosity of mind, and a shrewd eye for the weak points in his opponent's position; in addition, a ready wit and a happy turn of phrase make his writings much less dreary reading than those of many of his contemporaries.[14]

[11] The critics' position is stated (in order to be refuted) by Bishop Montagu of Winchester in his Preface to *The Workes of the Most High and Mightie Prince, James, King of Great Britaine.* See also Goodman, *The Court of King James the First,* I, 214, and James Ussher, *An Answer to a Challenge made by a Jesuite in Ireland,* Ep. Ded.

[12] E.g., Richard Crakanthorpe, *A Sermon at the solemnization of the happy inauguration of our most gracious and religious sovereign King James,* pp. 2–3; John Williams, *Great Britains Salomon, passim;* Donne, *Sermons,* I, 217–219; X, 161; Bacon, *Works,* III, 431.

[13] William Barlow, *The Sermon preached at Paules Crosse,* p. 28. Robert Burton, writing after James's death (when praise was consequently more disinterested), paid tribute to him not only as a king and a statesman, but as "a famous scholar and the sole patron, pillar and sustainer of learning."

[14] See C. J. Sisson, "King James the First as Poet and Political Writer" in *Seventeenth Century Studies presented to Sir Herbert Grierson,* pp. 47 ff.

Central to James's political theory was his doctrine of kingship, and he was fond of repeating the principal arguments that buttressed his position.

> First then I will set down the true grounds whereupon I am to build, out of the Scriptures, since monarchy is the true pattern of divinity, as I have already said: next, from the fundamental laws of our own kingdom, which nearest must concern us; thirdly from the law of nature, by diverse similitudes drawn out of the same.[15]

Monarchy, said James, was instituted by God himself. From him it derives its unique dignity.

> God gives not kings the style of God in vain,
> For on his throne, his sceptre do they sway.[16]

Thus the majesty of kings partakes of the splendor of things divine: monarchs have not earned it by their merit nor achieved it by their skill. "Remember, then, that this glistening worldly glory of kings is given them by God." [17] They are anointed of the Lord; they are "the breathing images of God upon earth." [18] With infinite ingenuity James varied the form while repeating the substance of his staggering claims. "The state of monarchy," he told the members of both Houses of Parliament in March, 1609/10, "is the supremest thing upon earth For kings are not only God's lieutenants upon earth and sit upon God's throne, but by God himself they are called gods." [19]

James inculcated the lesson so often that others learned to repeat it. "Your highness is more than an ordinary man," wrote John White; "God hath set his own image, as it were upon his gold, in an eminent manner upon you, which he hath not done upon other men." [20] The unique relation in which the king stood to God established the royal authority; it also defined the subject's obligation. James readily conceded that his dignities presupposed responsibilities of the highest order, but he was answerable, he argued, to God and not to men.[21] Unquestioning obedience was the proper response of the people. They were forbidden even to probe into the origin and meaning of royal authority. "That

[15] James I, "The Trew Law of Free Monarchies," *The Political Works of James I*, p. 54.
[16] James I, "Basilikon Doron," Dedicatory Sonnet, *ibid.*, p. 3; cf. also p. 54: "they sit upon God his throne in the earth."
[17] *Ibid.*, p. 12.
[18] James I, "A Speach to the Lords and Commons of the Parliament at Whitehall, on Wednesday the xxi of March, Anno. 1609," *ibid.*, p. 307. This speech is one of the full and mature statements of James's political theory.
[19] *Ibid.*
[20] John White, *A Defence of the Way to the True Church*, Ep. Ded. Cf. George Morley's epitaph for King James: "Princes are gods; O do not then / Rake in their graves to prove them men." Quoted in J. Spotswood, *The History of the Church and State of Scotland*, p. 547.
[21] Cf. James I, *Political Works*, p. 327: "kings are to accompt to God."

which concerns the mystery of the king's power is not lawful to be disputed; for that is to wade into the weakness of princes, and to take away the mystical reverence that belongs unto them that sit in the throne of God." [22] The Scriptures show that godly men have always submitted even to unjust and tyrannical rulers. Consequently we must remember that

> the duty and allegiance of the people to their lawful king . . . ought to be to him, as God's lieutenant in earth, obeying his commands in all things . . . as the commands of God's minister, acknowledging him a judge set by God over them, having power to judge them, but to be judged only by God, whom to only he must give account of his judgment; fearing him as their judge, loving him as their father; praying for him as their protector; for his continuance, if he be good; for his amendment if he be wicked; following and obeying his lawful commands, eschewing and flying his fury in his unlawful, without resistance, by sighs and tears to God, according to that sentence in the primitive church in time of the persecution. [23]

James believed that the law of nature, no less than the Word of God, confirmed the authority of kingship. Certain similes illuminated the preeminence that in the course of nature invests the throne. As the father is the undisputed head of the family, so the king must be the unchallenged governor of the state. The authority of a patriarch over his household was simple, direct, and absolute; the same must be true of the relation of the ruler to his subjects. Monarchs are therefore rightly "compared to fathers of families; for a king is truly *parens patriae,* the politique father of his people." [24] Similarly the ruler can appropriately be likened "to a head of a body composed of diverse members. . . . For from the head, being the seat of judgment, proceedeth the care and foresight of guiding, and preventing all evil that may come to the body or any part thereof. The head cares for the body, so doth the king for his people." [25] James stressed the parallel, but he did not fully explore its implications. He did, however, point out that anarchy is the only alternative to the orderly patterns that prevail throughout nature and that ought to be reflected in the affairs of men. At this point James was not exploring new possibilities. He was emphasizing a concept both common and popular in his own day. When Shakespeare ventured into political theory, he too dwelt on the role of

[22] James I, "A Speach in the Starre-Chamber," *ibid.,* p. 333.

[23] James I, "The Trew Law of Free Monarchies," *ibid.,* p. 61. James considered it the essence of a "free monarchy" that the ruler should have supreme and unchallenged power over all his subjects.

[24] James I, "A Speach to the Lords and Commons," *ibid.,* p. 307.

[25] James I, "The Trew Law of Free Monarchies," *ibid.,* p. 64. Cf. "A Speach to the Lords and Commons," p. 307: "And lastly kings are compared to the head of this microcosm of the body of man."

kings in preserving order and thus restraining anarchy.[26]

The authority of the king, established both by the will of God and by the law of nature, is confirmed by the evidence of history. Theory is thus validated by experience. In Scotland, said James, monarchy was established by King Fergus and his followers. By force of arms they won the rights conferred by conquest. The same was true of England: "when the bastard of Normandy came into England and made himself king, was it not by force and with a mighty army?" [27] But possession alone was not a sufficient title to the throne. Hereditary right was equally necessary, and James took strong objection to the views enunciated in the suggested canons of 1604. A man would greatly err, said Convocation, if he assumed that he might legitimately resist a government, established by successful rebellion, on the grounds that its authority lacked divine sanction.[28] James's response was prompt and vigorous. Archbishop Abbot drew a stinging rebuke for approving a view that would have guaranteed the king of Spain the loyal obedience of Englishmen, provided he successfully invaded their country and seized the throne. James believed too firmly in the principle of legitimism to sanction such dangerous doctrine. Abbot, he wrote, had "dipped too deep in what all kings reserve among the *arcana imperii*," and must never repeat the error.[29] The relation between history and doctrine thus seemed clear. Conquest bestowed power; inheritance confirmed it. The essential legal quality in monarchy must therefore always be associated with lawful descent from the previous legitimate ruler. To this position the Stuarts clung tenaciously throughout the seventeenth century.

The relation between royal prerogative and established law was important but far from clear. James asserted that one of the king's primary duties was to establish and execute good laws.[30] Originally the king's will *was* the law, but "how soon kingdoms began to be settled in civility and policy, then did the kings set down their minds by laws, which are properly made by the king only." [31] Is the king, then, restricted by the laws that he himself has made? The answer is confused. As sovereign the king has complete power, but the exercise of that power might well be constitutionally unlawful. As a matter of fact, the king has committed himself "by a double oath to the observation of the fundamental laws of his kingdom." Merely by being king he is "bound to protect as well the people as the laws of his kingdom," but in addition his coronation vows

[26] Cf. Shakespeare, *Henry V,* Act IV, Sc. i.
[27] James I, "The Trew Law of Free Monarchies," *Political Works,* pp. 61–63.
[28] John Overall, *Bishop Overall's Convocation Book,* p. 59 (Bk. I, Canon xxviii).
[29] David Wilkins, *Concilia Magnae Britanniae et Hiberniae,* IV, 405. James's letter to Archbishop Abbot is also reprinted in the *Library of Anglo-Catholic Theology* edition of *Bishop Overall's Convocation Book* and in James Welwood, *Memoirs,* p. 239.
[30] James I, "Basilikon Doron," *Political Works,* p. 18.
[31] James I, "A Speach to the Lords and Commons," *ibid.,* p. 309.

oblige him to rule in conformity with the settled patterns that the law has established.[32] The good king submits to this limitation, the tyrant does not. James realized that the common law might well constitute a restraint on his authority. The civil law, he claimed, had certain theoretical advantages, and a knowledge of it was necessary for the conduct of international affairs, but he insisted that he had no intention of quarreling with the common law. "For no law can be more favourable and advantageous for a king and extendeth further his prerogative than it doth. And for a king of England to despise the common law it is to neglect his own crown." [33]

James was not alone in his concern about prerogative. This issue, as much as any other, dominated political controversy in the seventeenth century. But, though James preached a high doctrine of royal authority, his writings and speeches really reflected a tendency rather than a fully developed theory. He was too cautious to be a revolutionary, and when his claims threatened to precipitate a clash, he retreated into generalities. He vaguely reasserted his authority, but reached an accommodation with his critics. In due course, however, other thinkers, both lay and clerical, gave his theories more explicit form, and other men tried to give them more resolute expression.

To complicate the problem, "prerogative" was a word used in more senses than one and it was not always exactly defined. On the one hand it pointed to certain rights, normally prescribed by law, that were conceded to anyone in a position of authority. "Prerogative," said John Selden, "is something that can be told what it is, not something that has no name. Just as you see the archbishop has his prerogative court, but we know what is done in that court, so the king's prerogative is not his will, or—what divines make it—a power to do what he lists. The king's prerogative, that is the king's law." [34] On the other hand it was admitted that certain conditions might arise in which neither law nor custom dictated what must be done. Here the sovereign was surely free to determine the proper course to follow. It was even admitted that under certain circumstances he might override the law in order to safeguard the welfare of the state. As constitutional development progressed, of course, the undefined area inevitably shrank, but in Stuart times it was still very extensive. As the monarchy asserted its right to operate in this indeterminate region, it gave the impression that it was enlarging its prerogative. When the representatives of the people challenged this apparent extension, a new problem emerged. Sir Thomas Smith, the Elizabethan theorist, had declared that "the most high and absolute power of the realm consisteth in the

[32] *Ibid.*
[33] *Ibid.,* p. 310.
[34] Selden, *Table Talk,* p. 112.

Parliament"—that is, the crown and the estates.[35] But what happened if king and parliament should disagree? To many observers in the early seventeenth century the answer seemed obvious: sovereignty reverted to the king alone. It is clear that in some of the most celebrated clashes between the early Stuarts and their parliaments both James and Charles believed that they had the authority of law on their side, and modern scholarship concedes their claim. In Bate's case (1606) and in the case of ship money (1638) the opinion of the judges upheld the right of the king to act independently of parliament when necessity required.[36] But the terms of the verdicts make it obvious that the judges assumed that such latitude could be claimed and exercised only in times of serious crisis. In the ship money case, in particular, the judgment of Sir Robert Berkeley was clear: he was defining the situation that would prevail in a grave emergency. Under such circumstances, he argued, the national interest demanded that the king be free to act alone; if necessary, he must be able to suspend the law. Moreover, it was the king himself who must determine if a crisis had arisen. Under normal circumstances, it was assumed, the exercise of such latitude could not be countenanced. Unfortunately, Charles insisted that an emergency had arisen, though there was little evidence to support the claim; what was much more serious, he then proceeded to use extraordinary measures to meet normal government needs.

Inevitably the exploration of the scope and implications of sovereignty became the chief preoccupation of many political theorists. Before pursuing this subject, however, we must turn to examine a separate but related issue.

II

When James I came to the throne of England, he had already propounded his theory of sovereignty. He was promptly compelled to clarify its implications in relation to other types of authority. The tension between royal claims and popular rights was to prove a persistent problem for the Stuarts, but it was in a different area that the debate began. The prerogatives of the king clashed with the pretensions of the pope, and the controversy raised issues that no one could ignore.

The contest was probably inevitable, though its occasion could not have been foreseen. James's right of succession had been injudiciously attacked by Fr. Robert Parsons, the great expatriate Jesuit, but most English

---

[35] Sir Thomas Smith, *The Commonwealth of England,* Bk. II, Ch. 2. Eight editions of this work were published in the early part of the seventeenth century.

[36] Bate's case concerned the king's right to levy duty; Hampden's case (ship money) involved the right to collect special taxes unauthorized by parliament. Full reports are given in W. Cobbett and T. B. Howell (eds.), *State Trials,* II, 387–394, and III, 1090–1101; the essential sections are quoted in J. P. Kenyon, *The Stuart Constitution, 1603–1688,* pp. 62–64, 111–114.

Catholics welcomed the new king. They trusted that his reign would inaugurate an era of happier relationships. Pleas for toleration multiplied. In effusive terms the Catholics praised the king's enlightened outlook. They emphasized their loyalty and argued that persecution weakened the fabric of society.[37] They hoped for better treatment, and their hopes seemed eminently reasonable. Before his accession the king had angled for Catholic support by promising concessions. In addressing his first parliament he had stressed his conciliatory aims. He had no intention, he said, of compelling his subjects to conform to all his own opinions; "nay," he added, "my mind was ever so free from persecution or thralling my subjects in the matters of conscience, as I hope that those of that profession within this kingdom have a proof since my coming that I was so far from increasing their burdens with Rehoboam, as I have, as much as either time, occasion or law would permit, lightened them." [38]

Treason, however, blighted the prospects of toleration. The Bye Plot, followed by the Main Plot, led to a stiffening of royal policy, and this in turn inspired a few Catholic fanatics to plan the Gunpowder Treason. The government replied by imposing on all Catholics a test of loyalty. In terms of what it demanded, the Oath of Allegiance of 1606 was not extreme, but to Catholics its language seemed gratuitously offensive. The penalties for refusing the oath were unquestionably harsh. Indeed, it is doubtful whether so inquisitional a measure, prescribing such severe punishments, could have been effectively enforced. What made the oath important was the controversy that it prompted. The archpriest George Blackwell decided that Catholics could, in good conscience, take the oath. He did so himself, and suppressed the papal injunctions that forbade the faithful to take it. He was called to account by Cardinal Bellarmine; as soon as the greatest of Catholic controversialists entered the fray, King James saw in him an opponent worthy of his own mettle. Already the scope of the controversy was rapidly expanding; it spread to practically every court and university of Europe. Every nation was eager to explore the significance of its sovereign freedom. The pope, it appeared, was insisting that under certain circumstances the nation-state must submit to the dictates of the Church of Rome. No prince could be indifferent to such claims. Most rulers were at least intrigued by the independence and authority that the English crown had seized; in Donne's words, "it is easy to be observed that all other princes of Christendom begin to shake off

---

[37] Cf. Cal. Salisbury MSS., XV, 131, 199; *A Petition Apologeticall presented to the Kinges most excellent Majestie by the lay Catholikes of England;* Simion Grahame, *The Passionate Sparke of a Relenting Minde;* Matthew Kellison, *A Survey of the new Religion,* Ep. Ded., pp. 8–10; M. C. P. [Michael Walpole], *A Briefe Admonition to all English Catholikes,* Ep. Ded.; William Bishop, *Maister Perkins Reformed Catholique,* Ep. Ded. There also appeared a spate of works warning James against tolerating papists. Note Donne's relief that James came to the throne without prior commitments to papists or Puritans, *Sermons,* I, 219.

[38] James I, "A Speach as it was delivered in the Upper House of the Parliament," *Political Works,* p. 274.

those fetters which insensibly and drowsily they had admitted, and labour by all ways which are as yet possible to them to return to their natural supremacy and jurisdiction." [39] The list of participants in the controversy embraces many of the most distinguished theologians and political theorists of the age: Bellarmine, Becanus, Bédé, du Perron, Gretzer, Lessius.

In this case King James fashioned royal policy and then expounded it. The oath, he wrote, was so framed that it was simply "the profession of natural allegiance, and civil and temporal obedience." It was exclusively concerned "with the civil obedience of subjects to their sovereign in mere temporal causes." [40] To treat it as a religious issue was to deflect it from its obvious and essential purpose. "For as for the Catholic faith, can there be found one word in all that oath tending or sounding to matter of religion? Doth he that taketh it promise there to believe or not to believe any article of religion? Or doth he so much as name a true or false church there?" [41] Those who framed the oath were consequently clear about its aim; it affirmed the king's "just supremacy"; from the subject it exacted an appropriate submission, and it repudiated, as far as the pope was concerned, "the superintendence of his authorities and the violence of his excommunications." [42]

It is obvious, however, that two kinds of jurisdiction were in conflict, and each claimed to be supreme. Ecclesiastical authority, though staggering under "heaps of ashes and dead doctrine,"[43] was disputing the powers that all princes were now determined to exercise. "This challenge of the pope," wrote Bishop Barlow, "in dethroning and deposing princes, is a temporal intrusion and no spiritual jurisdiction." [44] The champions of the civil power insisted that kings, no less than popes, derive their authority from God. "Only all lawful magistrates . . . are so many vicegerents of God Almighty, to govern and moderate their peculiar dominions in, for and according to God and his word." [45] Kings are answerable to no man, whether priest or pope; only God can challenge their decisions and he alone can punish their misdeeds.[46] The course of history had rendered obsolete the papal claim to intervene in the affairs of nations. There is one question, said Donne, that the bishop of Rome cannot evade: "Who made you judge of kings, that you should depose them in criminal cases? Or

---

[39] Donne, *Pseudo-martyr*, Preface, §7.

[40] *The Workes of the Most High and Mightie Prince, James* (1616 ed.), pp. 294, 292.

[41] *Ibid.*, p. 269.

[42] Thomas Ireland, *The Oath of Allegiance defended*, Ep. Ded.

[43] Donne, *Pseudo-martyr*, p. 374.

[44] Barlow, *An Answer to a Catholike Englishman*, p. 32; cf. R. Parr, *The Life of James Usher*, p. 22.

[45] Henry Burton, *The Baiting of the Pope's Bull*, p. 50. Cf. Donne, *Pseudo-martyr*, p. 83; "for magistracy and superiority is so natural and so immediate from God that Adam was created a magistrate"; cf. also [Richard Mocket?], *Deus et Rex: God and the King*, pp. 14–28.

[46] David Owen, *Herod and Pilate Reconciled*, p. 1.

who made you proprietary of kingdoms, that you should dispose of them as of civil inheritances?" [47] Certain natural and inalienable rights belong to princes; when the pope interferes with these he endangers the fabric of society. He also sets all Roman Catholic citizens in conflict with the state. "Their point of doctrine," said King James, "is that arrogant and ambitious supremacy of their head, the pope, whereby he not only claims to be spiritual head of all Christians, but also to have an imperial civil power over all kings and emperors." In practice, therefore, it becomes "no sin but rather a matter of salvation to do all acts of rebellion and hostility against their natural sovereign lord, if he be once cursed, his subjects discharged of their fidelity, and his kingdom given a prey by that three-crowned monarch, or rather monster, their head." [48]

The Catholics, of course, rejected so damaging an indictment, but they were embarrassed by conflicting views advanced by their own spokesmen. One group, represented by Carerius, claimed for the pope absolute authority over all the world, alike in civil and religious matters. Bellarmine, as spokesman for a more moderate party, admitted that the pope had no direct temporal power over kings and kingdoms; nevertheless, by an indirect prerogative, tending to the advancement of spiritual good, he had supreme authority to dispose of the temporalities of all Christians. Still others, like William Barclay, argued that though the pope undoubtedly had spiritual power to excommunicate even royal offenders, he had no temporal authority "directly or indirectly to afflict the persons of kings, to transpose their kingdoms, to persuade foreigners to make wars or subjects to rebel against them." [49] Among English Catholics these theoretical differences were aggravated by acute disagreements about practical policy. They all insisted that they were eager to render the kind of civil obedience that "any loyal and dutiful subject" owes his prince.[50] But what were the proper limits of their allegiance? The pope himself, said Parsons, urged legitimate submission; he merely insisted on reserving to the supreme religious authority the right and the duty to intervene in temporal affairs.[51] The pope had to possess "this supereminent power . . . over princes to punish them temporally"; without it, Christ would have

[47] Donne, *Sermons,* II, 327.

[48] James I, "A Speach as it was delivered in the Upper House of the Parliament," *Political Works,* p. 275. These same issues concerning the pope's authority had been debated during the French controversies on kingship; cf. J. W. Allen, *A History of Political Thought in the Sixteenth Century,* pp. 287–291, 352–355.

[49] D. Owen, *op. cit.,* Ep. Ded. Barclay's most important work on this subject was his *Of the Authoritie of the Pope.*

[50] M. C. P., *op. cit.,* p. 85. Cf. William Warmington, *A Moderate Defence of the Oath of Allegiance,* Preface; Robert Parsons, *The Judgment of a Catholicke English-man,* pp. 8–9; T. A. [Thomas Owen], *A Letter to a Catholicke Man beyond the seas,* p. 47.

[51] R. Parsons, *The Judgment of a Catholicke English-man,* pp. 50 ff., 62. Parsons had previously enunciated this position in 1592, when justifying rebellion against Queen Elizabeth; E. L. Taunton, *The History of the Jesuits in England,* p. 148.

insufficiently endowed his church with the disciplinary resources it requires.[52] Consequently, the more ardent Catholic apologists felt obliged to restate with some care the proofs of the pope's supremacy; they affirmed his authority over temporal rulers, and thus returned to the practical point at issue: the Oath of Allegiance must be refused.[53] Catholics might accede to the purely civil demands, but certain clauses of the oath "detract(ed) from the spiritual authority of the said highest pastor." By limiting what the pope could "do towards his Majesty or his successors in any case whatsoever," it touched "a point of doctrine and Catholic belief concerning the sufficiency of pastoral authority . . . for redressing of all inconveniences that may fall out."[54] High theory was fortified by practical considerations. The oath, it was argued, was defectively framed. The pope has a *probable* power to depose; it is unreasonable to deny that he has *any* power. The royal supremacy is a novel theory and its implications are far from clear; the king cannot compel his subjects to swear to uncertain matters. A valid oath must satisfy the criteria of truth, justice and necessity; the Oath of Allegiance fell short in all three respects. King James was not a Catholic sovereign; therefore Catholic subjects could not be bound by any oath he might require of them.[55]

It became increasingly clear, however, that English Catholics were agreed neither about the high theory of papal supremacy nor about the practical acceptability of the oath. The critics of the official Roman position appealed to the divine origin of temporal power. Like the Anglicans, they argued that civil authority has been instituted by God, and cannot be overturned by man—any man. The apostles never claimed any temporal power; certainly they never exercised it, and what they did not possess they could not transmit.[56] In Old Testament times ecclesiastical persons were subject to princes, and the coming of Christ certainly did not alter matters. To depreciate royal authority is to flout the Bible and fall into the most pernicious of heresies.[57] "The temporal power wherewith emperors and kings do govern their subjects is from God according to the most express texts of Scripture."[58] It was the confusion of spheres that caused so much trouble to Catholics who wished to be loyal both to the head of the church and to the head of the state. The archpriest Blackwell, under relentless cross-examination by royal officials, admitted that "he

---

[52] Richard Sheldon, *Certain General Reasons proving the Lawfulnesse of the Oath of Allegiance*, p. 5. Sheldon is stating a position that he himself repudiates.

[53] H. I. [Anthony Hoskins], *A Briefe and Cleare Declaration of sundry pointes absolutely dislyked in the lately enacted Oath of Allegiance*, pp. 8, 16–20, 26 ff., 43 ff.

[54] R. Parsons, *The Judgment of a Catholicke English-man*, pp. 10, 14.

[55] Martin Becanus, *The English Iarre*, pp. 51–60; M. C. P., *op. cit.*, p. 123; William Howard, *A Patterne of Christian Loyaltie*, To the Reader; James I, *Workes*, pp. 260, 301. James quotes Cardinal Bellarmine. Howard was a Catholic supporter of the oath.

[56] Barclay, *Of the Authoritie of the Pope*, pp. 11–12.

[57] Jean Bédé, *The Right and Prerogative of Kings*, pp. 35–46, 172–178.

[58] Sheldon, *Certain General Reasons*, p. 13.

was much grieved to see the pope's supreme authority in causes ecclesiastical so much entangled with these pretences of another supreme authority *in temporalibus.*" [59] It is utterly impossible, said Barclay, to prove that there is any kind of authority, direct or indirect, that the pope can exercise over princes; even if it existed in theory, it could not function in practice, because it would be blocked by the undisputed prerogative which belongs to Christian kings.[60] The pope has, indeed, "the first place amongst his brethren the bishops in feeding Christ's flock," and he can properly exercise a pastoral office with respect to wayward rulers.[61] He lacks the deposing power which some of his supporters treat as a matter of faith, and he cannot claim a dispensing power regarding a subject's allegiance to the prince, since this kind of obedience is enjoined both by the word of God and by the law of nature.[62]

None of the English Catholics questioned, even for a moment, the pope's spiritual primacy, but some of them felt confused about the way it functioned. Can a papal breve alone determine matters of faith? When a pope declares his judgment, is he not sometimes expressing his private opinion, and does not history prove that popes have committed disastrous mistakes? In matters not yet officially determined by the church, can the pope's private assertions be treated as binding until they have been confirmed by a Council? [63] No one, it was argued, is bound by any papal verdict if it is based on misinformation or misapprehension of the facts. The pope has no right to impose his verdict concerning any matter that is or has been disputed by learned Catholics, and certainly he cannot act as judge in his own cause by pronouncing on his own claims.[64] For reasons such as these, some at least of the English Catholics were not prepared to regard the inadmissibility of the oath as settled simply because the pope had condemned it. Moreover, it was apparent that many of those who objected to the oath had not really studied its terms. King James pointed out that Bellarmine had evidently failed to grasp the elementary distinction between the Oath of Allegiance and the Oath of Supremacy. Some Catholics shrank from taking the oath because they believed that it denied the pope's right to excommunicate, whereas it tacitly conceded that right but repudiated the inference that an excommunicated king could be deposed by his subjects or assassinated by anyone. In any case it was obvious that the terms of the oath threatened those who refused to take it with the loss of all their worldly goods, and under the prevailing

---

[59] George Blackwell, *A Large Examination taken at Lambeth . . . of Mr George Blackwell,* n.p.

[60] Barclay, *Of the Authoritie of the Pope,* pp. 28–32, 61–66.

[61] Sheldon, *Certain General Reasons,* p. 12; Barclay, *ibid.,* pp. 167–176.

[62] Roger Widdrington, *A Theological Disputation concerning the Oath of Allegiance,* An Admonition to the Reader. Widdrington, whose real name was Thomas Preston, was head of the Benedictine mission to England.

[63] Warmington, *op. cit.,* pp. 36, 39, 46 ff.

[64] Widdrington, *A New Years Gift for English Catholics,* pp. 52, 64.

circumstances it was argued that this kind of sacrifice could not be exacted as a matter of faith.[65]

The controversy gradually subsided; it could not be considered settled, since debate alone could not resolve the questions at issue. Most English Catholics did not take the oath, but relatively few of them suffered the full consequences of their refusal. As long as Catholic plans or policies were regarded as a menace, there were occasional reverberations of the controversy. But the significant results lay elsewhere. The controversy had brought into sharp focus certain issues which lurked in the whole problem of authority. Both sides conceded that government exists in order to maintain the law of God. But how was this divine law to be enforced? Above all, who was to interpret its demands? Obviously the secular ruler must administer the law, but who was to tell him what the law required? To the Catholics the church was the depository of divine wisdom, and consequently only the pope could unfold the meaning of the law of God. The champions of the modern state assigned this function to the prince; no one, they insisted, could take it from him. As the fountainhead of justice he was in a position to determine what was right. All jurisdiction was royal jurisdiction, and even church courts were his courts. These arguments, first forged in French controversies, were now invoked in order to buttress the theory of royal supremacy. The Tudors had contended that the prerogatives of the prince placed him beyond foreign interference. It was now possible to add that the king alone could interpret what the law of God decreed. The situation created by the controversy about the oath made it a great deal easier to commend the divine right of kings to many Englishmen.

The papal claims were rejected because they seemed excessive. "We may be bold to say," declared Donne, "that there is much iniquity and many degrees of tyranny in establishing so absolute and transcendent a spiritual monarchy." [66] The only way to resist the encroachments of this aggressive power was to erect an adequate barrier against it. So the controversy inevitably encouraged men to elaborate and to commend a theory of kingly authority strong enough to hold in check the pope's pretensions. The king must be regarded as the divinely instituted head of the state, commissioned by God to interpret what is right and wrong, and invested with the authority that such a task requires. When national states were eager to free themselves from the last vestiges of ecclesiastical control, the divine right of kings was the natural counterpart to a theory of national independence. It claimed much for the king in order to claim even more for the state. But this was not the only political doctrine demanding acceptance. Once fear of the pope subsided, men of strong

---

[65] Sheldon, *Certain General Reasons*, pp. 2–12; Widdrington, *A Theological Disputation*, To the Reader; Warmington, *op. cit.*, pp. 21–22, 36, 64, 87–119.

[66] Donne, *Pseudo-martyr*, p. 246.

convictions would remember that there were sufficient grounds for challenging the king's authority in the interests of the people's freedom.

III

As we have seen, James I consistently asserted the inviolability of the royal prerogative, but he was always careful not to define it. "It is dangerous," he said, "to submit the power of a king to definition." [67] But the risk was difficult to avoid. James constantly reminded his parliaments of the limited character of their power. To his judges he pointed out that he was entitled to rule on all disputed questions of law. He encouraged and promoted the churchmen whose doctrine coincided with his own political theories. These issues were potential sources of discord; all of them were aggravated under his successor. Discussion therefore was inevitable. James proclaimed a doctrine of royal authority that was novel to Englishmen and that fitted with difficulty into the pattern of English political practice. The Tudors had been too astute to allow the relative power of king and of parliament to become a matter of bitter dispute, but the problem existed, and it could not indefinitely be shelved.

It was still possible, of course, to discuss political theory on the basis of assumptions that no longer applied. Sir Walter Ralegh was a brilliant Elizabethan; most of his experience was gained and all his presuppositions were fashioned in the sixteenth century. But he was a seventeenth-century author, and, by a strange irony, one who carried unusual weight with the Puritans. His judgments were often shrewd; they were seldom systematic. He made random comments on political matters; he did not elaborate anything approaching a political theory. Like most of his contemporaries he believed that "kings are made by God and by laws divine; and by human laws only declared to be kings." From this it followed that "therefore the prince cannot be said to be subject to the laws." [68] When circumstances require, the ruler must be free to break the laws: "all binding of a king by law upon the advantage of his necessity makes the breach thereof lawful in a king." [69] From this Ralegh drew certain important inferences about the proper relations between the ruler and his subjects. "The bonds of subjects to their kings should always be wrought out of iron, the bonds of kings unto subjects but of cobwebs." [70] This is rhetorical but vague; fortunately Ralegh defined a little more precisely the nature of these bonds. The law is the product of the joint endeavor of king and parliament: parliament enacts it, the king promulgates it. It is right that the people should exercise their due share of responsibility. The king

[67] S. R. Gardiner (ed.), *Parliamentary Debates in 1610* (Camden Society), p. 24.
[68] Ralegh, *Works,* III, 144.
[69] Ralegh, *The Prerogative of Parliaments in England,* Ep. Ded.
[70] *Ibid.*

ought to allow the House of Commons to challenge the legality of monopolies or new impositions, and to permit such criticism is not an admission of weakness. "Shall the head yield to the feet? Certainly it ought when they are grieved; for wisdom will rather regard the commodity than object the disgrace—seeing if the feet lie in fetters the head cannot be free." [71]

In Ralegh we see Tudor theory virtually untouched by the new age. In Bacon we have the Tudor ideal modified by an attempt to incorporate the theory of King James. Under Queen Elizabeth, Bacon had learned to his sorrow that it could be disastrous to oppose the royal will, and in the new reign he ranged himself firmly on the king's side. He believed that good government presupposed a strong ruler, surrounded by wise counselors and advised by a cooperative parliament. The royal prerogative was the condition of effective rule. Bacon stressed both the divine origin of the kingly office and the human limitations of the man who held it. "I said ye are gods," declared the Scripture, but it added, "ye shall die like men." Kings "must be answerable to God Almighty"; this places them above rebellion, but not beyond criticism.[72] Bacon believed that an informed and effective House of Commons was an essential part of the constitution, and he carefully indicated the relationship in which it ought to stand to the king. Authority and freedom were nicely balanced, but authority clearly claimed precedence.

> The king's sovereignty and the liberty of parliament are the two elements and principles of this estate; which though the one be more active, the other more passive, yet they do not cross or destroy the one the other, but they strengthen and maintain the one the other. Take away liberty of parliament, the griefs of the subject will bleed inwards; sharp and eager humours will not evaporate, and then they must exulcerate, and so may endanger the sovereignty itself. On the other side, if the king's sovereignty receive diminution or any degree of contempt with us that are born under an hereditary monarchy . . . it must follow that we shall be a meteor or *corpus imperfecte mistum;* which kind of bodies comes speedily to confusion and dissolution.[73]

Bacon regarded with alarm any disposition to treat crown and parliament as competing parties. Each has its appropriate functions; both are essential elements in a single commonwealth.

Law was made by the king-in-parliament, but it was interpreted by the judges. Bacon was aware of the possible tension between the prerogative and the law. He believed that the best way to resolve it was to strengthen

---

[71] *Ibid.*
[72] Bacon, "Advice to Sir George Villiers," *Works,* III, 427–428.
[73] Bacon, "A Speech of the King's Solicitor," *Works,* III, 366.

the prerogative. Occasions might easily arise when the law could actually obstruct the public welfare, and the king must then be free to break the law for the benefit of the people. The judges were the interpreters of his wisdom and his will. In a celebrated passage which is more eloquent than precise, he urged the judges to "remember that Solomon's throne was supported by lions on both sides; let them be lions, but yet lions under the throne, being circumspect that they do not check or oppose any points of sovereignty." [74] The role of the judges was particularly important because the balanced system that Bacon desired was obviously insecure. If parliament refused to cooperate with the king, then the king must exercise his superior authority and teach the judges to interpret public issues as he understood them.

Bacon believed that the primacy of the king's authority should be restated in terms of the forces struggling to control the state, and in his comments we can detect traces of the new doctrine of the prerogative which was beginning to emerge. Bacon was convinced that only those qualified by practical experience were competent to expound political theory, and in this respect he stood in sharp contrast with John Cowell. Cowell's academic qualifications were above reproach—he was master of Trinity Hall and regius professor of civil law at Cambridge—and in 1607 he published a legal dictionary, *The Interpreter*, which quickly earned a place of recognized usefulness. On constitutional questions, his views were explicit and uncompromising. The authority of the king, he believed, was above challenge: "he is above the law by his absolute power." If he allows parliament to participate in the processes of legislation, that is of grace, not of obligation, "for otherwise were he a subject after a sort and subordinate, which may not be thought without breach of duty and loyalty." [75] Parliament thus plays a courtesy role that does not entitle it to challenge the purposes of the king. "And of these two, one must needs be true, that either the king is above parliament, that is the positive law of his kingdom, or else he is not an absolute king." [76] Cowell defined the royal prerogative as "that especial power, pre-eminence or privilege that the king hath in any kind, over and above other persons and above the ordinary course of the common law, in the right of his crown." On one point he was particularly emphatic: "the king of England is an absolute king." [77]

King James and his courtiers heartily applauded such doctrines. The parliamentary leaders and the common lawyers took a different view. The

---

[74] Bacon, "Of Judicature," *Essays*. See the very similar words in his speech to Justice Hutton: "weigh and remember with yourself, that the twelve judges of the realm are as the twelve lions under Solomon's throne: they must show their stoutness in elevating and bearing up the throne." *Works*, IV, 507.
[75] John Cowell, *The Interpreter*, "King (*rex*)."
[76] *Ibid.*, "Parliament (*parlamentum*)."
[77] *Ibid.*, "Prerogative of the King (*praerogative regis*)."

House of Commons attacked *The Interpreter* and specified as particularly objectionable the articles on king, parliament, prerogative, and subsidy. James reprimanded Cowell—in very gentle terms—and the book was temporarily suppressed. It was clear that Cowell had focused attention on certain issues that had already become contentious and around which controversy would increasingly revolve. On the one hand there were the rapidly diverging theories of the king and of the parliament as to where the supreme authority in the state was located. On the other hand there was a standing dispute between two legal systems. Behind the attack on Cowell was the pressure of the common lawyers.[78] The struggle between the champions of two types of law seemed much more serious at the time than it appears in the light of the subsequent triumph of the common law. The king, it was suspected, sympathized with the civil lawyers and was prepared to support them. In dedicating a legal work to James, Sir Thomas Ridley reminded him that he was well aware "of some differences that are in judicature between your ecclesiastical law and the temporal law of the land." [79] These differences Ridley undertook to explain as clearly as possible. The king was so delighted with the book that rumor reported "that Sir Edward Coke undertook from thence to prophesy the decay of the common law." [80]

In the early years of the seventeenth century there were ample grounds for uncertainty about the future role of the common law.[81] It was still far from clear how the relation of the common law to the executive government of the state would be defined. The doctrines of the common law concerning the power of parliament needed to be clarified. Its proper function in protecting the liberties of the subject had to be restated. In the mounting turmoil of the ensuing period the common law would play a crucial part. The striking gains registered by the common law were possible because of the steady consolidation of a pattern of thought to which appeal could successfully be made. The authority of an immemorial antiquity had been gaining ground. Those who cited "the ancient constitution" argued that certain rights were of such antiquity that no king could annul them. Law was rooted in custom, and custom antedated even the earliest princes. By slow growth and gradual process institutions had taken shape. The legal and political patterns of society rested on the tacit consent of many generations. English common law, in particular, was inseparable from the custom of the land. Statutory legislation reflected only the insight of those who framed it; at best it relied on the experience of a single generation. But the common law derived its complex and organic quality from its gradual evolution over many centuries. Conse-

---

[78] Thomas Fuller stressed the importance of the contest, Cowell's involvement in it, and James's sympathy with the civil lawyers. Fuller, *The History of the Worthies of England,* I, 420.

[79] Sir Thomas Ridley, *A View of the civile and ecclesiastical law,* Ep. Ded.

[80] David Lloyd, *State Worthies,* p. 423.

[81] Holdsworth, *A History of English Law,* V, 414, 420–422.

quently it was the deposit of a people's wisdom. It was perfectly adapted
to the nation's needs because from times antedating all written records it
had been tested and proved in the corporate life of men. In his celebrated
exposition of this point of view, Sir Edward Coke magnificently summarized the position of the champions of the common law.

> We are but of yesterday, (and therefore had need of the wisdom
> of those that went before us) and had been ignorant (if we had
> not received light and knowledge from our forefathers) and our
> days upon the earth but a shadow in respect of the old ancient
> days and times past, wherein the laws have been by the wisdom
> of the most excellent men, in many successions of ages, by long
> and continual experience, (the trial of light and truth) fined and
> refined, which no one man (being of so short a time) albeit he
> had in his head the wisdom of all the men in the world, in any
> one age could ever have effected or attained unto.[82]

When therefore a judge in a court of common law rendered a verdict, he
did not rely on abstract reasoning or philosophical reflection; he drew
upon the cumulative wisdom of a people's history.

Sir Edward Coke established himself as the great exponent of this
position. During a long and turbulent career he played a variety of roles.
He was a servant of the crown, Lord Chief Justice both of the Common
Pleas and of the King's Bench, an influential member of parliament, and
the great codifier of the common law. He was a man of fierce ambition
and of towering erudition. Truculent when in power, cringing when
threatened with its loss, he was highly respected as a lawyer though he
won little affection as a man.[83] "He plays with his case as a cat with a
mouse," said Aubrey, "and be so fulsomely pedantic that a school boy
would nauseate it. But when he comes to matter of law, all acknowledge
him to be admirable." [84] In these areas Coke's influence was decisive. In
the first place, he powerfully assisted the creation and diffusion of the
mythology that grew up around the common law. The interpretation of
the constitution advanced by the lawyers was ostensibly an appeal to
history. They pierced behind the frontiers of the known past into that
misty region where good laws had their origin. They contended that out
of that remote Germanic background the English people had emerged

[82] Sir Edward Coke, *The Reports of Sir Edward Coke* (Seventh Report, Calvin's Case), IV, 6.

[83] His widow's verdict, which says a great deal in a few words, is often quoted: "We shall
never see his like again, praises be to God!" S. E. Thorne, *Sir Edward Coke* (Selden Society), p.
4. It is only fair to add that his heroic struggle on behalf of the common law gained him a
respect that his personal qualities would not have won.

[84] Aubrey, *Brief Lives*, I, 179. Aubrey mentions that the play *Ignoramus*, presented before
James I at Cambridge, was so staged that Coke was made the butt of its ridicule. This,
Aubrey believed, united the lawyers against the clergy; he detected one result of this
antagonism in Selden's *The Historie of tithes*, with its attack on clerical pretensions.

already endowed with a sense of freedom and with a just legal system. Recorded history was interpreted as the story of how Englishmen had resisted all attempts to rob them of this birthright.[85] Certain events acquired a highly mythological significance. As early as the reign of Alfred, the king's subjects were fully protected against injustice.[86] In the Norman Conquest, William the Conqueror, aided and abetted by the pope, tried to subvert the basic liberties of the land.[87] Magna Charta was seen as a particularly important reassertion of the people's rights. The seventeenth-century interpretation of English constitutional development was much more than a sifting of antiquarian lore. In rewriting their history, Englishmen were laying the foundations for a certain kind of political theory. "The ancient and excellent laws of England," wrote Coke,

> are the birth-right and the most ancient and best inheritance
> that the subjects of this realm have, for by them he enjoyeth not
> only his inheritance and goods in peace and quietness, but his
> life and his most dear country in safety. (I fear that many want
> true knowledge of this ancient birth-right.) [88]

In a second area Coke's championship of the common law had significant results. By systematizing English law, Coke aggravated the tension that increasingly set the common law in conflict with the prerogative courts. The church courts in particular found themselves exposed to incessant harassment. There were practical as well as theoretical reasons for the attack mounted by the common lawyers. Of late the church courts had shown an efficiency and expedition that made them popular. Coke and his companions dismissed the court of the High Commission as a foreign intrusion into the native legal system, but they feared its expanding activity as much as they disliked its alien character.[89] There was disagreement about the origin of these courts. The common lawyers insisted that the High Commission had been established by statute in the reign of Queen Elizabeth; the civilians traced it to an earlier period and saw it as the creation of the royal prerogative. There was constant conflict about the extent of ecclesiastical jurisdiction. Whitgift had insisted that church courts had become royal courts, and the common law could not interfere with their operation. Richard Cosin contended that in

[85] See J. G. A. Pocock, *The Ancient Constitution and the Feudal Law* (especially Ch. II and Ch. III) for an excellent account of this development. See also Gardiner, *History of England, 1603–1642*, II, 77.

[86] In 1624, Andrew Horn's *A Mirror for Justices* was published. Horn lived in the reign of Edward I and drew on some very dubious Anglo-Saxon traditions. He tells us that Alfred hanged twenty-four unjust judges in one year. The appeal of his material to the seventeenth century is significant.

[87] Coke, *Third Institutes*, Preface.

[88] Coke, *Reports* (quoted by C. Hill, *Intellectual Origins*, pp. 257–258).

[89] See S. B. Babbage, *Puritanism and Richard Bancroft*, p. 286.

any conflict between various courts, the decision rested with the king; they were all his courts.[90] Bancroft adopted this argument and amplified it; in the "Articles of the Clergy" (1605) he stated at length the view that it lay with the king to resolve disputes about the jurisdiction of his courts.[91] A decision on the question was highly desirable. In the early years of James's reign the common law judges, on the plea that certain cases were concerned with temporalities, made it a regular practice to issue prohibitions that prevented the church courts from proceeding any further with the matter in hand. Bancroft was concerned to preserve his courts from this paralyzing interference; the gist of his argument heightened the royal prerogative. The judges, he claimed, were merely the delegates of the king; therefore the king could always lift cases out of their hands and determine them according to his own wisdom. The theoretical questions became entangled with a variety of urgent practical issues. The bishops used the church courts to compel the Puritans to conform; the Puritans appealed to the common lawyers for support. As a result an alliance rich in consequences was fashioned. But the Puritans and the common lawyers did more than give each other aid and comfort;[92] they combined to press for a definition of the practical limits of the royal supremacy when exercised in association with parliament. The king obviously sympathized with the champions of ecclesiastical jurisdiction, and the troubles that Nicholas Fuller, an aggressive Puritan lawyer, brought upon himself proved that it was dangerous to challenge constituted authority. When the Stuarts were eliciting from a rather submissive bench of judges rulings concerning the scope of their powers, there was little chance successfully to challenge the claims of the prerogative courts. But Coke's demonstration of the superiority of "the laws of England . . . over the civil and canon laws within this realm" was not forgotten, nor his warning that the ecclesiastical courts have "sought ever . . . to encroach and usurp in matters of jurisdiction and authority upon the king's prerogative and the laws and statutes and customs of England." [93] When the system of "thorough," upheld by Charles I and applied by Strafford and Laud, collapsed, the victory of Coke's ideas could be seen in the prompt overthrow of the prerogative courts.[94]

Coke was careful to suggest that the royal prerogative and the common law were engaged in a common cause, but it was obvious that his theories

[90] R. Cosin, An Apologie for Sundrie Proceedings by Jurisdiction Ecclesiasticall (1593), quoted by Allen, A History of Political Thought, p. 139.

[91] The Articuli Cleri are reproduced in J. R. Tanner (ed.), Constitutional Documents of the Reign of James I, pp. 177 ff. The articles were answered, one by one, by the barons of the Exchequer.

[92] [William Stoughton], An Assertion for true and Christian Church-policie, Ep. Ded.

[93] B. M. Cotton MSS. Cleopatra, F. 1, f. 116, quoted by Babbage, op. cit., p. 282.

[94] It was often assumed, both at the time and subsequently, that the High Commission was Laud's favorite instrument. This clearly misinterprets the facts. He relied primarily on the Star Chamber.

struck at absolute sovereignty and not merely at its instruments. Coke insisted that "the common law protecteth the king," but James recognized the true drift of Coke's argument and called it a "traitorous speech." [95] In 1610 the judges, led by Coke, declared that the king could not create any offense by proclamation; indeed, they added, he had no prerogative except that which the law of the land allowed him.[96] On this point Coke was explicit. "The common law," he said, "hath so admeasured the prerogative of the king that he cannot take nor prejudice the inheritance of any." [97] The king, indeed, was hedged about by the restrictions that the law imposed.

> I know that prerogative is part of the law, and sovereign power is no Parliamentary word. In my opinion it weakens Magna Carta and all our statutes; for they are absolutely without any saving sovereign power; and shall we now add it, we shall weaken the foundation of law, and then the building must needs fall; take we heed what we yield unto, Magna Carta is such a fellow that he will have no sovereign.[98]

With good cause the Stuarts distrusted Coke and feared the ends to which he might turn his massive learning. Implicit in his exposition of the common law was an attack on the Stuart view of kingly prerogative.

King James, as we have seen, held a high doctrine of royal authority. It was one that fitted uneasily into the English context. Certain questions clamored for an answer. Could his theory be adjusted to the forces that he faced? Could a compromise be found between royal claims and parliamentary susceptibilities? Where did ultimate authority reside? How should it be exercised and how could it be controlled?

During James's reign a royalist theory of the prerogative emerged which conceded to the king the position that he claimed and that nevertheless seemed to be compatible with English law. Its essential feature was a distinction between two aspects of the royal prerogative. On the one hand it attributed to the king an absolute prerogative, which could not be challenged and which he could exercise when and as he pleased; on the other it recognized an ordinary or personal prerogative which might legitimately be challenged. Lurking within this view was an implication which even its advocates did not initially perceive. Their theory of the constitution located supreme power in the king; the character of his prerogative would entitle him to act, if necessary, as an absolute monarch. As the struggle between Charles and his parliaments grew more intense, this latent implication gradually emerged. The interpretation reached its

---

[95] Allen, *A History of Political Thought,* p. 14.
[96] Gardiner, *History of England,* II, 104.
[97] Coke, *Second Institutes,* p. 63. I am indebted to C. Hill, *Intellectual Origins,* for this reference.
[98] John Rushworth, *Historical Collections,* I, 562, quoted by Holdsworth, *op. cit.,* V, 451.

full development when the foundations of royal power were already crumbling.

The theory had both important advantages and fatal defects. It removed certain ambiguities in the constitution. It provided a definite answer to the most urgent question of the period: where is sovereign power located? The political tensions of the age could not be resolved until uncertainty on this point had been removed, and no alternative solution dealt with the problem in such simple and explicit terms. By declaring that the king was supreme both in theory and in fact, the royalists gave efficiency as well as symmetry to the constitutional structure. "The authority of a king," as Wentworth told the Council of the North,

> is the keystone which closeth up the arch of order and government, which contains each part in due relation to the whole, and which once shaken and infirmed, all the frame falls together into a confused heap of foundation and battlement, of strength and beauty. . . . For whatever he be which ravels forth into questions the right of a king and of a people shall never be able to wrap them up again into the comeliness and order he found them.[99]

The theory attracted those who wished to keep their country abreast of current constitutional developments. On the Continent representative assemblies were suffering eclipse. Absolute monarchies seemed to promise the most efficient government, and Stuart theories coincided with the most progressive practices of the day. Not all the king's counselors were prepared to go so far. Wentworth believed in the people's liberties, even if he reacted against what he considered the excessive demands of parliament. "I ever did inculcate this," he declared at his trial, "that the happiness of a kingdom consists of a just poise of the king's prerogative and the subject's liberty; and that things would never go well till they went hand in hand together." [100] Doubtless the balance that he desired would have tipped authority far to the side of the king, but he still fell considerably short of Continental standards.

Belatedly the leaders of the rising opposition in parliament realized that they needed a theory of sovereignty to counterbalance the royalist claims. Initially many of them were content with the lack of precise definition which had served in medieval times. Coke was anxious to locate supreme authority in the common law. The first explicit formulation of a parliamentary theory was apparently provided in 1610 by James White-locke, in his speech in the House of Commons during the debate on impositions. As he pointed out, arguments about the control of trade raise the fundamental question of sovereign power—"a power that can control

[99] Gardiner, *History of England*, VII, 25–26.
[100] Cobbett and Howells (eds.), *State Trials*, III, 1465.

all other powers and cannot be controlled but by itself." Everyone admits
its existence; "then is there no further question to be made but to examine
where the sovereign power is in this kingdom." That power, he continued,

> is agreed to be in the king, but in the king is a twofold power, the
> one in parliament, as he is assisted with the consent of the whole
> state; the other out of parliament, as he is sole and singular,
> guided merely by his own will. And if of these two powers in the
> king one is greater than the other and can direct and control the
> other, that is *suprema potestas,* the sovereign power, and the other
> is *subordinata.* It will then be easily proved that the power of the
> king in parliament is greater than his power out of parliament,
> and doth rule and control it.[101]

If supremacy is exercised by two coordinate powers, they are jointly
stronger than either when it acts alone. But should they disagree, which
can claim superiority? To solve this question controversy alone was
insufficient.

The dispute about sovereignty became more and more acute as the
prerogative of the crown increasingly conflicted with the liberties of the
subject. Initially people protested not against the theory of royal
supremacy but against the way it was applied. Certain fiscal measures of
the king infringed what were regarded as popular rights. In the debates
on impositions, on monopolies, and on forced loans, the members of the
House of Commons insisted that they were not attacking royal prerogative; they were merely attempting to remedy the subjects' grievances. The
liberty of the subject seemed to be directly challenged by the king's claim
to imprison offenders at discretion. In the debates on the Petition of Right,
upholders of the prerogative seriously urged the need of preserving for the
crown some discretionary power to arrest those who in times of danger
might threaten the security of the state. The members of the House of
Commons rejected all qualifying amendments, whether suggested by the
king or by the upper house. "At this little gap," said Selden, "every man's
liberty may in time go out." [102] But the passing of the Petition of Right
proved a frail protection for the freedom of the subject. No sooner had
parliament been dissolved in 1629 than Charles imprisoned those who had
led the attack on his prerogative, and during his eleven years of personal
rule he ignored the Petition of Right whenever it suited him to do so. It
enacted nothing new, said the crown lawyers, and therefore the king was
free to act in exactly the same way as before.

Popular anger mounted as the nature of Stuart absolutism became

[101] G. W. Prothero (ed.), *Select Statutes and Other Constitutional Documents, 1558–1625,*
pp. 351–352; Kenyon, *op. cit.,* p. 70.
[102] Cobbett and Howells (eds.), *State Trials,* III, 170.

apparent. When ship money was added to forced loans, impositions, and monopolies, resentment reached a new intensity. "If it [ship money] does not altogether violate the laws of the realm, as some think it does," wrote the Venetian ambassador, "it is certainly repugnant to usage and the forms hitherto observed." [103] The king's legal advisers assured him that he was acting within the law, and in every case that he submitted to the judges he had some precedent or ancient right on his side. As we have already noticed, there was a serious flaw in his case. In a national emergency, his judges assured him, he could legally adopt such measures as the defense of the realm required; and he himself was the sole judge as to whether such an emergency existed. To his subjects it was obvious that in apparently normal times Charles was justifying illegal acts by appealing to a nonexistent crisis, and was using emergency measures to meet recurrent financial needs.

What Charles regarded as legal actions, his people branded as tyranny. The seventeenth century was acutely conscious of the distinction between subjects and slaves. Subjects owned property which could be taken from them only with their consent. Once the king ignored this basic fact he became a tyrant and thus reduced his people to slavery. The gravamen of the charges ultimately brought by parliament against the king and his ministers was that they had sought to overthrow the ancient liberties of freeborn Englishmen. Strafford and Laud had been guilty of an attempt to "subvert the fundamental laws and introduce an arbitrary and tyrannical government." At his trial Charles was accused of a "wicked design to erect and uphold in himself an unlimited and tyrannical power to rule according to his will." [104] Charles, of course, vehemently denied the charge. A king could not be a tyrant so long as his actions were sanctioned by law. Furthermore, he was fulfilling an obligation that everyone in the seventeenth century recognized, namely, that the duty of a ruler is to govern.[105] Charles, therefore, could not comprehend the charge that his authority was jeopardizing his subjects' freedom. "For the people," he said,

> truly I desire their liberty and freedom as much as anybody whatsoever; but I must tell you, their liberty and freedom consist in having good government, those laws by which their lives and their goods may be most their own. It is not their having a share in the government; that is nothing appertaining to them. A subject and a sovereign are clean different things; and therefore,

---

[103] Gardiner, *History of England,* VII, 376.

[104] Gardiner (ed.), *The Constitutional Documents of the Puritan Revolution, 1625–1660,* p. 372.

[105] Cf. Charles's speech to parliament in 1628: "If you (which God forbid) should not do your duties in contributing what this state at this time needs, I must, in discharge of my conscience, use those other means which God hath put into my hands, to save that the follies of particular men may otherwise hazard to lose." *Lords' Journals,* III, 687.

until you do that—I mean that you put the people in that
liberty—they will never enjoy themselves.[106]

But here Charles was clearly ignoring a conviction that, as we have seen,
was almost universally accepted: that it was slavery when a subject's
property was seized without his consent, even if this was done in the name
of efficient government and with the sanction of the law. The judges, in
ruling on the legality of the king's acts, had said nothing about the abuses
to which these legal rights might be exposed, and this was the theme of
Falkland's "Speech in the House of Commons Touching the Judges." By
leaving the king "the sole judgement of necessity," the judges "enabled
him to take from us what he would, when he would, and how he would,"
yet they tried to persuade the people "that they had left us our property."
From this, added Falkland, there followed "the transformation of this
kingdom from the estate of free subjects . . . into that of villanes." [107]

Two theories about the location of sovereign power in the state were
struggling for predominance. Each was strong precisely where the other
was weak. The advocates of royal supremacy were abreast of what seemed
to be the progressive tendencies of the age. They could offer a way of
resolving the impasse that would inevitably arise whenever king and
parliament were in conflict. They had the practical advantage that the
authority of the crown was on their side, and they could count on the
support of the ministers of state. But the champions of the parliamentary
position stood for the freedom of the subject, for control over taxation and
legislation, and for the supremacy of law over all subjects, including the
servants of the crown. Parliament could therefore appeal to very
influential segments of the nation. The common lawyers were pledged to
its support; so were the justices of the peace, who controlled local
government in the country as a whole, and the merchants, who dominated
the corporations of the larger towns.

These advantages on the side of parliament would prove decisive only if
its leaders could devise an effective method of pressing its claims. For this
reason the struggle to maintain the privileges of parliament was vital.
When the Stuarts tried to enlarge the royal prerogative they inevitably
aroused the hostility of the House of Commons. To James's initial
pronouncements on the authority of kingship, the House replied with its
famous Apology of 1604. The privileges of parliament, it declared, could
not be "withheld from us, denied or impaired but with apparent wrong to
the whole estate of the realm." Any attempt to infringe these privileges
jeopardized "the rights and liberties of your subjects of England." [108] The

---

[106] Gardiner, *History of the Great Civil War, 1642–1649*, IV, 322. This was Charles's last
speech.

[107] Lucius Cary, Viscount Falkland, *The Lord Falkland his learned speech in Parliament . . .
touching the Judges*, pp. 4–5.

[108] Prothero, *op. cit.*, 287–288.

issue reemerged under a variety of forms during the parliamentary session of 1610. The regular conjunction of popular freedom and parliamentary privilege should have given pause to the king and his advisers, but James was deaf to such warnings. Consequently, in the acrimonious exchange between the king and the Commons in December 1621, as the king's tone became more peremptory, the attitude of the House became more resolute.[109] The Protestation of 18 December declared "that the liberties, franchises, privileges and jurisdictions of parliament are the ancient and undoubted birthright and inheritance of the subjects of England," and it reaffirmed in uncompromising terms the right of the House of Commons to pursue its proper tasks without hindrance or intimidation.[110] James was so angry that "in Council, with his own hand [he] rent out this protestation" from the Journal of the House of Commons.[111] The leaders of the parliamentary opposition constantly recurred to this theme. "Now the whole power and virtue of parliament," said Sir John Eliot, "depends upon the privileges thereof. Her ancient franchises and immunities are that which has sustained her. A parliament without liberty is no parliament." [112]

Parliamentary privilege therefore became the retort to royal prerogative. By invoking the ancient liberties of the representatives of the people it was possible to challenge the absolutism of the king. James's anger at the Protestation of 1621 sprang from his perception that this position, if consistently applied, would destroy the basis of prerogative rule. Similarly in the long and indignant Declaration in which Charles justified his dissolution of parliament in 1629, he emphasized the threat to efficient government implicit in this insistence on parliamentary privilege. "Under pretence of privilege and freedom of speech," he pointed out, the leaders of the House of Commons had defied "all authority," and "their drift was to break, by this means, through all respects and ligaments of government, and to erect an universal over-swaying power to themselves, which belongs only to us, and not to them." [113] The privileges to which parliament appealed were varied. Four were constantly invoked: the right to decide disputed elections, freedom from arrest, freedom of speech, and the right to determine the order of business of the House. The last two, in particular, provided the means by which parliament effectively resisted the crown. But even successful opposition was not enough. The period of King Charles's personal rule convinced the critics of prerogative that royal supremacy had to be curbed. When parliament finally reassembled, John Pym and his colleagues were ready to launch the measures that would effectually restrict the powers of the king.

[109] *Ibid.*, pp. 307–314.
[110] *Ibid.*, pp. 313–314.
[111] *Commons' Journals*, I, 668.
[112] John Forster, *Sir John Eliot*, II, 446.
[113] Gardiner (ed.), *Constitutional Documents*, pp. 94–95.

IV

As the constitutional struggle intensified, it absorbed more and more attention. It never wholly eclipsed certain related issues. Churchmen had always been concerned about political theory; the persistent tensions between church and state allowed them no choice. In England the Reformation established the principle that the monarch was the supreme head or governor of the church, but this left many problems unsolved. To the Puritans and to the Catholics (especially the Jesuits) were attributed doctrines that the authorities regarded with dismay.[114] Political theory was widely and earnestly canvassed. The results were seldom strikingly original, but they played a significant role in current developments. Richard Hooker's calm and magisterial exposition of the way the church functions within a context of law—divine, natural, and political—made many problems seem less menacing, but serious issues still demanded attention.

On certain topics all churchmen were essentially agreed. Like most of their contemporaries, they treated political theory as a subdivision of theology. Naturally they believed that "the primary efficient cause of all government is only God." [115] Civil rulers must therefore be regarded as his vicars, entrusted with temporal affairs.[116] Their dignity is consequently without parallel: "the monarch is divine as only representing God's own power." [117] Thus we are prepared to understand the ordered regularity that runs throughout creation.

> God is the ordainer of the king, the king the image of God, the law the work of the king, judges interpreters of the law, magistrates with them dispensers, justice the fruit of laws dispensed, this fruit of justice the good of the people, this good of the people the honour of the king, this honour of the king the glory of God, the ordainer, orderer and blesser of all.[118]

[114] It was believed that under certain circumstances these groups sanctioned—even encouraged—resistance to the king. The role in the church that they assigned to the king seemed to imply that ecclesiastical power should take precedence over royal authority. Cf. Thomas Morton, *A Sermon preached before the King's Most Excellent Majesty,* pp. 3–4, 10, 25 ff.; Barlow, *Concerning the antiquitie and superiority of bishops,* To the Ministers of Scotland: "Papists and Puritans have the king but an honourable member, not a chief governor in the churches of his own dominion"; Robert Sibthorpe, *Apostolike Obedience,* p. 23.

[115] [Morton], *Christus Dei, the Lords anointed, or a theological discourse wherein is proved that regall or monarchicall power is not of humane but of divine right,* p. 5, also pp. 13, 15; Henry Valentine, *God save the king,* p. 407.

[116] Bartholomew Parsons, *The Magistrates charter examined,* pp. 4, 16.

[117] Ireland, *The Oath of Allegiance defended,* n.p.; Robert Pricke, *The Doctrine of superioritie and of subjection,* pp. 9, 16–19.

[118] William Pemberton, *The charge of God and the king to judges and magistrates,* Ep. Ded. Cf. R. Horn, *The Christian governour,* pp. 3, 28, 79, 130; John Lawrence, *A golden trumpet to rouse up a drowsie magistrate,* Ep. Ded.

The divine origin of the king's office imposes upon him an inescapable responsibility: he must enforce the righteous law of God. A corresponding duty, declared the churchmen, devolves upon the people: they must render unquestioning obedience to the king.[119] As Bartholomew Parsons reminded his readers, the Scriptures provide "an instruction to all, at all times." The prince ministers "judgement in [God's] name and place; thereof of necessity ye must be subject—ye, every soul." [120] For subjects to usurp the magistrate's function would be sacrilege, since "what God doth by his deputies, he doth as it were by himself." [121] In God's providential government of the world, political order is the alternative to anarchy, and the citizen who disregards his due subjection opens the floodgates to social chaos. "In vain," exclaimed Ussher, "do Christian princes bear the sword, if their subjects' conscience may question their power." [122] Should the king forget his duty, subjects dare not plead that they may forsake their obedience. We accept just rulers as a divine blessing; in the same spirit we must submit to wicked rulers as a divine judgment. "Good kings are God's images, and evil kings are his executioners." [123] Moreover, experience fully vindicates the value of subjection. "Obedience is the mother of well doing. Nothing can be well done without obedience." [124]

From the king's divine authority and the subject's duty of unvarying obedience it was an easy transition to the king's responsibility to safeguard and supervise the household of God. "To preserve the church," wrote William Wilkes, "is a special prerogative belonging to the supreme power of the highest commander." [125] Admittedly this right had temporarily been obscured by papal usurpation, but the Reformation had restored the proper balance.[126] "As therefore their office stretcheth to reform doctrine, to order ecclesiastical officers, to see to their executing their offices according to God's ordinance, to order the divine worship and to cause people to live according as God's word commandeth, . . . so they are to judge in all these things what is to be done, what not." [127] Serious dangers lurked within this doctrine. The church had been gravely troubled by the tendency of influential laymen to plunder it for their own advantage, and Laud found that all his influence could not rectify deep-seated evils.[128]

[119] F. Dillingham, *A goodly and learned sermon concerning the magistrates dutie and death*, pp. 5–10. Cf. William Loe, *The kings shoe*, 3, 16, 23–27; Pricke, *op. cit.*, pp. 34–38.

[120] B. Parsons, *op. cit.*, p. 18.

[121] Thomas Hurst, *The descent of authoritie*, p. 22; see also p. 30. Cf. Proctor, *The right of kings*, p. 28; William Wilkes, *Obedience or ecclesiasticall union*, p. 4.

[122] Ussher, *The soveraignes power and the subjects duty*, p. 1.

[123] Ireland, *op. cit.*, n.p.

[124] Dillingham, *op. cit.*, p. 5.

[125] Wilkes, *op. cit.*, p. 5.

[126] Proctor, *op. cit.*, p. 1.

[127] *Ibid.*, p. 14. Cf. [Sir John Hayward], *A Reporte of a discourse concerning supreme power in affaires of religion*, pp. 11–12.

[128] Cf. C. Hill, *Economic Problems of the Church, passim;* Stone, *The Crisis of the Aristocracy*, pp. 405–408.

Churchmen deplored "this unhappy age wherein the tribe of Levi is so little respected," [129] but meanwhile they felt that the only way to contain priestly pretensions (as represented by the bishop of Rome) was to exalt the civil authority.

It was generally assumed that church and state should be united in the most intimate association. As the two parts of a single whole each should support the other. "Magistrates are God's deputies, ministers are his ambassadors"; when these cooperate "both the temporal and the spiritual swords are effective." [130] If the magistrate fails to "adjoin the sword to defend the word," he is guilty of gross negligence.[131] But exactly how this desired unity might be achieved was far from clear, and, as the period progressed, the answers put forward by the Puritans increasingly diverged from those advanced by the Arminians.

At the beginning of the seventeenth century the Puritans found themselves in a disconcerting position. They were Calvinists, and it was widely assumed that their theology implied a political theory that subordinated civil power to churchly authority.[132] James rebuked those who "must have a kind of liberty in the people . . . ; and in every cause that concerns prerogative give a snatch against a monarchy, through their itching after popularity." [133] "You see," he wrote to Lord Cranborne, "I have daily more and more cause to hate and abhor all that sect, enemies to all kings, and to me only because I am a king." [134] He believed that they were intent on circumscribing his authority. "I have learned," he said, "of what cut they have been who, preaching before me since my coming into England have passed over with silence my being supreme governor in causes ecclesiastical." [135] It was an easy step to the belief that Puritan convictions tended to sedition.[136] What the king said, his counselors were quick to echo. The archbishop of York, writing to his brother of Canterbury, pointed out that popular government in the church could hardly be reconciled with royal prerogative in the state. "Therefore the King's majesty," he continued, "as he is a passing wise king and the best learned prince in Europe, had need to take heed how he receiveth into his kingdom such a popular government ecclesiastical as is that of the presbytery." [137]

[129] B. Parsons, *op. cit.*, Ep. Ded.

[130] Hurst, *op. cit.*, p. 26. Cf. *Bishop Overall's Convocation Book*, which assumed that the church helps to create this unity as the religious teachers enter fully into the nation's life.

[131] Dillingham, *op. cit.*, Ep. Ded.

[132] Henry King, *A Sermon preached at St Pauls*, pp. 27–28.

[133] James I, *Political Works*, p. 340.

[134] James I, Letter to Lord Cranborne, 22 Nov. 1604. Hist. MSS. Com. R., Cecil MSS. Pt. XVI, 363.

[135] C. H. McIlwain (ed.), *The Political Works of King James I*, p. xc.

[136] Goodman, *The Court of King James the First*, I, 313.

[137] Matthew Hutton to John Whitgift, 9 Oct. 1603. J. Strype, *The Life and Acts of John Whitgift*, III, 392–402. Cf. Swan, *A Sermon*, p. 12.

The Puritans insisted that the charges leveled against them were unfounded and manifestly unfair. They assured the king that "we . . . the ministers . . . neither hold in opinion nor entertain in practice any matter prejudicial to your royal state, supremacy and prerogative." [138] They objected to "the imputation of puritanism, disloyalty, innovation and faction . . . laid upon the faithful ministers and people of the land." [139] To advocate a modified pattern of church government was a very different matter from threatening the civil power: the "discipline by pastors and elders" might be instituted "without any derogation to the king's royal prerogative, and indignity to the three estates in parliament, or a greater alteration of the laudable laws." [140] They pointed to their record: no group had supported Queen Elizabeth with greater loyalty or played a more important part in repelling the Armada. They had always preached obedience; they did so still. They exalted the position of the king. "Magistrates," wrote Robert Pricke, "are in the highest degree of preeminence next unto God, above all other persons." [141] "God is an invisible king," said Thomas Adams, "the king is a visible god." [142]

The Puritans did not add, of course, that the obedience they inculcated was compatible with an ingenious program of passive resistance. In Elizabeth's reign they had shown considerable skill in devising types of pressure (both in parliament and out of it) that never amounted to active resistance but that certainly contained a veiled threat. Under the early Stuarts there was a pause, then a slowly mounting crescendo of resistance, and finally civil war. Theory hardly kept pace with events, but Puritan writers increasingly stressed the supremacy of law. According to Thomas Beard, the law is above the prince; rulers are not only subject to the law of God but to the civil laws which command justice and equity.[143] The Puritans were likely to emphasize the king's duties rather than his prerogative.[144] Their critics bitterly remarked that Puritans exalted the law above the prince, and the people above the law.[145] And here we must remember that though the ministers were often the most vocal spokesmen for Puritanism, they were not always its most resolute representatives. Many of them, when threatened by Bancroft or by Laud, drew back. They were particularly vulnerable, of course, because they had no other means of livelihood, and as discontent increased, many of them left

[138] *An humble supplication for toleration and liberty* (1609), pp. 17–18. Cf. William Bradshaw, *A protestation of the king's supremacie, passim.*

[139] Hist. MSS. Com. R. Lord Montagu of Beaulieu, p. 33.

[140] [W. Stoughton], *An Assertion for true and Christian Church-policie,* title page.

[141] Pricke, *The Doctrine of superioritie and of subjection,* p. 16. Cf. William Gouge, *God's Three Arrowes: Plague, Famine, Sword,* pp. 93, 245.

[142] Adams, *Sermons,* p. 16. Cf. Matthew Griffith, *Bethel, or a forme for families,* p. 429.

[143] Thomas Beard, *The Theatre of God's judgements,* pp. 12–13. Cf. Josias Nichols, *The Plea of the Innocent,* pp. 58 ff.; H. Burton, *An Apology of an appeale,* p. 72.

[144] Cf. Gouge, *The Whole-armour of God,* p. 81.

[145] King, *A Sermon preached at St Pauls,* p. 28.

England for the New World. As the resistance to the Stuarts mounted, the leadership came from lawyers, country gentlemen, and merchants as well as from ministers. An alliance developed that achieved unexpected results. It showed, among other things, that Puritan political theory could develop into something very different from passive acceptance of kingly authority.

The Stuart kings disliked and distrusted the Puritans. Theologically, aesthetically, politically they were attracted to the Arminians. That rising school of churchmen needed royal support, and gave ardent and often uncritical assent to the doctrine of kingly prerogative. Royal authority was rooted in the gift of God, "so that hereby we see the sovereign power vindicated from all controlment." [146] Beyond even the customary measure, the Arminians emphasized the duty of obedience: "nothing is more ancient in the laws of God, nothing more pregnant to advance the common good than obedience." [147] "To preserve the peace of the church is a special prerogative belonging to the supreme power of the highest commander," and high churchmen appealed confidently to the king to trample down their enemies. "Let not the cry of the Edomites prevail, that would down with church, chancel, steeple, bells and all, that cry, Down with ecclesiastical policy, down with prelates, down with foundations." [148]

The Arminian position, of course, was not free of embarrassment. Bancroft did his utmost to establish the fact that the right to legislate for the church lay with the clergy. What convocation decided, the king would doubtless ratify, and Bancroft tacitly assumed that the king would always cooperate with his bishops. But what would happen if a king by divine right clashed with bishops by divine right? Many of the sermons preached by high churchmen presupposed a kind of holy Erastianism.[149] A good deal of the mounting opposition of the House of Commons to tendencies in the church also presupposed Erastianism—appealing to parliament rather than to king, and anticlerical rather than churchly, but still Erastian. Laud wrestled with this problem in his speech in the Star Chamber, but without conspicuous success. The divine right of bishops, he argued, in no way infringed the king's prerogative. "For though our office be from God and Christ immediately, yet may we not exercise that power, either of order or jurisdiction, but as God hath appointed us, that is not in his Majesty's or any Christian king's kingdoms, but by and under the power of the king given us so to do." [150] It was generally assumed in church circles that in all that pertained to religious responsibilities—the determination of doctrine, the settling of the ministry, the enforcement of discipline—the

---

[146] Loe, *op. cit.*, p. 23.

[147] Wilkes, *op. cit.*, p. 4.

[148] Wilkes, *op. cit.*, p. 14; Loe, *op. cit.*, pp. 14–15.

[149] Cf. Francis Mason, *The Authoritie of the Church in making Canons and Constitutions*, pp. 12–13, 15; John Buckeridge, *A Sermon preached at Hampton Court, ad fin.*

[150] William Laud, *A Speech delivered in the Starr-chamber*, p. 7.

clergy would indicate the proper solution and the king would implement their decisions. Church and state, though intimately related, were distinct in nature, purpose, and function. The division of function should be maintained, however close the union might be.[151]

As feeling mounted and views became more extreme, the extravagant spokesmen for the High Church position achieved an importance far beyond anything that their inherent significance deserved. Richard Montagu began by affirming, with an emphasis bordering on arrogance, the exclusive right of the clergy to interpret Scripture and to determine doctrine.[152] With an impartial disregard for the feelings of many of his fellow countrymen he denounced both Calvinism and Romanism. He attacked the former with greater venom than the latter, and his type of religion was clearly more compatible with the beliefs and practices of Rome than with those of Geneva. Catholicism inspired fear and hatred among Englishmen for political reasons no less than for religious ones. To complicate the matter, the convictions that Montagu advocated had already become entangled in the struggle between king and parliament. James, and then Charles, encouraged, supported, and protected Montagu. The House of Commons attacked him and denounced his views. Charles found himself embroiled in the disputes that the High Churchmen precipitated, but he contributed little to the political theory that was ostensibly at issue. He held to a high doctrine of the royal prerogative and defended those who preached it, but he cared little for the niceties of political speculation. Perhaps he did not understand them. What he contributed to the controversy was a heightened emotional intensity; among Laudian clerics he inspired a passionate loyalty that both prompted extreme statements about kingship by his partisans and aroused a corresponding indignation in parliament.[153]

Robert Sibthorpe inevitably got into difficulties because he used the pulpit to show "the duty of subjects to pay tribute and taxes to their princes according to the Word of God, in the law and the gospel, and the rules of religion." King Charles himself, he tells us, suggested the subject, and he adds that the Church of England was deeply involved in the debate about arbitrary taxation. "Oh! let not the people stand so much upon pretence of liberty as to lose safety." There can be no better example of an overly scrupulous conscience than to withhold tribute where tribute is due.[154] Sibthorpe's main concern was to show that the duties of the prince must be balanced by the obligations of the people, and at this point he merely repeated what many had said.[155] The startling feature of a rather

[151] Cf. especially, George Carleton, *Jurisdiction, regall, episcopall, papall, passim;* Richard Field, *Of the Church,* Bk. V.
[152] Richard Montagu, *A New Gagg for an Old Goose,* pp. 14 ff.
[153] Cf. Valentine, *op. cit.,* pp. 32–33.
[154] Sibthorpe, *op. cit.,* Ep. Ded., p. 19.
[155] Cf. *ibid.,* pp. 6 ff.

dull sermon was the confidence with which a clergyman invested the king's controversial tax proposals with the authority of religious obligation. He was aware of the danger; he had no intention of making "religion the stalking horse of the state." "Nor speak I," he declared, "as a sychophantical time-server nor as a statizing court orator or one who has left God to preach for the king, as some are too apt uncharitably to censure." [156]

Roger Mainwaring was not an original thinker nor even a very distinguished man, but his gift for extreme statement earned him considerable notoriety. As to kingly power, he argued, "even God himself gives from heaven most full and ample testimony; and that this power is not merely human but superhuman and indeed no less than a divine power." [157] For the sake of emphasis, Mainwaring reiterated to the point of weariness his doctrine of the high and exclusive prerogatives of kingship. "That sublime power therefore which resides in earthly potentates is . . . a participation of God's own omnipotency which he never did communicate to any multitudes of men in the world, but only and immediately to his vicegerents." [158] No one can dispute royal commands, "nor search into the discourse and deep counsel of kings, seeing their hearts are so deep by reason of their distance from common men." [159] Mainwaring then turned to the controversial topic of the day. Even the highest representative assemblies of the kingdom were not entitled to challenge the rights that belong to the crown. When the king asks for a subsidy, parliament may distribute the burden, but it cannot dispute the right to impose it. With something bordering on contempt, Mainwaring dismissed the pretensions of "those who cross the just and lawful designs of their wise and gracious sovereigns; and that under the plausible shows of singular liberty and freedom, which, if their consciences might speak, would appear nothing more than the satisfying either of private humours, passions or purposes." [160]

In view of the mounting constitutional tensions of the time, parliament could hardly ignore either the tone or the content of Mainwaring's sermons. It seemed intolerable that a clergyman, apparently with royal approval, should preach "that the king is not bound to observe the laws of the realm concerning the subjects' rights and liberties." [161] In opening the case against Mainwaring, Francis Rous denounced "this plot and practice to alter and subvert the frame and fabric of this estate and commonwealth." He detected not merely a distortion of time-honored constitu-

---

[156] *Ibid.,* pp. 20–21.

[157] Roger Mainwaring, *Religion and Alegiance,* p. 10.

[158] *Ibid.,* p. 11.

[159] *Ibid.,* p. 17.

[160] *Ibid.,* p. 28; cf. pp. 24–25, 26–27.

[161] *The Proceedings of the Lords and Commons in the year 1628 against Roger Mainwaring,* p. 3. I have used a reprint of 1709; on the title page Mainwaring is described as "the Sacheverell of those days."

tional practice, but also an attack on the property rights of the subject.[162]
The House of Commons adopted a declaration stating in the strongest
terms the seriousness of the offense, and John Pym followed with a superb
speech in which he drove home the gravity of the challenge Mainwaring
had posed. With remorseless logic he dissected the offending sermons. He
laid bare their theological presuppositions as well as their constitutional
and political implications. He cited a mass of precedents and statutes that
proved the irresponsibility of Mainwaring's position. The Commons, Pym
pointed out, considered it "a great presumption for a private divine to
debate the right and power of the king, which is a matter of such a nature
as to be handled only in this court, and that only with moderation and
tenderness." [163] Parliament condemned the offending cleric. The king
agreed to suppress the printed sermons, and then promoted the preacher.
Mainwaring himself made his humble submission to parliament. "May it
please this honourable house," he declared, "I do here in all sorrow and
true repentance acknowledge the many errors and indiscretions which I
have committed in preaching and publishing those two sermons of mine,
which I called Religion and Allegiance." [164] Perhaps it was not an
excessive price to pay for a bishopric.

The doctrine taught by Sibthorpe and Mainwaring formed the
substance of the sermons that Laud preached at the opening of parliament
in 1625/6 and 1628. He repeated the commonplaces of clerical rhetoric in
describing the king as "God's lieutenant upon earth." [165] Like Mainwaring, he dwelt on the intimate interrelation of church and state, and this
was a subject to which, in his various works, he repeatedly returned. In his
first sermon before King Charles he stressed the chain of authority that
runs from God, to the king, to the state.[166] In preaching to parliament in
February 1625/6 he varied the sequence to embrace the church. "These
three," he said, "God, the king, and the church, that is, God, his spouse,
and his lieutenant upon earth, are so near allied—God and the church in
love, God and the king in power, the king and the church in mutual
dependence upon God and subordination to him—that no man can serve
any one of them truly, but he serves all three." [167] When Laud got into
trouble it was not for enunciating these theories but for applying them. In
the early seventeenth century, doctrines were not always sharply defined.
Everyone professed to be a supporter of the ancient constitution, and a
good deal of rhetoric could safely be used to embellish so vague an ideal.
But when clerics tried to apply their theories in ways that threatened the
liberty or the property of the people, the answering protest was immediate,
vehement, and formidable.

[162] *Ibid.,* pp. 4–5.
[163] *Ibid.,* p. 21.
[164] *Ibid.,* p. 24.
[165] Laud, *The Works of William Laud,* I, 94.
[166] *Ibid.,* I, 99.
[167] *Ibid.,* I, 79.

IV

HOOKER, ANDREWES,
AND THE SCHOOL OF LAUD

The ELIZABETHAN SETTLEMENT rested on a theory that was clear and relatively simple. The church embraced the whole nation; it was coterminous with the commonwealth. But it was not easy to translate the theory into fact. The Catholic recusants repudiated the church as now reformed, and resolutely stayed outside. The Separatists, still a tiny minority, had already begun to leave. The Puritans remained within the establishment, but they were clamoring for change; the structure and the ceremonies of the church, they argued, ought to correspond more closely to the Calvinist theology which was widely accepted in the Elizabethan age. The appropriate organization of the Church of England and its future course were matters of fierce debate. Initially most of Elizabeth's leading churchmen had regarded the Settlement of 1559 as an interim arrangement, subject to further modification as the political situation permitted a more complete reform. The queen disagreed. Changes were consistently blocked. Late in the reign an alternative position, distinguishable from both Romanism and Puritanism, began to emerge. But it established itself slowly and amid intense debate.

I

To Richard Hooker belongs the credit of providing the Church of England with a position strong enough to meet its rivals on equal terms. Though *Of the Laws of Ecclesiastical Polity* arose out of the demands of controversy, the intellectual grasp and the spiritual power of the work lifted it high above the circumstances of its origin. Hitherto the Church of England had borne only too clearly the marks of a political expedient; at last it could appeal to a massive statement of fundamental religious principles. Hooker died in 1600. The greater part of his book appeared during the last decade of Elizabeth's reign; the remainder, under circumstances that have inspired endless controversy, was published in the

97

seventeenth century. The book so clearly initiates a new phase in English religious thought and so obviously increased in influence during this period, that it must be taken as our point of departure in considering the emergence of a new approach to religious problems.

Hooker did not represent a radical breach with many of the principles of Calvinist theology.[1] He was engaged in controversy with the Puritans, but the points at issue concerned church order rather than church doctrine. He quietly assumed a large measure of agreement on matters of belief, and then proved that marginal questions (the "indifferent" matters) could satisfactorily be dealt with in such fashion as the royal supremacy might dictate. But Hooker set his discussion of church organization and church government in a magnificently comprehensive context. A discussion of ecclesiastical and political institutions presupposed a discussion of man and his nature; that in turn led to a consideration of more ultimate matters, and these to an examination of the constitution of the universe and to the purposes of God. Beneath the diversity of phenomena Hooker detected the uniformity of order. Here lay the secret of intelligibility in human life. With the help of a philosophy of law, he was confident that he could unfold the meaning of existence.

Hooker was explicit about his basic task: he undertook "the necessary justification of laws." [2] He believed that laws were of various kinds, corresponding to the ascending spheres of a universe that is hierarchically ordered. "All things therefore do work after a sort according to law." Even "the being of God is a kind of law to his working," and from this it follows that God "is a law both to himself and to all other things besides." [3] If God himself is not exempt from the rule of law, we can well understand how it regulates every aspect of the universe—the functioning of nature, the life of each individual, the formation of political societies, the functioning of governments. Some of these laws are fixed, others are not. Natural laws are eternal and immutable; positive laws vary according to external necessity and expediency. But Hooker was convinced that the laws that can be altered derive increased authority from their association with the laws that are abiding. "Let that law eternal be always before our eyes, as being of principal force and moment to breed in religious minds a dutiful estimation of all laws, the use and benefit whereof we see; because there can be no doubt but that laws apparently good are (as it were) things copied out of the very tables of that high everlasting law." [4]

Hooker explained with care that human affairs are subject to "the law rational"; since "human nature knoweth itself in reason universally bound unto" this law,[5] we can appreciate the prominent place he assigned to

[1] Note the generous terms in which he speaks of Calvin and of his work. Cf. Hooker, *Laws of Ecclesiastical Polity*, Preface, ii, 1–6. Cf. Field, *Of the Church*, pp. 92–127.
[2] Hooker, *Laws of Ecclesiastical Polity*, Ep. Ded.
[3] *Ibid.*, I, ii, 2 and 3.
[4] *Ibid.*, I, xvi, 3.   [5] *Ibid.*, I, viii, 9.

reason. "The rule of voluntary agents on earth," he wrote, "is the sentence that reason giveth concerning the goodness of those things which they are to do." [6] By using his intelligence man establishes a standard of judgment and gropes his way through the perplexities that surround him. "Wherefore the natural measure whereby to judge our doings is the sentence of reason, determining and setting down what is good to be done." [7] Hooker was always sensitive to the tensions that keep the religious life taut and resilient, and he never forgot that reason must be balanced by revelation. "There are but two ways," he wrote, "whereby the Spirit leadeth men into all truth; the one extraordinary, the other common; the one belonging but unto some few, the other extending itself unto all that are of God; the one that which we call by a special divine excellency, revelation; the other reason." [8] Revelation, it must be remembered, is interpreted by reason. "Scripture indeed teacheth things above nature, things which our reason by itself could not reach unto. Yet those things also we believe, knowing by reason that the Scripture is the word of God." [9] On some questions the Bible speaks clearly and without equivocation; then we have no choice but to acquiesce. But on many issues God has not explicitly declared his will. For resolving these "indifferent matters" we fall back on other resources. Reason helps us; so does the cumulative wisdom of the race. Tradition must be assigned its proper weight. "The general and perpetual voice of men is as the sentence of God himself; for that which all men have at all times learned, nature herself must needs have taught; and God being the author of nature, her voice is but his instrument." [10] The church also plays its part; "the church being a body which dieth not, hath always power, as occasion requireth, no less to ordain that which never was than to ratify what hath been before." [11]

Hooker thus displayed the complex nature of the authority on which a religious system must rest. The foundation is a rule of law that unifies and orders all things. For the resolution of particular problems he relied not on one but on three types of authority: the Bible, reason, and tradition. "What Scripture doth plainly deliver, to that the first place both of credit and obedience is due; the next whereunto is whatsoever any man can necessarily conclude by force of reason; after these the voice of the church succeedeth." [12] Beyond this, among the questions not determined by law nor laid down by Scripture, he expected that custom, the approval of the majority, and the decision of the prince would equitably resolve disputed points. He granted the state considerable authority in determining

[6] *Ibid.*, I, viii, 4.
[7] *Ibid.*, I, viii, 8.
[8] *Ibid.*, Preface, iii, 10. Cf. H. Tozer, *A Christian Amendment*, p. 19.
[9] Hooker, *Laws of Ecclesiastical Polity*, III, viii, 12.
[10] *Ibid.*, I, viii, 3.
[11] *Ibid.*, V, viii, 1.
[12] *Ibid.*, III, viii, 13.

ecclesiastical questions, but the decisions of the prince ought always to deserve the approval of the people. Hooker took care not to restrict freedom in the interests of authority. Admittedly the liberty he was anxious to preserve was not that of the individual but of men in society. This was the kind of freedom that seemed to be threatened by a false conception of supernatural authority. His interpretation both of freedom and of authority was profoundly affected, of course, by his view of the relation of church and state. He believed that the two were composed of "the selfsame multitude": "there is not any man of the Church of England but the same is also a member of the commonwealth; nor any member of the commonwealth which is not also of the Church of England." [13]

To his successors Hooker bequeathed a twofold legacy: a reasonable and enlightened outlook, and a courteous and charitable temper.[14] "And the good man would say," reported Isaac Walton, " 'the Scriptures were not writ to beget pride and disputations, and opposition to government; but moderation, charity, and humility, obedience to authority and peace to mankind; of which virtues,' he would as often say, 'no man did ever repent himself upon his death-bed.' " [15]

II

Hooker criticized the polity of the Calvinists, not their doctrine; though he was not writing a theological treatise, his work profoundly affected subsequent developments in English thought. It coalesced with a number of other influences to create a new temper and outlook. In philosophy a strain of Platonism had begun to modify the character of English thought. It was clearly present in the works of Thomas Jackson; in due course it inspired the group of writers known as the Cambridge Platonists. Mysticism (represented by Jacob Boehme's writings) was unobtrusively widening its influence in England. Particularly important was the reaction against Protestant Scholasticism. Latter-day Calvinism had hardened into a rigid and inflexible system; its formidable logic seemed to force intolerable conclusions on the Christian mind, and heart and conscience began to protest. This reaction was European in scope, and it became vocal in England about the time that Hooker published his great work. In 1595, William Barrett of Caius College preached a sermon before the University of Cambridge that set the academic community in an uproar. In the citadel of Calvinist orthodoxy, this audacious young

[13] *Ibid.*, VIII, i, 2.

[14] For the way authority was being interpreted early in the seventeenth century, see L. H. [Leonard Hutten], *An Answere to a Certaine Treatise of the Cross in Baptisme*, pp. 19–24, 105–130, where his appeal is to reason, nature, Scripture, and tradition (represented by the fathers and history).

[15] I. Walton, *The Life of Mr. Richard Hooker*, in Hooker, *Works*, I, 25. Cf. Hooker, *Laws of Ecclesiastical Polity*, Preface, vi, 1.

theologian argued that the doctrines of assurance and predestination bred a false security in the Christian soul, and he insisted that "sin is the true exclusive and first cause of reprobation." [16] A university sensation erupted into a controversy of national significance. Archbishop Whitgift (formerly master of Trinity), Lord Burghley (the chancellor of the university), even the queen became involved. In trying to calm the troubled waters, Whitgift, with the aid of William Whitaker and others, drew up the Lambeth Articles. These were designed to guide university authorities in arbitrating sensitive doctrinal matters, and Whitgift did not intend them to be made public. They represent the farthest point of Calvinist penetration of the Church of England, and they became matter of general knowledge through the indiscretion of Peter Baro, the Lady Margaret Professor of Divinity at Cambridge. After commenting publicly (to the queen's intense annoyance) on what had been intended to be a confidential document, he mounted a full-scale attack on the Calvinist doctrines of election, reprobation, and grace.

Normally Barrett and Baro would only have created a nine days' wonder in the little world of Cambridge. But the critics of Calvinism took heart from their forays, and Baro had friends and followers who were already becoming figures of national importance. Lancelot Andrewes, master of Pembroke, had moved away from his youthful Puritanism, and his famous lectures on practical divinity clearly contravened certain principles that the Calvinists cherished. Andrewes, unlike his younger contemporary William Perkins, survived to be a notable figure in the reign of James I, and his contributions to English "Arminianism" will be examined in a later section of this chapter. Like Andrewes, John Overall, master of St. Catherine's and regius professor of divinity at Cambridge, rose to be a bishop in the Jacobean church, and his *Bishop Overall's Convocation Book* contains the stillborn canons of 1606. Whereas Andrewes taught moral theology with universal applause, Overall got entangled in the controversies about predestination that had made Cambridge such a hotbed of contention. He ran foul of the Calvinism of some of the other leading heads of houses, and the problems of assurance, persevering grace, election, and reprobation kept the university in continual turmoil. The sensitiveness to criticism shown by the leaders of Cambridge Calvinism betrays an insecurity that belies their confident dogmatism. Here again the stage was set for the controversies of the seventeenth century. The wrangles in Cambridge accurately anticipated the debates at the Hampton Court Conference in 1604. The same subjects—grace, assurance, predestination—were discussed. Some of the same participants—Overall, Chaderton, Knewstubb—were involved. The Calvinists won few concessions at Hampton Court, and one of the most vociferous of their opponents at the conference was to lead the attack against them in other areas.

[16] Cf. H. C. Porter, *Reformation and Reaction in Tudor Cambridge*, pp. 344 ff.

102

Richard Bancroft, bishop of London and soon to be archbishop of Canterbury, intervened in the debates at Hampton Court with the obvious purpose of discomposing the Calvinists and compromising their cause.[17] In this he achieved some success. But it was not a theological victory. Nor is there much evidence that Bancroft objected to Calvinist doctrine. His sermons, his writings (which are not extensive), even the contents of the library at Lambeth show that he kept a careful watch on the Puritans and on their practices. But his concern was that of an ecclesiastic, not of a theologian. He wished to bring them into conformity, and he harried without mercy those who deviated from the straight path of uniformity.[18] The canons of 1604, largely Bancroft's work, were so designed that no man dissatisfied with the discipline of the Church of England could honestly remain among its clergy.[19] During the early years of King James's reign the Puritans were subject to considerable pressure, but the motives that inspired the attacks were seldom clearly associated with the rise of a new theological temper. The king made no secret of his dislike of Puritan ways,[20] but he prided himself on his theological competence, and in this sphere his convictions were clearly Calvinist. He put considerable pressure on the Dutch to silence Vorstius, the successor to Arminius at Leyden.[21] In 1617, when the court was at Newmarket, he summoned the leading figures from Cambridge to attend him, and he cross-examined them about their reaction to an Arminian confession that had been imported from Holland. Those who had approved the document suddenly found themselves in serious trouble, "especially Dr. Richardson, the King's [i.e., the Regius] professor, for which he either hath already or is in some danger of losing his place." [22] James could claim some credit for the convening of the Synod of Dort; he sent as English delegates a team of convinced Calvinists, and their reports show that (barring questions of order) they solidly supported the anti-Arminian side.[23]

While the king was attacking liberal theology in Holland, a parallel trend began to appear in England. Its representatives were reluctant to be labeled as Arminians. Montagu, one of the most prominent (and controversial) members of the new school, emphatically repudiated the

[17] Cf. Barlow, *The Summe and Substance of the Conference,* pp. 11, 13, 26–28, 49, 55–57. "The bishop of London," reported Dudley Carleton, "spake well to the purpose, but with too rough boldness." *Cal. S. P. Dom., James I,* 14, Vol. VI, No. 21.

[18] Cf. especially R. G. Usher, *The Reconstruction of the English Church,* and Babbage, *Puritanism and Richard Bancroft.*

[19] Cf. especially Canons IV, V, VII, XXXVI. Kenyon, *The Stuart Constitution,* pp. 79, 83; James I, *Political Works,* pp. 6 ff., 15, 24, 126, 151, 296.

[20] Cf. Barlow, *The Summe and Substance,* pp. 79, 83; James I, *Political Works,* pp. 6 ff., 15, 24, 126, 151, 296.

[21] James I, *The Workes of the Most High and Mightie Prince, James* (1616 ed.), pp. 347–380.

[22] Letter of Sir Henry Bourgchier to James Ussher, in R. Parr (ed.), *A Collection of Three Hundred Letters,* p. 61.

[23] Cf. John Hales, *Golden Remains,* pp. 460, 581.

designation. He had never even read an Arminian book; "I disavow the name and title of Arminian," he said, "I am no more Arminian than they are Gomarians." [24] The objection was sound; in England the theological phase of the struggle was over. During the contentions at Cambridge, the opponents of Calvinism had defined their position on such sensitive subjects as election and reprobation. It was now sufficient to appeal to the views of Andrewes and Overall. Andrewes had argued that the doctrines implicit in the Thirty-nine Articles and the Book of Common Prayer antedate the rise of Calvinism. They reflect Cranmer's position, and rely on the theology of the early days of the Reformation. Andrewes went behind the Reformation and appealed to the practice of the early church. From this treasury he proposed to bring out things that were old though they might seem new to his contemporaries. He believed that the devotional life of the church could be greatly enriched by incorporating elements from many ancient sources. He believed that the worship of the church could be beautified by laying under contribution ceremonial practices that admittedly were not commanded by Scripture but that were certainly not forbidden by it. And he believed that the relation between church and nation should be exemplified in every sphere of thought and practice.

To these areas an increasing number of Jacobean clerics devoted their attention. Andrewes' *Preces Privatae* showed how greatly scholarship could enrich the life of devotion. He drew on the Greek and Latin fathers, on Eastern liturgies as well as on the Missal, the Breviary, and the Manual. He laid various Reformation sources under contribution, but he also showed that the ancient pagan writers could serve the ends of Christian piety. The spirit that pervaded his book was exemplified in his life; in its literary form his contribution to this field was published only after his death. Donne's *Devotions upon emergent occasions* was a less eclectic work, but not necessarily a less profound one. George Herbert's *A Priest to the Temple: or the Country Parson* proved that the contributions of many traditions of ministry could be fused into an ideal that was widely representative yet typically English. Daniel Featley's *Ancilla Pietatis* was used by Charles I. The devotional ideals of the Arminian school found their most complete expression in Nicholas Ferrar's family retreat at Little Gidding. The ordered life, the unceasing devotions, the monastic atmosphere epitomized much of the sedate and gentle spirit of this revival. Its remedy for the disorders of the time was the training of the character by the life of disciplined devotion. But it is scarcely surprising that under the guise of "The Arminian Nunnery" it invited attack.[25] It had lost touch with the spirit of the age. It could not enter with sympathy into the thoughts and aspirations of the mass of mankind.

[24] Montagu, *Appello Caesarem*, p. 10. Gomar was the leader of the Dutch Calvinists.
[25] *The Arminian Nunnery, or a briefe description and relation of the late erected monasticall place called the Arminian Nunnery at Little Gidding.*

The most celebrated (because the most controversial) work of this type was John Cosin's *A Collection of Private Devotions*. Cosin took care to forestall the kind of criticism that he must have anticipated. His material, he pointed out, was "taken out of the Holy Scriptures, the ancient Fathers, and the Divine Service of our own church." The Lord's Prayer was the pattern of all devotion, and "ancient piety" merely built on that foundation. He felt that four reasons justified his decision to make readily accessible the kind of material he provided. "The first is to continue and preserve the authority of the ancient laws and old godly canons of the church, which were made and set forth for this purpose, that men, before they set themselves to pray, might know what to say and avoid, as near as might be, all extemporal effusions of irksome and indigested prayers which they use to make, that herein are subject to no good order or form of words, but pray both what and how and when they list." The ancient church forbade all prayers except those she authorized, and this prohibition applied particularly to extemporary prayer. The second reason was the desire to let the whole world know how wrong they are who believe the English "to have set up a new church and a new faith, to have abandoned all the ancient forms of piety and devotion, to have taken away all the religious exercises of our forefathers, to have despised all the old ceremonies and cast behind us all the blessed sacraments of Christ's Catholic Church." His work was also designed to help those prevented from joining in public worship; instead of reading endless disputations about "many unnecessary questions" they would be able "to spend some hours of the day at least . . . in God's holy worship and service." Finally, those who might be little inclined to devotion would by this means be awakened to their religious duty.[26] No reader of Cosin needed to complain of dearth of material. He suggested patterns of thought based on the seven virtues, the seven deadly sins, the seven sacraments, the fruits of the Spirit, and so forth. He provided psalms, collects, litanies, and general prayers. In introducing the canonical hours, he explained their origin, meaning, and value. He reproduced the church calendar, explained the rules for movable feasts, and listed the days of fasting and abstinence. He assumed that his readers would have unlimited time and an inexhaustible enthusiasm for the practices of the ancient Catholic Church.

Many of his contemporaries were suspicious of his zeal. Englishmen feared anything that smacked of popery; to the ordinary person the practices that Cosin advocated bore all the marks of Romish infection. His manual of devotions prompted a most undevotional uproar. Henry Burton, rector of St. Matthew's, Friday Street, and a vehement Puritan, accused Cosin of plotting to reduce the Church of England "to an union with the Church of Rome, as your only mother, and to entertain again a conformity and communion with her in her superstitious rites and

---

[26] John Cosin, *A Collection of Private Devotions,* Preface.

ceremonies." [27] He flatly declared that this was "a popish book," [28] and proceeded to establish the point with some verve but in tedious detail. The Reformation, he pointed out, had reduced the "sacraments of the Gospel" to two; Cosin had reverted to the Catholic number of seven. Clearly the purpose of the work was to bring back "the whole tower of Babylon in England." [29] Burton had no doubt that he was dealing with a "most pernicious, pestilent and popish book." [30] The specter of Romanism also summoned to the fray William Prynne, a young barrister of Lincoln's Inn. So began a collaboration that was to reach dramatic proportions. Prynne, spurred on by a pathological fear of Rome and an irresistible itch to write, published *A Briefe Survay and Censure of Mr Cozen his Couzening Devotions*. His aim was to "prove both the form and matter" of the book "to be merely popish." Prynne covered much the same ground as Burton. On every page of the *Private Devotions* he detected the "mark of the Beast." Arminianism was clearly a conspiracy to deliver the Church of England into the hands of the pope of Rome.

The enrichment of devotion implied the reform of worship. To men of Catholic sympathies the simplicity favored by many Puritans seemed stark to the point of crudity. They believed that those who cared little for form would also care little for decency. If there was no special reverence for the altar, there would be no respect for the building that contained it.[31] The Arminians were horrified at the way secular activities often intruded into sacred places. Holiness meant separateness. The altar (not the "table") was to stand permanently against the east wall, and in token of its sanctity it should be raised above the level of the nave and railed off even from the rest of the choir. Behind this lay various motives, theological and aesthetic, and it had a number of consequences. If you raised the altar above the church, did you not raise the priest above the people? The separateness of the altar implied the separateness of the ministrant, and the dormant anticlericalism of the Englishman took alarm. Lay antipathy to High Church ways was compounded of many ingredients; distrust of the ecclesiology of the Arminians was certainly one. Vague resentment found expression in the famous case of the altar at Grantham. The Elizabethan injunction seemed to imply that the communion table should be kept at the east end when not in use, but should be brought forward when the sacrament was celebrated. Andrewes' influence had strengthened the disposition to keep the altar at the east end, and before many years had passed, Laud, as dean of Gloucester, would defy his bishop by insisting that the altar in the cathedral be moved to the east end and kept there.

[27] H. Burton, *A Tryall of Private Devotions*, p. 3.
[28] *Ibid.*, p. 8.
[29] *Ibid.*, p. 36.
[30] *Ibid.*, p. 52.
[31] Cf. Walter Balcanquall, *The Honour of Christian Churches*, p. 12; Francis Mason, *The Authoritie of the Church in making Canons and Constitutions*, pp. 8–10.

The vicar of Grantham merely defied his parishioners, but the case gained sufficient notoriety to require the attention of the bishop of the diocese. The incumbent of the see of Lincoln was John Williams, an astute and able ecclesiastic who never allowed zeal to outstrip discretion. He had a competent grasp of theological principles. As an undergraduate at Cambridge he had been deeply influenced by John Overall, but he had also faithfully attended the ministry of William Perkins, the foremost Puritan preacher of the day.[32] He was thus familiar with both positions in the current debates. His ruling in the Grantham case was a reasonable interpretation of what he took to be the exact meaning of the Elizabethan injunction. But he also contributed to the general controversy on the subject by publishing a work entitled *The Holy Table, Name or Thing*. In cool, analytical fashion he examined the presuppositions of the Arminian school. Temperamentally he was favorably disposed to their claims: he loved magnificence, and the services in his chapel at Buckden, we are told, were models of dignity.[33] As the argument of his book unfolded, it became clear that he was not merely advising an indiscreet vicar; he was exposing the weaknesses inherent in the policy of men like Laud, and criticizing them with considerable effect.[34] As Clarendon remarked, "it was a book so full of good learning, and that learning so close and solidly applied . . . , that it gained him reputation enough to do hurt. . . . He used all the wit and all the malice he could to awaken the people to a jealousy of those agitations and innovations in the exercise of religion." [35]

The dismay caused in some quarters by liturgical reform is fully illustrated by the case of Peter Smart, prebendary of Durham. Cosin was also a member of the chapter, and had introduced into the worship of the cathedral a wide variety of ancient practices. Smart watched in angry silence till he could contain himself no longer. In July 1628 he denounced Cosin from the pulpit of the cathedral, and then published his sermon as *The Vanitie and Downe-fall of Superstitious Popish Ceremonies*. The world, said Smart, had heard of Cosin's "speculative and theoretical popery, which he hath audaciously broached in his Book of Private Devotions"; let it now observe Cosin in action. So Smart enumerated twelve separate changes which Cosin had introduced at Durham, all based merely on "human traditions." In the process "the plain simplicity and modest attire of that grave matron, Christ's holy spouse" have "been despised," and "the whore of Babylon's bastardly brood, doting upon their mother's beauty, that painted harlot, the Church of Rome, have laboured to restore her all her robes and jewels again." [36] Smart found himself in serious trouble. He

[32] John Hacket, *Scrinia Reserata*, Pt. I, pp. 9–10.

[33] Cf. Anthony Cade, *A Sermon necessary for these Times*, Ep. Ded. Hacket, *op. cit.*, Pt. II, 30.

[34] Cf. Laud, *Works*, VII, 355.

[35] Edward Hyde, Earl of Clarendon, *The History of the Rebellion and Civil Wars in England*, I, 150.

[36] Peter Smart, *The Vanitie and Downe-fall of Superstitious Popish Ceremonies*, p. 11. For a similar

was resisting a tide flowing much too strongly to be checked by isolated protests, but this was not the last that was heard of him. The Long Parliament restored him to his prebend "after his eleven years imprisonment and fourteen years persecution in the several High Commissions of Durham, London and York for preaching against the superstitious innovations in Durham." [37]

Slowly but steadily the Arminians gained in influence under James I. In the succeeding reign they reached a position of precarious eminence, and then their fortunes crashed with the collapse of Stuart absolutism. James I admired the preaching of Lancelot Andrewes, but, as we have seen, he distrusted the new theology, and when the see of Canterbury fell vacant, he passed over Andrewes in favor of George Abbot, a man of moderate Calvinistic views. James was loath to advance William Laud; when the Duke of Buckingham and Bishop Williams urged his claims, the king offered a shrewd assessment of Laud's character: "I see he has a restless spirit, and cannot see when matters are well, but loves to toss and change, and bring things to a pitch of reformation floating in his own brain, which may endanger the steadfastness of that which is in a good pass, God be praised." [38] Charles I, however, was in complete agreement with the ideals and aspirations of the Arminians. He adopted their theological position; he shared their liturgical aims; he wholeheartedly applauded their political theories; he approved of their policy in the administration of the church. He was blind to the perils of open partisanship in an area so sensitive as this, and boldly invited a conflict with the House of Commons. Early in the new reign Laud gave Buckingham a list, to be transmitted to the king, of the clergy who should or should not be advanced; each name was identified as O (orthodox) or P (Puritan).[39] But the issue was not wholly of Charles's making. In the last year of the reign of James I, Richard Montagu, a man of considerable learning and of proven skill in controversy, found that a Catholic pamphlet, *The Gagge of the Reformed Gospell,* was circulating in his parish. In it Matthew Kellison of the Douai college attacked Calvinism, which he tacitly equated with the official theology of the Church of England. With some wit and much invective, Montagu replied in *A New Gagg for an Old Goose.* The Catholic criticisms, he argued, were loose and inexact. Many of the doctrines and practices attributed to Anglicans were repudiated by them, while on other disputed matters it could be shown that the Church

---

reaction to ceremonial enrichments, see Thomas Brightman, *A Revelation of the Revelation,* p. 905.

[37] Smart, *A Catalogue of Superstitious Innovations.* Cf. *The Articles or Charge exhibited in Parliament against D. Cozens of Durham.* Note William Prynne's attack on Cosin's Durham reforms in *Anti-arminianisme,* Ep. Ded., p. 8.

[38] Hacket, *op. cit.,* Pt. I, p. 64.

[39] William Laud, *The History of the Troubles and Tryal of . . . William Laud, wrote by Himself,* I, 16.

of England followed the example of the primitive church. Montagu attacked the Puritans on the one hand and the Catholics on the other.[40] To Puritan sympathizers in the House of Commons the book seemed as popish in tenor as the pamphlet it refuted. Archbishop Abbot was asked to rebuke Montagu, and did so. Montagu appealed to the king, who authorized him to expound his views at greater length. The result was *Appello Caesarem,* one of the most controversial works of the period. As before, Montagu maintained the intermediate position of the Church of England by denouncing both papists and Puritans. It can hardly be claimed that he did so impartially. He dismissed Calvinism as "a desperate doctrine of predestination," and insisted that it could not be found in the official formularies of the Church of England.[41] Man was created good, and even the Fall had not vitiated this original endowment, nor robbed him of his free will. "If this be Arminianism," he added, "I must profess it." [42] Montagu claimed that he was "opposed to popish doctrines," [43] but his contemporaries felt that he handled them somewhat gently. "I am absolutely persuaded," he wrote, ". . . that the Church of Rome is a *true,* though not a *sound,* Church of Christ," and it must be remembered, he added, that everything that the papists say is not necessarily popery.[44] Images have a legitimate as well as an illegitimate use. It is by no means certain that the pope is Antichrist. Controverted rites like signing with the cross have a proper place. Confession is not a new popish custom, but the ancient and pious practice of the church.[45] He claimed that the canons of the Council of Trent were not entirely incompatible with the teaching of Calvin; at some points, he added, he agreed with Perkins and at others with Aquinas.

If Montagu had been less provocative in manner, he might have given less offense. As it was, he thoroughly aroused the fears of the country gentlemen who sat in the House of Commons. King Charles, however, immediately intervened; he made Montagu a royal chaplain, and then informed the House that "he had taken the business into his own hands." [46] By the time the second parliament of the new reign assembled, certain important developments had emphasized the new trend. Dr. Robert Sibthorpe and Dr. Roger Mainwaring had preached and published sermons setting forth an uncompromising view of the king's authority, and thus had underlined the link between High Church theology and high prerogative theory (cf. Chapter III). Meanwhile, Charles had promoted Montagu to the see of Chichester, and had

[40] For this stress on the *via media,* see Field, *op. cit.,* Ep. Ded.
[41] Montagu, *Appello Caesarem,* pp. 31, 48.
[42] *Ibid.,* p. 65.
[43] *Ibid.,* p. 225.
[44] *Ibid.,* pp. 113, 116.
[45] *Ibid.,* pp. 145 ff., 248 ff., 265 ff., 297 ff.
[46] Rushworth, *Historical Collections,* I, 174.

completed his defiance of parliament by granting all three men anticipa-
tory pardons. The challenge was too blatant to be ignored. "For an
Arminian is the spawn of the papist," Mr. Rous assured the House of
Commons, ". . . and if you mark it well, you shall see an Arminian
reaching out his hand to a papist, a papist to a Jesuit, a Jesuit gives one
hand to the pope and the other to the king of Spain." [47]

Montagu alarmed others besides apprehensive members of parliament.
Arminianism had chiefly made headway among clerics, especially among
those of scholarly tastes, familiar with antiquity and attracted by it. But
the great body of Calvinist opinion remained loyal to its convictions, and
Montagu inspired a rash of answers. Nor were his critics insignificant
nonentities. George Carleton was bishop of Chichester—Montagu's
predecessor in that see. Daniel Featley was a man of learning and a
distinguished controversialist. Montagu, they said, had shown himself
fundamentally disloyal to the accepted doctrines of the Church of
England. He had revived the discredited errors of Barrett, Baro, and
Thomson. He had ridiculed the Lambeth Articles, and had thus
impugned the memory of archbishops Whitgift and Hutton. He had
departed from the Augustinianism on which the doctrine of the Church of
England rested, and had resuscitated the bland imbecilities of Pelagianism. In particular, by casting aspersions on the doctrine of predestination
he had clearly shown that he was an Arminian in sympathy, if not a papist
at heart.[48] So with great care the traditional beliefs of the Church of
England were restated. Often in parallel columns the offending novelties
taught by the Arminians were contrasted with the true faith received by
the Church of England. The authority of King James was repeatedly
invoked, and tedious quotations from his writings proved how emphatically he repudiated Arminian errors.[49] This seems slightly superfluous;
James had apparently approved of Montagu's first work and had
authorized the second one, and in any case there was no doubt about the
sympathies of his son, the new king. The Calvinists were on sounder
ground in protesting against the slurs cast by Montagu on the Synod of
Dort; the English Church had been officially represented, and its
spokesmen had supported all the doctrinal articles of the synod.[50]
Montagu's opponents objected to his careless controversial methods, and
they were alarmed at the possible results of his activities. Clearly he would

---

[47] W. Notestein and F. H. Relf (eds.), *Commons' Debates for 1629*, p. 13.

[48] These points represent the core of the following works: G. Carleton, *An Examination of
those things wherein the author of the late Appeale holdeth the doctrines of Pelagians and Arminians to be the
doctrines of the Church of England;* Francis Rous, *Testis Veritatis;* [Anthony Wotton], *A dangerous
plot discovered;* [John Yates], *Ibis ad Caesarem;* [Featley], *A Second Parallel; An Appeal of the orthodox
ministers of the Church of England against Richard Mountague.* Cf. also D. Maxey, *Five Sermons
preached before the King.*

[49] Cf. Rous, *op. cit.*

[50] Cf. *A Joynt Attestation of several Bishops and Learned Divines of the Church of England.*

"make divisions where there were none." [51] The English Church had been united in doctrine; he was fomenting faction. The Reformed Churches—of England, Scotland, Holland, Geneva, the Palatinate—had differed on matters of discipline, but they had been united on questions of faith. Montagu was driving a wedge between them. Even more serious dangers threatened. Rous enumerated six ways in which Arminianism was "a policy to loose religion, land and all." It favored Spain; it would leave England vulnerable to its traditional foe.[52] "It is to be feared," wrote Daniel Featley, "that the error of the universalists is too universally dispread. Many men have too much free will, and take to themselves too free liberty now-a-days to advance and maintain free will." What had emerged was simply a "new Pelagianism, varnished over with a fair gloss by the pencil of Arminius and his scholars." [53]

The controversy at least proved that the country was not simply divided between Laudians and Puritans. Between the new Arminians and the vigorous advocates of reform there was a large middle body of opinion, Calvinist in doctrine but not Puritan in sympathy. When Montagu posed as a spokesman for the church, these men of intermediate position suddenly found their voices.[54] The new policy, of which Montagu was the symbol, gave good ground for the fears rising in the minds of these men. Samuel Ward's letters to James Ussher reflected his growing dismay. Ward, who had been a member of the delegation to Dort, was Lady Margaret Professor of Divinity and master of Sidney Sussex College, Cambridge. He did not like what was happening in the university. Men hoping for promotion were beginning to "look in the Arminian direction, because preferments at Court are conferred upon such as incline that way." The vice-chancellor "favoureth novelties, both in rites and doctrines." Concerning university affairs, "I may truly say," he remarked, "I never knew them in worse condition since I was a member thereof, which is almost forty-six years. Not but that I hope the greater part is orthodox; but that new heads are brought in, and they are backed in maintaining novelties." [55] Before long George Morley, when asked what the Arminians held, would reply that they held the best bishoprics and deaneries in England.

To his contemporaries William Laud was the incarnation of the Arminian revolution. Certainly he provided the most complete demonstration of the way the new school interpreted authority in practical terms; many felt that he also showed within what narrow limits it would sanction

[51] Carleton, *An Examination*, p. 78.

[52] Rous, *op. cit.*, p. 106.

[53] [Featley, tr.], *Pelagius Redivivus*, Translator to the Reader.

[54] Cf. *An Appeal of the orthodox ministers of the Church of England.*

[55] R. Parr (ed.), *A Collection of Three Hundred Letters*, pp. 394, 407 f. Cf. O. N., *An Apology of English Arminianisme*, Ep. Ded., p. 5. The author maintains that Arminianism has made great headway in the universities and cathedral chapters.

freedom. King Charles delighted to honor him. He advanced him as rapidly as possible to the highest position in the church, and promoted him to a corresponding place of power in the state. King and archbishop were united by similar tastes in worship, similar views on theology, and common objectives in government. Laud—fussy, efficient, incorruptible—filled a real void in Charles's system of personal rule. With Strafford he became joint head of the king's government. While the system lasted he was in large measure responsible for its success; when it collapsed he had to bear a large share of the blame for its failure.

Laud saw no incongruity in the twofold responsibilities he discharged. He accepted without question Hooker's doctrine of the unity of church and nation. The divine right of kings and the divine right of bishops were complementary doctrines, and he did not greatly trouble himself to make sure that they were really compatible. Frontiers need to be defined only when the areas they divide must be kept separate. Laud believed that in this case the areas had been joined together by God. He did not neglect his duty as a churchman when he devoted himself to matters of state. A bishop, he assured Lord Saye and Sele, "may preach the Gospel more publicly, and to far greater edification, in a court of judicature or at a council table, where great men are met together to draw things to an issue, than many preachers in their charges can." [56] He placed clerics in high government offices—a fatal blunder in Clarendon's eyes—because "he did really believe that nothing more contributed to the benefit and advancement of the church than the promotion of churchmen to the places of the greatest honour and offices of the highest trust." [57] "The church and state," Laud insisted, "are so near united and knit together, that though they may seem two bodies, yet indeed in some relations they may be accounted as but one." [58] Controversy in the church encouraged unrest in the state, and Laud and his friends enforced a ban on the discussion of sensitive subjects. Laud was reputedly responsible for the form of the royal declaration prefixed to a new edition of the Thirty-nine Articles. "We will that all further curious search be laid aside, . . . and that no man hereafter shall either print or preach to draw the article aside any way, but shall submit to it in the plain and full meaning thereof." [59] Laud was deeply concerned to preserve peace, and he regarded the maintenance of uniformity as an essential means to that end. He believed that he was enforcing the law of the land. Among the various reasons for his exasperation with Prynne, not the least was his conviction that this pestilent fellow claimed that he was within the letter of the law, whereas

[56] Laud, *Works*, Vi, 188.

[57] Clarendon, *History*, I, 133. Cf. Strafford, *The Earl of Strafford's Letters and Dispatches*, II, 12; Thomas May, *History of the Long Parliament*, Bk. I, Ch. ii, pp. 23–24.

[58] D. Wilkins, *Concilia*, IV, 471.

[59] Gardiner (ed.), *Constitutional Documents of the Puritan Revolution*, p. 76. Cf. the similar terms of the royal declaration of 1622, Kenyon, *The Stuart Constitution*, pp. 145–146.

Laud had constituted himself as the interpreter and guardian of its true intent.[60]

In enforcing the law, Laud was maintaining a certain view of the church and of its place in the national life. With every fiber of his being he resisted all who challenged that place. In retrospect it is clear that when Laud came to power the challenge from Rome was already subsiding, but contemporaries were not aware of this, and the proselytizing zeal of the Jesuits still made popery seem a dangerous threat. The most substantial of Laud's writings was *A Relation of the Conference between William Laud . . . and Mr Fisher the Jesuit*. The form and pattern of the book are serious drawbacks; nevertheless, this is unquestionably one of the ablest books produced in this period. Behind Fisher stood the redoubtable figure of Cardinal Bellarmine, and Laud seldom forgot him. He accepted most of Bellarmine's presuppositions; on that basis, with great clarity and cogency he attacked his position. In more ways than one the book looked to the past rather than to the future; it can be accounted one of the last triumphs of Scholasticism. It was an unusually able defense of Anglican principles. In view of this, the persistent rumors that Laud was a cryptopapist are manifestly unfair. Even in his Oxford days he had been accused of halting between two positions.[61] Twice he was approached by emissaries from Rome, so blind to his real aims that they offered him a cardinal's hat. To the Puritans it seemed natural to attribute popish sympathies to a man so devoted to ritualism and episcopacy. Prynne was not a neutral witness, nor was he an isolated one, and in Laud's policies he detected a plot "to undermine our Protestant religion, reduce both us and all our dominions back to Rome by insensible degrees." To put it more bluntly, he believed that Laud's aim was "reconciliation with this Babylonish strumpet." [62] Laud, of course, denied the charge, vehemently and repeatedly. "I take it now on my death," he declared on the scaffold, "that I never endeavoured the subversion of the laws of the realm, nor never any change of the Protestant religion into popish superstition." [63]

The Puritans found it difficult to be dispassionate in their judgment of Laud's intentions. They were his chief victims. To few tasks did he devote himself with such singleness of purpose as to the reduction of the Puritans to due obedience. He detested their views, but it was not on this account that he harried them. They were breaking the law, both of the church and of the state; they were undermining that unity on which the national stability depended. His efforts to preserve—or rather to restore—uniformity were varied and incessant.[64] Incumbents who took liberties with the

---

[60] Cf. [Prynne], *A New Discovery of the Prelates Tyranny*, pp. 19 ff.

[61] Laud, *Works*, VII, 3.

[62] Prynne, *A Breviate of the life of William Laud*, Ep. Ded.

[63] [Laud], *The Archbishop of Canterbury's Speech*, p. 14.

[64] The Laudians often used visitation sermons to enforce their views. Cf. Edward Boughen, *Unanimity in Judgment and Affection necessary to Unity of Doctrine and Uniformity in Discipline, passim;*

prescribed liturgy were brought to heel. Sometimes a little pressure, a blunt warning, an unvarnished threat convinced the offender that his convictions on a given question were more flexible than he had imagined. Laud wanted to change the pattern, not to punish the individual, and if there were signs of amendment he was prepared to suspend proceedings. He considered Puritan "lecturers" to be a special menace. They had access to the pulpit but were not responsible for worship. They were not appointed by the bishops and were therefore less amenable to their control. In 1629 Laud secured from King Charles a declaration that severely limited the activities of lecturers. He tried to bar the door to a favorite refuge of disgruntled Puritans—the chaplaincies in the mansions of the nobles and the gentry. He stepped in to terminate the activities of feoffees who had bought up impropriations in order to place godly preachers in strategic parishes.[65] Having brought the University of Oxford to what he regarded as a satisfactory state, he attempted the much more difficult task of reducing the University of Cambridge to a similar condition. His reports to the king leave the impression that he and his fellow bishops were primarily engaged in the task of harrying those who refused to conform.

Laud had at his disposal the authority he needed and the instruments necessary to effect his ends. As bishop of London, then as archbishop of Canterbury, he was ideally placed to control the press. The High Commission and the Star Chamber provided him with the means to pursue offenders and to punish those who refused to capitulate. Here, as elsewhere, Laud's motto was "thorough." The persistence with which he pursued his goal suggested a rancor that he did not always feel. The impression that he created may have been false; it was confirmed by the cases in which the offender's recalcitrance had aroused in Laud something that bore all the marks of vindictiveness.[66] Alexander Leighton invited some kind of retribution; Laud saw that he got it. Leighton's *An Appeal to the Parliament; or Syons Plea against the Prelacie* was an unmeasured attack on episcopacy and those who upheld it. "The prelacy is the mother of all sin"; currently it was buttressed by Arminianism, a correlative evil "which, we know, is the very elixir of popery, the mystery of the mystery of iniquity, . . . the quintessence of equivocation, the oracle of Delphos, the cabinet of the pope's secret."[67] Leighton was imprisoned; when he

---

John Randol, *A Sermon . . . concerning the Kingdoms Peace,* pp. 2–3, 8; William Quelch, *Church Customs Vindicated,* pp. 12–15, 44–47.

[65] Cf. I. M. Calder, *Activities of the Puritan Faction of the Church of England,* Introduction.

[66] Cf. [Henry Parker], *A Discourse concerning Puritans,* p. 10: "My lord of Canterbury, in all his invectives against Puritanism, ever made fury and turbulence the ground of all his hatred and enmity against it, and yet the whole world would judge if the earth ever brought forth anything more furious and turbulent than himself."

[67] Alexander Leighton, *An Appeal to the Parliament; or Syons Plea against the Prelacie,* pp. 241, 234.

escaped, Laud pressed the search; when Leighton was recaptured, Laud demanded one of those savage mutilating sentences that in the seventeenth century even churchmen did not shrink from inflicting.

It would have been difficult to justify Laud's policy, even if it had been completely successful. As it was, Laud found himself frustrated at every turn. In practice he could seldom be as inflexible as his theory demanded. The shortage of clergy was such that in prosecuting delinquents he often had to be satisfied with a vague promise of conformity. Laud's persecution of the Puritans was ill-conceived because in the long run it was so ineffective. Its failure was the more certain because Laud extended his disciplinary activities to the laity as well as to the clergy, and thus drove his two types of victims into alliance. He used the High Commission court—his instrument in compelling Puritan ministers to conform—to coerce laymen into morality. "Persons of honour and great quality were every day cited into the High Commission Court, upon the fame of their incontinence or other scandal in their lives." One must admire his determination that the law of the church "should be applied to the greatest and most splendid transgressors, as well as to the punishment of smaller offences and meaner offenders," [68] but it was a policy guaranteed to alienate the best and the worst elements among the laity.

This was serious because simultaneously Laud was giving the gentry economic cause for apprehension. The Reformation had created a class of landowners who owed their wealth to the plunder of the church. Queen Elizabeth had had no compunction about squeezing concessions from bishops. She had offered to elevate Andrewes to the sees of Ely and of Chichester, but on terms that no conscientious churchman could accept. Where the queen set the example, her needy (and greedy) servants were quick to follow. When the Bishop of Durham tried to resist these predatory raids on church property, Sir Robert Cecil wrote him a letter full of incredulity and angry threats.[69] Many of the church's problems were caused, all its difficulties were aggravated, by economic stringency due to these repeated losses. "So in very truth," declared Andrewes, "unless we would have the universities to be broken up, the clergy to be trampled on, and all that is holy come to ruin, there lies a necessity to plead for the church's patrimony." [70] Many shared Andrewes' alarm. Thomas Adams and Richard Bernard, both Puritan preachers, were as deeply concerned as any bishop. Laud, as was natural, spoke against the evil, and then acted as resolutely as circumstances allowed. The church, he reminded Charles, was like a hive of bees. "And men that care neither for the hive nor the bees have yet a great mind to the honey. . . . Now in

---

[68] Clarendon, *op.cit.,* I, 146.

[69] Cf. Matthew Hutton, *The Correspondence of Matthew Hutton,* p. 94

[70] Lancelot Andrewes, *Sacrilege a Snare,* p. 5. Cf. Henry Leslie, *A Treatise of the Authoritie of the Church,* Ep. Ded.

this great and busy work the king and the priest must not fear to put their hands to the hive, though they be sure to be stung, and stung by the bees whose hive and house they preserve." [71] Laud made a heroic effort to reverse the recent trend, and if possible to recover what had been lost. His efforts had only a limited success, and no one thanked him for his pains.[72]

Laud raised up enemies on every side. He alienated so many people in so many ways that no man in England was so thoroughly hated. To Laud's obvious bewilderment his critics regarded him as a tyrant. Where they saw an attack on freedom of conscience, he intended merely an effort to enforce the law. He demanded that men should abide by the rules, but these rules, he insisted, were regularly established and allowed as wide a latitude as was desirable. He was largely responsible for the canons of 1640; "never any synod sat in Christendom," he boasted, "that allowed more freedom either of speech or vote," but he believed that liberty of interpretation ended once the synod's decision was made. He claimed that the Scottish canons (also his handiwork) did not establish a tyranny either over worship or "over the souls of men; for they are left free in all things, save to commit sin and disorder." [73] It would have been impossible, he insisted, for him to countenance dictatorial rule, "my knowledge and judgement going ever against an arbitrary government in comparison with that which is settled by law." [74] His diary is full of honest perplexity. He was puzzled that he should be so misunderstood, but on every page there is evidence that he could not comprehend the motives of those who differed from him. There is no doubt that Laud believed in intellectual freedom. He did not propose to interfere with any man's convictions. "Nor will I ever take it upon me," he said, "to express that tenet or opinion, the denial of the foundation only excepted, which may shut any Christian, the meanest, out of Heaven." [75] He expected, however, that people who differed from him would disseminate their beliefs only with the most subdued discretion, and certainly he did not intend that anyone's ideas should be so expressed as to endanger established institutions. So even friends like John Hales and Joseph Hall were called to account for injudicious statements. Under such circumstances what kind of freedom could Puritans expect? Laud himself showed no consuming interest in the world of ideas. He was a scholar, with a taste for manuscripts. He was an academic administrator who wished to see his university under tight control, and he saw no reason why the whole nation should not be run like Oxford. He was vulnerable to criticism because his contemporaries did not believe that he applied with equity the laws by which he set such store. The regulations to prevent discussion of sensitive ideas were strictly

---

[71] Laud, *A Relation of the Conference,* Ep. Ded.
[72] Cf. C. Hill, *Economic Problems of the Church,* where the whole subject is fully treated.
[73] Laud, *The History of the Troubles,* pp. 80, 83.
[74] *Ibid.,* p. 150.
[75] Laud, *Works,* II, 402.

enforced against those who preached predestination, laxly against those who denied it. It was easy for Montagu or Mainwaring to get their books licensed, even when they advanced controversial and inflammatory theses; their critics had to resort to the clandestine presses. Partiality, tinged with vindictiveness, was responsible for the belief that he was narrow-minded and oppressive. Laud, said Thomas Fuller, "was observed always to concur with the severest side, and to infuse more vinegar than oil into his censures." [76] Those who noted the fate of Laud's victims found it hard to believe in his intellectual tolerance.

Laud failed to understand his critics, just as they failed to understand him. His failure had the more immediately disastrous results, because great power was concentrated in his hands. He so effectually confused the actions of the state with the objectives of the church that he drew down on both the opprobrium that each alone might easily have survived. The measure of Laud's failure can be read in the fierce attacks on prelacy that marked the early months of the Long Parliament. Falkland, for example, was a devoted churchman, but he could no longer stomach what Laud had made of the church.[77]

Laud failed not because of his ideals but because of the way he pursued them. His sincerity was above question; he felt it should have placed him beyond reproach. "For my care of this church," he said, "the reducing of it into order, the upholding of the external worship of God in it, and the settling of it to the rules of its first reformation, are the causes (and the sole causes, whatever are pretended) of all this malicious storm which hath lowered so black upon me and some of my brethren." [78] In his naïveté "he believed innocence of heart and integrity of manners was a guard strong enough to secure any man in his voyage through this world, in what company soever he travelled and through what ways soever he was to pass." [79] That Laud constantly aggravated the problems of his journey was due to the methods he employed. He trusted in authoritative documents—instructions, injunctions, decisions, records. He was not content to apply a policy; he wanted it defined in some official way. He relied on the power of organization. He believed in the value of systems. He never questioned that the church, by inculcating certain habits, training men in certain responses, fostering certain attitudes would move toward its essential objectives. Uniformity was not merely a device for minimizing trouble, it was a training in a certain kind of life. An obedient people would be a happy people. And what if people should prove reluctant to be organized? In that case they must be compelled to acquiesce. His solution to most problems was coercion. He believed that

---

[76] Fuller, *The Church History of Britain*, Bk. XI, Sec. IX, 75. Cf. *Cal. S. P. Dom.* 1633–1634, xxv.

[77] Cf. Falkland, *A Speech made to the House of Commons concerning Episcopacy.*

[78] Laud, *A Speech delivered in the Starr-chamber*, p. 4.

[79] Clarendon, *op. cit.*, I, 139–140. Cf. p. 102.

the church must enforce spiritual unity. He even tried to make people play games on Sunday. With unflagging resolution he did his utmost to compel his fellow countrymen to accept his ideals of decency, decorum, uniformity, reverence, sound learning, and obedience to authority. It never occurred to him that people might wish to be free to pursue their own ideals. The greatest defect in his method was his inability to recognize its faults. He confided to his diary his honest bewilderment that others were so often wrong. His perplexity was natural, since he apparently believed that he was always right. Even in prison, when inaction gave him leisure to review his policy, he could see in his troubles nothing of his own making.

Laud failed, not for the lack of great qualities but of small ones. His virtues and ideals, so inflexibly, so relentlessly, so unimaginatively pursued, alienated him from one group after another in both church and state, and at last left him isolated and defenseless. He was sincere; he could not see that his opponents were equally so. He was untouched by the folly and corruption of the Court; he completely lacked the social graces that might have made him a less incongruous figure among the courtiers who feared and hated him. "He had usually about him," said Clarendon, "an uncourtly quickness if not sharpness, and did not sufficiently value what men said or thought of him." [80] He saw troubles approaching, but did not know how to prevent them. "Methinks," he wrote, "I see a cloud arising and threatening the Church of England. God of his mercy dissipate it." [81] In his attempt to control the world of great affairs even his virtues hastened his overthrow. "And his mishaps in this last action were," he wrote of Strafford, "that he groaned under the public envy of the nobles, served a mild and gracious prince who knew not how to be, or to be made great." [82] Laud was exposed to the same jealousies and served the same inept master, but he made his position the more desperate by his own defects.

III

The English "Arminians," or the school of Laud—no name is wholly satisfactory—registered an important change in the intellectual outlook of the age.[83] It can hardly be claimed that they created a new system of thought. Few of them were systematic thinkers. Hooker, indeed, is a notable exception. He inaugurated a new way of considering the problems of church and state, and in so doing he produced one of the major works of

[80] Clarendon, *op. cit.*, I, 234.

[81] Laud, *The History of the Troubles*, I, 26.

[82] Laud, *Works*, III, 443.

[83] Cf. Allen's claim that the rise of Arminianism was the most important intellectual and religious development of the early seventeenth century. Allen, *English Political Thought, 1603 to 1644*, pp. 159–160.

the period. Thomas Jackson wrote on a massive scale, but much of his work is bemired in the controversy with Rome. Richard Thomson had gifts that might have made him an important writer, but he failed to use them to their full effect. Field's *Of the Church* was an influential work that fell short of the highest category. For the most part the members of the school produced sermons, controversial writings, and letters. Their pattern of thought was eclectic rather than original, but it was consistent and coherent and it showed remarkable powers of survival.

Authority was the dominant issue of the age. It was also the manifest need of the Church of England. The crown provided the kind of coercive power necessary to sustain the institution and to preserve its outward unity. It was scarcely surprising that churchmen leaped to the defense of the royal prerogative. But the chief deficiency of the church was a lack of moral authority. The times demanded more than coercive jurisdiction. On either flank the Church of England faced antagonists whose view of authority was clear and persuasive. Rome relied on an infallible church. The Puritans appealed to an infallible Bible. Though so different in many ways, the two closely converged in their treatment of authority. There was nothing novel in either their methods or their approach. As Donne perceived, both the Jesuits and the Calvinists had long historical antecedents: "these two kinds of false Puritans we find in the primitive church; and Satan, who lasts still, makes them last still too." The duty of the churchman was clear: "leave no means untried as may work on their understandings and remove their just scruples. Preach, write, confer." [84]

Whereas the Jesuit and the Puritan appealed to a forthright and unequivocal doctrine of authority, the Laudian relied on a complex and composite interpretation. Andrewes distinguished between two different degrees of moral constraint. On the one hand there are certain truths that unquestionably can claim to be matters of faith, since they have been communicated by revelation. On the other, there are questions to which the answers are probable at best; when resolved, they remain matters of opinion. Authority, therefore, is derived from a clear reliance on the true objects of man's faith, hope, and reverence—in other words, on the great certainties enunciated in the Creeds. The resources that we need have been given us by God. "Those [truths] that are necessary he hath made plain; those that are not plain, not necessary." [85] Laud's position was similar: all the principal elements of Christian truth contribute in due proportion to a comprehensive view of authority. Scripture, he declared, is normative, but requires the illuminating interpretation provided by the tradition of the early church. That in turn must be fortified by the example and practice of the church in every age, so that the witness of the apostles, the fathers, and the ecumenical councils may coalesce with

[84] Donne, *Sermons,* I, 186, 188.
[85] Andrewes, *Works,* II, 35.

the total experience of all Christians. The testimony of the church must be combined with the demands of conscience, and the whole must be tested by the light of reason.[86]

A structure of authority so carefully balanced required neither an infallible church nor an infallible Bible. So its champions insisted. But their assertions left a vital problem unresolved. Of these various elements, which one could claim precedence over the others? And how, it might be added, could men tell that it was entitled to do so? As to the first question, the answer was never in doubt. The Scriptures are the primary source of authority; they are our unfailing guide on all matters of faith and conduct. But since the infallibility of the Bible had already been denied, the precise character of its authority was difficult to define. Initially the disposition among the Laudians was to enumerate the various authorities to which they appealed and to trust that the gradations among them would automatically emerge. We have, said Andrewes, "one canon of Scripture given us by God, two testaments, three creeds, the first four councils, and the fathers of the first five centuries, for our guidance." [87] In this statement the Bible does not stand alone, but its preeminence is clearly implied. Often it was even more explicitly expressed. "No Christian," said Thomas Jackson, "is bound to admit or receive any doctrine or proposition as an article of his faith unless it be contained in the Old or New Testament." [88] According to Ussher, it is within the bounds of the holy Scriptures that "the utmost extent of all our faith and knowledge must be contained." [89] But this, it might be objected, is mere assertion, and in no sense constitutes any kind of proof. At this point Laud and his friends began to interrelate the various elements in their system of authority so that each might lend support to the others. Laud was much too sophisticated a logician to imagine that you can use Scripture to confirm tradition and then appeal to tradition in support of Scripture.[90] It is reason, he pointed out, that suggests even to an uninstructed mind the likelihood that there should be a divine and inspired guide. It is tradition that points to Scripture as that guide. But neither reason nor tradition is powerful enough to make a man embrace that teaching and bend his will in submission to that guide. So faith enters as an essential partner in the process of erecting the structure of authority. Reason might suggest that revelation is a precondition of religious knowledge, but it takes more than reason to convince us that this is so. Fortunately there is inherent evidence that the Bible is such a revelation. "The truth of the mysteries contained in [the Scriptures] may

---

[86] Laud, *A Relation of the Conference*, pp. 40 ff., 53, 73.

[87] Andrewes, *The Collected Works of Lancelot Andrewes*, IX, 91. Cf. Laud's very similar statement, *A Relation of the Conference*, p. 234.

[88] Jackson, *Works*, IX, 18.

[89] Ussher, *A Briefe Declaration*, p. 60. Ussher was more liberal than some of the Arminians and more Calvinist than others, but he clearly belonged to the circle around King Charles.

[90] Laud, *A Relation of the Conference*, pp. 38, 63.

be sufficiently manifested by their own light. . . . Their light is of itself sufficient to enable you to discern all truths expedient for your salvation." [91] We are then able to draw upon confirmatory evidence. "To prove that the book of God which he honours as his Word is this necessary revelation of God and his truth . . . comes in a cloud of witnesses." [92] The testimony of the church confirms the intuition of faith.

> So then the way lies thus. The credit of Scripture to be divine resolves itself finally into that faith which we have concerning God himself and in the same order. For as that, so this, hath three main grounds to which all other are reducible. The first is the tradition of the church, and this leads us to a reverent persuasion of it. The second is the light of nature—and this shows how necessary revealed learning is, and that no other way can it be had. The third is the light of the text itself, in conversing wherewith we meet with the Spirit of God inwardly inclining our hearts and sealing the full assurance of the sufficiency of all three into us. And then, and not before, we are certain that the Scripture is the Word of God both by divine and by infallible proof. But our certainty is by faith and so voluntary, and not by knowledge of such principles as in the light of nature can enforce assent whether we will or no.[93]

The Laudians asserted the supremacy of Scripture, but their own controversial methods required them to explain how it should be used. They had denied the Catholic claim that an infallible church is the only interpreter of the Bible. Their reaction against Calvinism convinced them that they must examine with some care the nature of reason as an instrument for exploring the character of authority. Hooker had shown how this might be done; Andrewes, Overall, Field, and Laud followed his lead. Jackson boldly pushed to its limits the role that reason must play in a system where the Bible, the church, and tradition were involved. Scripture, he declared, "is the only infallible rule of rectitude or obliquity in opinions concerning God or man's salvation; yet are we not hereby bound to reject reason." Nor, he added, are we "to suspect reason in others to be unsanctified because it is accompanied with rules of profane sciences." [94] Religious faith commends itself to reason, and reason responds by demonstrating the cogency of faith.[95] To Laud it was clear that revelation is not proved by argument, but once the necessity and reality of revelation are conceded, then reason enters to prove that "the Scriptures which we now embrace as the Word of God is that revela-

[91] Jackson, *Works*, VI, 366. Cf. Laud, *A Relation of the Conference*, p. 73.
[92] Laud, *ibid.*, p. 74.
[93] *Ibid.*
[94] Jackson, *Works*, V, 315–316.
[95] *Ibid.*, I, 13. Cf. IX, 146.

tion." [96] Laud carefully weighed the distinctive roles of faith and reason. In any science, progress depends on accepting certain presuppositions; once this has been done, reason can begin to advance our knowledge in the given area. This is no less true in religion; a man may believe the Bible to be the Word of God, and if he begins to doubt its authority, he must judge its claims by reason. This is perfectly proper; "the danger is when a man will use no other scale but reason, or prefer reason before any other scale. . . . Reason then can give no supernatural ground into which a man may resolve his faith, that Scripture is the Word of God infallibly; yet reason can go so high as it can prove that Christian religion which rests upon the authority of this book stands upon surer grounds of nature, reason, common equity and justice than anything in the world." [97] Laud, indeed, was prepared to submit to the test of reason all the arguments by which he buttressed his understanding of the faith. He had abandoned the barren form of disputation in which rival infallibilities usually met in the clash of dogmatic assertion. By insisting that the claims of Scripture and of tradition should be submitted to the test of reason he made an important contribution to the intellectual outlook of his age. In this respect the position of Laudians can well be regarded as a landmark in the progress of thought.

The Scriptures contain the truth. Reason interprets its meaning. Who can teach us to apply its lessons? The answer was simple: the church. "For as the Scripture is the perfect rule of faith, so the judgement of the church is a special means to direct us in applying this rule." [98] There is a balance in these questions of authority, difficult to maintain but essential to assert. "We do not therefore so make the Scripture the rule of our faith as to neglect the other, nor so admit the other as to detract anything from the plenitude of the Scripture, in which all things are contained that must be believed." [99] No sensible man, said Leslie, denies that the church has a certain power to direct and command; "all the controversy is touching the extent of that power." [100] The church is entitled to make laws concerning "indifferent" or marginal matters; when she has done so she ought to be obeyed.[101] At this point, of course, we touch a very characteristic emphasis of Laud and his friends. They stressed discipline rather than doctrine. Even when the bishop's will seemed arbitrary, his authority was to be accepted as absolute. Whereas Hooker found the authority of the church in the law of a divinely guided reason, Laud believed that it must be recognized in the regulations of the ecclesiastical society of which he was an officer. In the decrees of councils, in the canons and rubrics that

[96] Laud, *A Relation of the Conference*, p. 73.
[97] *Ibid.*, p. 49; cf. pp. 39, 48, 51, 165.
[98] Leslie, *A Treatise of the Authoritie of the Church*, p. 22.
[99] Field, *op. cit.*, p. 225.
[100] Leslie, *A Treatise of the Authoritie of the Church*, p. 17.
[101] F. Mason, *The Authoritie of the Church*, pp. 10–15.

control the life and worship of the church, he believed that the will and purpose of God were clearly reflected. Such a view of authority reduced to a few simple directions the complexities of faith and discipline. The Christian was under obligation to obey; if he wavered, the bishop should compel him to submit. In due course when adversaries multiplied upon him, Laud asserted that he had always acted according to law. He had never discouraged, still less suppressed, the preaching of God's Word, but only the dissemination "of schism and sedition." [102] Laud and his Puritan opponents, having traveled full circle though in opposite directions, met on common ground but refused to admit the similarity of their basic principles.

Current ecclesiastical injunctions, however, could be regarded as valid only when confirmed by the authentic testimony of the early church. Tradition was one of the subjects hotly debated between the Protestants and the papists. The Arminians were as unwilling to repudiate all traditions as they were to accept many of those to which their Roman opponents appealed. As Francis White pointed out, "the reformed churches reject not all traditions, but such as are spurious. . . . Genuine traditions agreeable to the rule of faith, subservient to piety, consonant with holy Scripture, derived from the apostolic times by a successive current . . . are received and honoured by us." [103] Richard Field drew a sharp distinction between "the uncertain and vain traditions of the papists" and such as serve to clarify the meaning of Scripture. [104]

The primitive church was the source of all reliable tradition. To the judgment of the earliest centuries the Arminians submitted with profound deference. The Church of England, they insisted, conformed in every significant detail to the most ancient patterns. [105] The canons of 1604 asserted that the English Church was a true and apostolic church. Its apologists consistently argued that it differed from Rome only insofar as Rome had deviated from the doctrine of the apostles. Montagu declared that he belonged to a church that was "the absolute representation of antiquity this day extant." [106] This reverence stopped well short of subservience. As Field pointed out, the fathers had to be used with discrimination; in interpreting Scripture their general drift was usually right, but few of them knew Hebrew, and on details they were often wrong. [107] The same reservation appears in Samuel Hoard: "For albeit I make not the decisions and determinations of the Fathers or councils the rules of my faith (because they are but men and therefore subject to error), yet I honour their grey hairs and their grave assemblies." [108] Of more

[102] Laud, *The History of the Troubles*, I, 164.
[103] Francis White, *A Treatise of the Sabbath-day*, Ep. Ded.
[104] Field, *op. cit.*, p. 238. Laud drew the same distinction in *A Relation of the Conference*, p. 34.
[105] Cade, *A Sermon necessary for these Times*, p. 30.
[106] Montagu, *Appello Caesarem*, p. 48.
[107] Field, *op. cit.*, pp. 228–229.
[108] S. Hoard, *Gods Love to Mankind*, p. 6.

importance than a specific doctrine of authority was a general approach to intellectual questions. The Arminians were steeped in antiquity. Jackson approached current scientific problems with a panoply of classical quotations and with no awareness of current developments.[109] Andrewes discussed eucharistic doctrine largely in terms of the sacrificial language of the fathers. The Little Gidding Story Books abound in tales about the desert fathers, and the example of those early ascetics clearly affected Ferrar's conviction that the religious life presupposed retirement from the world. The appeal to antiquity was in part a reaction against the rigidities of doctrinaire Calvinism. It involved "a signal enlargement of the intellectual horizon of the English Church." But, as Mark Pattison sadly remarked, "this hopeful beginning led to little or no substantial results." [110]

The appeal to tradition was a claim to catholicity. It was important that "all men [should] know that we have not departed from the ancient faith or forsaken the full fellowship of the Catholic Church, but that we have forsaken a part to hold communion with the whole." [111] The essential fact was that the faith accepted by the Church of England was the faith enunciated by the early Christians. Rome had distorted the meaning of apostolic succession; the English Church preserved it in a valid form.[112] At every point the ancient church remained the guide in matters of faith and order. "What is sound [the English Church] retains; what is old she restores; what newly emanates from Rome or Trent she refuses to accept as catholic." [113] The early church was not disfigured by the marks of a spurious catholicity—prayers in an unknown tongue, denial of the cup to the laity, image worship, solitary masses. Where England dissents from Rome, Rome has departed from the practice of antiquity.[114] But meanwhile legitimate Catholic practices were fostered. Ussher pointed out that confession, both private and corporate, was enjoined and practiced. Edward Knott, the Jesuit, observed that in vocabulary, in devotional practice, and in theological interpretation, many English Protestants were moving in a Catholic direction.[115] The Puritans noticed the same thing and abused Donne for reverencing the Virgin Mary.[116] The conflated version of the Gospels produced by Nicholas Ferrar's community at Little Gidding was illustrated with steel engravings obviously imported from

---

[109] Cf. Jackson, *Works*, I, 111 ff. Ussher's correspondence graphically illustrates the intense (but by no means exclusive) preoccupation of Anglican scholars with antiquity. In his *Answer to a Challenge made by a Jesuite*, he quoted from or referred to 318 classical or patristic authors. Cf. also Egeon Askew, *Brotherly Reconcilement*, pp. 257–353.

[110] Mark Pattison, *Essays*, II, 287.

[111] Field, *op. cit.*, Ep. Ded. Ussher (in *A Briefe Declaration*, pp. 9–10) stressed the identification with the wholeness of the church as the mark of Catholicity.

[112] Laud, *The History of the Troubles*, pp. 248–250; Andrewes, *Works*, VIII, 277.

[113] Andrewes, *ibid.*, p. 163. Cf. also pp. 208, 209, 347, 450, 457.

[114] *Ibid.*, VII, 96; VIII, 69–70, 159.

[115] Cf. William Chillingworth, *The Works of William Chillingworth*, pp. 12–13.

[116] Donne, *Sermons*, V, 23.

abroad. Their artistic quality may be moderate, but there is no mistaking the Tridentine type of piety that inspired them.[117] But in affirming the essential Catholicity of their church, the Arminians had no intention of abandoning the intermediate position which they had adopted. They admitted that Rome was a true church, though sadly in need of reform.[118] They insisted that they were Catholic though not Roman, and this left them free to maintain their distinctive character. "Trouble not thyself," said Donne, "to know the forms and fashions of foreign particular churches; neither of a church in the lake, nor of a church upon the seven hills; but God hath planted thee in a church where all things necessary for salvation are administered to thee, where no erroneous doctrine (even in the confession of our adversaries) is affirmed and held." [119]

A catholic church will, of course, be characterized by certain marks. Disciplined order, so essential to effective function, naturally leads to a graduated system of authority. "That which magistrates do in civil matters, the chief pastors of the church are to do in matters of religion," [120] so the ancient forms of government persisted. "I would have them remember," said Laud of his critics, "that we live in a church reformed, not in one made new. Now all reformation that is good and orderly takes away nothing from the old, but that which is faulty and erroneous." Bishops are the essence of catholicity; to remove them would introduce "parity (the mother of confusion)." [121] The doctrine of the Church of England, he maintained, is that "the calling of bishops is *jure divino*, by divine right." [122] With learned ingenuity Andrewes proved that the distinction between bishops and priests can be traced back to Biblical sources: the apostles appointed the first bishops in their own lifetime.[123] Jackson insisted that a Christian who defied the authority of his bishop had relegated himself to the same category as ancient heretics or modern Turks.[124]

Catholicity and a regard for ancient ways engendered a concern for decency and seemliness in the ordering of the church's life and worship. Beauty has its proper place in the house of God, and there is no harm in

[117] The British Museum has three of these carefully executed "scrap books." The most important for our purposes is *The Actions, Doctrines and Passages Touching our Lord and Saviour Jesus Christ as they are related by the Four Evangelists, Reduced into one complete body of History, . . . To which are added sundry pictures.* When Charles I, on a visit to Little Gidding, saw the work, he asked that a copy be made for him.

[118] Cf. Field, *op. cit.*, p. 72; Montagu, *Appello Caesarem*, p. 113.

[119] Donne, *Sermons*, V, 251. Laud also stressed the *via media* in *A Relation of the Conference*, Ep. Ded. Cf. Boughen, *Unanimity in Judgment and Affection*, p. 2.

[120] Leslie, *A Treatise of the Authoritie of the Church*, p. 25.

[121] Laud, *The History of the Troubles*, pp. 139, 142.

[122] Laud, *Works*, IV, 310–311.

[123] Andrewes, *Works*, IX, 173 ff.

[124] Jackson, *Works*, XI, 174.

spending the money necessary to provide it.[125] Did not St. Paul himself commend order and decency as means to edification? Ceremonies are important; "they cover the nakedness of public actions, both civil and religious, and procure reverence and esteem unto them. . . . They serve to preserve religion, as salt doth meat, or the bark the tree, or the leaves the bud." [126] The High Churchman was distressed that worship was so often without dignity and the sanctuary itself in slovenly disarray. "Comeliness requireth that not only gravity and modesty do appear in the performance of the works of God's service, that beseemeth actions of that nature, but also that such rites and ceremonies be used as may cause a due respect unto and regard of the things performed and thereby stir men up to greater fervour and devotion." [127] So Laud insisted on conformity because it promoted "the things of decency and uniformity," and he was puzzled when men thought him harsh and peremptory.[128] When God had such a very high regard for sanctified buildings, should not his servants be governed by his wishes? [129]

It may well appear that for many of the Laudians theology was a means of approaching important questions rather than a systematic way of answering them. This is only partly true. Many of the problems that concerned them most were related to authority, and the theoretical issues seemed to have been settled in the debates of the late sixteenth century. But English Arminianism retained a strong antipathy to Calvinism, it repudiated the forensic quality that distinguished so much of the discussion of grace, predestination, and free will. In an earlier age these had been subjects for debate in the Schools; of late they had been eagerly canvassed by the general public. They could not be wholly ignored, though Andrewes insisted that he had seldom preached on them, and had no desire to do so. He regarded predestination as a great mystery, a fit subject for wonder but not for analysis.[130] "God's 'judgments,' " he said, "which are the fountain of reprobation, are *abyssus magna;* and his mercy, extended to all that by faith apprehended the same, is *abyssus et profunditas,* 'a great depth.' Therefore we are not curiously to enquire and search out God's secret will touching reprobation or election, but to adore it." [131] Where Andrewes was reserved, Laud was outspoken: "That Christ died for all men is the universal and constant doctrine of the Catholic church in

---

[125] Balcanquall, *The Honour of Christian Churches,* p. 7; Boughen, *A Sermon concerning decencie and order in the Church, passim.*

[126] Leslie, *A Treatise of the Authoritie of the Church,* pp. 47, 49. Cf. Laud, *A Relation of the Conference,* Ep. Ded.

[127] Field, *op. cit.,* p. 268. Cf. Holyoke, *A Sermon of Obedience,* p. 21.

[128] Laud, *The History of the Troubles,* p. 104. Cf. also pp. 121, 156.

[129] Balcanquall, *op. cit.,* p. 12.

[130] Andrewes, *Works,* VI, 294–295.

[131] *Ibid.,* V, 398.

all ages, and no error of Arminius." [132] It is no wonder that the redoubtable Puritan champion, William Ames, regarded with dismay "those who broach new doctrines of justification, such as Dr. Jackson doth in his book of Justifying Faith." [133] The Laudians assembled the resources for dealing in a new way with fundamental ruligious issues. They showed how the appeal would lie to reason, nature, history, scripture, tradition, and the fathers.[134] In many of them we find a more expansive outlook, a more generous and imaginative approach to perennial problems than had hitherto prevailed. The result was a new temper but not a new theology. The promise of a renaissance proved elusive and failed to materialize. The new doctrine of authority showed a distressing tendency to harden into an authoritarian mood.

[132] Laud, *The History of the Troubles*, p. 90. For a defense in dialogue form of the views of the Arminians on grace, election, predestination, and all the related subjects, see O. N., *An Apology of English Arminianisme*, pp. 82–188. It was designed for popular consumption, but is complete with appeals to reason, to tradition, to the fathers, and ends in a complete capitulation by the spokesman for Calvinist views.

[133] William Ames, *A Fresh Suit against human ceremonies in God's worship*, p. 116.

[134] Cf. L. H. [Leonard Hutten], *An Answere*, pp. 19–24, 105–130.

V

THE PURITANS:
THE AUTHORITY OF THE WORD

THE CHASM between the ideal and the feasible is painful to accept but almost impossible to eradicate. This was the problem that beset the advocates of further reform in the Church of England. When the seventeenth century opened, the struggle had already lasted for more than a generation. No sooner, indeed, had Queen Elizabeth mounted the throne than tensions developed. During Queen Mary's reign the leaders of English Protestantism had fled for refuge to Geneva, to Zurich, to Strassburg; with the example of those reformed churches before their eyes, could sincere men accept the halting compromise provided by the Elizabethan settlement? Many of the queen's religious leaders—many even of her bishops—wanted to move more rapidly than her caution would permit. Initially the demands of these reformers were relatively moderate. They criticized the "popish vestments" still in use, and they asked that certain offensive ceremonies be modified. When Convocation rejected the Six Articles presented in 1563, the advocates of reform turned for help to their sympathizers in parliament.[1] The queen, however, was determined that no one should infringe her right to decide ecclesiastical policy. In the words of a message that she sent by the Speaker to the House of Commons, "Resolutely, she will receive no motion of innovation, nor alter or change any law whereby the religion or church of England standeth established at this day." [2] Three features of the religious struggle of the later sixteenth century had already emerged: the attack on rites and vestments, the Puritan alliance with certain elements in the House of Commons, and the queen's determined resistance to change.

At the outset the Puritan protest was restricted to externals.[3] The scope of the debate rapidly widened. In 1569 Thomas Cartwright, an unflinch-

---

[1] For the Six Articles, see G. R. Elton, *The Tudor Constitution*, p. 437. For the various Puritan attempts to gain their ends by means of parliamentary aid, see Sir J. E. Neale, *Elizabeth I and her Parliaments, passim.*

[2] Neale, *op. cit.*, II, 74.

[3] [Parker], *A Discourse concerning Puritans*, pp. 6–7.

ing Calvinist and the great Elizabethan champion of Presbyterianism, became the Lady Margaret Professor of Divinity at Cambridge. His tenure of the chair was brief. He was expelled from it in 1570, and the following year he was deprived of his fellowship at Trinity College, but meanwhile he and his associates had launched a major attack against episcopacy. The Puritan controversy was thus expanded to embrace the crucial area of church order. In the famous *Admonitions to Parliament*,[4] certain Puritans described the reconstituted church they hoped to achieve and pled for its adoption. They mounted an intensive campaign to get the necessary legislation passed by parliament. In books and pamphlets they elaborated their case and pressed their attack on the existing system.[5] By means of the "prophesyings" they tried to develop the preaching skills that their projected system presupposed. The "classis" movement surreptitiously began to create the presbyterial network that would ultimately be required.

The effort failed. Ever since 1583 a reaction against Puritan demands had been gaining ground. In that year John Whitgift became archbishop of Canterbury, and he steadily increased the pressure on the advocates of change. In 1590 the authorities felt confident enough to arrest Cartwright and eight other Puritan leaders. Both before the High Commission and in the Star Chamber the accused defended themselves with great resourcefulness. The authorities finally felt compelled to drop the cases. Cartwright and his friends were neither sentenced nor acquitted; they were simply released. This might appear a rebuff to Whitgift, but he had given fair warning to all Puritans of his intentions, and many of his opponents took notice. The Separatists also felt the full weight of official disapproval. In 1593 three of their ablest leaders, Barrow, Greenwood, Penry, were hanged. In the same year parliament, veering away from a proposed measure against the papists, passed a vicious act "for the preventing and avoiding of such great inconveniences and perils as might happen and grow by the wicked and dangerous practices of seditious sectaries and disloyal persons."[6] Thus by the end of Queen Elizabeth's reign both the Presbyterians and the Separatists had at certain points been checked. The clamor for specific reforms had been silenced; most of the advocates of change had decided that it was wiser as well as safer to conform. But the issues had been raised; many felt that important questions had not been answered. Under more favorable circumstances the problems were certain to recur.

The accession of James I rekindled Puritan hopes. The would-be

---

[4] *An Admonition to Parliament* and *A Second Admonition to Parliament* are reprinted in W. H. Frere and C. E. Douglas (eds.), *Puritan Manifestoes.*

[5] The Marprelate Tracts are the most famous and the most extreme examples of Puritan pamphlets of this period.

[6] An Act to retain the queen's subjects in obedience (35 Eliz. I, c. 1). Elton, *op. cit.,* pp. 447 ff.

reformers noted that the new king had firsthand knowledge of a properly reconstituted church, and forgot that he had disliked what he had experienced. James had scarcely reached London when he was presented with the Millenary Petition—"the humble petition of the ministers of the Church of England desiring reformation of certain ceremonies and abuses of the church." [7] The document was intended to be moderate in tone and purpose; its authors saw themselves "neither as factious men affecting a popular parity in the church, nor as schismatics aiming at the dissolution of the state ecclesiastical." They adroitly quoted the king in support of his duty to reform the church; pointed out that though the petitioners had subscribed to the Prayer Book with a variety of reservations, they were "all groaning under a common burden of human rites and ceremonies," and requested "that [of] these offences following, some may be removed, some amended, some qualified." Their grievances fell into four categories. The first concerned "the church-service," and many of the familiar Puritan objections reappear—to the cross in baptism, and other aspects of the administration of the sacraments; to the cap and surplice; to the ring in marriage; to the lectionary; and to the lax observance of the Lord's Day. The second group concerned "church ministers"—an adequate supply of men who could preach, and the removal of those who could not; the curbing of nonresidence; and the enforcement of subscription only so far as the statutory requirement extended. Next they specified the evils of pluralism and the need for providing adequate maintenance for the ministry, and so reached their final category of abuses: the lack of a proper application of church discipline. The recital of evils in the church led to an appeal that these problems be considered at a conference that the king was urged to call.

The document, it was clear, revived many of the traditional complaints of the Puritans. Most of its points would be argued and debated, enforced and repealed during the course of the seventeenth century. By its humble tone and its cautious approach it implied a desire to deal with the minor grievances of the Puritans, not with the revolutionary demands of those who insisted on radical changes. It might be argued, of course, that the section on church discipline presupposed a church very differently constituted from the Elizabethan Church of England. It was also apparent that inactivity had not robbed the Puritans of their gifts for clandestine organization. The early months of James's reign saw a revival of the attempt to awaken public opinion and so to apply its pressure that concessions would be forthcoming.

The object of the latter exercise was to ensure that radical views would gain a hearing when the king summoned the conference at which he had promised to consider Puritan demands. The fact that James had agreed to

[7] The Millenary Petition is given in Prothero, *Statutes and Other Constitutional Documents,* pp. 413–416, and in Kenyon, *The Stuart Constitution, 1603–1688,* pp. 132–134.

such a meeting was in itself important. The Puritans professed complete loyalty to the crown, but there was a serious possibility that they might be driven into permanent opposition. If the Church of England was to be genuinely national in scope, it was desirable that the grievances of an important minority should at least be heard. James did not lack counselors who recommended a conciliatory approach to the problem. Bacon was prepared to take a balanced view of the dissidents. Only the narrow-minded or the hardhearted would despise their ministrations: "I know the work of exhortation doth chiefly rest upon these men, and they have zeal and hate sin: but again, let them take heed that it be not true which one of their adversaries said, that they have but two small wants, knowledge and love." [8] It was anomalous that reform was a good thing in the state but a bad one in the church. "I would only ask," he said, "why the civil state should be purged and restored by good and wholesome laws, made every third or fourth year in parliament assembled, devising remedies as fast as time breedeth mischief, and contrariwise the ecclesiastical state should still continue upon the dregs of time, and receive no alteration now these five and forty years and more." [9] Doctrine might well be considered "immutable," but "for rites and ceremonies and for the particular hierarchies, policies and discipline of churches, they be left at large." [10] Bacon then suggested a range of concessions that the king might profitably consider, and that constituted a program strikingly similar to that advanced by the Millenary Petition.

The Hampton Court Conference brought a very small group of moderate Puritans face to face with the king, his counselors, and a number of his bishops. The account of its proceedings that has usually been accepted was written by William Barlow, then dean of Chester, subsequently bishop, first of Rochester, then of Lincoln.[11] James gave his unofficial imprimatur to the book, and it proved to be very popular. It is hard to believe that, even in that age of unblushing sycophancy, the bishops heaped on the king such unmeasured adulation as the work suggests—but of course James had an insatiable appetite for praise, and perhaps the churchmen (and Barlow as their reporter) knew the appropriate note to strike. The account dwells on Bancroft's efforts to harry and interrupt the Puritans, and as a climax leads up to the famous outburst attributed to James. "If this be all, quoth he, that they have to say, I shall make them conform themselves, or I will harry them out of the

---

[8] Bacon, "An Advertisement touching the Controversies of the Church of England," *Works*, II, 505.

[9] Bacon, "Certain Considerations touching the better pacification and edification of the Church of England," *Works*, II, 510.

[10] *Ibid.*, II, 512.

[11] Barlow, *The Summe and Substance of the Conference . . . at Hampton Court*. Barlow's account was commissioned by Bancroft, and it has been accused of reflecting a certain propaganda bias.

land or else do worse." [12] But the general tenor even of Barlow's record points to a somewhat less acrimonious debate, and it has been argued that other documents create a rather different impression.[13] Admittedly, in a letter to a correspondent in Scotland, James claimed that at "a revel here with the Puritans this two days" he had "peppered them as soundly as ye have done the papists there." [14] The Bishop of Durham also mentioned that the king "disputed and debated" with the Puritans, "with some sharp words among," but he made it clear that the bishops also received some blunt and unvarnished exhortations from the governor of the church.[15] Patrick Galloway, a Scottish minister, sent an eyewitness account to the presbytery of Edinburgh (King James gave his approval to this document also) and in it he gave a detailed catalog of twenty-five points on which it was agreed that reform was necessary. Some of these represented concessions to the Puritans; some were matters to which James himself insisted that the bishops must give their attention.[16] It seems reasonable to conclude that the conference was more amicable and constructive than has sometimes been supposed; that the Puritans were promised some relief and that the bishops were faced with some demands. Certainly Thomas Sparke, a Puritan who finally conformed with some reluctance, was greatly encouraged by the Hampton Court Conference; he was convinced that the unity of the church would appreciably be promoted "if the things his Majesty there resolved would quickly be put into effect," and he specified nine points at which progress had been made.[17]

The resolutions of a conference do not, of course, necessarily become the law of the land. Many of the Hampton Court recommendations were allowed to slip into oblivion, and the Puritans gained less than they had hoped they would. Moreover, in religious matters the initiative passed at once to Convocation.[18] Of the canons of 1604, the first twelve tried to define with some precision what subscription meant and who could properly be considered members of the national church. To this threat the Puritans responded by reviving pressure in parliament. The House of Commons was willing to cooperate. The House of Lords was not, and a royal proclamation (16 July 1604) showed how little the Puritans could

[12] *Ibid.*, p. 83. Cf. James's famous attack on Scottish Presbyterianism, "which, saith he, as well agreeth with a monarchy as God and the devil" (p. 79).
[13] Cf. especially Mark H. Curtis, "The Hampton Court Conference and its Aftermath," *History*, xlvi (1961).
[14] E. Cardwell, *A History of Conferences*, p. 161.
[15] *Ibid.*, pp. 164, 161–169.
[16] *Ibid.*, pp. 212–217.
[17] Thomas Sparke, *A Brotherly Perswasion to Unitie and Uniformitie*, pp. 2–3.
[18] Convocation: an assembly of the clergy. There have been (and are) two convocations in England (Canterbury and York). At times that of Canterbury, in particular, has played an important part in the church history of the country, and the sixteenth and seventeenth centuries were the periods of its most significant activity. Like parliament, the convocations are summoned by royal writ and are dismissed when the sovereign dissolves parliament.

expect from the king. James reminded his people of his concern to establish in the church "an uniformity as well of doctrine as of government, both of them agreeable to the Word of God, the doctrine of the primitive church, and the laws heretofore established." He reminded his subjects that at the recent conference "no well-grounded matter appeared to us or our said Council why the state of the church here by law established should in any material point be altered"; yet in spite of this, parliament had taken up precisely the questions so satisfactorily settled at Hampton Court. So the king resolved to notify his subjects that there was

> no cause why the form of the service of God . . . should be changed; and consequently to admonish them all in general to conform themselves thereunto, without listening to the troublesome spirits of some persons who never receive contentment, either in civil or ecclesiastical matters, but in their own fantasies, especially of certain ministers who, under pretended zeal of reformation, are the chief authors of divisions and sects among our people.

Wise men, conceding the weakness of their case, would immediately submit; for others the warning was clear: "we must advertise them that our duty towards God requireth at our hands that what intractable men do not perform upon admonition they must be compelled unto by authority." [19]

The king's demands seemed to leave no middle ground between conformity and deprivation. For the Puritan ministers this created a crisis of conscience. They indignantly denied that they were inclined to insubordination. No less than others, they made a virtue of obedience to the king. But what happened when the king's demands seemed to conflict with the requirements of Scripture? It might legitimately be asked "whether a minister of God's Word, being forbidden to preach by the magistrate, [is] to forbear to execute this his office of preaching, seeing the Apostles did not, though straitly charged?" The question seems to invite the answer No. But the writer (a conforming Puritan) believed that the situation in the seventeenth century was totally different from that which prevailed in the first. "The ordinary ministers of these times are bound in this case to obey the magistrate, as touching the public execution of their office; because, that howsoever they have an inward calling from God, yet their outward, to the public place, is from man and may be taken away by man; but it was not so with the Apostles, who, as the other ministers of those times, were immediately and extraordinarily set awork by God only." [20] Could men of Puritan sympathies conscientiously subscribe?

[19] Kenyon, *op. cit.*, pp. 134–136.
[20] John Mayer, *The Englishe Catechisme*, p. 330.

After an agonizing reappraisal many decided that they could. Sympathetic discussion of their scruples often cleared the way. Thomas Hutton tells us that Bishop Cotton of Exeter met for three days "in godly learned conferences" with ministers in his diocese who "privately dissented from the present state and government of the church, . . . answering doubt after doubt, sometimes distinguishing, other whiles expounding, anon again returning one argument or other, always instructing." [21] The ministers of Devon and Cornwall cited the usual objections to the Book of Common Prayer: the defects in the liturgy, the imperfections of the lectionary, the offense caused by certain rites. Many found their doubts resolved.

Another kind of issue, however, emerged. Gabriel Powel complained that the Puritans deliberately shifted their ground. Originally the controversy concerned "subscription, ceremonies, the strict observation of the Book of Common Prayer and other conformity unto the discipline and order of our church"—matters of "indifference and small moment in themselves." But "now they seem to account it, forsooth 'the cause of God, the ministry of the Gospel, the salvation of the people, the main cause of the land, of all the states of this kingdom and all their posterity.' " [22] Actually this shift in emphasis represented an important stage in moving to a less intransigent position. It was precisely when compared with "the ministry of the gospel [and] the salvation of the people" that the rites began to seem genuinely indifferent matters. If nothing is enjoined that is clearly contrary to Scripture, "it is the duty of every modest and Christian minister to yield rather his conformity than (at what wrong to the church, himself and his) to be kept from entering the ministry or be deprived of place." [23] Thomas Sparke, a Puritan who was sensitive to the charge that he had expediently changed his mind, carefully examined the measure of liberty that the individual can claim in a well-regulated system. Wherever possible, he argued, we must submit to "God's ordinance, to bind us, in all things not contrary to his revealed will in Scripture, to obey our superiors." The great reformers all agreed that a church is entitled to make rules about ceremonies; once it has done so, the private man cannot refuse to conform, "for that the public judgment of the church in such matters is always to be preferred before the private opinion of this man or that. . . ." The individual has not forfeited his Christian freedom; he merely sees that he may not exercise it.[24] So the controversy resolves itself into a relatively simple question, "whether any of the things whereunto our conformity on pain of deprivation is thus required be so intolerable for unlawfulness or inconveniency, as that rather than we will be drawn to

[21] Thomas Hutton, *Reasons for Refusal of Subscription to the Booke of Common Praier, with an Answere* . . . , Ep. Ded.
[22] Gabriel Powel, *A Consideration of the deprived and silenced ministers arguments*, p. 12.
[23] T. Sparke, *op. cit.*, p. 7.
[24] *Ibid.*, pp. 10–13.

yield obedience thereunto, we by our persisting in refusal thereof to suffer that sentence of deprivation or but suspension from our ministry to pass upon us." [25] Sparke pointed out that he had preached against the rites, and had done his utmost to get them changed; having failed, the decisive consideration with him was the apostolic cry, "Woe is me if I preach not the Gospel." [26]

John Sprint's case was very similar to Thomas Sparke's. He managed to postpone for a good deal longer the evil day, but after being indicted at the quarter sessions and required by his archdeacon to state his mind, he found himself obliged to face the question whether his nonconformity was more precious to him than his ministry. In considering the ceremonies, "I asked myself," he said, "whether I would rather suffer death than use them in a church professing the foundation and urging them as things indifferent, not pressing them as binding conscience in themselves or as needful to salvation? And whether the execution of my ministry (which was pressed on my conscience with a woe if I neglected it) should not be as dear unto me as my life." [27] The real issue was not whether the ceremonies were evil, but whether conformity was worse than deprivation. So he announced his decision: though "confessing ingenuously my unwillingness thereto if by any means I might avoid it," he consented to conform.[28]

Many shared Sprint's position: they disliked the prescribed ceremonies, and refrained from using them as long as possible, but when the pressure became severe they submitted. Lawrence Chaderton, the first master of Emmanuel College, had kept the chapel services free of the obnoxious practices, but he was not doctrinaire about the matter. At the Hampton Court Conference it was complained "of sitting communions in Emmanuel College; which (Chaderton) said was so, by reason of the seats so placed as they be," but he added that some knelt also.[29] Chaderton, though a patriarch among the Puritans, was essentially a conformist. He wanted to purify the church, not disrupt it. Those "who dislike the government of the church by bishops," he said, "will substitute something far less beneficial both to church and state." [30] Chaderton, of course, was treated with forbearance by the authorities. It is interesting to note how many of those who accepted the government's position did so when they were allowed time to discuss their problems and to reconcile themselves to an uncongenial view.[31] A surprisingly high proportion felt that they would

[25] *Ibid.,* p. 39.

[26] *Ibid.,* p. 44.

[27] John Sprint, *Cassander Anglicanus,* To the Reader.

[28] *Ibid.,* Ep. Ded.

[29] Barlow, *The Summe and Substance of the Conference,* p. 103.

[30] Dillingham, *Life of Chaderton,* p. 10, quoted by Porter, *Reformation and Reaction in Tudor Cambridge,* p. 240.

[31] Cf. Sprint, *op. cit.,* Ep. Ded.; T. Sparke, *op. cit.,* Ep. Ded.; Parker, *A Discourse concerning Puritans,* p. 39.

give way though they could not agree. Some found it impossible to compromise with their convictions. Arthur Hildersam, one of the most highly respected of the Puritan leaders, was suspended at least seven times. He was fined and he was imprisoned. Many others were suspended. The exact numbers have been a matter of some dispute.[32] Bacon felt that many of the nonconformists were difficult and unreasonable men, but the bishops too seemed open to criticism. "As for their easy silencing of them in such great scarcity of preachers, it is to punish the people and not them . . . shall every inconsiderate word, sometimes captiously watched and for the most part hardly enforced, be as a forfeiture of their voice and gift in preaching?" [33] There is no doubt that in some quarters the silencing of ministers (often men who could preach) stirred up disaffection among the laymen. As time went on it became increasingly difficult to shelter nonconformists from official pressure, but Gabriel Powel found it expedient to point out that in refuting the arguments of "the deprived and silenced ministers" he was not casting aspersions on any peer or member of parliament.[34]

The victims insisted that they would gladly recover "that liberty of preaching which once we had, wherein we showed not ourselves so unwilling and negligent as many of our opposites do," [35] but a certain number considered the obstacles insuperable. Sprint and Sparke found that they could yield when the question of authority was restated in a different form. At first they had asked, Are the rites and ceremonies compatible with Scripture? They shifted to, Can the king impose uniformity in things indifferent? They believed he could, but they felt it necessary to reexamine the ceremonies in tedious detail. The debate sometimes subsided; it never wholly died.

As the national disagreements grew more bitter, William Prynne, though busy with many other issues, thought it worth his while to launch a characteristically bitter attack on bowing at the name of Jesus.[36] Late in the seventeenth century, when the Restoration had again made the conditions of conformity a vital issue, the original objections to the ceremonies were revived. This was inevitable; whatever prevented men from pursuing their profession—and thus jeopardized their livelihood— was certain to be discussed. It was also natural that the men whose ties with the established church were tenuous should always be most vocal in criticizing its worship. Shortly after the Hampton Court Conference, William Bradshaw published a couple of short but telling works in which

[32] The best discussion of the number and pattern of the deprivations is in Babbage, *Puritanism and Richard Bancroft.*
[33] Bacon, *Works,* II, 500.
[34] Powel, *op. cit.,* To the Christian Reader.
[35] Anon., *An Answere to a Sermon,* p. 24.
[36] Prynne, *Certaine Quaeres propounded to the bowers at the name of Jesus.* This was answered by William Page, *A Treatise of Justification of bowing at the name of Jesus.*

he attacked the controverted rites. He quoted King James's definition of superstition—"when one restrains himself to any other rule in the service of God than is warranted by the Word, Bas. Dor. p. 15"—and proceeded to show that the king's words perfectly described the ceremonies the king was now enforcing.[37] Even more uncompromising is the series of *Twelve General Arguments* in which Bradshaw epitomized his case. "All human traditions and rites"—so runs his eleventh point—"enjoined to be performed in God's worship as necessary to salvation are unlawful. These ceremonies in controversy, being but human traditions, are enjoined to be performed in God's worship as necessary to salvation. Ergo these ceremonies are unlawful." [38]

William Ames quoted with approval Bradshaw's definition of religious worship: "that which is done to the honouring of God: and if it be according to God's commandments then it is true; if not, then it is false." [39] Ames, however, greatly amplified Bradshaw's position. He felt that a couple of works by Bishop Morton of Durham required an answer. With all the wealth of his learning and all the cogency of his logic, he undertook the demolition of Morton's views. He attacked the bishop's doctrine of the church. He showed how feeble was the appeal to the fathers, how unconvincing the claim that the ceremonies were instituted by the apostles. Against the authority of the bishops, Ames set the claims of the instructed conscience. "What authority have our prelates to obtrude unnecessary ceremonies upon the church, which must be declared before they can be used? Is it fit that the people should be troubled with men's inventions when they are hardly brought to hear willingly the main things of the Gospel?" [40] The chief defect of the ceremonies, Ames argued, was their lack of Scriptural warrant, but equally serious was the fact that they encouraged superstition.[41] The defenders of the rites appealed to order and seemliness, but the Puritans contended that the true character of a church is determined by its purity and the vigor of its life. Could a dignified liturgy compensate for the pluralism, the nonresidence, the simony, the distortion of discipline, and all the abuses that disfigured the church? [42] Ames was concerned about important questions—the nature of worship, the place of ritual, the organization of the church—but all too often his argument loses its way in the intricacies of his refutation of his opponent.

Early in the reign of James, when the demand for conformity agitated a great many anxious minds, the debate on ceremonies was most intense. The cross in baptism, kneeling at communion, the use of the surplice, the

---

[37] Bradshaw, *A Consideration of certain positions archiepiscopal*, pp. 1 ff.
[38] Bradshaw, *Twelve General Arguments proving that the ceremonies . . . are unlawful*, p. 68.
[39] Bradshaw, *Divine Worship* (1604).
[40] Ames, *A Reply to Dr Mortons general defence of three nocent ceremonies*, p. 77.
[41] Ames, *A Fresh Suit against human ceremonies in God's worship*, pp. 99–101.
[42] Ames, *The Dispute about human ceremonies*, pp. 402–422.

ring in marriage were earnestly canvassed.[43] Then such subjects fell into comparative neglect. Those able to conform had done so; the rest had fled abroad or lapsed into silence. Many men found that when the ceremonies ceased to be a matter of fierce contention they actually proved to be a great deal less offensive than they had seemed. A widely respected Puritan, whose counsel was eagerly sought, pointed out that external rites must be judged in the light of the meaning the participant attaches to them. "When there is no apparent scandal," wrote Paul Bayne to an inquirer,

> you may kneel [in receiving communion]. Latent things which cannot with moral certainty be presumed, must not hinder us. My reason: first, it is a gesture sanctified of God, to be used in his service; secondly, it is not unbeseeming a feaster, when our joy must be mingled with reverent trembling; thirdly, it neither is an occasion, nor by participation, idolatry. Kneeling never bred bread-worship. And our doctrine of the sacrament, known to all the world, doth free from suspicion of adoration in it.[44]

But the grievance still lurked just beneath the surface of public attention. When, late in the period, Lewis Hughes published an attack on the prescribed forms of worship, his book met with an immediate response and rapidly passed through five editions. The Book of Common Prayer, he claimed, is "no good book, because it hath the seeds of superstition and idolatry in it, and doth open a gap to all profaneness and ungodliness and doth father an untruth upon God." It was, in fact, "full of popish errors and doth appoint horrible blasphemies and lying fables to be read to the people instead of God's holy Word." [45] But during the early part of the seventeenth century, changes in the ceremonies seemed remote and the agitation for reform died down.

So did the demand that the polity of the church be altered. Early in the period, before the hopes raised by the Hampton Court Conference had faded, William Stoughton published a bold plea for a radically reconstituted church. The apostolic church, he insisted, was governed by presbyters and elders. Then corruption crept in, and stagnation engulfed the Christian community. The results that would now follow a reformation would be as dramatic as the need for it was obvious. "For if all dross, filth and corruption be cast out; if all lets and impediments be done away, it cannot be but that the Gospel must needs have a freer and larger passage, as whereunto a wider door cannot be but opened for the bringing in of a more plentiful harvest." [46] Episcopacy was clearly the obstacle to a purer church; therefore let episcopacy be abolished. Stoughton's plea fell

---

[43] Cf. S. Hieron, *A defence of the ministers reasons for refusall of subscription; idem, The second part of the defence of the ministers reasons; idem, A dispute upon the question of kneeling.*

[44] Bayne, *Christian Letters*, p. 201.

[45] Lewis Hughes, *Certaine Grievances or the popish errors and ungodliness of the service book*, pp. 1, 9.

[46] [W. Stoughton], *An Assertion for true and Christian Church-policie*, p. 13.

on deaf ears. This was so obviously a forlorn hope that for most of the period few were bold enough to press for it. Only when discontent with Charles's personal rule began to mount was the clamor against the bishops revived, and then it was initially taken up not by the sober Puritans but by the agitators on the fringes of the movement (cf. Chapter X).

The clamor for reform subsided. The bishops, with the full encouragement of the Stuart kings, bent all their energies to stamp out nonconformity, and the prospects for change grew dim. So the Puritans concentrated their efforts on the achievement of other goals. If they could not change the system, they would change the men within it. This was the golden age of Puritan preachers. William Perkins of Great St. Andrew's Church, Cambridge, died just as the seventeenth century began, but his influence, spread abroad by Cambridge men molded by his example, was powerful throughout the period. Certainly no other author was so widely read or so earnestly imitated. John Dod—"Decalogue Dod" to his contemporaries by virtue of his celebrated treatise on the Ten Commandments—confirmed the pattern of copious exposition of Scripture.[47] This was the age of Richard Sibbes and John Preston, of John Cotton and Thomas Goodwin. There was an apostolic succession of men whose lives were touched and changed by the preaching of the Word. Perkins converted Paul Bayne, who succeeded him at Great St. Andrew's. Bayne converted Richard Sibbes. Sibbes converted John Cotton. Cotton converted John Preston. The influence of these men spread far and fast. Sibbes filled the lectureship at Holy Trinity Church till ejected by Laud; there he was succeeded in due course by Thomas Goodwin, while he himself found a place of influence as preacher at Gray's Inn. Cotton had a memorable ministry at Boston, Lincolnshire, until Laud's pressure drove him to a new career, no less influential, in the Boston beyond the seas. Thanks to the Puritan habit of keeping a diary of the soul, we know in detail about the transformation that in each case changed a man's outlook and gave a new direction to his life.[48] This kind of change was a contagion, passed from preacher to hearer in ever-widening circles. For the moment, the Puritans spent little time or effort on reforming the liturgy or the polity of the church. They were fully occupied in the task of creating the new man. This, as it proved, had revolutionary consequences far beyond anything that could have been foreseen. The authorities were worried. It was "observed in England," remarked Peter Heylyn, Laud's faithful henchman, "that those who hold the helm of the pulpit always steer the people's hearts as they please." [49]

It would be misleading to imply that the Puritans turned to the pulpit

[47] Among the many examples of detailed exposition, see William Perkins' *A faithful and plaine exposition upon the first two verses of the second chapter of Zephaniah* (1606).
[48] One of the fullest examples is the autobiography of Thomas Goodwin in his *Works*, II, li–lxxv.
[49] Reported by Thomas Fuller, and quoted by W. Haller, *The Rise of Puritanism*, p. 81.

because this seemed a promising tactical maneuver. They regarded preaching as the most important single means of discharging their primary task. "Thus we feel that preaching is God's ordinance," declared William Gouge, "whereunto especially he will give blessing." [50] It is the instrument by which faith is awakened; it is our principal encouragement to godliness, and the unfailing support of a satisfying life.[51] It lifts Christ up for his people to behold; consequently, it is the chief means of our salvation.[52] "Therefore God, who hath appointed us to be saved by Christ, hath also ordained preaching, to lay open the Lord Jesus, with the heavenly treasures of his grace and glory." [53] It was a commonplace among Puritans that salvation begins with preaching and progresses with the help of prayer and the sacraments. Christ "is present after a spiritual manner in the midst of his public ordinances; in the Word, in the sacraments. Where Christ is truly preached, there is he truly present." [54] The Scriptures provided the materials that the preacher used; the Holy Spirit illuminated their meaning, and thus the resources to which the Puritan primarily appealed coalesced in the activity on which he principally relied.[55]

When the significance of the sermon was exalted, the importance of the preacher was emphasized. The exacting character of the task eliminated the temptation to pride. The true minister knew that reliance on his own powers invited failure. Here the humbling effect of experience reinforced the lessons of Scripture, and he was constantly reminded that his "sufficiency was of God." But even so the standards were high and the demands exacting. With approval as well as gratitude, John Randall's friends referred to him as "that famous, learned, judicious, orthodoxal, holy, wise, and skilful preacher and servant of God." [56] The minister was a herald; he received his message from on high. To the servants of his Word, said Thomas Tuke, God "hath committed the keys of his treasure, the dispensation of his secrets, the promulgation of his promise, the interpretation of his oracles, and the administration of his sacraments." In the terser comment of Gouge, "God reveals his mind to his ministers." [57] The embellishments of carnal wisdom had no place in such a task. Preaching had to be plain in order to be effective. "Nothing," said William Ames, "is

[50] Gouge, *The Whole-armour of God*, p. 218. Cf. Mayer, *The Englishe Catechisme*, p. 9.

[51] Richard Sibbes, *The Complete Works of Richard Sibbes*, VI, 526; John Downame, *A Guide to Godlinesse*, p. 479; John Norden, *A godlie man's guide*, p. 10.

[52] Gouge, *The Whole-armour of God*, pp. 259, 509; Sibbes, *op. cit.*, V, 508–510; John Randall, *The Necessitie of Righteousness*, p. 17; Hieron, *Three Sermons* (1607), p. 38; John Rainolds, *The Discoverie of the Man of Sinne*, p. 17; Mayer, *op. cit.*, p. 509.

[53] Sibbes, *op. cit.*, IV, 116; cf. V, 507.

[54] John Brinsley, *The Glorie of the Latter Temple*, p. 15.

[55] Tuke, *The Picture of a true Protestant*, p. 73; Arthur Hildersam, *Lectures upon the Fourth of John*, To the godly Reader (by I. C.—John Cotton).

[56] Randall, *op. cit.*, To the Reader. The work was published posthumously.

[57] Tuke, *The Picture*, p. 94; Gouge, *God's Three Arrowes*, p. 12.

to be admitted which doth not make for the spiritual edification of the people, neither anything to be omitted whereby we may in a sure way attain to that end." [58] To master a style of preaching that would be simple in form but powerful in its appeal to the conscience, the Puritan knew that he needed help. Gradually there developed a whole library of homiletical aids. Perkins led the way with his *Prophetica*, a manual whose influence was further extended when Thomas Tuke translated it under the title of *The Arte of Prophecying, or, A Treatise concerning the sacred and onely true manner and methode of preaching.* Richard Bernard, a preacher of proven effectiveness, published *The Faithful Shepheard* in order to share with his brethren the skills he had learned by experience. John Brinsley explained at length the complementary duties of pulpit and pew.[59] "I account preaching the most principal part of my function," said Gouge.[60] Naturally men spent time and effort perfecting so necessary an art, and their pains were amply repaid. As Professor Haller has pointed out, much of the dynamic of Puritanism was generated by its preachers.[61]

The authority of the pulpit was paramount but not exclusive. A deep pastoral concern permeated all that the preacher said because it inspired all that he did. Late in the Elizabethan age, Richard Greenham of Dry Drayton, Cambridgeshire, had firmly established the Puritan tradition of the devoted pastor. He faithfully dispensed the Word of God and diligently shepherded his flock. "It is a greater thing in a pastor," he wrote, "to deal wisely and comfortably with an affected conscience, and soundly and discreetly to meet with an heretic, than to preach publicly and learnedly." [62] The minister, as Bernard pointed out, must settle among his people and stay there; he must feed his flock and not fleece it.[63] The results can be seen in the affection that often bound pastor and people together.[64] But more was involved than a kindly human relationship. Ministers were required to rebuke as well as to comfort. "Their office," said Sibbes, "is to discover the works of darkness. They are husbandmen to break up the fallow grounds of our hearts." [65] Sir Anthony Cope, we are told, valued ministers "by how much the more freely and plainly they reprove us." [66] This required an intimate understanding not only of

---

[58] Ames, *The Marrow of Sacred Divinity*, p. 183. Cf. Ward, *A Collection of such sermons*, No. 3, pp. 75–76.

[59] Brinsley, *The Preachers Charge and the Peoples Duty*. Cf. Gouge, *The Whole-armour of God*, pp. 483 ff.; Tuke, *The Arte of Prophecying*, pp. 1 ff.; J. Preston, *The Golden Scepter*, p. 202.

[60] Gouge, *The Whole-armour of God*, Ep. Ded.

[61] Haller, *op. cit.*, p. 15.

[62] Richard Greenham, *The Works of the reverend and faithful servant of Jesus Christ, Mr Richard Greenham*, p. 322.

[63] Bernard, *The Faithful Shepheard*, pp. 7–8. Cf. J. Preston, *Life Eternall*, p. 147.

[64] Cf. Timothy Rogers, *Good News from Heaven*, Ep. Ded.; J. Rogers, *A Treatise of Love*, Ep. Ded.

[65] Sibbes, *op. cit.*, V, 49. Cf. Bernard, *The Isle of Man*, Ep. Ded.

[66] Harrice [Harris], *Samuels Funerall*, To the godly Reader.

human nature but of the specific needs of the individual. "Who," demanded Paul Bayne, "can fit a shoe that knoweth not the foot? How can I fit you with helpful counsel while you conceal from me your daily condition?"[67] In Bayne's letters of advice we find much diagnosis and probing of sin, a keen awareness of the interrelation of physical and spiritual ailments, great stress on repentance and on the effort without which progress is impossible. "Canst thou not minister to a mind diseased?" asked Macbeth, and every Puritan was aware of the uncomfortable thrust of that question. Naturally a literature grew up designed to help pastors who felt the need of guidance. William Gouge's *Of Domesticall Duties* is an early example; Baxter's *A Christian Directory* is the culmination, and perhaps the climax, of the type.

The fashioning of the new man was the enterprise to which the Puritan ministers bent their energies. They accomplished much, but the clergy alone are never likely to convulse a nation. The preachers found sympathetic hearers, and though the records of Puritanism were disproportionately produced by ministers, the effective power of the movement was in the laity. As the influence of the Puritans expanded, it increasingly found expression in ways that demanded the participation of laymen. This can clearly be seen in politics. The Stuart kings created a network of opposing alliances. James ranged the bishops, the council, and the prerogative courts against the House of Commons, the common law, and the Puritan congregations. Charles pushed the process considerably farther; to many people it seemed that he had changed the monarchy from a parliamentary institution into an ecclesiastical one. The Puritans found allies among the common lawyers; when the inns of court looked for a preacher they turned to men like Sibbes and Preston. Lawyers and Puritans alike found associates in the House of Commons.[68] With the City of London the Puritans developed important ties; in commerce and colonization Puritans found new spheres of endeavor.[69] Puritans "were at first ecclesiastical only," remarked Henry Parker, "so called because they did not like a pompous or ceremonious kind of discipline in the church like unto the Romish; but now it is come about, by a new enlargement of the name, the world is full of nothing else but Puritans, for besides the Puritan in church policy, there are now added Puritans in religion, Puritans in the state, and Puritans in morality."[70]

By all available means the Puritan consistently pursued his goal of religious reformation. He challenged existing institutions in order to

[67] Bayne, *Christian Letters*, p. 302.

[68] Cf. J. D. Eusden, *Puritans, Lawyers, and Politics in Early Seventeenth Century England, passim;* [Parker], *A Discourse concerning Puritans*, p. 50.

[69] The importance of the tie with commerce and with the gentry who comprised the House of Commons can be seen in the dedications of many Puritan works. Those to Preston's works read like a roll-call of the noblemen and gentry who supported the Puritan cause.

[70] Parker, *A Discourse concerning Puritans*, p. 13.

subject them to the cleansing rigor of his ideal. If necessary, he resisted kings and bishops "that the Church of England . . . might more and more grow forward into such perfection as in this frail life might be attained." [71] To sustain this fixed resolve there was a massive theological system; this in turn rested on a doctrine of authority that was relatively simple, but that to the Puritan appeared completely sufficient and utterly impregnable. His opponents might invoke other authorities; the Puritan returned insistently to the Bible. "Let them chant while they will of prerogatives, we shall tell them of Scripture; of custom, we of Scripture; of acts and statutes, still of Scripture, till the quick and piercing word enter to the dividing of their soul, and the mighty weakness of the Gospel throw down the weak mightiness of man's reasoning." [72]

To the Puritan the Bible had a unique and self-authenticating quality. "Whence hath the Scripture authority?" asked Sibbes. "Why, from itself. It is the Word; it carrieth its own letters testimonial with it. Shall God borrow authority from men? No; the authority the Word hath is from itself. It hath a supreme authority from itself." [73] No restriction can be placed on the Bible's jurisdiction. "Scripture," said Ames, "is not a partial but a perfect rule of faith and manners." [74] Nor can the general position be reaffirmed too often. "I believe that [the Scriptures] are of divine authority," said Elnathan Parr, "whereby we are infallibly certain of the doctrine contained in them, and necessarily bound to believe and obey the same. Being therefore called the Word of God, and the perfect and only canon of our faith and life." [75] The peril of exalting a book into an infallible authority was obviously present, and the history of Puritanism shows that it was real enough. Initially, however, the more perceptive writers guarded against the danger. Gouge realized that the Bible could mislead as well as guide. The Word of God, he pointed out, is "that part of God's will which in the holy Scriptures he caused to be recorded. . . . This Word is properly and truly the right sense and meaning of the Scriptures; for except that be found out, in many words there may seem to be matter of falsehood." [76] To a certain extent the content of Scripture is self-authenticating: read it, and you are convinced that it is true. But more important is the confirmation of the Holy Spirit. It "bears witness with our spirit," and its testimony is vindicated by experience.[77] This sounds simple, but the Puritans knew the sense of Scripture could easily be misunderstood. With great care they enumerated the principal means—

[71] Nichols, *The Plea of the Innocent,* p. 3.

[72] Milton, "The Reason of Church Government urg'd against Prelaty," *Works* (Columbia ed.), III, 246.

[73] Sibbes, *op. cit.,* II, 493; cf. VII, 195.

[74] Ames, *The Marrow of Sacred Divinity,* p. 170.

[75] Elnathan Parr, *The Grounds of Divinity,* p. 75.

[76] Gouge, *The Whole-armour of God,* p. 308. Cf. Sibbes, *op. cit.,* IV, 210; II, 494–495.

[77] E. Parr, *op. cit.,* p. 81; Gouge, *God's Three Arrowes,* Ep. Ded.

seven in number, said Gouge—by which true understanding comes. They specified the classes of people who too often go astray at this point. They described the various wiles by which Satan tried to persuade even the devout that the Scriptures are not God's Word.[78]

So great an authority was expected to produce commensurate results. As we shall see, in the long run Scripture affected almost every aspect of Puritan belief and conduct. But certain immediate consequences could be detected, some in the experience of the individual, others in the life of the church. "Let us therefore examine ourselves," said Sibbes, "what power and efficacy the Word hath. It is a Word that changeth and altereth the whole man. It transforms the whole man. It is a word of life." [79] So each person must turn to the Scripture for direction in the ordering of his life. In more primitive days, men perforce relied on dreams and visions. "Now we have the written Word of God to be our rule, how God must be served, an exact and perfect rule." [80] The Scriptures govern our minds, and teach us how to think of God and ourselves. They direct our consciences, and tell us how to act.[81] They are a means of salvation, "clear and plain to every humble and teachable heart." [82] As the Bible "is the only register of true wisdom, so it is a most sufficient rule for man's life": therefore "think nothing, conceive nothing, know and resolve nothing, until thou findest it in the holy Scriptures." [83]

The Bible guides the individual. It also constitutes the church. It is "God's voice by which he calleth us into the company of his people; it is that whereby we must find out his church." [84] God reigns where his Word is given preeminence. His oracles constitute the richest endowment of the Christian fellowship, and by their means every aspect of its corporate life should be controlled. By the Scriptures we are to settle controversies in divinity and so determine the true pattern of theology. They supply the only standard of judgment and the only source of insight. "As the sun is to the world, so is the Word of God to his church and people, the light of their lives, the life of their souls." [85]

The connection between the Bible and the church was so intimate that it was impossible to examine the authority of the one without also discussing the authority of the other. Current controversies made this doubly true: a distinctive feature of the rival Arminian position was the exalted place it assigned to the church. The Puritans, of course, also had a

---

[78] Gouge, *The Whole-armour of God*, pp. 310–313, 318–330; J. Downame, *The Christian Warfare*, pp. 382, 431; E. Parr, *op. cit.*, pp. 10–57; Sibbes, *op. cit.*, VI, 489 ff.

[79] Sibbes, *op. cit.*, III, 368.

[80] *Ibid.*, VI, 499.

[81] E. Parr, *op. cit.*, pp. 95, 190.

[82] J. Rogers, *A Treatise of Love*, p. 3.

[83] R. Horn, *The Christian Governour*, p. 62; Mayer, *op. cit.*, pp. 111–112.

[84] Mayer, *op. cit.*, p. 109.

[85] E. Parr, *op. cit.*, p. 1. Cf. *ibid.*, p. 78; Ames, *The Marrow of Sacred Divinity*, p. 171; Gouge, *God's Three Arrowes*, p. 7; Nichols, *op. cit.*, p. 14.

high doctrine of the church. It is the creation of God, and the recipient of his mercy. It is the spouse of Christ and the object of his love. To it every Christian must belong, and while he believes in the invisible and eternal church, he must participate in the life of that imperfect institution which is the visible church on earth.[86] The church is cared for and kept by men, but the source of its life is in God. A divine vitality is mediated to it through Jesus Christ. To this intimate relation the church owes whatever authority it possesses. We should follow the church, said Mayer, only insofar as the church itself follows Christ.[87] There is little doubt that for the Puritan the authority of Scripture was primary, that of the church derivative. "The testimony of the church," said Parr, "is to be reverenced and is good, but not infallible. The authority of the Scripture is better and infallible." [88] Sibbes was even more emphatic. It is "an improper phrase," he suggested, "to say that the church gives authority; . . . the church allures us to respect the Scriptures, but then there is an inward power, an inward majesty that bears down all before it." [89]

The church is a fellowship of love; it should also be a community of concern. It will therefore admonish as well as console. Consequently it will recognize that discipline is one of its inescapable duties.[90] "Holy discipline," said Ames, "is a personal application of the will of God by censures, either for the prevention or taking away of scandals out of the church of God." [91] The obligation to enforce discipline is clearly laid down in the gospel. Christ explicitly commanded his disciples to eradicate corruption from their fellowship. He even specified the procedure they should follow in dealing with offenders. Why, asked the Puritans, have the leaders of the church been so remiss? The reason seemed clear: the bishops were obsessed with "the pomp, pride and power" of their empire.[92] They neglected their duty and delegated the exercise of discipline to lay subordinates. But these officials were not only oppressive and inquisitorial in method, they were preoccupied with the wrong questions. As a result the injunctions of our Lord were ignored, and consequently the life of the church suffered.[93] In the process the authority of Scripture was treated with contempt. But this was not merely an administrative problem. It involved the temper and spirit of each member of the fellowship. As the church must be ready to enforce discipline, so every Christian must be

[86] Sibbes, *op. cit.*, I, 374, 390; II, 12, 231–272; VII, 123; Ames, *The Marrow of Sacred Divinity*, p. 147; Mayer, *op. cit.*, p. 92; E. Parr, *op. cit.*, p. 496.

[87] Mayer, *op. cit.*, pp. 111–112.

[88] E. Parr, *op. cit.*, p. 83. Cf. J. Preston, *Life Eternall*, pp. 59–60.

[89] Sibbes, *op. cit.*, III, 9; cf. III, 374, 523.

[90] J. Rogers, *op. cit.*, p. 173; E. Parr, *op. cit.*, p. 498.

[91] Ames, *The Marrow of Sacred Divinity*, p. 188.

[92] Parker, *op. cit.*, p. 18.

[93] Thomas Whetenhall, *A Discourse of the abuses now in question, passim;* Hieron, *Three Sermons* (1609), p. 21.

willing humbly to submit to it.[94]

The Puritans made the authority of the church subordinate to that of Scripture, and naturally they assigned an even more modest place to the testimony of tradition. As they were well aware, this was one of the sensitive points in seventeenth-century controversy. They deliberately took their stand against the Roman exaltation of tradition. They attacked the Arminians because of what seemed an excessive reliance on the words and wisdom of men. Richard Sibbes scornfully dismissed "mere tradition, a thing from hand to hand, that is questionable and uncertain." It could hardly be otherwise, since "that that comes from men" cannot be "infallibly the word of God." [95]

The position of reason was more ambiguous. The Puritans appealed to it, relied on it, feared and distrusted it. They were familiar with Scholastic philosophy—Preston, we know, used to read Aquinas in the barber's chair—and they did not forget that for centuries natural religion had held an honored place in theological speculation. Preston regarded "the strength of our natural reason" as one of the two ways by which we prove the existence of God.[96] "God having made man an understanding creature, guides him by a way suitable to such a condition," said Sibbes, and added that true religion and right reason cannot ultimately be in conflict.[97] The critics of the Puritans accused them of placing too much reliance on logic; indeed, they dismissed Ramus, the French exponent of this discipline, as "this liquor of Puritanism." [98] Many of the ponderous folios of the period show that Calvinism was perfectly compatible with a pronounced fondness for metaphysics. Yet a deep distrust of reason shadowed the Puritan mind. The intellect was safe only when disciplined by faith. "A man hath reason to guide him, and he hath grace to guide reason." [99] Once this due subordination is disturbed, reason becomes a menacing threat. Pelagianism, a heresy particularly sinister in Puritan eyes, was seen as a symptom of the arrogancy of the unregenerate mind.[100] There are certain mysteries that we cannot fathom. "Faith therefore must be placed above our reason and we must believe more than we can conceive." [101] Though the Puritan used reason as a tool, he repudiated reliance on it as a method. "The knowledge we have of God must not only be speculative in the brain, but must pass into the heart, to be put into practice in our conversation." [102]

---

[94] Bayne, *Briefe Directions*, p. 178; Hildersam, *A Doctrine of Fasting and Praier*, p. 106.
[95] Sibbes, *op. cit.*, III, 523.
[96] J. Preston, *Life Eternall*, p. 3. Cf. *idem*, *The Breast-Plate of faith and love*, p. 9.
[97] Sibbes, *op. cit.*, I, 80, 245.
[98] Oliver Omerod, *The Picture of a Puritane*, p. 36.
[99] J. Preston, *The Breast-Plate of faith and love*, p. 32. Cf. Sibbes, *op. cit.*, V, 467.
[100] J. Preston, *Plenitudo Fontis*, p. 11.
[101] Gouge, *The Whole-armour of God*, p. 490. Cf. E. Parr, *op. cit.*, p. 453.
[102] Randall, *The Mysterie of Godliness*, p. 6.

This emphasis on experience was important. It carried the life of faith out of the realm of theory and set it firmly in the world of conduct. "The practice of religion and godliness," said John Downame, "is an infallible sign of the sincerity of our knowledge and profession." [103] "We must have an experimental knowledge," said Gouge.[104] Academic learning had little value unless confirmed by practical experience. Religious authority, beyond all others, had to be verified by being tested amid the problems and complexities of life. The certainty of the verdict that experience returned was inescapably related to the doctrine of the Holy Spirit. At one point after another the Spirit represented the unifying, vitalizing element in the Puritan concept of authority. "That heavenly and pure knowledge of God" contained in Scripture is made available to us by the Holy Ghost.[105] The Spirit is the vivifying force in faith. It takes the words of Christ and makes them vital to his followers. It establishes peace as the guardian in the believer's heart. It ministers comfort and grace, and confirms the disciple in holiness. Because "the spirit of God is the author of the spiritual life," neither the Bible, nor the church, nor tradition, nor experience can speak with authority without its help.[106] "And hence," said Sibbes, "the work of the Holy Ghost is distinguished from illusions and delusions, that are nothing but frantic conceits of comfort that are groundless. The Holy Ghost fetcheth all from Christ in his working and comfort, and he makes Christ the pattern of all; for whatsoever is in Christ, the Holy Ghost, which is the spirit of Christ, works in us as it is in Christ." [107]

The authorities that the Puritan accepted determined the kind of life he lived. Scripture and the stress on experience were directly responsible for many of the features most characteristic of Puritanism. The disciplined and organized life of the godly was the result of an attempt to translate Scriptural imperatives into a pattern for Englishmen to follow. The strong emphasis on vocation sprang from the conviction that God summons each man to walk in the way of his commandments. "A good calling is that way wherein God setteth a man and wherein he hath appointed him to walk." [108] To be in a calling that is "lawful, agreeable to the Word of God, honest or necessary for the use and society of men" is the best way to fulfill the positive demands of the Eighth Commandment.[109]

This earnest and upright way of walking presupposed unremitting

[103] J. Downame, *A Guide to Godlinesse*, p. 2. Cf. J. Preston, *A Heavenly Treatise of the divine love of Christ*, To the Reader.

[104] Gouge, *The Whole-armour of God*, p. 236.

[105] J. Preston, *Summe of Divinity* (Emm. Coll. MSS.), f. 1. Cf. the close conjunction between Spirit and Word in Sibbes, *op. cit.*, II, 62; III, 427; VII, 190.

[106] J. Downame, *A Guide to Godlinesse*, p. 7.

[107] Sibbes, *op. cit.*, I, 18.

[108] Gouge, *God's Three Arrowes*, p. 100.

[109] Norden, *A godlie man's guide*, p. 125; Mayer, *op. cit.*, p. 392.

personal discipline. "Let your loins be girded about," said the Scripture, "and your lights burning; and ye yourselves like men that wait for their lord." Without vigilance the precious gift of faith languishes. With a profusion of metaphors Preston indicated the strenuous character of our calling. "Is it not a hard thing," he asked, "to keep watch and ward day and night against a spiritual enemy; to keep up the banks against the sea of lusts continually assaulting and breaking in; to take up and to bear daily the cross without stooping; to carry the cup of prosperity without spilling; to climb the hill of good duties without fainting; to abstain from the waters of pleasure when we are most thirsty and they are at hand?" [110] So with meticulous care the pattern of the well-disciplined life was laid down.[111] Hard work is the corollary that follows from the privilege of the Sabbath rest. "Only observe," said Thomas Adams, "that the Father commands every son to work. There must be no lazy ones in God's family." [112] Time must be carefully apportioned and conscientiously used. Recreation may have its place, provided it be seemly, but sloth, gluttony, drunkenness cannot be tolerated. "Diligence invites a blessing, but idleness allures temptation." [113] The Biblical imagery of the Christian wakeful and well armed is repeated with endless variations.

We are no sooner born Christians than we enter ourselves soldiers. This world is the field, the faith of Christ is the quarrel, the army against us is large and strong, led on by that grand general of all mischief, the devil. The main body of it consists of sinful flesh and many thousands of noisome lusts. The world flanks it on the right hand with many brave troops of honours, riches, and favours, on the left hand with many legions of disgraces, contempts, troubles, losses and death. The service of a Christian against these is honourable, but withal very dangerous.[114]

The Puritans observed that the paths of pleasure often led to most unpleasant results. "Young men without obedience, old men without devotion, Christians without charity, it would make one's heart mourn to consider seriously the calamity of our times." [115] So the wise man examined with scrupulous care the hazards that beset his way. He

[110] J. Preston, *The Golden Scepter*, p. 230.
[111] Cf. Griffith, *Bethel, or a forme for families;* Richard Rogers, Perkins, *et al., A Garden of Spiritual Flowers*, n.p.
[112] Adams, *Sermons*, p. 201. Cf. Mayer, *op. cit.*, p. 289.
[113] E. Sparke, *The Christians Map of the World*, p. 25. Cf. Robert Bolton, *Some General Directions for a comfortable walking with God*, pp. 299–380; Randall, *The Description of Fleshly Lusts*, pp. 17–21; Gouge, *God's Three Arrowes*, pp. 141–154.
[114] Obadiah Sedgwicke, *Military Discipline for the Christian Souldier*, p. 2. Cf. Christopher Sutton, *Disce Vivere; Disce Mori*, ch. 28; J. Downame, *A Guide to Godlinesse*, pp. 778–803.
[115] Sutton, *Disce Vivere*, To the Reader.

avoided oaths; when the Bible is so explicit on the matter, "it is a most ungodly thing to use common swearing." [116] Dancing was a more ambiguous practice. Holy David, as the Bible tells us, danced mightily before the Lord, and though his wife rebuked him, God apparently did not. But this gave no warrant "to dance mixtly lascivious and wanton dances, men and women together." Stage plays were an offense to godly men. It was clearly a transgression of the Seventh Commandment to be "present at obscene and filthy stage plays; for here the way and manner of uncleanness is commonly acted and so taught to the spectators." At this point temptation came in an attractive guise; therefore explicit Scriptural warning was necessary. For two reasons plays were abominable: "the disguising of sexes, boys being apparelled like women, against what is commanded (Deut. 22.4); the acting of men's and women's sins, to the delighting of such as be present, against which also there is an express precept (Eph. 4.3–4)." [117] It would be well, added Mayer, for the public to reconsider the nature and virtue of modesty.

In discussing the claims of godliness and the incitements to sin, the Puritan assigned a special place to two subjects: prayer and the observance of the Sabbath. Obviously the pattern of the devout life must allow an important place to prayer. The Bible commanded it; the Puritan did his utmost to obey. But the cultivation of the inner life is never easy, and the Puritan leaders found that exhortation and advice were needed in equal proportions. The fainthearted often abandoned the practice before they had time to discover its benefits; therefore constant discipline was necessary. Without zeal the effort involved was largely wasted; therefore the close connection between prayer and "fervency" was emphasized. Since prayer plays so vital a part in the life of faith, the various types of prayer were analyzed and explained. The numerous popular manuals on the religious life provided practical hints, helpful suggestions, and explicit instructions.[118] Detailed expositions of the Lord's Prayer taught the novice how to adapt that model to his personal needs.[119] Because formalism leads to apathy and deadness, the Holy Spirit ought to be our constant companion and counselor. Then the seeker can expect to become a finder. He learns that the result of prayer is what the Puritans called "familiarity with God." "There is an inward kind of familiar boldness in the soul," said Sibbes, "whereby a Christian goes to God, as a child when he wants anything goes to his father." [120]

Sabbath observance was a form of discipline hardly less important than prayer and no less characteristic of the earnest Puritan. It was a

[116] Mayer, *op. cit.*, p. 238.
[117] *Ibid.*, pp. 365–367; cf. Rainolds, *The Overthrow of Stage-playes*, pp. 2, 17, 19.
[118] Cf. Lewis Bayly, *The Practise of Pietie, passim;* Norden, *A load-starre to spirituall life*, pp. 213–264; Gouge, *The Whole-armour of God*, pp. 331–372, 410–475.
[119] Cf. Gouge, *A Guide to go to God, passim.*
[120] Sibbes, *op. cit.*, III, 457.

distinguishing mark, though not an exclusive one. In a famous passage in his autobiography, Richard Baxter tells us that his father, who had never met a Puritan, earned the nickname simply because he preferred to read the Bible in his cottage rather than to participate in Sunday games on the village green.[121] The authority of the Bible made it difficult to evade the problem of Sabbath observance. The commandment was clear; should it not be obeyed? Some moralists argued that it was merely a formal obligation, characteristic of the covenant of law and consequently abrogated by grace. Where, asked the Puritans, was the record of its revocation? "Remember the Sabbath day to keep it holy"; to the Puritan these were the very words of God. Surely they should be heeded! [122]

A sensitive subject became doubly controversial when both King James and King Charles tried to promote Sunday diversions by royal edict. *The Book of Sports* touched off a fierce debate. With the Puritans, Christian obedience merged into social criticism. Consider, cried Samuel Ward, "how little attention the Sabbath often receives. How perfunctorily and fashionably is it slubbered over, . . . divided between the church and the ale-house, the maypole commonly beguiling the pulpit? What man would not spue to see God thus worshipped? This want of devotion makes the foul-mouthed papists to spit at us; this want of reformation makes the queasy-stomached Brownists to cast themselves out of the church." [123] Here, as in so many other aspects of his life, the Puritan tried to adjust the pattern of his daily life to the exacting standard that the Scriptures provided. When asked why the servants of God should "be singular in respect of abstinence from sin, purity of heart and holiness of life," Robert Bolton was ready with his answer: "God's holy Word exacts and expects from all that are newborn and heirs of heaven an excellency above ordinary." [124]

Scripture prescribed a pattern of life. Its authority also fashioned a highly characteristic theology. The Puritans claimed that their system of thought was distinctive only because others had deviated from the truths laid down in the Bible. Calvin profoundly affected their thinking; but they submitted to his authority because they believed that he had derived his system directly from Scripture. Their definition of the theological enterprise indicates the sources on which they relied. Theology, said Preston, "is that heavenly wisdom, or form of wholesome words, revealed by the Holy Ghost in the Scripture, touching the knowledge of God, and of ourselves, whereby we are taught the way to eternal life." [125] The Puritans stressed the majesty of God because they believed that the Biblical account of his holiness, his righteous purpose, his eternal will left them no

[121] Richard Baxter, *Reliquiae Baxterianae*, Bk. I, Pt. I, p. 2.
[122] Gouge, *The Whole-armour of God*, p. 194.
[123] Ward, *op. cit.* (no. 5), p. 83.
[124] Bolton, *Some General Directions*, p. 2.
[125] J. Preston, *Life Eternall*, pp. 1–2.

alternative. They searched the Scriptures, and in its pages they found no evidence of the genial accommodating deity that so many men seemed to want. God's justice was "a great deep"; they had no intention of making it a shallow puddle. All men ought to submit to God's purpose; in any case they lived under his judgment. "We must bring forth against the proud high minded men of this world an army of God's terrible judgements." [126] This points to the true meaning of that much misunderstood phrase, "the wrath of God." "Anger attributed to God," said Gouge, "setteth out his dislike of evil and his resolution to punish evil-doers." [127] The stern elements in the divine nature often seemed to obscure all other attributes, but this is not entirely fair to Puritan thought. As Sibbes pointed out, we ought "to think on God, not as all justice and power, hating sin and sinners, but as a Father, now laying aside terrible things that may scare us from drawing nigh to him, and as a God stooping down to our human nature, to take both it and our miserable condition upon himself, and see our nature not only suffering with Christ, but rising, nay, now in Heaven united to God; and this will feed the soul with inestimable comfort." [128]

"Our nature," indeed, was the subject of much earnest thought. The Puritan was aware that the Bible spoke of both the grandeur and the misery of man, and sad experience emphasized the strange paradox of his nature.[129] Arthur Hildersam, it was said, "deciphered the scornful vanity of corrupt nature, the loathsomeness and desperate danger of sin, . . . the trial of a man's own deceitful heart," but he also dwelt on "the wonderful power of God's grace in the conversion of a sinner, . . . the amiable life of God's grace in the regenerate, . . . sundry sweet consolations of a troubled spirit." [130] The explanation, of course, lay in the Fall; the Puritans "read and marked in Holy Scripture the tale of the loving purpose of God from the first days of our disobedience unto the glorious redemption brought us" by Jesus Christ, and they worked out an appropriate doctrine to explain both man's need and his deliverance. Here Puritan thought was wholly traditional. But the issue raised a wider question. Sin and salvation could be discussed only in the context of the purpose of God, and in particular of the way this purpose operates. The Puritan believed that ultimate issues cannot be explained by whim or impulse. So he put forward the doctrine of election to account for the ultimate destiny of every man. Predestination sent the elect to heaven and the damned to hell. This was a complex doctrine; in many Puritan treatises it was developed with sophisticated skill. It was certainly regarded as a characteristic Puritan tenet, though it was held, of course, by many conformists who remained convinced

[126] Beard, *The Theatre of God's judgements,* p. 6.
[127] Gouge, *God's Three Arrowes,* p. 67.
[128] Sibbes, *op. cit.,* VII, 72.
[129] Cf. Bolton, *A Discourse about the state of true happinesse,* p. 32.
[130] Hildersam, *Lectures upon the Fourth of John,* To the godly Reader (by I. C.).

Calvinists.[131] It is not necessary at this point to expound the content of the doctrine. For our purposes it is sufficient to note that the Puritans emphasized it so vigorously because they believed that it was derived directly from Scripture. Admittedly it was a doctrine difficult to understand and to apply. The Puritans were never sure how to draw the line between the elect and the damned; "yet can we not say of any particular man that he belongeth not to God's election." [132] They were often in an agony of apprehension as to whether they were of the number of the saved, and it was not always reassuring to be told "that the unsearchable wisdom of God . . . hath reserved his eternal counsel concerning the election of men as a secret unto himself." [133] Nor was it helpful to learn that your doubts on the subject were a temptation sent by Satan.[134] The theologians, of course, could point to certain grounds of confidence. Only the elect have faith; if you have faith, you have good grounds for believing that you are among their number. In page after page of serious discussion John Downame advanced a score of "signs and infallible notes" that ought to convince us that we are among the elect, and "the testimonies of Scripture" were clearly the most important.[135] The Puritans readily admitted that this was a difficult and unpalatable doctrine. We should never ask, said William Twisse, "whether this will attract or alienate the infidel," but whether such a doctrine "be agreeable to God's Word or no." [136]

Considerably less controversial yet no less characteristic of Puritan theology was the doctrine of the covenant. Its Biblical sources were clear. William Ames traced the development of the covenant, first in the Old Testament, then in the New. Preston regarded it as a vitally important doctrine because it was so clearly derived from Scripture.[137] By this unique compact God and his people are bound together. God's grace is its source; our awareness of his all-sufficiency and of our own need prompts our response.[138] With all who are faithful God enters into covenant, and this is the foundation of whatever is sincere and genuine in our religious life. "The sum of the covenant between God and us is this: God in Christ saith, he will take us for his people, we promise him that we will have him for our God. This therefore doth comprise all our duty to God, that we set

[131] Cf. Leslie, *A Treatise tending to Unitie*, pp. 11–15. Leslie was a staunch anti-Puritan but a convinced Calvinist.
[132] Gouge, *The Whole-armour of God*, p. 373.
[133] *Ibid.*, p. 227.
[134] J. Downame, *The Christian Warfare*, p. 232.
[135] *Ibid.*, p. 237; cf. the whole passage, pp. 222–315.
[136] Twisse, *The Doctrine of the Synod of Dort*, pp. 34–35; see Ames, *The Marrow of Sacred Divinity*, pp. 116 ff.; Tuke, *The Highway to Heaven, passim*.
[137] Ames, *The Marrow of Sacred Divinity*, pp. 193–205; J. Preston, *The New Covenant*, Pt. I, p. 3.
[138] *Ibid.*, Pt. I, p. 107; *idem, Life Eternall*, Ep. Ded.

him up in our hearts as God." [139] Because the covenant is of grace, we can predict with accuracy the change that it will produce in the sinner's life. "His opinion, his disposition and affection is altered, he looks not upon God now as upon a hard and cruel master, but he looks upon him now as a God exceeding full of mercy and compassion; whence this follows, that his heart melts towards the Lord." [140] The condition of the covenant is simple belief in God; because it is confirmed in a wide variety of ways, we know that it cannot be shaken by any doubt. Since it is a twofold agreement, we may be sure that the daily sins into which we fall cannot invalidate it. "The particular branches and parts or gifts and privileges of this covenant" can best be understood if we regard them in conjunction with Christ's offices as prophet, priest, and king.[141] Deliverance from sin, of course, does not mean immunity from sin. In dealing more specifically with "the privilege and prerogative of the saints by virtue of the covenant," Preston set forth four doctrines, "plainly proved both by Scripture and reason, and pithily applied, viz. 1. That he that is in the state of grace lieth in no known sin, no sin hath dominion over him. 2. That sin, though it doth not reign in the saints, yet it doth remain and dwell in them. 3. That the way to overcome sin is to get assurance of the love and grqce and favour of God, whereby it is forgiven them. 4. That whosoever is under the law, sin hath dominion over him." [142] The covenant embraced both sin and grace. It spoke of man's deepest need and of his glorious redemption. It was derived from Scripture, and it was verified in experience.

In addition the doctrine of the covenant had certain merits that were less immediately obvious but that were of deep psychological significance. It preserved the austere Puritan conception of God but modified it in subtle and important ways. Instead of stressing his incomprehensible being, it emphasized his declared will. It did not deny his eternal and immutable decree, but it made his demands intelligible to the consciences of ethically sensitive men. It did not minimize justice, but it exalted mercy and grace. Since the covenant was a mutual agreement, man had to accept it voluntarily, and thus his moral freedom was preserved. The inflexible determinism that haunted orthodox Calvinism was sufficiently modified that "the glorious liberty of the children of God" became more than a rhetorical phrase from Scripture. "Every man," said Preston, "hath a free will to do that, for the not doing of which he is condemned." [143] Furthermore, it made man a partner in a joint enterprise, and opened the way for that spirit of restless endeavor so

---

[139] Bayne, *Christian Letters*, pp. 340 ff. Cf. E. Parr, *op. cit.*, pp. 68–69; Sibbes, *op. cit.*, VII, 481–483.

[140] J. Preston, *The New Covenant*, Pt. II, p. 75.

[141] *Ibid.*, Pt. II, pp. 127–138.

[142] J. Preston, *The Christian Freedom*, title page.

[143] J. Preston, *The Saints Qualification*, p. 225.

characteristic of Puritanism in its prime. "As soon as God's grace hath seized on us," said Sibbes, "presently it puts us on doing; what God worketh in thee, thou must work thyself." [144] Sibbes was typical of the Puritans in allowing no place for desultory service or for profession that did not go beyond words. "The estate of a Christian is a working estate, not idle. Christianity is not a verbal profession, nor speculative." [145] To this theme he constantly recurred. "For religion is a living and trade. It must be maintained with continuance in labour, and working in a constant course of goodness 'all the days of our life.' " [146] Though strenuous effort is the mark of discipleship, the Christian is delivered from reliance on the specious merit of good works. Endeavor is the fruit of faith, not the precondition of salvation. We are "fellow-labourers with God": "in every work that is done there is God's power and man's joined together." [147]

Scriptural authority, touching almost every aspect of the Puritan's life and thought, was bound to affect his approach to social questions. In the early part of the seventeenth century much economic doctrine was traditional and the appeal to Scripture often supported conventional views. The Puritan saw himself as the heir to the prophetic tradition, and this involved him in the difficult task of social criticism. "If we take the words spoken in the person of the prophet, let us observe that he is no good preacher that complains not in these sinful days." [148] So Thomas Adams denounced the evils that churchmen had attacked for generations: "Usuries, oppressions, exactions, enclosings, rackings, pleasing gobbets of avarice." [149] He was suspicious of wealth, since it easily leads men astray, but he realized that it could be a blessing conferred by God. He was sensitive to the injustices that the powerful often inflicted on the poor. "The labourer's hire cries in the gripolous landlord's hand, James 5.4. The furrows of the encloser cry, complain, nay, weep against him." [150]

The Puritans were gravely concerned about poverty. The Poor Laws were more carefully administered where Puritans were strong than where they were weak. Merchants and the gentry were active in endowing philanthropies that would assist the poor. They established schools, built almshouses, assisted apprentices. [151] To relieve the poor is a Scriptural obligation, said John Rogers; "we are but stewards in respect of God (though owners among men)." [152] But the problems of dispensing charity

[144] Sibbes, *op. cit.*, VII, 510.
[145] *Ibid.*, V, 6.
[146] *Ibid.*, V, 8.
[147] *Ibid.*, V, 15.
[148] Adams, *The Sermons of Thomas Adams*, p. 125.
[149] *Ibid.*, p. 27.
[150] *Ibid.*, p. 58. Cf. Mayer, *op. cit.*, pp. 368 ff.
[151] W. K. Jordan, *Philanthropy in England, 1480–1660.*
[152] J. Rogers, *A Treatise of Love*, p. 185.

were always present. There was much sympathy for the deserving and industrious poor, none at all for the indolent and lazy.[153] There is a good deal of truth, said Dekker, in the claim that the poor were responsible for their own misfortunes, but he also admitted that social causes were often to blame; the enclosing landlords and the heartless rich had much to answer for.[154]

True love, said Rogers, will prompt Christians to give freely to the very needy and to lend to those who have skills but who lack capital. He expected that loans would be free of interest; like many a Puritan, he was bitterly opposed to usury.[155] "That biting sin," complained Roger Turner, had "grown now to a profession," though it was "clean opposite unto God's Word." [156] The social results were deplorable: "that cursed and cruel trade of usury hath eaten up and banished out of the country this Christian duty of free lending." [157] Though there was much horrified denunciation, there were also signs of a new approach. Robert Bolton was opposed to lending money on interest, but he discussed the whole subject with care.[158] Much more remarkable was Ames's contribution to the subject. He denied that interest was forbidden either by Scripture or by natural reason. He dismissed as irrelevant many of the restrictions that tradition had imposed, though he added a number of his own. No interest should be charged the needy, and in ordinary transactions the lender and the borrower ought to share the risks and divide the profits.[159] Ames's work was widely quoted; books were written to attack or to defend his views.[160] Yet Ames was still a very cautious critic of economic problems. The Puritans were using the Bible as a guide to social behavior, but as yet with little sense of the exciting and revolutionary possibilities that lurked within its pages. They were unaware that they were standing on the eve of a vast social upheaval; in the new day the Puritans of the left would discover in the Bible doctrines that would horrify the Puritans of the right.

During the approaching revolution Englishmen were to show that they could be passionately concerned with almost every aspect of human freedom. It is tempting to look for the beginning of this preoccupation in the years before 1640. On examination, the situation seems more confused than we might expect. The early part of the century was marked by a caution that hardly presages the explosion of radical ideas during the Interregnum. At this point, the term "Puritan" reveals its deficiencies. It

[153] *Ibid.,* pp. 212, 237. But note Bernard's plea that some system of useful employment be devised for prisoners, *The Isle of Man,* To the Reader.

[154] Thomas Dekker, *Greevous Grones for the Poore,* p. 17.

[155] J. Rogers, *A Treatise of Love,* p. 62.

[156] Roger Turner, *The Usurers Plea Answered,* pp. 1, 5. Cf. R. Wakeman, *The Poore-mans Preacher,* pp. 79–84.

[157] J. Rogers, *A Treatise of Love,* p. 72.

[158] Bolton, *On Usury, passim.*

[159] Ames, *Conscience with the power and cases thereof,* n.p.

[160] Cf. Nathanael Holmes, *Usuary is Injury.*

indicates a common outlook; as soon as official pressures are removed, it ceases to stand for common convictions. Its earliest representatives demanded relatively modest reforms. Its leading Elizabethan radicals were Presbyterians—who in due course would form the right wing of a movement that was steadily moving to the left. By 1640 the revolutionaries had barely emerged. Even those who would constitute the center party of the victorious Puritan movement were still a small minority. But even those who proved to be the conservatives helped to pave the way for revolutionary doctrines. They said relatively little about freedom, but they fostered certain habits of thought that ultimately led their hearers to new and unexpected positions. The great Puritan preachers of the early seventeenth century were not revolutionary thinkers, but they taught men to search the Bible for themselves. They encouraged an outlook that judged both the structure of society and the lives of individuals by the content of Scripture—and Scripture, as it proved, had very revolutionary implications.

The ingredients of a doctrine of freedom were clearly present in the New Testament. "Stand fast therefore in that liberty wherewith Christ hath set you free," said St. Paul, "and be not entangled again with the yoke of bondage" (Gal. 5:1). Luther expounded the meaning of the passage, and stressed its importance. "Every word hath here a certain vehemency . . . ," he said. "Let us learn therefore to magnify this our liberty." [161] Christian freedom had consequently become an integral part of the Reformation heritage. All subscribed to the doctrine; they were by no means agreed about its meaning. Clearly it emphasized conscience rather than conformity. By contrasting the Gospel with the Law, it penetrated beyond the outward patterns of human institutions to their fundamental purpose. It delivered the believer from the burden of life governed by rules into the emancipation that rests on a gracious personal relationship and is directed by insight. In the world of the spirit the effects were immediate and far-reaching. But how far did they extend in the practical realm of church and politics? The more cautious Puritans admitted the difficulties inherent in the doctrine. "The knowledge of this question is very necessary, yet dangerous," said Samuel Torshell, ". . . because carnal men do wantonly abuse it." [162] The advocates of reform did not intend that misguided people should be free to follow their mistaken beliefs—otherwise what would become of reform? When the pattern of truth is so clearly prescribed, heresy should not be able to invoke the benefits of liberty. Toleration was a doctrine at which the right wing Puritan always looked askance. Obviously freedom ought to be the exclusive prerogative of the elect. But how, it might be asked, could the concept of freedom be reconciled with an unshakable belief in predestina-

---

[161] Martin Luther, *A Commentary on . . . Galatians,* pp. 441, 443.
[162] Samuel Torshell, *The Three Questions of Free Justification, Christian Liberty, the Use of the Law,* p. 48.

tion? The question was beset with difficulties. God's decree, said Parr, does not make the wicked any less guilty, "because there is no force used towards them, but they follow their sins with great pleasure and a very willing mind." [163] Nor had the wicked any latitude for maneuver. "If a man be reprobated, he shall certainly be damned, do what he can: 'tis most true. But remember, such an one can (nay will) do nothing but that which shall more and more bring damnation upon him." [164] Parr tried to escape from the determinism in which his rigid definitions had trapped him. As far as the reprobate were concerned, he had little success. He was not even very explicit about the measure of freedom he conceded to the elect.

The Puritan appealed to the conscience, and by this very fact he raised the problem of freedom. When conscience dictates a course of action, surely a man must be allowed to follow it? Those who resisted Laud posed the question in a form embarrassing to the authorities. The champions of order had always denied that the individual had a right to disrupt the settled order of church and state. In attacking the Puritan preachers, John Swan, a very conservative Laudian, charged that they would "rather disgorge their stomach to excite their disciples against superiors, than study to reduce them to a more quiet and dutiful way. They therefore startle them with fears, as if both tyranny and popery were coming in." [165] But the Puritans were quite aware of the dilemma. Not every conscience could claim the prerogatives of freedom, but only such as were duly instructed in the truth. Even after 1640, when the scope of the discussion had been immeasurably extended, the problem was recognized. "There are two things contended for in this liberty of conscience," declared a tract published in 1645: "first to instate every Christian in his right of free, yet modest judging and accepting what he holds; secondly, to vindicate a necessary advantage to the truth, and this is the main end and respect of this liberty." [166] Puritanism released the turbulent forces of individualism, but in doing so it tried to impose certain effective restraints. It believed that a man must obey his conscience, but it insisted that that conscience could be guided and trained.

By teaching that all men stand on the same footing in the sight of God, the Puritan preachers had struck a mighty blow on behalf of human equality. "God hath made every man a governor over himself," said Sibbes. "The poor man, that hath none to govern, yet may he be a king in himself." [167] This does not mean that all men are equal; that would ignore

---

[163] E. Parr, *op. cit.,* p. 204.

[164] *Ibid.,* pp. 489–490.

[165] Swan, *A Sermon,* p. 12.

[166] "The Ancient Bounds," in A. S. P. Woodhouse (ed.), *Puritanism and Liberty,* p. 247. Woodhouse is mainly concerned with the period after 1640, but his valuable introduction is relevant to Puritanism as a whole.

[167] Sibbes, *op. cit.,* II, 149.

the distinction between the just and the unjust, between the elect and the reprobate. A good man is equal to any other good man, and both are vastly superior to an unregenerate nobleman or an unjust king. Initially this was an assessment of a man's spiritual worth. In time it inevitably affected the estimate of each man's place in society. We are still a long way from Colonel Rainborough's famous comment during the Putney Debates of 1647, "that the poorest he that is in England hath a life to live, as the greatest he," [168] but the spiritual groundwork has already been laid. Liberty in the Gospel became liberty in the state: "nor is this," said Milton, speaking of the freedom Christ conferred, "to be understood of inward liberty only, to the exclusion of civil liberty." [169] The Puritan easily passed from the religious to the civil aspects of a question. The two were in continual interaction. Liberty in the spirit is the gift of Christ; freedom in society is its inevitable sequel. "When we are treating of worldly affairs," said Henry Parker, "we ought to be very tender how we seek to reconcile that to God's law which we cannot reconcile to man's equity: or how we make God the author of that constitution which man reaps inconvenience from." [170]

The Puritan emphasis on experience (which we have already noted) encouraged a willingness to experiment. This fostered tensions within Puritanism. The conservatives believed that revelation had been reduced to appropriate patterns in Calvinist theology and Presbyterian polity; the more adventurous believed (in the words attributed to John Robinson) that "the Lord hath yet more truth to break forth out of his holy word." The full consequence of this willingness to experiment with new forms appeared only when the Civil War had released all the forces working for change, but the way had already been prepared by much earnest Puritan preaching.

In all its forms the Puritan demand for greater freedom drew its inspiration from the Bible. In one of its more extreme manifestations it rested explicitly on a particular strain in Scripture. Millenarianism among the Puritans reached its zenith during the eventful years when the new age seemed about to dawn. This was always a small, sometimes an extreme, but never a negligible element in Puritanism. The new heaven and the new earth were defined in terms of deliverance from every kind of oppression, and of the fulfillment of the expectation that a new order in church and state was at hand.[171] In that day, said Hanserd Knollys, the poor despised people of God "shall not be ashamed of religion, for it shall be glorified before the sons of men." [172] Apocalyptic expectations of this

---

[168] Woodhouse (ed.), op. cit., p. 53.
[169] Milton, "Pro Populo Anglicano Defensio," in Works (Columbia ed.), VII, 145.
[170] Parker, Jus Populi, p. 57.
[171] Cf. T. Collier, "A Discoverie of the New Creation," in Woodhouse (ed.), op. cit., pp. 390–396. Millenarian expectations, which were widely diffused during the years of mounting crisis, were particularly strong among the groups that proliferated on the Puritan left wing.
[172] [Hanserd Knollys], "A Glimpse of Sion's Glory," in Woodhouse (ed.), op. cit., p. 239.

kind would find full and free expression during the exciting days when all institutional forms had been thrown into the melting pot of revolution. But there were earlier anticipations. Hanserd Knollys acknowledged his debt to Thomas Brightman, and this is hardly surprising. After all, Brightman's *A Revelation of the Revelation* was one of the most influential works of the early seventeenth century. In form it is an exposition of the Apocalypse of John. It contains vast stretches of dreary exegesis, but whenever the author related his text to current developments the level of excitement perceptibly heightened. The ancient seer, he believed, had clearly foreseen the sins of the Church of Rome. "The pope," he categorically declared, "is the Beast." [173] He saw the Constantinian era as one notable period of deliverance from oppression, and the Reformation as another. But freedom had been forfeited. The Church of England had subsided into a lifeless replica of the church of Laodicea. The new age, however, would remove the blight of spiritual inertia.

> From hence we may observe that that church is most glorious wherein the sun of righteousness shineth most brightly and openly, not covered over with the clouds of misty and mystical ceremonies. Let them therefore see what a foul error they live and lie tumbling in, who bring into the church pompous and garish ceremonies of their own heads and that to this end forsooth, that they may procure more authority and reverence unto the service of God among the people.[174]

Brightman was like a man who saw through a glass darkly. Liberty of worship would lead to other kinds of liberty. He indicated their scope; he did not define their nature. He was certain that the freedom foreseen in the Revelation would mean that God would "come to converse with men most familiarly, as it were face to face." [175] From this, as an inevitable consequence, every other needful kind of freedom would follow.

[173] Brightman, *A Revelation of the Revelation*, p. 608.
[174] *Ibid.*, p. 905.
[175] *Ibid.*, p. 912.

VI

THE AUTHORITY OF ROME
AND THE CLAIMS OF CANTERBURY

In THE EARLY seventeenth century, most intellectual issues had theological overtones. Debates about religion invariably raised the problem of authority. In the massive controversy between Protestants and Roman Catholics this question was not always explicitly invoked, but it was never far from mind. The struggle engrossed attention to a degree that a later age can grasp with difficulty. It touched the issues of church and state, of faith and reason, of theory and practice, of present experience and eternal destiny. It was one of the chief preoccupations of seventeenth-century Englishmen. "The studies in fashion in those days," wrote John Aubrey, "were poetry and controversy with the Church of Rome."[1] A debate that consumed so much time and aroused so much passion must be given its proper place in any study of seventeenth-century thought. We shall first consider its general character—the contemporary estimate of its importance, the spirit in which it was conducted, the temper it engendered, the methods it employed, and the assumptions that determined its course. We shall then examine the specific issues about which earnest men contended so strenuously: the essence of the faith, the nature and authority of the church, the limits of free inquiry, and the measure of liberty that should be conceded to the Catholic recusants of England.

No one denied the urgency of the issues involved in the debate. The gravest conflicts in the history of Christianity, said Richard Hooker, concerned the person of Christ, "and the next of importance those questions that are this day between us and the Church of Rome, about the actions of the Church of God."[2] The controversy emphasized the chasm that religious differences had cut across English life. An Anglican saw in his fellow countrymen of the Catholic faith "our historical enemies and

[1] Aubrey, *Brief Lives*, I, 150. For this reference I am indebted to Prof. N. J. Endicott of Toronto. Cf. T. Birch, "The Life of Mr. Chillingworth," in *The Works of William Chillingworth*, p. ix.
[2] Hooker, *Laws of Ecclesiastical Polity*, Bk. V, Ded. §3.

159

our prophetical enemies; historically we know that they have attempted
our ruin heretofore, and prophetically we may be sure that they will do so
again whensoever any new occasion provokes them or sufficient power
enables them." [3] Protestants, dismayed at "the impudent lies and
slanders" of Catholic authors, felt summoned to "oppose with all their
power against the bloody torrent of Popery and rage of Antichrist." [4] To
the Catholics the situation seemed equally grave: when the recusants were
exposed to relentless pressures (social, political, and economic) it was the
primary duty of every Catholic writer to confirm the faithful.[5]

The sense of urgency was heightened by the variety of levels at which
the participants found themselves involved. The controversy had a deeply
personal quality; it touched the springs of loyalty and commitment, and
only Biblical parallels could illuminate its nature. "Papists to Protestants
are as Amalakites to Israelites," was the verdict of William Gouge.[6] Every
act of Protestant worship was, for every person present, a rededication to a
holy cause: "as often as you meet here," said Donne, "you renew your
band to God, that you will never be reconciled to the superstitions of
Rome." [7] A debate that thus demanded personal decision also related the
participants to the gravest issues of thought and conduct. As men argued
about Scripture and tradition or about presbyter and pope they touched
problems that were in the forefront of contemporary intellectual concerns.
Even more obvious and much more insistent was the connection between
popery and politics. Could Catholics ever be loyal subjects? Did not their
faith inevitably involve them in treason against a Protestant ruler? This
was a problem inherited from the Elizabethan age; as we shall presently
see, it was hotly debated in the reign of James I. Many Englishmen
concluded that the triumph of Catholicism would subvert their most
cherished institutions. Consequently, the controversy with Rome never
seemed theoretical or remote. The public bought and read the books that
poured from the presses because they bore directly on some of the most
pressing problems of the day.

Because the issues at stake were important, the tone pervading the
debate was intense. Those who believed that they were absolutely right
were satisfied that their opponents were completely wrong. The note of
conviction was always strident. Often it became abusive. The Catholics
declared that Protestantism was "a religion defending all turpitude of sin
and vice, as also discouraging men from the exercise of all virtue." It was
a faith at once "profane, vicious and blasphemous." [8] The Protestants

[3] Donne, *Sermons*, IV, 238; cf. VII, 165.
[4] Beard, *Antichrist the Pope of Rome*, Ep. Ded.; Bolton, *A Discourse about the state of true happinesse*, Ep. Ded. Cf. Featley, *The Practice of Extraordinary Devotion*, Ep. Ded.
[5] John Floyd, *A Plea for the Reall-presence*, pp. 4–5.
[6] Gouge, *God's Three Arrowes*, p. 188.
[7] Donne, *Sermons*, IV, 370.
[8] B. C., *Puritanisme the mother, sinne the daughter*, p. 112.

retorted that "the Papists are vile and abominable in God's sight." [9] The Bible clearly implies as much; why should we hesitate to echo its very words? "What means the Holy Ghost by the terms of Antichrist, the man of sin, the son of perdition, the seat of iniquity, the whore of Babylon, the strumpet upon the beast with seven heads and ten horns . . . if we may not use the same terms and be at defiance with God's enemies?" [10] The acrimony of the debate was sometimes due to the pugnacity of certain individuals;[11] more often it reflected the accepted patterns of religious debate. The Catholics believed that "the more you maintain heresy the deeper a lodging you bespeak yourself in Hell," and they said so without reserve.[12] "All false religions are lies," replied Robert Abbot, "but there is no religion in the world which makes lying a part of their religion but that of Rome." [13] It was elementary prudence therefore "to shew unto the people aforehand the filthy, black, infernal stuff which lies at the bottom of the whore's cup, which they must one day drink off assuredly if they will become her disciples and followers." [14]

The attack on the system of thought was usually reinforced by an attack on the thinkers who defended it. It was standard practice to defame the opposing leaders. Edmund Campion, it was recalled, had described the precursors of the Reformation as "the dregs and bellows and fuel of Hell," [15] and vilification of the great Reformers became a favorite theme of Roman controversy. Luther was a whoremonger. Calvin was a sodomist. "By this," remarked a pamphleteer who had just noted Zwingli's graphic descriptions of the power of sin, "we may conjecture of the extraordinary sensuality of Zwinglius and of his incredible thirst after a woman." [16] Protestant controversialists replied in kind. They branded Catholic priests as "Satan's winnowers"; they regarded "the unmasking of all popish monks, friars and Jesuits" as a religious duty and a patriotic obligation.[17] Where every priest was feared, the Jesuit was hated with a unique

[9] Gouge, *God's Three Arrowes*, p. 45.

[10] *Something written by occasion of that fatal and memorable accident in the Blackfriars*, pp. 6–7.

[11] As soon as Fr. Robert Parsons read the fifth part of Sir Edward Coke's *Reports*, he itched (he tells us) to answer it, and so two very contentious writers confronted each other. [R. Parsons], *An Answere to the Fifth Part of Reports lately set forth by Syr Edward Cooke, Kt.*, Ep. Ded.

[12] [Edmund Lechmere], *A Disputation of the Church*, Ep. Ded.

[13] R. Abbot, *The danger of popery detected*, p. 12.

[14] T. B., *A Preservative to keep a Protestant from becoming a Papist*, p. 44.

[15] George Abbot, *The Reasons which Doctour Hill hath brought for the Upholding of Papistry Unmasked*, p. 65.

[16] B. C., *op. cit.*, p. 98. Cf. also pp. 7, 71 ff.; Lawrence Anderton, *The Non-entity of Protestancy*, pp. 148–154. Cf. Lancelot Andrewes' reply to such charges in *Responsio, Works*, VIII, 46 ff. The effect of such charges varied considerably. Francis Walsingham, a convert to Rome, was impressed by these attacks and repeated them. Sir Edwin Sandys felt they did the Roman cause more harm than good. The evidence to which they appealed usually came from tainted sources. Sandys, *A Relation of the State of Religion*, p. 30.

[17] T. B., *op. cit.*, To the Reader; Lewis Owen, *The unmasking of all popish monks, friers, and Jesuits, passim;* Anon., *Speculum Jesuiticum.*

intensity. "The Jesuit lays his plot (with no small cunning) how to reduce
a state to popish superstition." [18] He belonged to "the order which
envenoms poison itself and makes the Roman religion more malignant
and turbulent than otherwise it would be." His doctrine was "the
sublimation of Pharisaism, mixed with malignant atheism." [19] When the
pope plotted treason and rebellion, the Jesuits were "his only factors"; by
"their devilish wisdom" they contrived "the death of princes and the
downfall of states"; by their wicked practices true Christianity was "most
filthily corrupted, the public peace disturbed, and the bands of human
society dissolved." [20] The skepticism that they inspired was aggravated by
the doctrine of equivocation which they taught. Father Parsons, the most
influential of the English Jesuits, had defined equivocation as "nothing
else but when a speech is partly uttered in words and partly reserved in
mind, by which reservation the sense of the proportion may be diverse."
He volunteered an example: a priest under interrogation by a magistrate
might legitimately answer "I am no priest"; provided he mentally added,
"so as I am bound to tell you." [21] The Protestant reaction was immediate
and vehement: this merely invested a blatant lie with a pretentious
name.[22] A violent controversy erupted. In the course of it Thomas
Morton stressed two basic points. "Our first conclusion is this: every
equivocation by a mental reservation is not a hidden truth but a gross lie.
The second conclusion is this: every equivocation (whether it be mental or
verbal) if it be used in an oath, though it be no lie, yet is it an abominable
profanation of that sacred institution of God." [23] Morton advanced seven
arguments to support the first conclusion and four to support the second.
He pointed out, however, that equivocation poses a practical, not a
theoretical, question, and experience condemns the practice. It "dissol-
veth the natural policy of all kingdoms." Because it makes even the oaths
of Catholic priests completely worthless, it compels the government to use
the rack to elicit the truth. Those who practice equivocation gain only
"the infamy of deceit and lying." Finally "it begetteth scandal to souls,
blasphemies against Christ in the profession of the holy faith." [24] Can any

[18] Anon., *Look About You*, To the Reader. Cf. Thomas Reeve, *The Churches Hazard*, p. 24;
William Freake, *The Doctrines and Practices of the Societie of Jesuites*, Ep. Ded.
[19] Chillingworth, *The Religion of Protestants a Safe Way to Salvation*, Ep. Ded.
[20] H. Burton, *The Baiting of the Pope's Bull*, To the Duke of Buckingham; F. White, *London's
Warning*, p. 52; Anon., *Aphorismes or certain selected points of the doctrine of the Jesuits*, To the
Reader. Cf. Nichols, *The Plea of the Innocent*, Ep. Ded.; Alexander Chapman, *Jesuitisme
described*, p. 19.
[21] R. Parsons, *A treatise tending to mitigation*, pp. 382, 424. Cf. *idem, Apologie of Ecclesiastical
Subordination*, Ch. 12.
[22] Henry Mason, *The New Art of Lying*, pp. 15, 106; Morton, *A Preamble unto an Incounter with
P. R.*, pp. 42 ff.
[23] Morton, *A Full Satisfaction concerning a double Romish iniquitie*, p. 49.
[24] *Ibid.*, p. 97. Cf. Alexander Cooke, *Worke, More Worke and a little More Worke for a Masse
Priest*, p. 17.

possible advantages, he asked, offset such palpable defects?

The early seventeenth century was a contentious age, but most men recognized the dangers of religious controversy.[25] A bitter spirit banished charity. The books it inspired were "more fraught with malice and bitter speaking than with truth and learning." [26] Evil rather than good was usually the result, for "the bitter dissension in religion hath been the springhead of all our miseries." [27] Neither side had escaped the contagion of a vindictive attitude. "And verily in this kind," remarked Sir Edwin Sandys, "both Protestants and Papists seem generally to be both to blame, though both not equally, having by their passionate reports much wronged the truth, abused this present age and prejudiced posterity." [28] There was a better way open, if only men would follow it. If a great divine, said John Earle, is compelled to attack popish errors, he "cuts them with arguments, not cudgels them with barren invectives, and labours more to show the truth of his cause than the spleen." [29] Contestants ought to avoid personal recriminations; "as they are beside the cause, so they do not further the affections of any honest mind, and are most disgraceful to those that use them." [30] Christian forbearance presupposed a more charitable spirit. Elementary prudence demanded it; opponents were more likely to respond when treated with common courtesy.[31]

As a method of confirming waverers or of winning converts, reliance on argument was exposed to criticism. Apostasy was often due to ignorance; people properly grounded in their faith would not forsake it when confronted with specious arguments. James I recognized the nature of the problem and suggested the appropriate solution. "It was the observation of the learnedest king that ever sat hitherto in the English throne," said Joseph Hall, "that the cause of the miscarriage of our people into popery and other errors was their ungroundedness in the points of catechism." [32] A feature of the period was the proliferation of simple aids for the ordinary person. Even distinguished churchmen—writers as eminent as Lancelot Andrewes—did not feel it beneath their dignity to produce such works. The catechisms that appeared in such numbers[33] were seldom avowedly

[25] Occasionally a writer admitted that he enjoyed the war of words: it was "not only most needful, but delightful also to them that are therein exercised." Featley, *The Practice of Extraordinary Devotion,* Ep. Ded.

[26] G. Abbot, *The Reasons,* To the Reader.

[27] *The Catholic Moderator,* Ep. Ded.

[28] Sandys, *A Relation,* p. 32.

[29] Earle, *Micro-cosmographie,* p. 2; cf. R. Parr, *The Life of James Usher,* p. 10.

[30] John Favour, *Antiquitie Triumphing over Noveltie,* Ep. Ded.

[31] John Dove, *A Perswasion to the English Recusants,* p. 35.

[32] Joseph Hall, *The Old Religion,* in *Works,* IX, 307.

[33] Catechisms were usually produced in a uniform size; older libraries often have rows of compact volumes, each containing half a dozen catechisms. The proliferation of catechisms contravened the injunctions of the Hampton Court Conference: "One catechism to be made and used in all places." Strype, *Whitgift,* II, 501.

anti-Roman in their content, but they were often explicitly anti-Roman in their aim. They were clearly designed as a "further help to stay the honest-hearted Protestants from apostasy." [34]

Much of the literature inspired by the feuds between Catholics and Protestants can hardly be called attractive, but we know that it gained converts. The reminiscences that occasionally enliven the controversy let us follow the process, usually slow and often painful, by which a man was persuaded to change his faith. Francis Walsingham, a young clergyman of the Church of England, found himself seriously unsettled by reading Catholic works. There must, he felt, be some satisfying answer to his doubts, and who was better qualified to provide it than the supreme governor of the church? So he carried his perplexities to King James himself. This was exactly the kind of case, one might have thought, to which the king would have responded sympathetically; after all, Walsingham was asking precisely the kind of question about which James delighted to write books, and the "British Solomon" was inordinately susceptible to the vanity of authorship. But he could spare no time for the troubled young man. Walsingham found himself passed from one clerical courtier to another, and all were too insensitive to his perplexities or too preoccupied with their own interests to give him any help. Mounting discouragement aggravated his doubts. When no satisfaction was forthcoming from the Anglican side, he became a Roman Catholic—and an effective apologist for his new faith.[35] Walsingham described his pilgrimage in detail; many who turned to Rome left only occasional references to the motives responsible for their change.

The testimonies of ex-Catholics survive in larger numbers and were usually written in greater detail. In comments scattered throughout his prose writings, John Donne has left us a graphic picture of the torturing anxieties, the slow resolution of doubts, the careful examination of opposing arguments which finally persuaded a sensitive but ambitious man of Catholic upbringing to renounce his ancestral faith. Henry Yaxlee, a Norfolk recusant, tells us that he was first shaken by Cardinal Bellarmine's admission that even popes had fallen into error, even into sin. He was deeply troubled by the internecine strife between the secular priests and "the violent faction of the Jesuits." His reading broadened in scope till it embraced all aspects of the controversy, and he finally decided that it was safest to be "a 'Catholic' without the addition of 'Roman.' " [36] Christopher Musgrave had been a Carthusian for twenty years. The high-handed tyranny of his superior, the apparent indifference to flagrant immorality, the ignorance and superstition among his fellow monks forced

[34] Bernard, *Looke Beyond Luther,* p. 38.

[35] [Francis Walsingham], *A Search made into matters of Religion by Francis Walsingham.* On King James's bishops, see H. R. Trevor-Roper, *Historical Essays,* Ch. XX.

[36] Henry Yaxlee, *Morbus et Antidotus, the Disease with the Antidote.*

him to reexamine the practices that he had always thought to be inseparable from the true faith. He compared the primitive church with both the Church of England and the Church of Rome, and concluded that he was already an Anglican at heart.[37] A Spanish monk named Ferdinando Texeda decided that both the liturgy to which he was accustomed and the faith in which he had been reared were gravely defective. In his own country, he assures us, he had golden prospects; he was acutely conscious of "the poverty, nakedness, perpetual exile, hatred of parents, country, friends, and in brief the want of all necessary things toward the preservation of life which I must needs endure if I quit my former religion." He decided to accept the consequences, made the change, and came to London, "where every man praiseth God in the sunshine of the Gospel." [38] Even more detailed is the account written by Father Richard Sheldon. He divided the motives for "his just, voluntary and free renunciation of communion with the bishop of Rome" into categories. First he enumerated ten "pontificious erroneous doctrines" that he regarded as detrimental to true faith. Next he specified a few of "the wicked laws and customs" that corrupted the Roman Church. Finally he pointed to "the dangerous spirits of sundry chief English Romanists." Only one conclusion could be drawn: the Church of Rome "necessarily ought to be forsaken." [39]

Those who changed their faith professed a disinterested concern for right order, pure worship, and true faith. Sometimes they were swayed by motives that were considerably more mundane;[40] in that case they often discovered that the pastures on the other side of the fence were not so green as they had hoped. As we might expect, converts were sometimes reconverted. The most celebrated example of an Anglican who defected to Rome and then reverted to the Church of England was, of course, William Chillingworth. Many attacked his judgment, a few impugned his motives.[41] Rather different, and probably more typical, was Theophilus Higgons. As censor of Christ Church, Oxford, he had shown himself an ardent Puritan; he had insisted, it was said, on cutting down a maypole "because it came out of a Romish forest." The prospect of preferment tempered his zeal, but having modified his views he was disappointed of his hopes. Malicious critics said that he was tired of his wife and embarrassed by his creditors; by defecting to Rome he escaped from both. But he found his new life on the continent even more frustrating than his

---

[37] *Musgroves Motives and Reasons for his Succession and Dissevering from the Church of Rome and her Doctrine.*

[38] *Texeda Retextus, or the Spanish Monke, his Bill of Divorce against the Church of Rome.*

[39] *The Motives of Richard Sheldon Pr. for his Just, Voluntary and Free Renunciation of Communion with the Bishop of Rome.* Cf. Thomas Bell, *Motives Concerning Romish Faith and Religion.*

[40] Cf. Donne, *Sermons*, X, 161.

[41] Chillingworth wrote an account of his reasons for changing his religious allegiance, Bodleian Library, Tanner MSS. 233.

old, so he returned to England and to the ignominious necessity of publicly recanting at Paul's Cross.[42]

Marc Antonio de Dominis, who made the return journey in the opposite direction, was a much more colorful figure, and a much more important convert—for each side in turn. As archbishop of Spalato he was a man of some consequence. When difficulties in the Roman orbit persuaded him of the advantages of the Anglican system he was welcomed in the highest quarters in England and was showered with promises of preferment. He signaled his conversion with an attack on his former church and a defense of his current one; thereby he released an avalanche of pamphlets from Catholic controversialists. But his estimate of the honors and emoluments to which he was entitled was inordinately high, and his expectations were not satisfied. In due course, therefore, he decided to consolidate his English gains and to return to Rome. This time also he published a book to justify his change, and once more he drew down upon himself the wrath of his recent associates. The lot of the twice-converted was not a happy one, but at least de Dominis could not complain that his antics were ignored.[43]

Too often these narratives of conversion were thinly veiled appeals for financial compensation. Both sides were apt to parade the convert as a prize exhibit in the propaganda war;[44] perhaps it was natural that he himself should regard some material assistance as the appropriate sequel. After the faintly unpleasant kind of apologia that this inspired, it is refreshing to read the correspondence of two college friends, whose ways had parted but whose respect for each other remained undimmed.[45] William Bedell and James Wadsworth had been contemporaries at Emmanuel College, Cambridge. Wadsworth, troubled about the visibility and continuity of the church, turned to Romanism and received a pension from the Holy Inquisition in Seville. Bedell, ultimately a bishop in Ireland, described himself as "a minister of the Gospel of Christ in Suffolk." An exchange of views was difficult. At best, communication was slow. Sometimes letters were lost. What emerges from the correspondence is a vivid picture of two men sharing their concerns and expounding their

---

[42] [Theophilus Higgons], *A First Motive to Adhere to the Romish Church* (1609); *[idem], A Sermon preached . . . by T. H. in Testimony of his Hearty Reunion with the Church of England* (1610); Sir Edward Hoby, *A Letter to Mr T. H., late minister, now Fugitive.*

[43] *A Manifestation of the Motives whereupon the Most Reverend Father, Marcus Antonius de Dominis, Archbishop of Spalato, Undertook his Departure Thence;* and (seven years later) *M. Antonius de Dominis, Archbishop of Spalato, Declares the Cause of his Return out of England.* His major contributions to the debate were, of course, in Latin, as were most of the innumerable replies.

[44] Cf. the comments about de Dominis: "In my mind you will be able to make no other use of him, but only to shew him for a time up and down the streets" (C. A., *Monsigr. fate voi, or a discovery of the Dalmatian apostate,* p. 1); "By halting between two he hath much obscured his worth with all parties" (R. Parr [ed.], *A Collection of Three Hundred Letters,* p. 321).

[45] [William Bedell and James Wadsworth], *The Copies of Certain Letters which have passed between Spain and England in the matter of Religion.*

convictions with charity, forbearance, and mutual respect. In Anglicanism, Wadsworth found no satisfactory answer to the problem of authority. Uniformity of faith, purity of doctrine, proper succession of pastors, the fullness of ecclesiastical order all seemed to belong to one side in the controversy. He forsook the Protestant religion "for very fear of damnation and became a Catholic with good hope of salvation." But he shrank from disputation; let him end his life quietly in the practice of devotion. Bedell replied, and the tone of affectionate regard is unmistakable. He saw that Wadsworth wanted no further arguments. His first impulse was to keep silence, "but how," he asked, "could I approve to my own soul that I loved you if I suffered you to enjoy your own error?" Moreover, Wadsworth might misinterpret silence as an admission that Catholic arguments could not be answered.[46] So the debate began and gradually extended its scope till it embraced most of the points at issue between the two churches. But the final word was one of peace.

> I account we hold one and the same faith in our Lord Jesus Christ and by him in the blessed Trinity. To his judgments we stand or fall. Incomparably more and of more importance are those things wherein we agree than those wherein we dissent. Let us follow therefore the things of peace and mutual edification.[47]

So extensive a controversy, engaging so many men of such varied gifts, conformed to no single format. The participants had all been trained in the traditional logic of the schools, and in verbal debates one side or the other usually demanded that all arguments be couched in syllogistic forms. This was like dancing in chains, and after a flurry of interruptions ("I deny your major," "I refute your minor") formal debate collapsed, and the participants withdrew, each side confidently claiming the victory. But when the arguments were committed to writing, the Scholastic method ponderously dragged its burden through interminable volumes. The syllogism was regarded as a valuable technical device for achieving what everyone was eager to do. If you could catch your opponent in an inconsistency or prove that a logical fallacy lurked in his argument, it was assumed that you had fatally compromised his position, and as a result the search for minor flaws often obscured the essential points. It was also assumed that to accumulate authorities and multiply quotations ensured an author against defeat. So the margins of books grew black with references printed in small type, and the argument wound its dreary way through such a morass of quotation that it lost both its impetus and its sense of direction. Apart from overwhelming your opponent with authorities, there were other uses for quotations. It was considered astute

[46] *Ibid.*, pp. 14–15.
[47] *Ibid.*, pp. 160–161.

tactics to confound your opponent with his own words. You might twist
his arguments to serve your purposes. Bishop Hall drew on a wide range
of Catholic writers to show that their vaunted unity was an illusion; their
own works proved conclusively that they were riven by dissension.[48] James
Maxwell demonstrated that Catholics themselves had foretold in detail the
apostasy into which their church would fall; these prophecies had now
been fulfilled to the minutest detail.[49] For the opposing side, Richard
Broughton gathered a formidable mass of extracts from laws, decrees, the
proceedings of parliaments, the writings of bishops, doctors, and ministers
—all to prove that even Protestants admitted that it was wicked for
Catholics to participate in any way in the worship of the Church of
England. He went further; his quotations showed, he claimed, that
Protestants conceded that their religion was utterly damnable and their
ministry "void, false and usurped." [50] This was a form of controversy that
appealed to those who practiced it, but carried little conviction to
opponents. Each side complained about the unscrupulous tactics of the
other. Matthew Sutcliffe insisted that Father Parsons consistently used
incomplete and distorted quotations.[51] The Protestants accused the
Catholics of appealing to authorities whom even their own scholars
accounted spurious.[52] The Catholics claimed that Protestants quoted
Catholic writers in support of doctrines that, in the very passage cited, the
Catholics had repudiated as false.[53]

A particularly tedious kind of work was the one in which the author
refuted his antagonist passage by passage, even clause by clause. This
often entailed quoting the opponent's book in its entirety; the reader thus
got two works sandwiched together, and it must have required great
concentration and unflagging attention to detail to disentangle the two sets
of arguments. Books of this kind made no concessions to the weakness of
the reader. William Bishop began his examination of William Perkins' *A
Reformed Catholike* with a reassuring promise: "I mean not," he said, "to
entertain thee here with needless words." After more than eight hundred
tightly packed pages, he ended with an ejaculation of praise: "Laus Deo."
The reader can truthfully respond, "Amen." When Francis White refuted
John Fisher's *Answere* to the questions put to him by James I, he pursued
the Jesuit's errors through nearly six hundred folio pages. The controversy

---

[48] Joseph Hall, *The Peace of Rome,* in *Works,* IX, 1–305.

[49] Maxwell, *Admirable and Notable Prophecies . . . concerning the Church of Rome's Defection,
Tribulation, Reformation.*

[50] Broughton, *Protestant Demonstration for Catholicks Recusancie.*

[51] Sutcliffe, *The subversion of Robert Parsons,* pp. 110–119. Cf. Morton, *A Preamble unto an
Incounter with P. R.,* pp. 71–118.

[52] Bernard, *Looke Beyond Luther,* Ep. Ded. Bishop Andrewes accused Bellarmine of appealing
to documents he himself had admitted to be spurious. Andrewes, *Tortura Torti, Works,* VII,
197.

[53] [Lechmere], *The Conference Mentioned by Dr. Featley,* p. 4; [Floyd], *The overthrow of the
protestants pulpit-babels,* p. 261; B. C., *The First Part of the Protestants Proofs,* pp. 17, 28.

between Kellison and Sutcliffe wound its interminable way through volume after volume of dreary refutation. Robert Abbot's *The true ancient Roman catholike* leaves the impression of a skirmish in a dense jungle on a dark night; the antagonists crawl about in the underbrush, shooting noisily at anything that they mistake for their opponents' position.

In comparison, there is something almost casual about the various dialogues that proposed to resolve the basic questions at issue. The situations often seem artificially contrived; the spokesman for superstition or heresy is invariably overthrown, and the champion of truth is consistently victorious. Possibly these books were not taken too seriously either by their authors or by their readers. The same cannot be said of the reports of the disputations that were so characteristic of the period. Sir Edwin Sandys noted that it was a favorite practice of the Roman Catholics to encourage this kind of debate.[54] In describing a Continental country where heretics "enjoyed liberty of conscience," a Catholic author reported that "the Masters [doctors] on sundry occasions entered into public disputation with the principal heretics, and always came out victorious and triumphant, leaving the heretics quite confounded and vanquished." [55] Naturally the Catholics in England adopted the same tactics. The debates were often held in the presence of distinguished and influential people. On one occasion King James himself was present.[56] "Fisher the Jesuit" was a particularly aggressive disputant, and there grew up an extensive literature designed to establish or destroy the myth of his invincibility. King James, having listened for some time to the debate that he attended, jotted down nine points on which he felt that the Jesuit was being evasive. Fisher studied the king's questions and in due course published his answers. Then Dr. Francis White replied with an interminable refutation. The most celebrated work inspired by the Fisher disputations was *A Relation of the Conference between William Laud . . . and Mr Fisher the Jesuit*. This is an important book in its own right; Fisher realized as much and published a reply. The Puritan radicals were also alarmed, and Henry Burton rushed into print to expose the fallacies in Laud's position.[57] Dr. Daniel Featley, a redoubtable opponent of popery, was inevitably drawn into the debate with Fisher, but his chief contribution (*The Fisher Catched in his owne net*) does not fulfill the promise of its title.[58]

---

[54] Sandys, *A Relation*, §29.

[55] J. McCann and H. Connolly (eds.), *Memorials of Father Augustine Baker and other Documents Relating to the English Benedictines*, p. 270.

[56] The fact that the priests usually had no legal right to be in the country made little difference.

[57] H. Burton, of course, needed no special provocation to attack Laud.

[58] *The Fisher Catched* inspired a number of replies. It was one of the works that started a kind of chain reaction. Featley had already attacked Romanism in such books as *The Grand Sacrilege of the Church of Rome*. It was not uncommon for Catholic controversialists to use assumed names. Fisher's real name was John Percy.

Nor should we forget the Rev. George Walker, who dashed in and out of the fray, each time supremely confident that he had demolished his antagonist.

The popish controversy was not restricted to the press; it continually intruded itself into the pulpit. Samuel Torshell found it impossible to expound the Protestant doctrine of justification by faith without attacking the Roman attitude toward good works.[59] Henry King, preaching at an Act Sunday at Oxford, checked himself after a long digression on Catholic practices and resumed the thread of his argument with the comment, "I have almost lost myself in this labyrinth of papal usurpation." [60] Donne's sermons provide revealing evidence. From time to time he undertook systematically to expose some Catholic deviation from the truth. He once felt it necessary, for the space of a whole year, to devote his evening sermons to "the vindicating of some such places of Scripture as our adversaries of the Roman Church had distorted in some point of controversy between them and us, and restoring those places to their true sense." Usually a casual comment is enough to show that his mind was never far from the subject of "popish corruptions." [61]

When we turn from the general character of the controversy to the subjects under debate, we must first allow for certain presuppositions that affected every argument. Both sides believed that God's judgments are made manifest in the earth: the Lord of history declares his purpose (and his preferences) in the pattern of events. On 23 April 1623 a Catholic meeting place in Blackfriars collapsed. A large congregation had gathered in an upper room to hear a celebrated preacher. The floor beams gave way beneath the weight, and scores of worshipers were killed. Was this accident, asked a Protestant, "a judgement of God or no?" Should we "put it into the catalogue of his wrath and violence?" "With fear and trembling," he concluded that we could only answer Yes; "and then it is a memorable fatal punishment not only for [their] main opposition to God's Word but for their presumptuous affronting the true church of God." So he proceeded to expound, under seven headings, the substance of divine judgment.[62] The purposes of God could be traced in past events no less than in present experiences. Thoughtful men should consequently give heed to the lessons of history. For controversial purposes, the court of

[59] Torshell, *op. cit.*, p. 15.

[60] King, *David's Enlargement*, p. 26.

[61] Donne, *Sermons*, II, 325; IV, 359; IV, 133 ff.; VII, 166. Once, after remarking that when abroad "the drums of war sounded in every field," it behoved Protestants to "beat the drum in the pulpit," he launched into an attack on the doctrine of purgatory. Ussher, when preaching each Sunday afternoon in Dublin, "made it his practice to treat of the chief points in controversy between the Romish Church and ours." R. Parr, *The Life of James Usher*, p. 8.

[62] [Anon.], *Something written by occasion*, pp. 13–14. William Crashaw's *The Fatall Vesper in the Black-Friers* is very similar in form and argument; so is Goad's *The Dolefull Evensong*. John Floyd, the famous Catholic writer, published *A word of comfort* to reassure troubled Catholics.

appeal was restricted to comparatively recent events. The whole pattern of the English Reformation, said Donne, should be read as the revealing of a light, as the declaring of a mercy, which God would withdraw only from a people willfully blind to his great deliverance.[63] The closer that men came to their own times, the more compelling they found the lessons of the past. The Armada and the Gunpowder Plot were the events to which every Protestant appealed. "If God," said Donne,

> have delivered us from destruction in the bowels of the sea, in an invasion, and from destruction in the bowels of the earth, in the powder-treason, and we grow faint in our publication of our thanks for this deliverance, our punishment is but aggravated.[64]

The controversy also compelled men to face a yet more comprehensive issue: what was the temper that ought to characterize the religious enterprise? In the full flood of his eloquence, Donne could interject a comment on "the uncharitableness of the Church of Rome towards us all," and pause to elaborate it before resuming his theme.[65] Why, asked an exasperated pamphleteer, should Protestants judge leniently of Catholics,

> seeing the Papists are so uncharitable to repute us all damned heretics, to detest and abhor our congregations, to hate and malign our persons, to scoff and deride our profession, and to take advantage of every petty overthrow or misfortune which seems to depress us?[66]

When confronted with "the angry face of Rome, murdering and torturing," the Protestant response was sometimes equally intransigent: will not all papists, they asked, be damned? [67] The Catholics replied that to charge them with lack of charity was entirely unjust. Admittedly they declared that Protestantism, if unrepented, destroyed the possibility of salvation. At worst, Catholics might be accused of excessive zeal for souls or of a mistake in judgment. But they felt that they were untouched by the attack. Their real motive was "the religious and just care they have to awake men toward the saving of their souls, in the right ways, by procuring that they see that they are to perish if they continue in the wrong." [68] Catholics dislike insisting on unpalatable truths, but they have

[63] Donne, *Sermons*, IV, 98.
[64] *Ibid.*, p. 306. Cf. Adams, *Works*, I, 114–136.
[65] Donne, *Sermons*, VI, 246. Cf. Selden's comment on Catholic charity in *Table Talk*, p. 29.
[66] *Something written by occasion*, pp. 27–28.
[67] *A Gagge for the Pope and the Jesuits*, pp. 16, 20.
[68] Edward Knott, *Charity Mistaken*, p. 10. Knott's real name was Matthew Wilson. He also used the pseudonym Nicholas Smith. This was part of an extensive debate. *Charity Mistaken* was answered by Christopher Potter in *Want of Charity*. Knott's second contribution was *Mercy and Truth, or Charity maintayned by Catholiques;* his third was *Christianity Maintained.* Chillingworth replied to *Charity Mistaken,* and John Floyd answered Chillingworth in *The Church conquerant over humane wit* and in *The totall summe.* William Lacey joined the fray with

no choice. They know that Protestantism is a sin that deprives the soul of the grace of God; those beguiled by it "estrange themselves from the right means of applying the merits of Christ our Lord to their souls whereby they might be saved." It is frivolous to pretend that the Apostles' Creed and the Thirty-nine Articles are a sufficient summary of the faith.[69]

Each side was certain that the other had fallen into heresy. But heresy had to be defined. It is, said John Dove, an opinion stubbornly held that challenges a fundamental article of faith, and it is one that is "publicly, not privately determined." [70] A disputed point, remarked Edward Knott, might concern a minor matter, but when held contrary to the church's teaching it becomes heresy. A refusal to submit to authority is decisive; heresy springs from pride and disobedience.[71] General definitions paved the way for explicit accusations. "Are not the Papists then good Catholics? No, but rather gross heretics. . . . Do the Papists err in the fundamental points of religion? They do teach and maintain many false opinions against the very grounds of religion." [72] The Roman Church, said the Anglicans, had forsaken primitive Christianity. The Council of Trent had authorized a serious modification of the ancient creeds, and such Romish innovations could justly be branded as "absolute and formal heresy." [73] The Roman Catholics naturally retorted in kind. All the chief doctrines of Protestantism, they said, are "old condemned heresies; and the most damned heresies that ever were hatched in any age have been fostered, cherished and defended by the Church doctors of the Protestant Church." Therefore "no Protestant . . . can be said (if he follows the doctrines of his chief doctors) to believe aright any one article of the Apostles Creed." [74]

The scope of the controversy was wide; could its concerns be defined with greater precision? Gordon-Huntley, the Jesuit, recognized two areas of dispute: the Word of God and the Church. Francis White, dean of Carlisle, also isolated two principal points: "the one is about doctrine and manner of divine worship; the other concerning the monarchy of the pope." John White, Francis' brother, believed that four questions constituted the core of the conflict: the Bible, the justification of the sinner,

---

The Judgment of an university-man concerning Mr. William Chillingworth's late Pamphlet. In 1652, long after Chillingworth's death, Knott published a final and lengthy attack on him in *Infidelity Unmasked.*

[69] Knott, *Charity Mistaken,* pp. 13–14, 43 ff., 86–90. Cf. Bedell, *An examination of certaine motives to recusancie,* pp. 30–32; John Fisher, *The Answere unto the nine points of controversy,* pp. 20, 36–37.

[70] Dove, *A Perswasion,* p. 14.

[71] Knott, *Charity Mistaken,* pp. 48–49.

[72] [John Mico], *A Pill to Purge out Poperie,* p. 2. Cf. T. Rogers, *The Roman Catharist,* pp. 6 ff., 25, 37.

[73] Donne, *Pseudo-martyr,* p. 374. Cf. *Sermons,* III, 132; Boughen, *An Account of the Church Catholic,* p. 7.

[74] O. A., *The uncasing of heresie,* To the Reader; [Edward Maihew], *A Treatise of the Groundes of the old and newe Religion,* Preface i, 24–28.

good works, and images, but he added that the pope and his supremacy were also inescapable issues.[75] Cardinal du Perron believed that worship was the area of decisive difference. Catholics and Protestants, he said, were divided on four principal points—"the real presence of the Body of Christ in the sacrament, the offering of the sacrifice of the Eucharist, prayer and oblation for the dead, and prayer to saints"; if agreement could be reached on these questions, other differences could quickly be resolved.[76] But such patterns seemed much too simple to many of the controversialists. Richard Bernard listed twelve major areas of disagreement, Anthony Champney thirty-five, Matthew Kellison fifty-two. Knott roundly declared that Catholics and Protestants differed on every important doctrine of the Christian faith.[77] Dearth of subject matter was no problem for eager controversialists.

The participants in this debate focused their attention primarily on the nature and authority of the true church. The Church of Rome, said Knott, is "the spouse of our Lord"; whatever it may "propound and command me to believe," I must submit to its demands; they are "fundamental to my salvation."[78] With few exceptions, Catholic authors insisted that truth was enshrined in the arbitrary pronouncements of authority. Thomas Jackson, president of Corpus Christi College, Oxford, and dean of Peterborough, dismissed the Roman position as "an extravagant doctrine of authority," but he gave a succinct account of what the Anglicans understood it to mean. It embraced, he said, three essential points:

> The first that the pope (live as he list) cannot err in matters of faith and manners when he speaketh *ex cathedra;* that we are bound to believe whatsoever he so speaks, without examination of his doctrine. . . . The second, that we cannot assure ourselves the Scriptures are the oracles of God but by the infallible testimony of the visible church. The third, that the true sense and meaning of Scripture in cases doubtful or controversial cannot be undoubtedly known without the infallible declaration of the same church.[79]

The Anglicans felt that the Romans were much too prone simply to announce their claims and then assume that they had been accepted. Too

[75] James Gordon-Huntley, *A Summary of Controversies,* p. 1; F. White, *The orthodox faith and the way to the church,* Ep. Ded.; J. White, *The Way to the True Church,* Preface.

[76] *A Letter written . . . by the Lord Cardinal of Perron,* pp. 40, 43. For a view of the issues as seen by a convert from Catholicism, see the works of Thomas Bell, especially *The Woeful Crie of Rome, The Downefall of Poperie, The Popes Funerall, The Catholique Triumph.*

[77] Bernard, *Looke beyond Luther,* Ep. Ded.; A. C. S. [Anthony Champney], *A Manual of Controversies, passim;* Kellison, *The Touchstone of the Reformed Gospel, passim;* Knott, *Charity Mistaken,* pp. 46 ff.

[78] Knott, *Charity Mistaken,* p. 74.

[79] Jackson, *Works,* II, 309–310. Cf. also [Lechmere], *A Disputation of the Church,* Ep. Ded.

many complex issues were involved for this to be a tolerable attitude. Every church, said Lancelot Andrewes, must be prepared to show that it corresponds in some recognizable degree to the ancient Catholic church. It must go a step farther; it must prove that it conforms to the pattern provided by Scripture.[80]

Before examining the nature of primitive Christianity or the authority of the Bible, some Anglicans found it necessary to scrutinize more closely the character of the church with which they were in controversy. They believed that actually there were two Romes—not merely "the Church of Rome, but the court and kitchen of Rome," and the latter was "not for the heart but for the belly; not the religion but the policy, not the altar but the exchequer of Rome." [81] Thomas Ailesbury felt that "pagan Rome and papal Rome" were "so mutually intermixed and folded into one mass or chaos" that it was almost impossible to disentangle the heathen from the Christian elements.[82] When a church has grown corrupt can it still claim to be a church? No, said some. To Henry Burton the Church of Rome was merely a sink of iniquity. He challenged Bishop Hall's admission that Rome, though unreformed, was still a church. When Robert Butterfield and Hugh Cholmley came somewhat feebly to the bishop's aid, Burton demolished them as well.[83] But Hall and his friends could appeal to the authority of Hooker. Admittedly Rome was marred by "sundry gross and grievous abominations"; nevertheless there were certain "main parts of the Christian truth wherein they constantly still persist," and therefore to this extent, concluded Hooker, "we gladly acknowledge them to be of the family of Jesus Christ." [84] A vicious man, said Edward Boughen, is still a man; a defective church (like Rome) is still a church; "though we see her errors we deny not her essence, but wish she were cleansed of her corruptions." [85] But, replied the Catholics, you admit that ours is a true church (though corrupt), while we deny that yours is a church at all; should not wisdom therefore compel you to submit to us? [86]

In any case, continued the Catholics, it was absurd to charge their church with corruption. An institution that is infallible by nature cannot become defective by accident. There is one truth, and "one only true church wherein it is conserved and of whom it must be learned." [87] Father Champney defined the Roman position with care and precision: "The

[80] Andrewes, *Works*, VIII, 69.

[81] Donne, *Sermons*, VI, 248; cf. X, 172. See also Favour, *Antiquitie Triumphing*, p. 452: "Rome was a church, but she is a court."

[82] Thomas Ailesbury, *Paganisme and Papisme*, Ep. Ded.

[83] Joseph Hall, *The Old Religion*, in *Works*, IX, 318 ff.; H. Burton, *The Seven Vials* and *Babel no Bethel;* Robert Butterfield, *Maschil;* H. C. (Hugh Cholmley), *The State of the Now Romane Church.*

[84] Hooker, *The Laws*, III, i, 11.

[85] Boughen, *An Account of the Church Catholic*, p. 12. Cf. Laud, *Works*, II, 114.

[86] [Floyd], *The totall summe*, pp. 33, 44–52; Knott, *Mercy and Truth*, p. 5; [Maihew], *op. cit.*, p. 203.

[87] Bedell, *An Examination*, p. 39. Bedell is quoting a Catholic controversialist.

sense and meaning of holy Scripture given and approved by the holy Catholic Church is infallibly true, as are also the definitions and declarations of faith delivered by the same, and everyone is bound upon his damnation not to reject the same." [88] This was explicit; few Anglicans found it convincing. Thomas Jackson complained that "the Church of Rome both advances her decrees above the laws and ordinances of the Almighty, her words . . . above all divine oracles, written and unwritten," but under careful scrutiny infallible authority resolved itself into unsupported human claims.[89] It was admittedly desirable, said Lord Falkland, to prove the infallibility of the church, but it was clear that no church had in any degree succeeded in establishing its claims.[90]

The true church can be recognized, of course, only by those who know its distinguishing marks. What are these marks, and which churches possess them? The position of the great reformers was simple: the true church is present where the gospel is faithfully preached and the sacraments are duly administered. But these, protested the Catholics, are the offices of the church, not its marks. A definition more ample and precise was needed. "That the Roman Church only is the true Church of Christ is proved by the properties of the true church. The Church is the spouse of Christ; it is the inheritance of Christ; the city of Christ." [91] These terms also did not encourage exact definition. The marks of the church most vigorously debated were its visibility, its catholicity, its antiquity and continuity, its unity, its diversity, its freedom from schism.[92]

The visibility of the church seemed easy to define; its necessity, said the Catholics, was impossible to deny. There must be granted some visible church on earth; had not even Calvin admitted as much? [93] The church must be endowed with perpetual visibility; otherwise its position would become impossible, and the entire scheme of man's salvation would be placed in jeopardy.[94] But it was far easier to assert this than to prove it. Some Protestants conceded that the church had always been visible; at Oxford in 1602 Laud argued that from apostolic times till the Reformation the Roman Church had provided the outward form of the church.[95] Lord Falkland questioned whether any church could prove its uninterrupted visibility. "Neither of our churches has always been visible," he said, "only this is the difference, that we are troubled to show our church in the latter and more corrupt ages, and they theirs in the first and purest, that we can least find ours at night and they theirs at noon." [96] Once again,

[88] A. C. S. [Champney], *A Manual of Controversies*, p. 31.

[89] Jackson, *Works*, II, 307, 287.

[90] Falkland, *Discourse of Infallibility*.

[91] Gordon-Huntley, *A Summary of Controversies*, pp. 255 ff., 274 ff.

[92] On all of these, see Field, *Of the Church*, Bk. II (Concerning the Notes of the Church).

[93] Becanus, *A defence of the Roman Church*, p. 263.

[94] Knott, *Charity Mistaken*, p. 24.

[95] Peter Heylyn, *Cyprianus Anglicus*, p. 49.

[96] Falkland, in *A Coppy of a letter sent from France by Mr Walter Mountagu*, pp. 25–26.

any progress in the debate presupposed a more precise definition of the key words. According to Robert Sanderson, "the true church has always been visible in the body of those who have resisted the errors, superstitions and corruptions of their times." [97] Though the whole catholic church can never be visible to men at once, parts of it may and must. You must not assume that it can always be seen in a given place, since it is often hidden under a bushel. "The church of God is always visible, yet not to every eye; sometimes it is invisible not only to ordinary eyes but even to the best of men." [98] The visible church, moreover, cannot be equated with a hierarchical system manifestly and universally at work. You must allow for the situation in the days of greatest distress. "We maintain," said George Abbot, "that although when the most godly are most driven to extremities by heresies or persecutions, they will be visible each to other and acquainted with some other brethren," even though they remain unknown to other men. When Elijah fled to the wilderness, who could have identified the church of God? Had not St. Augustine compared the church to the moon? It waxes and wanes; sometimes it is invisible, sometimes it is shadowed from men.[99] Protestants have not been alone in insisting on a doctrine that allows for the invisibility of the church. Catholic scholars admitted that in the day of Antichrist the church will hardly be visible to men. The Jesuit Valentinianus conceded the possibility of as large a measure of invisibility as any Protestant could wish. So Anglican spokesmen claimed that their position was neither novel nor eccentric; they could both explain the fact that Christian witness has sometimes been eclipsed, and demonstrate that their church had always been as visible as the church of Christ ought to be.[100]

A church everywhere visible must be a church dispersed throughout the world. Universality is obviously a mark of the Catholic Church, but it proved more difficult to define the designation than to claim it. The Catholic Church, said Roger Fenton, has two determinative qualities: it is built upon Christ as its sole foundation, and it is "universal not because it is spread over the face of the universal world, but because it is not limited to any place or nation . . . it is scattered and dispersed without bounds." The inference seemed obvious: "If Rome be not the true Catholic Church, the true Catholic church and tradition is hidden." But this is a contradiction in terms; either Rome is the Catholic Church, or none exists. The implications of universality could profitably be clarified. Every Catholic must accept certain beliefs, and Bellarmine specified three:

[97] Robert Sanderson, *Two Treatises on the Church*, p. 218.

[98] Cade, *A Justification of the Church of England*, p. 139; Boughen, *An Account of the Church Catholic*, p. 8.

[99] G. Abbot, *A Treatise of the perpetuall visibilitie and succession of the true church in all ages*, pp. 3, 22. Cf. Kellison, *The Touchstone of the Reformed Gospel*, pp. 15 ff.

[100] F. White, *op. cit.*, p. 42; Cade, *A Justification of the Church of England*, pp. 146–147, 149 ff. Cf. Chillingworth, *The Religion of Protestants*, Ch. V, §§13–26.

transubstantiation, the supremacy of the pope, and the invocation of the saints. A church that repudiates any of these ceases to be genuinely universal. For various other reasons all rival bodies had forfeited any claim to the designation. The Church of England, for example, was disqualified because of the radically defective character of its orders. Only Rome remained, said its champions; it alone was universal.[101]

The Anglicans countered first by offering a more adequate definition of catholicity, then by denying the Roman claim to its exclusive possession. "Thus must we conceive of the Catholic church as one entire body," wrote James Ussher,

> [which is] made up by the collection and aggregation of all the faithful into the unity thereof, from which union there ariseth unto everyone of them such a relation to and dependence upon the Catholic Church as parts are use to have in respect of their whole. Whereupon it followeth that neither particular persons nor particular churches are to work as several divided bodies by themselves (which is the ground of all schism), but are to teach and to be taught and to do all other Christian duties as parts conjoined unto the whole, and members of the same commonwealth and corporation.[102]

Similarly William Bedell defined the catholic church as "the fellowship of saints dispersed throughout the whole world." [103] Judged by such a standard the claims of certain Roman authors seemed trivial or absurd. Dr. Hill had argued that those who hold the true faith are called Catholics; members of the Roman Church are invariably called Catholics; therefore the Roman Catholic Church must be acknowledged as the true Catholic Church. But, replied George Abbot, to appropriate a name is not to prove a case. Many a person disguises a shabby life by a pretentious title.[104] The Church of Rome cannot be equated with the Catholic Church. Churches existed before the Roman Church arose. Churches as ancient and as orthodox as she have not acknowledged her claims. The exclusiveness of Rome compels her to pretend that she is the sole root, whereas she is actually borne by that root. This arrogance is the true source of schism, and Rome is chiefly guilty of it. She refuses, said Ussher, to play her due part "with the rest of the churches of Christ, and to have a joint dependence with them upon the whole body of the church catholic, which is the mother of us all." By her attitude she proves that she is a

[101] Roger Fenton, *A Treatise against the necessary dependance upon that one head*, pp. 9–10; Fisher, *The Answere unto the nine points*, p. 44; R. Bellarmine, *Apologia pro responsione sua*; Richard Broughton, *A Demonstration by English Protestant pretended Bishops and Ministers*, pp. 136 ff.

[102] Ussher, *A Briefe Declaration of the Universalitie of the Church of Christ*, pp. 9–10.

[103] Bedell, *An examination of certaine motives to recusancie*, p. 29. Cf. Jenney, *A Catholike Conference between a Protestant and a Papist*, pp. 19–20.

[104] G. Abbot, *The Reasons . . . for the Upholding of Papistry Unmasked*, pp. 71–78.

particular church and not the Church Catholic.[105]

A church everywhere dispersed throughout the world will be a church active throughout the ages. Antiquity and continuity are as truly the marks of the church as catholicity or visibility. Here the Catholics claimed a decisive advantage. Protestantism was a "new-fangled religion," "a church which began only yesterday." [106] Hence the persistence with which they pressed what Laud called "that idle and impertinent question of theirs" [107]—where was your church before Luther? It was absurd, said Fisher the Jesuit, for Protestants to pretend that they are descended from the apostles. They can trace ancestry to Luther, who was commissioned to preach only by the devil; beyond him they have no antecedents.[108] Parliamentary action could "invent or give allowance unto a new but not a true religion"; it could certainly not invest it with a past that did not belong to it.[109] The charge often carried conviction. When Walter Mountagu wrote to his father, the Lord Privy Seal, about his change of faith, this was the point he chiefly stressed: he had found no answer to the Jesuits' taunts.[110] Sutcliffe conceded that "the shew of antiquity in the matters of religion" was "plausible to the multitude" and "forcible to persuade the simple," but he dismissed the argument as specious and false.[111] There is a "usurped pretence of antiquity," just as there is an unjust "imputation of novelty," and by such devices "the truth of God is deluded and error supported among the children of unbelief." The appeal to antiquity has always been the favorite device of those who resist reformation.[112] Actually the appeal of Protestantism is to other standards. Luther was not "the founder of our religion, but God the ancient of days." Luther derived the truths he taught from Scripture and the fathers, but if you appeal to predecessors, he had them in every age.[113] "For we do not imagine," said Richard Field,

> that the church began at Wittenberg or Geneva, but that at these and sundry other places of the Christian world it pleased God to use the ministry of his worthy servants for the necessary reformation of abuses in some parts of that Catholic Church, which beginning at Jerusalem spread itself into all the world.[114]

[105] Ussher, *A Briefe Declaration*, pp. 13, 17. Cf. Morton, *The Grand imposture of the (now) Church of Rome*, Chs. IV, V, XV.
[106] Kellison, *A Survey of the new Religion*, p. 17.
[107] Laud, *Works*, II, xiii.
[108] Fisher, *The Answere*, pp. 73–74; John Brereley, *The Apologie for the Romane Church*, pp. 76–156. Cf. Bédé, *The Masse Displayed*, Preface (by E. C.).
[109] Broughton, *A Defence of Catholikes persecuted in England*, p. 12.
[110] *A Coppy of a letter sent from France by Mr Walter Mountagu.*
[111] Sutcliffe, *The subversion of Robert Parsons, his worke*, Ep. Ded. Cf. Ussher, *An Answer to a Challenge made by a Jesuite in Ireland*, Ep. Ded.
[112] Favour, *Antiquitie Triumphing over Noveltie*, pp. 1, 3.
[113] Sampson Price, *Londons Warning by Laodiceas Lukewarmness*, pp. 41–42.
[114] Field, *op. cit.*, p. 55.

Consequently, though it does not primarily rely on the testimony of antiquity, the Church of England can appeal to it. Reformation does not destroy continuity. The Protestants keep the ancient saving faith; they merely remove the "super-seminated tares" which the adversary has sown.[115] "The field is the same, but weeded now, unweeded then." A tree when pruned is not a different tree, "neither is the church *reformed* in our days another church than that which was deformed in the days of our forefathers." [116] If it wished, Protestantism could claim an ancient and honorable lineage. Some writers traced it back through three centuries, some through five, some throughout Christian history. Others merely proved that in every generation there had been those who derived from the Scriptures the essentials of the gospel.[117] To Lancelot Andrewes the vital task was to show that his church retained an unbroken continuity with the Christianity of the purest period. "Our religion," he wrote, "you miscall sectarian opinions. I tell you, if they are modern, they are not ours; our appeal is to antiquity—yea, even the most extreme antiquity. We do not innovate; it may be we renovate what was customary with those same ancients but with you has disappeared in novelties." [118] This argument, partially developed by various writers, was reduced to systematic form by Richard Bernard. The Protestant appeal to antiquity, he said, is sound and valid, because (1) the holy Scriptures prove it; (2) it is the religion that has the testimony of the martyrs; (3) the writings of the fathers confirm it; (4) even Roman Catholic works prove that Protestantism long antedated Luther; (5) it was in England before Austin came; (6) "that religion which is of God was before Luther's time. . . . But our religion is of God, which I prove thus." [119] Moreover, the charge of novelty could be turned against its originators. Rome is the real innovator. The corruptions that have crept into the Roman Church have made it a new and different institution. The Council of Trent has modified both the faith and the practice of the church.[120] "It would be much harder for them," said Donne, "to name men in every age that have professed all the doctrines of the present Roman Church than for us to find men that have opposed those points that we oppose." [121]

Unity, it was generally agreed, is also a mark of the true church. Where

[115] Cade, *A Justification of the Church of England*, p. 3.

[116] Ussher, *A Briefe Declaration of the Universalitie of the Church of Christ*, pp. 48–49.

[117] Cf. Thomas Bedford, *Luthers Predecessours*, p. 2; I.P.P.L., *Luther's Forerunners*, esp. pp. 450–460; G. Abbot, *The Reasons . . . for the Upholding of Papistry Unmasked*, pp. 62 ff.; *idem, A Treatise*, pp. 89–90.

[118] Andrewes, *Tortura Torti, Works*, VIII, 96. For a Catholic retort to this kind of argument, see Nicholas Smith, *An Ecclesiastical Protestant Historie of . . . the Popes of Rome*, p. 3.

[119] Bernard, *Looke beyond Luther*, pp. 2–37.

[120] Cade, *A Justification of the Church of England*, pp. 23–27, 74–126; O. E., *A new challenge to N.D.*, pp. 27–43; Bell, *The Jesuits Antepast*, Ep. Ded.; Carleton, *Directions to know the true church*, pp. 60–65; *The Catholic Moderator*, pp. 26–57; Donne, *Sermons*, IV, 139, V, 72, IX, 361.

[121] Donne, *Sermons*, IX, 338.

can it be found in necessary measure? Within what limits could diversity be allowed? When did permissible differences about things indifferent become intolerable disagreement about essentials? The Catholics answered these questions with confidence. "The entire unity of the church is proved here by the exact obedience which we are obliged to exhibit to the same church." Such differences as exist within the Roman Church concern matters of opinion; they never touch the basic questions of faith or doctrine. The spokesmen of the church (e.g., the Jesuits and the Dominicans) are permitted to disagree on "matters of greater probability and private opinion"; if they exceed this limit, they are promptly brought to heel by the threat of excommunication.[122] The Catholics have this kind of discipline; the Protestants do not, and the difference is decisive. "We see that first the Protestants are divided; secondly, they are without any means of union in controversies; there is no jurisdiction among them." [123] The results are plain for all to see: Protestants attack each other with a virulence born of bitter divisions.[124] But the Protestants denied both the accuracy and the relevance of most of the evidence the Catholics adduced. Much of it came from Continental sources and had no bearing on the English situation. In any case, the Roman controversialists had greatly exaggerated the differences among foreign Protestants and had grossly distorted the facts. Protestant differences were neither so many nor so profound as those among Catholics. Historically, many of the Protestant differences resulted from the pope's refusal to call a council to reform the church; each state had been compelled to remove abuses as best it could, but the work was done without consultation and so without uniformity.[125] The authors admitted that there were differences in England also, but these, they insisted, did not concern essentials. The distinction between things fundamental and things indifferent, which the Catholics tended to dismiss, was valid and useful.[126] The papists postulate a kind of uniformity that smothers creative investigation; in the form in which they demand it, it cannot be a mark of the church, since the apostolic church itself was clearly divided.[127] Moreover, they achieve agreement by methods inconsistent with the nature of the church. The unity that Rome demands presupposes political absolutism; what God gave his church was "one Lord, one faith," and what keeps his people in this faith is "the unity of the Spirit," not political coercion. Actually the Catholics fail to reach even

[122] Knott, *Charity Mistaken*, p. 24; Fisher, *The Answere*, pp. 74–75.

[123] *The First Part of the Protestants Proofes*, p. 29.

[124] O. A., *The uncasing of heresie*, p. 206. The author quotes a fierce attack by a Lutheran theologian on the Calvinists. Cf. Kellison, *A Survey of the new Religion*, pp. 364–365.

[125] G. Abbot, *The Reasons*, pp. 87 ff., 97, 120–127; Cade, *A Justification of the Church of England*, pp. 243–250.

[126] Cf. Chillingworth, *op. cit.*, Ch. III.

[127] F. White, *The orthodox faith and the way to the church*, pp. 51 ff., 132; Ussher, *A Briefe Declaration*, pp. 18–20.

their own standard. Read their books, and you see at once that the Jesuits and the Dominicans fight—and fight bitterly—about important doctrines. "Let me see a Dominican and a Jesuit reconciled, in doctrinal papacy, for free will and pre-destination; let me see a French papist and an Italian papist reconciled, on state papistry, for the pope's jurisdiction; let me see the Jesuits and the secular priests reconciled in England; and when they are reconciled to one another, let them press reconciliation to their church." [128] Bellarmine admitted that Catholic doctors disagreed on over two hundred points. "And yet 'tis a wonder to see with what a face of brass and impudence the Romanists of these times are wont to upbraid us with the quarrels of our church, as if Rome had engrossed all the unity." [129] Joseph Hall claimed that "all the busy raking of the Jesuits" among Protestant differences had produced fewer examples of sharp contention than he had found simply by comparing two Catholic authors with each other. "We want only their cunning secrecy in the carriage of our quarrels. Our few and slight differences are blazoned abroad with infamy and offence; their hundreds are craftily smothered in silence." [130] The question was serious because it was directly associated with the issue of schism. The Catholics accused the Protestants of rending the seamless robe of Christ. The charge, replied the Protestants, was groundless. Their worship was not schismatic; church history shows that Rome has always admitted that variant "uses" do not necessarily create division.[131] Nor was it a schismatic act to repudiate the pope's supremacy. "The head of that church is the very grand Antichrist, the man of sin"; the doctrine of the Church of Rome rests on human traditions; in practice it withholds the Word of God from the people; it imposes ecclesiastical laws on men's consciences; it permits false sacraments; it encourages idolatry. Is it schism to separate from such a church? [132]

It is not enough to identify the true church by its marks; you must heed its teaching and obey its commands, and you do so only if it appeals to indisputable authorities. In the seventeenth century three of these were the objects of intensive scrutiny: Scripture, tradition, and the papacy. Both the Church of England and the Church of Rome claimed to rest on the Word of God, but from it they drew very different inferences. "And this," said Andrewes, "is the main question between them and us: who have the true means to interpret?" [133] In any controversy, the Bible must

---

[128] Donne, *Sermons*, IV, 312. Cf. VII, 123: "half the Roman Church goes one way and half the other"; the Jesuits take one line "and their very heavy and very bitter adversaries, the Dominicans," another. Chillingworth often speaks of the contentions between Jesuits and Dominicans.

[129] Quelch, *Church Customes Vindicated*, pp. 9–10.

[130] Joseph Hall, *Works*, IX, 16.

[131] Bedell, *op. cit.*, p. 33.

[132] Bernard, *Plaine Evidences*, p. 55.

[133] Andrewes, *A Pattern of Catechisticall Doctrine*, p. 109.

provide the decisive criterion, since "the Scripture hath been the rule of faith which must rule the church in teaching."[134]   Actually, if you could settle the question of the meaning and authority of Scripture, you would be well on the way to solving everything else.[135]   Protestant authors spent an immense amount of time defining and justifying the role of Scripture in their life and thought. "The Scripture according to our doctrine," wrote Thomas Jackson, ". . . is the only infallible rule of faith. First, in that it contains all the principles of faith and points of salvation. . . . 2. These principles of faith are plainly, perspicuously and distinctly set down to the capacities of all that faithfully" try to understand them. The Bible speaks clearly to the man who humbly seeks its meaning, and so there is no need of any interpretation beyond that made generally available by a learned ministry. This makes it possible to know whether or not God has spoken to his church, and it shows us how to discover the sense and meaning of Scripture.[136]

The Catholics acknowledged the importance of the Bible but refused to give it the exclusive position assigned to it by the Protestants. The Roman Church took the view,

> 1. That such articles as by her and the Protestants themselves believed and holden for articles of faith are not so expressly contained in holy Scripture as out of them only full proof may be made thereof. . . .
> 2. All such articles as are of faith and so holden by the Protestants themselves are not contained so much as indirectly or implicitly in holy Scripture, but only so far as the Scriptures contain and testify the authority of the church and traditions.[137]

Sometimes a Catholic writer boldly declared that all the doctrines of his church are "evidently and strongly confirmed out of the written Word of God," while no such claim could be made for any Protestant teachings. But the representative Catholic position was that which held Scripture and tradition in judicious equipoise. "The total and full rule of our faith," wrote Martin Becanus, "is Scripture and tradition both together, tradition being of equal authority with the Scripture."[138]

Each side, having stated its own view of the authority of Scripture, attacked its opponent's position. Obscurity, said the Catholics, disqualified the Bible for the use to which the Protestants proposed to put it.[139]

---

[134] Carleton, *Directions*, pp. 46–47. Cf. Jackson, *Works*, II, 106.

[135] J. White, *The Way to the True Church*, Ep. Ded.

[136] Jackson, *Works*, II, 421.

[137] A. C. S. [Champney], *A Manual of Controversies*, pp. 15–16, 18–19. Cf. [Maihew], *A Treatise of the Groundes of the old and newe Religion*, pp. 61–86.

[138] Gordon-Huntley, *A Summary of Controversies*, p. 3; Becanus is quoted by J. White, *The Way to the True Church*, Preface.

[139] Fisher, *The Answere*, pp. 23–24; A. C. S., *op. cit.*, p. 26.

But this, replied Jackson, is less a reflection on the Book than on the men who wrote it, and do the Catholics really intend to cast aspersions on "the penmen of the Holy Ghost"? Nor is the Bible really a difficult work for those who use it as they should.[140] But Scripture, objected the Catholics, is neither a reliable nor an independent authority: it has not "light to shew itself with *evident certainty* to be the Word of God," and many a man finds it a confusing guide. It is an insufficient authority: without some external testimony we cannot be sure that it is the Word of God. The plea that the Spirit will divulge its meaning is worthless; consider the confusion rife among Protestants. The Bible has been the source of heresy as well as of truth, and the Protestants consistently demonstrate that they have no rule by which they can prove anything from Scripture without "adding, diminishing, chopping or changing it by some interpretation or other."[141] The Protestants were no less convinced that the Catholics were arbitrary and inexact in their use of the Bible. Sometimes the distortions seemed so perverse that they could be explained only by ignorance of the text. But to minimize the importance of the Bible was to erode the foundations of the church. By a strange lapse in critical acumen, the Catholics insisted that the Vulgate was a more reliable source than the Greek and Hebrew texts. More serious still, the Church of Rome "expunges and interlines articles of faith upon reasons of state and emergent occasions."[142] But the crux of the matter remained the unique authority of Scripture, and here all Protestants subscribed to Hooker's words:

> When the question thereof is, whether we be now to seek for any revealed law of God otherwhere than only in the sacred Scripture; whether we do now stand bound in the sight of God to yield to traditions urged by the Church of Rome the same obedience and reverence we do to his written law, honouring equally and adoring both as divine? Our answer is, No.[143]

Catholic apologists insisted that as sources of authority Scripture and tradition were complementary and equal. Some assigned a kind of practical priority to tradition: it is "the sole ordinary means on which to ground faith." It cannot be otherwise. Belief is founded on the Word of God, not as written in Scripture, but as delivered by tradition and the church. Tradition antedates the Bible; it assures us what writings and doctrines are apostolic in origin.[144] William Bishop realized that in

[140] Jackson, *Works,* I, 463. Cf. Bernard, *Rhemes against Rome,* Ep. Ded.; J. White, *The Way to the True Church,* pp. 155–158.

[141] Fisher, *The Answere,* pp. 14, 21–22; A. C. S., *op. cit.,* pp. 1–10; Anderton, *The Non-entity of Protestancy,* pp. 115–116; Kellison, *The Touchstone of the Reformed Gospel,* Preface.

[142] Donne, *Sermons,* III, 129; also VI, 253; VII, 94, 123; IX, 330; R. Abbot, *The true ancient Roman catholike,* pp. 308–402; Beard, *Antichrist the Pope of Rome,* p. 396.

[143] Hooker, *Laws of Ecclesiastical Polity,* Bk. I, 13.

[144] Fisher, *The Answere,* pp. 76–77, 69, 44–52.

practice many Protestants allowed a certain place to tradition and that
consequently there were points of agreement as well as of difference.
Protestants, he noted, usually restrict tradition's role to transmitting
"ceremonious rites for the more seemly and decent administration of
divine service, sacraments and government of the church," and they
usually restricted this role to matters of secondary importance. "The main
matter of our dissent," continued Bishop,

> is this: they teach no one point of faith necessary to be believed
> to salvation to have been delivered by tradition, but all to be
> particularly and expressly set down in the Written Word. We
> affirm the flat contrary, to wit, that many things necessary to
> salvation be not particularly and expressly written in the holy
> Scriptures but are taken from apostolic tradition.[145]

To make his position perfectly explicit he set down five propositions that
ought to govern our treatment of the subject.

> 1. All things necessary to be believed of all Christians be not
> particularly set down in the holy Scriptures, nor can henceforth
> be deduced by necessary collection. . . . 2. That some articles of
> faith are not so fully set down in Scriptures but that they need
> the aid of tradition. . . . 3. That we cannot convince that which
> is plainly written without traditions; . . . without the help of
> traditive doctrines, no one article of faith, how plainly soever it
> be delivered in the Scriptures, can be convinced against obsti-
> nate heretics. . . . 4. That absurdity follows them who except
> against tradition. . . . 5. That in all ages traditions have been in
> use.[146]

Protestants remained unconvinced. To erect an authority correlative to
Scripture seemed sacrilegious; it was a defiance of the mercy that in Holy
Writ provided a unique revelation. Even Laud, who conceded a
legitimate role to tradition, felt that the Romans built an unwarranted
superstructure on a very precarious foundation. Many Protestants contended that the corruptions characteristic of Romanism could be traced
directly to the ills bred by reliance on tradition.[147] It was a "Jewish
disease" to neglect the Scriptures in order to follow "the traditions and
precepts of men for the rule of their faith." [148] Reliance on tradition has
always led men astray. "The additions and traditions and superedifica-
tions of the Roman Church" explain the unreliable nature of so many of
the principal elements in the Roman system.[149]

[145] Bishop, *Maister Perkins Reformed Catholique*, p. 712.
[146] *Ibid.*, pp. 715–735.
[147] Bernard, *Rhemes against Rome*, pp. 60 ff.; R. Abbot, *The danger of Popery detected*, pp. 19 ff.
[148] Jackson, *Works*, I, 441.
[149] Donne, *Sermons*, III, 370. Cf. Cooke, *op. cit.*, p. 23.

On Scripture and tradition there was much difference but some agreement. On the pope's authority there was no agreement at all. This issue aggravated all others in the controversy. "The matter then which principally and without hope of reconciliation divideth Christendom is the pride and usurpation of the pope. And no doubt other doctrinal controversies are kept on foot to be a stalking horse for this." [150] The Catholics, of course, were unanimous in pressing the pope's claims. He was the successor of St. Peter and the vicar of Christ. His authority was the sole foundation of true religion. In England there were particularly cogent reasons for submitting to his sway. St. Peter had preached in Britain; he had founded the Catholic church in these islands, and it has been here ever since. Even the mythical origins of Oxford and Cambridge received some highly picturesque embellishments from this story.[151] But such claims carried little conviction. St. Peter had never been in Britain; it could not be proved that he had ever been in Rome.

> And if he was never there, then he was not the bishop of Rome; then the pope is not St. Peter's successor there; then not Christ's vicar; then not the head of the church; then his supremacy usurped; his power of no force; the terrors of his excommunications babish; his pride tyrannical and his proceedings antichristian; then his yoke is to be shaken off.[152]

In any case apostleship was a personal office; it was neither transferable nor hereditary. There were no grounds for assuming that St. Peter established any formal preeminence among the apostles, and it is only in comparatively recent times that the bishop of Rome advanced such extravagant claims.[153] This unhappy development took place only when "the pope began to play the masterly servant in the household of God and to strike his fellow servants and cast out whom he list out of the family." [154]

Though the Protestants had no single explanation of how the pope gained his primacy, they were entirely agreed in their interpretation of what it meant. The Roman ecclesiastical system, as it culminates in the pope's unchallenged authority, is really Antichrist.[155] The papal claims indicate as much: "he that professeth himself the supreme head of the church of Christ and yet forceth men, upon pain of death, to blaspheme Christ, he is Antichrist." [156] Papal policies confirm the charge: he "taketh

---

[150] F. White, *The orthodox faith and the way to the church*, Ep. Ded.

[151] N. Smith [M. Wilson], *An Ecclesiastical Protestant Historie*, pp. 4, 8, 37, 51, 203 ff.

[152] Bernard, *The Fabulous Foundation of the Popedom*, n.p. Cf. John Panke, *The Fal of Babel*, passim.

[153] Dove, *An Advertisement to the English Seminaries and Jesuites*, p. 10; Joseph Hall, *Works*, IX, 381; Favour, *op. cit.*, pp. 374–376.

[154] Bedell, *An Examination*, p. 53.

[155] Rainolds, *The Discoverie of the Man of Sinne*, pp. 8–9.

[156] Edmund Gurnay, *The Demonstration of Antichrist*, p. 1. Cf. L. Andrewes, *Responsio, Works*,

186 FREEDOM AND AUTHORITY

upon him to dispense with the Word and law of God"; he sets "to sale all manner of sin"; [157] he deceives the world with his claims about miracles, relics, purgatory, papal excommunications, and pardons.[158] Moreover, when put to the acid test of experience the pope's authority was incapable of resolving precisely those religious problems that an absolute system might reasonably be expected to answer. The anxious Protestants believed that the Roman church was exalting the pope's authority above that of God himself. This could have only one end: "great Antichrist exaltation, utterly overthrowing the whole foundation of Christian religion, preposterously inverting both law and gospel, to God's dishonour and the advancement of Satan's kingdom." [159]

For much of the time controversy skirted doctrinal issues without specifically coming to terms with them. Almost any subject, of course, had theological overtones, but these were more often implied than actually developed. Ultimately the representatives of both sides had to answer the question, Do our opponents maintain the true faith in its integrity? Catholic writers often provided a thorough analysis of Protestant teaching, to show that at almost every point it was fatally defective. Matthew Kellison proved that every major doctrine was held by the Protestants in a seriously distorted form. God, Christ, the church, the duty of the Christian in this world and his destiny in the next—all were so warped by Protestant theologians that their readers would be led at best into heresy, in all likelihood into atheism.[160] In fact, wrote Anderton, "Reformation consisteth only in utterly subverting and destroying most of our affirmative Catholic articles of faith; and in lieu of them in introducing the negative." [161] The Protestants retorted that Rome's "doctrines (for the most part) are injurious to Almighty God and contumelious to the redeemer of the world," [162] and some authors were prepared to prove this both in general and in detail.

The theological debate tended, however, to concentrate on a few doctrines or practices that seemed particularly characteristic of the one side or the other. The Catholics seized on election, predestination and free will, on good works, merit, and justification. The Protestants stressed the sacraments and transubstantiation, the saints, superstition, dispensations and indulgences, and purgatory. From the Catholic point of view predestination and its complementary doctrines bound man in a determin-

---

VIII, 405 ff.; also pp. 299, 386, 465; Brightman, *A Revelation of the Revelation*, pp. 587, 608, 622–770.

[157] G. Downame, *A Treatise concerning Antichrist*, pp. 77, 88, 92–100.

[158] Beard, *Antichrist the Pope of Rome*, pp. 36, 301–380. Cf. [George Walker], *The Summe of a Disputation*.

[159] Jackson, *Works*, I, 447; II, 202, 501.

[160] Kellison, *A Survey of the new Religion, passim.*

[161] Anderton, *The Non-entity of Protestancy*, p. 4; also pp. 148–154.

[162] Butterfield, *op. cit.*, p. 3.

ism from which there was no escape. Thus it "made God the principal cause of all sins and wickednesses, and reputed the devil but his agent or instrument." [163] But this was too unsophisticated a treatment of a very complex doctrine. Election, said the Protestants, must be seen in due perspective. God has declared his will in three books—of nature, of grace (the Bible), and of life, "which is his secret counsel, and it he reserveth to himself in his own bosom. In it we cannot read particularly whose names are written, because it is not published as the other two are." This is a strange mystery, added John Dove; you can understand it only if you follow the seven steps that Scripture indicates: "purpose, foreknowledge, predestination, election, vocation, justification, glorification." In this context the believer can begin to see that "predestination is [God's] eternal and immutable decree, proceeding only from his will and pleasure, that he will be glorified by the salvation of some particular men above the rest." [164] This was a "mystery," and some Catholics realized that it touched upon problems that they too had to face. Edward Knott knew that because of the Fall man cannot simply turn to God and serve him; "we have no power to do good works pleasant and acceptable to God without the grace of God preventing us." But the Protestants did not say whether, when God inspires him, man has the power to do good works; the Catholics claimed he has. [165]

The Catholics claimed that Protestantism inevitably leads to a repudiation of good works. How can men do what they should if they are told that their best works are no better than sin? [166] Admittedly Protestants like Robert Abbot insisted that "the good works and sufferings of this life are not meritorious or worthy of the bliss of the life to come"; [167] Catholics assumed that "consequently [Protestants] bear a favourable eye to vice and sensuality"; indeed, they "loathe to practise good works." [168] But, as so often during this period, the controversialists were arguing at cross-purposes. Protestants believed that the Catholic doctrine of good works usurped the prerogative of God by giving man a share in his own redemption. "That religion which derogateth from the glory of God in the work of our redemption and giveth part thereof unto man cannot be the truth of God." [169] Donne insisted that

> there is more devotion in our doctrine of good works than in that
> of the Roman Church, because we teach as much necessity of
> them as they do, and yet tie no reward to them. And we

[163] O. A., *The uncasing of heresie*, p. 206; also pp. 102 ff. Cf. Kellison, *A Survey of the new Religion*, pp. 295 ff.
[164] Dove, *An Advertisement*, pp. 24–25.
[165] Knott, *Charity Mistaken*, p. 90.
[166] *Ibid.*, p. 120.
[167] R. Abbot, *The true ancient Roman catholike*, p. 295.
[168] [B. C.], *op. cit.*, p. 14; Anderton, *The Non-entity of Protestancy*, p. 119.
[169] Beard, *A Retractive from the Romish Religion*, p. 88. Cf. Walker, *Fisher's Folly Unfolded*, p. 6.

> acknowledge that God doth not only make our faith to fructify
> and produce good works as fruits thereof, but sometimes begins
> at our own works and in man's heart morally inclined to do good
> doth build up faith.[170]

But how do you define the relation between good works and justification?
This was the crux of the problem. Do good works merit a new standing in
God's sight, or are they the inevitable consequence of the new relationship
once it has been achieved? Canon 32 of the Council of Trent taught that
good works merit an increase of grace. The Protestants insisted that such
works follow justification and are the outward expression of a mercy that
man cannot deserve. "Good works are the true effects of a predestination,
by which the children of God make their salvation sure unto themselves
and manifest unto the world, but not the cause of predestination or
justification, nor can they merit eternal life." [171] Or as the same author
expressed it elsewhere, "good works do follow justification, but go not
before the same." [172]

Justification by faith was the great watchword of early Protestantism.
To justification the canons of the Council of Trent devoted more space
than to any other subject. Inevitably the repercussions continued to
reverberate through seventeenth-century controversies. "Justification by
faith *is* the great Protestant doctrine," said John Fisher, "and as such
heretical." Four points, he felt, epitomized the Protestant interpretation of
the doctrine: (1) every man is justified by the justice of Christ, he being (as
it were) vested therewith; (2) this justice of Christ is formally imputed to
every man, not through repentance and mortification, but through faith
only; (3) this faith is not dogmatical or historical faith, but a special faith
whereby a man persuades himself that the justice of Christ is imputed to
him for the full remission of his sins; (4) without such assurance a man is
not justified, even though he believes all the dogmas of the faith.[173] Fisher
conceded that many Protestants would not accept his summary as an
accurate interpretation of their beliefs, but usually seventeenth-century
controversialists were not unduly troubled by such complaints. Protestants
felt it all the more necessary to explain in detail what they actually meant
by justification and (since this was vital to their understanding of the
doctrine) what they meant by faith. In the course of a long and closely
reasoned volume, Thomas Jackson pointed out that the Catholics had
consistently refused to admit that the Protestants (because they appeal to
Scriptural usage) defined both the key words differently from the
Schoolmen. It is not enough blithely to assume that "the Holy Ghost has

---

[170] Donne, *Pseudo-martyr*, p. 99. Cf. *idem, Sermons*, IX, 120; II, 300.

[171] Bell, *The Downefall of Poperie*, p. 61.

[172] Bell, *The Catholique Triumph*, p. 239. On the Roman doctrines of merit and good works,
see R. Wakeman, *The Poore-mans Preacher*, pp. 54–65.

[173] Fisher, *The Answere*, p. 113.

been scholar to Aquinas." [174] To be justified is not to be "vested with justice"; it is to receive a new standing, to be brought into a gracious personal relationship. This is possible through faith—not as the intellectual apprehension of certain doctrines but as the response in trust of the whole man. Given this view of justification, merit and good works fall naturally into their proper place.[175]

Controversy was sometimes concerned with doctrines accepted by both churches but differently interpreted; at other times it dealt with beliefs accepted by the one church but repudiated by the other. Purgatory was a constant offense to Protestants. So was transubstantiation. The latter was dismissed as "absurd and erroneous both by Scripture and by common sense and reason." [176] With patient care, Thomas Beard exposed forty-four contradictions lurking in the doctrine of transubstantiation. Alexander Cooke laid bare its absurdities and anomalies. If, for example, you really perform a miracle and then reserve the elements, you have created a relic—but whoever heard of God as a relic? [177] To a devout Catholic many of Cooke's points must have reflected complete incomprehension, or even blasphemy mingled with bad taste. The role of the saints was also fiercely debated. The natural man, as the Gentiles proved, multiplied his gods without restraint; but, said the Protestants, the Roman Church has done the same with the saints.[178] In both cases, remarked Donne, the motives and dangers were alike. "A man may flatter the saints in heaven if he attribute to them that which is not theirs; and so a Papist flatters." Donne regarded the invocation of the saints as a practice shot through with inconsistencies. On certain days (e.g., Easter and Whitsunday), prayers are not offered to the Virgin Mary or to the saints, because then we need no mediator save Christ or the Holy Spirit. But why on some days only? If on some, why not on all? [179] Can you avoid the impression, asked Bell, that "popish invocation doth not only make the saints the mediators of intercession, but also of redemption"? Are they not then "joint purchasers of salvation with Christ's most sacred blood"? [180] "The principal crime whereof we accuse the Romish Church," wrote Jackson, ". . . is her open, professed, direct intendment to honour them which are no gods with those prayers or devotions, with those elevations of mind and spirits, wherewith they present the only wise immortal King." It was clearly "an ascription of that honour to the creature which is only due to the Creator." Protestants found it difficult to distinguish the reverence paid by Catholics to their saints from the worship offered by the heathen

---

[174] Jackson, *Works*, III, 183. Most of this volume is devoted to *Justifying Faith*.
[175] *Ibid.*, III, 286 ff.; Favour, *op. cit.*, p. 518.
[176] W. T., *Vindiciae Ecclesiae Anglicanae*, p. 48.
[177] Beard, *A Retractive*, pp. 242–296; Cooke, *Worke, More Worke*, pp. 37 ff.
[178] J. King, *David's Strait*, p. 6.
[179] Donne, *Sermons*, V, 38; VIII, 329–331.
[180] Bell, *The Catholique Triumph*, p. 303.

to their gods; and the charge of idolatry seemed to be confirmed by "that
image service, which the primitive church had abandoned as the liturgy of
hell." [181] But could you expect a different result? "The first main ground
of Romish faith leads directly unto atheism; the second unto preposterous
heathenism or idolatry." [182]

"By their fruits ye shall know them," and much of the controversy
centered on the practices associated with the Roman Church. "Their
doctrines are devilish," said Robert Butterfield, "but their practice much
worse." [183] According to Donne, the Reformation had become inevitable
because the church was "bed-ridden in the corruptions of Rome," and he
believed "all their errors proceed from their covetousness and love of
money." The source of this creeping infection was the practice of granting
dispensations. "It hath been said of Rome, . . . there a man may know
the price of a sin before he do it; and he knows what his dispensation will
cost; whether he be able to sin at that rate, whether he have wherewithall,
that if not he may take a cheap sin." This disturbed Donne. It inspired
his bitter comment about "the farmers of heaven and hell, the merchants
of souls, the Roman Church." [184] Corruption led to violence. The
Counter-Reformation had not been content with meek and gentle
methods, and an Englishman, examining the record of the past half
century, was apt to infer that the marks of papal policy were treason,
murder, perjury, lying, slander, and forgery.[185] Apparently "the Roman
Church thinks it necessary to her greatness to inflict more tortures now
than were inflicted upon her in the primitive church." The "massacres of
millions" seemed to be part of customary practice.[186] The conversion of
the New World, even as described by Catholic writers, appears as a
process of calculated cruelty and barbarism.[187] A popular preacher like
Robert Bolton, in urging his hearers to repentance, is momentarily
checked by the thought that a nation of sinners is escaping the retribution
that its wickedness deserves. But the answer is ready to hand: God stays
his just anger against England because "the cruel and implacable
insolency of our enemies" is so clear that "he is loth to make us a prey to
the wolves of Rome and matter of triumph to such a merciless and
murtherous generation." [188]

The debate was embittered by the fact that many seventeenth-century

[181] Jackson, *Works*, IV, 233, 291; also pp. 211, 214, 225, 329 ff., 355. Cf. Ussher, *An Answer to a Challenge made by a Jesuite in Ireland*, pp. 377 ff.
[182] Jackson, *Works*, II, 545. Cf. *Purchas his Pilgrimage*, Ep. Ded.
[183] Butterfield, *op. cit.*, p. 4.
[184] Donne, *Sermons*, VI, 132; X, 172; V, 202; IX, 130; X, 158.
[185] Beard, *A Retractive*, pp. 419–497.
[186] Purchas, *op. cit.*, pp. 746 ff.
[187] Bolton, *A Discourse of the state of true Happinesse*, To the Reader.
[188] *Ibid.*

Englishmen believed that the Roman Church encouraged many practices that seemed to have no relation whatever to God's law as set forth in the Bible.[189] The charges were many and varied. The Mass in Latin meant so little to the people that most of the worshipers would get as much benefit if they were a thousand miles away. Clerical celibacy ran directly counter to God's initial command, to be fruitful and multiply. Monasticism, by erecting discipline into a system, often encouraged the very vices that it attempted to subdue. The Index was a tissue of inconsistencies, and had surely become merely an embarrassment to those who devised it. Fasting, as usually practiced, was neither a physical hardship nor a spiritual benefit. Experience showed that pilgrimages chiefly encouraged hypocrisy, vagabondage, and immorality. The prevalence of popular superstition explains the persistence of these evils. The Church of Rome, said Daniel Featley, is prolific in certain religious practices, "but her devotions are blear-eyed with superstition." [190] Protestants saw this as the result of withholding the Scriptures from the common people;[191] they also regarded it as the product of a radically false system of belief and practice.

The controversy with Rome was concerned with issues that are never settled by argument. The uncommitted might be won over; the waverers might be confirmed; but the contestants seldom converted each other. Both sides developed elaborate arguments that rarely touched the essentials of their opponents' beliefs. "When a Protestant and a Papist dispute," said John Selden, "they talk like two madmen, because they do not agree on their principles." [192] The massive diatribes often attacked positions that no one occupied. John Floyd complained that Lancelot Andrewes wasted much time without really touching the essential issues; he was engrossed in verbal quibbles that ignored the heart of the Catholic position. But Floyd himself could be equally obtuse about essential Protestant convictions.[193] John Dove claimed that the Catholics argued endlessly about a distorted view of Protestantism that rested on the uncritical acceptance of second-hand myths.[194] Each work seemed logical and convincing, provided you accepted the author's presuppositions. Usually his opponents did not. The assumptions of the two sides seldom coincided; often they did not even touch. The sense of unreality that finally overtook this bitter controversy may explain the waning interest in it. The issues, however, remained unresolved. From time to time they stimulated a fitful debate. Then, late in the seventeenth century, James II's policies revived all the latent

[189] [Mico], *A Pill to Purge out Poperie,* pp. 29–31.
[190] Featley, *The Practice of Extraordinary Devotion,* Ep. Ded. The charge is a favorite one with almost all Protestant controversialists.
[191] R. Horn, *The Christian governour,* p. 70; cf. Beard, *A Retractive,* p. 396.
[192] Selden, *Table Talk,* p. 97.
[193] [Floyd], *The overthrow of the protestants pulpit-babels,* p. 7.
[194] Dove, *A Perswasion to English Recusants,* p. 7.

Protestant fear of Rome. The controversy erupted into fierce activity. After producing an impressive library of political works,[195] it subsided into the sober unconcern of the eighteenth century.

[195] These works were collected and republished by Bishop Gibson as *A Preservative Against Popery* (3 vols., 1738), 18 vols. 1848–1849. Supplement, 8 vols., 1849–1850.

VII

THE ENGLISH CATHOLICS
AND THE PROBLEM OF AUTHORITY

EARLY in the seventeenth century, Catholic fortunes in England reached their lowest ebb. As applied to English problems, the political strategy of the Roman see had failed at every point. The pope had excommunicated the queen; her people had responded with a mighty surge of loyalty to the crown. The attempts to invade her realms, mounted by a Catholic power with papal blessing, had ended in costly and ignominious collapse. The plots against her life had not achieved their purpose but had seriously compromised the Catholic cause. The schemes to promote a Catholic successor had done more harm than good. Even the most sanguine of optimists no longer looked for dramatic changes. Political expedients would neither overthrow the government nor change at a stroke the people's faith. The problem of authority remained. Could Catholics be loyal citizens of a Protestant monarchy? Did their religious allegiance to the pope modify their civil obedience to the king? Moreover, a religious minority had problems of its own regarding religious authority, and the period witnessed a series of bitter and paralyzing conflicts among Catholics concerning the exercise of that authority in England. But this was not the entire story. The English mystical strain persisted; in its serene atmosphere, unclouded by the bitterness of controversy, a select company of Catholics discovered the full intensity of religious experience. By its means they found that the authority of faith was most persuasively mediated.

I

The English Protestant owed allegiance, both civil and religious, to a single person, his prince. The English Catholic was in a more difficult position. He pledged his loyalty to the king, but in all religious matters he obeyed the pope. He saw nothing inconsistent in his position, but he found it difficult to convince his government that a divided allegiance could be reconciled with good citizenship. The argument was not settled by theoretical considerations. The events of Queen Elizabeth's reign were recent; no one could ignore them. Protestant writers constantly cited the pope's excommunication of the queen, his support of the invasion of Ireland, and his encouragement of the Spanish Armada.[1] The highest authority in the Catholic world had, so it seemed, deliberately mounted an attack on the English throne and people. Yet the Catholics insisted that their missionaries were in England on a purely religious enterprise; they never meddled in affairs of state—they were exclusively concerned with matters of faith.[2] This reflected the cruel dilemma that papal policy imposed upon its representatives. The pope was engaged in political designs; the Society of Jesus participated in international maneuvers.[3] The individual Jesuit might protest that he was entirely innocent of any political involvement. To the English authorities the evidence convincingly pointed the other way. "From you have come," wrote Donne, "the subtle whisperings of rebellious doctrines, the frequent and traitorous practices, the intestine commotions, and the public and foreign hostile attempts." Under such circumstances, had the government any choice but to strike at the agents of subversion? "Nor is it so harsh and strange as you use make it, that princes should make it treason to advance such doctrines, though they be obtruded as points of religion, if they involve sedition and ruin or danger to the state." [4]

The plea of noninvolvement was difficult to sustain. England was at war with Spain from 1595 to 1604, yet Jesuit emissaries traveled regularly (though secretly) between the two countries. In 1593, Father Walpole came directly to England from Madrid, and he came with the personal blessing of King Philip II. English Catholics, remarked Samuel Harsnet, were engaged in Spanish designs against their own country.[5] It was an acknowledged fact that throughout most of the war, Father Parsons, the ablest and most influential of the English Jesuits, had been in Spain; he had encouraged the invasion of his native land, and he had insisted that Philip II was the rightful king of England. His Spanish sympathies had made him notorious. A secular priest reported from Rome a comment which showed that Parsons was generally regarded there as a traitor who advocated intervention.[6] He had made it almost inevitable that English writers should identify papal religious policies with Spanish political goals. The Jesuits were commonly regarded as "the trading factors for the pope

[1] Cade, *A Justification of the Church of England*, Pt. II, pp. 89 ff.

[2] Fisher, *The Answere unto the nine points of controversy*, Preface, p. 5.

[3] Cf. Trevor-Roper, *Historical Essays*, pp. 109–110, 114–116.

[4] Donne, *Pseudo-martyr*, Preface, §§25–26. In writing this work, Donne was acting virtually as an official spokesman.

[5] Harsnet, *A Declaration of egregious popish impostures*, p. 7.

[6] John Colleton, *A Just Defence of the slandered priestes*, p. 241. A secular priest would not be prejudiced in Parsons' favor. On Parsons' pro-Spanish activities, see Donne, *Pseudo-martyr*, Preface, §7.

and the king of Spain, to extol the sanctity of the one and the power of the other." [7] Matthew Sutcliffe spoke of "the hostile actions of the pope and Spaniard, and treacherous practices of Romish priests and Jesuits." He could depreciate the arguments of his great opponent, Matthew Kellison, by remarking that "his heart is become Spanish." [8] The English government insisted that its policy toward Catholics was governed by political, not by religious, considerations. The recusancy laws were spasmodically enforced. But to give aid and comfort to the enemy was treason, and it was generally believed that there were altogether too many links between the emissaries of Rome and the foes of England. When Catholics were executed, the authorities insisted that it was for treason, not for "mere matters of religion." "Your consorts," wrote Sutcliffe to Parsons, "have been executed for treason most justly and not for religion." [9] There was a growing conviction that the government had shown considerable forbearance—"patience and moderation" is Donne's phrase—in its treatment of the leaders of English Catholicism. Early in the seventeenth century this interpretation seemed to be confirmed by the declaration of allegiance proffered to the government by thirteen Catholic priests. They would refuse, they said, to obey any papal command to support the enemies of England, because Catholics are obliged to obey the ruler "in all civil causes." They tacitly accepted the government's defense of the penal acts: Catholics had plotted against Elizabeth and had attempted to invade the country. The document drew a sharp distinction between the spiritual jurisdiction of the church and the temporal jurisdiction of the state.[10]

Catholic hopes rose with the accession of James I. During the months of confused maneuvering before Elizabeth's death, the Catholics had been deeply divided over the question of a successor. It was an axiom of papal policy that a legitimate ruler must accept the true faith, and the possibility of a Catholic claimant was earnestly canvassed. This accounts for the publication of Father Parsons' extremely controversial work, *A Conference about the next succession*. Parsons hoped that the English throne would be occupied by a Catholic ruler amenable to Spanish control, and his choice finally settled on the Infanta of Spain. But English Catholics had also supported the claims of James VI of Scotland. Early in the new reign Father William Watson reminded the lords of the Privy Council that he had worked hard to rally Catholics behind the candidacy of James.[11] Catholics who had been less prescient about the successful claimant

---

[7] L. Owen, *The unmasking of all popish monks, friers, and Jesuits*, p. 4; also p. 159. Cf. Fr. William Watson's charge against the Jesuits, *Important Considerations*, Ep. Ded.

[8] Sutcliffe, *A briefe replie to a certaine odious and slanderous libel*, Ep. Ded.; idem, *The Examination and confutation*.

[9] O. E. [Sutcliffe], *A new challenge to N.D.*, p. 93; Sutcliffe, *A briefe replie*, Ep. Ded.; cf. *ibid.*, p. 153.

[10] Printed in *The Archpriest Controversy*, II, 246–248.

[11] The letter is reproduced in Goodman, *The Court of King James the First*, II, 60–64.

hastened to point out that they had at least supported the new king's
mother, "who was known and reputed throughout Christendom to have
died for this Catholic doctrine." Indeed, added Parsons, it was the loyalty
of the English Catholics to Mary Queen of Scots that explained and
justified their resistance to Queen Elizabeth—though he had just proved
that Catholics always obeyed constituted authority, never interfered in
civil matters, and kept themselves free from the slightest taint of treason.[12]
James himself had given the Catholics firm grounds for hope. When his
prospects were still uncertain he had negotiated with Rome for papal
support. Sixtus V had been generous in his promises: if want of means
hindered James from granting concessions to the English Catholics, the
pope would exhaust the treasures of the church and sell the papal plate to
supply his needs. James, of course, had not sought help in this quarter
without Catholic encouragement. Godfrey Goodman, the crypto-Roman
bishop of Gloucester who caused Laud so much trouble, was well-informed
about the intrigues of the early Stuart court, and he believed that Catholic
pamphleteers had deliberately launched a campaign to frighten James
about his chances. As Parsons put it, "knowing the king to be fearful, they
put jealousies into him." They hoped to make him turn to the Catholic
powers for support, "and so engage to favour Catholics. And certainly
they had very great promises from him." [13]

Catholic appeals for toleration were a feature of the early part of
James's reign. Recusants began to write to the earl of Salisbury about the
possibility of greater freedom.[14] A Franciscan, living in exile and homesick
for England, was inspired to compose bad verses by his loyalty to James
and by the hope of religious liberty that the new reign aroused.[15] Matthew
Kellison, praising "the wisdom and lenity" of the king, touched on the
widespread expectation of a change in policy.[16] The Catholics, said
Michael Walpole, only ask for "the recalling and repealing of such
proclamations against them." [17] William Bishop appealed to James to
suspend the penal laws and then to assess dispassionately the superior
advantages of Roman Catholicism. The persecution of recusants, he
pointed out, could be of no advantage to anyone. In England toleration
would be feasible; in Spain or Italy, of course, it was not—there
Protestants were so few that it promoted peace to stamp them out as soon

---

[12] [R. Parsons], *The Judgment of a Catholicke English-man*, pp. 11, 99. Donne fiercely attacked
Parsons for the inconsistencies, misrepresentations, and disingenuousness which he detected
in this work: *op. cit.*, pp. 216–218. Cf. Hunt, *An Humble Appeale*, Preface, and [Broughton], *A
Defence of Catholikes persecuted in England*, p. 170.

[13] Goodman, *The Court of King James the First*, I, 83, 84, 96. Concerning James's explicit
promises of toleration, see *The Correspondence of King James VI of Scotland with Sir Robert Cecil*, pp.
36, 75.

[14] Cal. Salisbury MSS., XV, 131, 199.

[15] S. Grahame, *The Passionate Sparke of a Relenting Minde*.

[16] Kellison, *A survey*, pp. 8–10.

[17] M. C. P. [Michael Walpole], *A Briefe Admonition to all English Catholikes*, Ep. Ded.

as they appeared. "There they have more reason to crush the serpent in the head and to beat it down at the first before it hath any fast footing or hath spread itself abroad." But Catholics, he argued, were too numerous to justify such a policy in England, and toleration would firmly attach to the throne this large and law-abiding body.[18]

Protestants were alarmed. Had not the pope warned English Catholics not to accept toleration if it implied any recognition of the Church of England? The pleas for freedom struck Andrew Willet as incongruous; did the Catholics not realize that "the ark and Dagon cannot dwell together"?[19] George Downame, with a nervous glance at the Catholics' reputation for treason, anxiously remarked that their demands "have grown more insolent than in former times," and that a menacing note had crept into their petitions. Then came the Gunpowder Plot. It is impossible to exaggerate the extent to which this unhappy episode dashed the Catholics' hopes of more lenient treatment. For at least a generation it poisoned the public response to the Roman question. Since it firmly established the popular view of popish treason, it affected the relations of Catholics to civil authority and determined the measure of freedom they could expect.

As an immediate result of the Plot, the government imposed on Catholics the Oath of Allegiance, and thus provided one of the most fertile topics of debate in the seventeenth century (cf. Chapter III). But the Plot also inspired an extensive literature of anti-Catholic polemic. Year after year, as the anniversary returned, the pulpits rang with denunciations of popish treason. Upon the vast majority of English recusants—especially the Catholic squires who lived aloof from public life—the Plot fell like a bolt of lightning from a clear sky. But to Protestants also, preoccupied with arguments about a small extension of toleration, the shock was paralyzing. On the Sunday following the discovery of the Plot, Bishop Barlow preached at Paul's Cross. It was the sermon of a man who had obviously not regained his equanimity. "First in the plot observe, I pray you, a cruel execution, an inhuman cruelty, a brutish immanity, a devilish brutishness, and a hyperbolical yea an hyperdiabolical devilishness." The bishop was horrified at the thought of the slaughter, so narrowly averted, of all the leaders of the nation's life. With dismay he depicted what would have happened, as scattered fragments of king, lords, and commoners were hurled skyward in indiscriminate confusion—and he himself (O awful thought!) would have been among the victims. "And in that black powder plot (the eternal shame of popery) for the advancement of the Catholic cause Papists and Protestants both together . . . pell mell must all be blown up." By any standard it was "an immanity barbarous and matchless."[20] The horror awakened by the Plot echoed for years even in

[18] Bishop, *Maister Perkins Reformed Catholique*, Ep. Ded.
[19] Andrew Willet, *An Antilogie*, Preface.
[20] Barlow, *The Sermon preached at Paules Crosse*, p. 11.

casual references to the event. To Daniel Featley it was "this monster of all treasons, which no age can parallel." [21] William Gouge described it as "the matchless, merciless, devilish and damnable Gunpowder treason." [22] It was a design, said Donne, "that even amazed and astonished the Devil and seemed a miracle even in Hell." [23] Eleven years after the Plot, Donne was keeping it fresh in the memory of his hearers; after a further six years it was still a theme to which he constantly returned.[24] Perhaps Robert Bolton best illustrates the lingering dismay created by the Plot. More than a generation after the event, he spoke with all the freshness of recently awakened passion about "those breathing devils, the Gunpowder Papists." "Who knows," he asked, "what those busy and bloody heads are even now hammering in the same kind." [25] The Catholics, naturally enough, began to deprecate this annual regurgitation of an ancient grievance. The Plot, they argued, had been the work of "a few private Hotspurs"; "in justice [it] is rather to be buried with the offenders than objected and imputed to innocent men who generally with great sorrow abhor the memory of it." [26] But Parsons, who from his security abroad had the unhappy gift of making things more difficult for his coreligionists at home, argued that the fault really lay with the government, not with the Catholics. The plotters acted because "all those pressures both of conscience and of external affliction which since that time they have suffered and do at this present were designed before that and begun to be put into execution (as indeed they were) and that the Powder Treason was not the cause of these afflictions, but an effect rather." [27]

The Gunpowder Plot stirred national feeling to its depths. It did more than fortify deep-seated prejudices. It raised in a dramatic form the relation of the Catholics to constituted authority. It was immediately responsible for the Oath of Allegiance, which, as we have seen, precipitated that massive controversy about the right of the pope to intervene in the affairs of individual nations. But it also resuscitated the question that had vexed the Elizabethans: was disloyalty entailed upon the English Catholics? Could they acknowledge the royal authority sufficiently to behave as dutiful subjects, or was treason their inevitable posture? The record, said the Catholic apologists, disproves the popular assumptions. The Catholic need not be—and never has been—a traitor. The recusants have always been a particularly loyal community. The evidence identifying them with plots against Elizabeth's life was either inapplicable or unconvincing. Most of them genuinely deplored the pope's interventions

---

[21] Featley, *Clavis Mystica*, p. 815.

[22] Gouge, *God's Three Arrowes*, p. 360.

[23] Donne, *Sermons*, I, 219.

[24] *Ibid.*, III, 148; IV, 235–263, 368.

[25] Bolton, *A Discourse about the state of true happinesse*, To the Reader.

[26] P. D. M. [M. Patterson], *The Image of bothe churches*, p. 14.

[27] [R. Parsons], *The Judgment of a Catholicke English-man*, p. 6.

in English affairs. There were three questions which (if answered) would clarify the situation: "1. Whether to be a Catholic who professes due reverence to the Church of Rome and to be a true subject to his prince and country be compatible or no? . . . 2. If they be incompatible, whether that incompatibility be generally in all states, or but in some particular states? . . . 3. Whether Lutheranism or Calvinism be not more incompatible with loyalty?" Examine the record; it proves that the Protestants have amassed a far blacker record of subversion than the Catholics.[28] It is "untrue, indiscreet and pernicious," said Parsons, to assert that Roman Catholics are "not tolerable in a Protestant commonwealth in respect of rebellion and conspiracy."[29] Throughout this period the Catholics insisted, with mounting emphasis, that loyalty to the king was one of their distinguishing traits.

The Protestants were not convinced. From the same facts they drew opposite conclusions. The whole Roman system, fortified by the doctrine of the church, made it impossible for Catholics to be good citizens. The acts of treason that they have committed are simply "the effects of their doctrine."[30] Parsons himself confessed that the Jesuits held themselves "bound with no oath than can be devised for them, if the observance be to the hurt or hindrance of their religion"—from which it seemed reasonable to conclude that "this general doctrine of theirs of the lawfulness and obligations of treason and whatsoever practices for the good of their church affords them a boundless liberty in all their thoughts and actions."[31] Thomas Morton pointed out that the Catholic doctrine that all Protestants are heretics and consequently excommunicated provides an ideal theoretical justification for treason against a Protestant ruler.[32] It was not surprising that "conspiracy is the pope's only weapon, treason the last refuge of Rome."[33] So the charge was repeated with every resource of emphasis. "And therefore," declared John White, "I still say and write it in capital letters, that THE CHURCH OF ROME TEACHES DISLOYALTY AND REBELLION AGAINST KINGS AND LEADS HER PEOPLE INTO ALL CONSPIRACIES AND TREASONS AGAINST STATES AND KINGDOMS." White proceeded to substantiate this charge with page after page of quotations from Roman Catholic authors.[34] The arguments of serious controversialists became the accusations that popular writers bandied about without proof. John Earle is particularly revealing. In his character sketches, he offered urbane descriptions which he expected the reader immediately to recognize as true to type. Having

[28] P. D. M. [M. Patterson], *op. cit.,* pp. 338, 347–374, 395, 18.
[29] R. Parsons, *A Treatise tending to mitigation,* p. 31.
[30] Chapman, *Jesuitisme described,* p. 21.
[31] *Ibid.,* p. 23.
[32] Morton, *A Full Satisfaction concerning a double Romish iniquitie,* p. 1.
[33] Reeve, *The Churches Hazard,* p. 16.
[34] J. White, *A Defence of the Way,* p. 15.

portrayed the nominal English Catholic, "we leave him," he concluded, "hatching plots against the state and expecting Spinola." [35]

Under the early Stuarts the position of the English Catholics probably improved. Their relations with the monarchy were usually friendly. Their doctrine of obedience to the king did not get entangled too often with the question of their submission to the pope. Both by temperament and by conviction James I was opposed to persecution. He began his reign by insisting that he would reward loyalty with leniency. Unfortunately, for the first decade royal policy fluctuated unpredictably between conciliation and repression. Circumstances were partly responsible, but James must accept some of the blame for the vicious alternation between laxity and severity. He was repressive enough to embitter the Catholics; he was lenient enough to alarm the Protestants. James was seldom successful in devising a wise policy and applying it consistently. The Catholics did not notice that the same instability was present (though to a less marked degree) in the king's treatment of the Puritans. But factors that did not operate in favor of the Puritans predisposed James to treat the Catholics well. He admired the great Continental powers. He was anxious to come to terms with Spain. He was in favor of the marriage of his son Charles to the Infanta—the "Spanish match" that aroused such widespread popular disapproval. He yielded too willingly to the persuasive influence of the very adroit Spanish ambassador, Count Gondomar. James also respected property, and Catholicism survived among the landowners and under their protection. The recusancy laws were sporadically enforced. Those who could afford to pay were occasionally fined, but seldom to the full measure permitted by the law (never to the point of impoverishment), and in many cases the fines were never paid. In 1621 the officer responsible for collecting such fines was a "Church" Catholic—one who fulfilled legal requirements by occasional conformity —and his wife was an avowed and ardent Catholic. The Protestant gentry who were locally responsible for enforcing the law did not wish to penalize their neighbors the Catholic squires, and in districts where the old faith was strong the persecuting laws were often in abeyance.

However, the fact that James was friendly to the Catholics worked to their disadvantage in some respects. In the constitutional struggles of the period, Protestant fears added momentum to the rising parliamentary demand for a more effective role in government. Religious issues had a prominent place among the grievances of which parliament complained. In 1610 the House of Commons petitioned the king to enforce "without dread or delay" the "good and provident laws which have been made for the maintenance of God's true religion and safety of your Majesty's royal person, issue and estate, against Jesuits, seminary priests and popish

---

[35] Earle, *Micro-cosmographie*, 11. (Spinola was the commander of Spanish forces in the Low Countries.)

recusants." Yet, they added, these "laws are not executed against the priests, who are the corrupters of the people in religion and loyalty." [36] Eleven years later, it was apparent that Englishmen were increasingly disturbed about James's ineffective foreign policy; the disastrous course of the Thirty Years' War seemed to confirm their most pessimistic apprehensions as to what would happen if the Protestants on the Continent were abandoned to their fate, while at home the Catholics were encouraged. On 3 December 1621 the House of Commons reminded the king that foreign princes had taken advantage of his good will to promote their interests and to endanger his. As a result, the Catholics had taken "encouragement, and are dangerously increased in their number and in their insolencies." Under fourteen headings the Petition of the House enumerated the signs of Romish revival, and concluded the list by pointing to "the swarms of priests and Jesuits, the common incendiaries of all Christendom, dispersed in all parts of your kingdom." [37] The House then proposed a comprehensive program for checking the spread of this corrupting influence. The king was furious. Like Queen Elizabeth, the early Stuarts regarded church policy as an area where the royal prerogative must not be infringed by parliamentary interference. James sharply rebuked "the fiery and popular spirits of some of the House of Commons" who ventured "to argue and debate publicly of matters far above their reach and capacity, tending to our high dishonour and breach of prerogative royal." [38] For the moment, the nervous Protestants in parliament gained nothing from this encounter, nor in the long run did the Catholics.

Anne of Denmark, James's wife, was a crypto-Catholic. Henrietta Maria, the wife of Charles I, was an avowed Catholic, with certain religious privileges guaranteed to her by treaty. The terms of the marriage settlement were negotiated by the Duke of Buckingham. Though originally the religious clauses were secret, they soon became known. They certainly did nothing to improve relations between Charles and his parliaments, and they probably did more harm than good so far as the Catholics were concerned. By treaty Charles was committed to tolerate Roman Catholics in the country and to admit Catholic priests as members of Henrietta Maria's household. In due course anxious Protestants saw the queen's chapel thronged with English worshipers. They noticed that Catholic priests were moving about the country without restraint. They suspected that Catholic sympathizers—for so they considered Laud, Montagu, Cosin, Neile—had gained the king's favor and were replacing true Protestants in the positions of greatest influence in the Church of England. The court was never typical of the country, and as the reign of

[36] Prothero, *Statutes and Other Constitutional Documents*, p. 300.
[37] *Ibid.*, pp. 307–308.
[38] *Ibid.*, p. 310.

Charles progressed it probably became less so, but it was always conspicuously in the public eye. The favor shown to Catholics could not pass unobserved. Charles himself was deeply committed to the Anglican Church, but he was increasingly dependent on the queen, and Henrietta was not a wise woman. She did nothing to restrain the exuberance of the court Catholics. She and her circle had a very superficial understanding of Catholic evangelism, but they secured conversions. In high circles there was an unmistakable rise in defections to Rome. Charles did not improve matters by admitting to positions of prime responsibility men whose Catholic sympathies were undisguised.[39] Moreover, he encouraged his wife to send an agent to the court of Rome, and permitted her to receive a papal emissary in return. He was favorably impressed by Father Gregorio Panzani, whom the pope had sent to moderate differences among the English Catholics, and who became a very popular figure at Charles's court. Bishop Montagu assured him that most of the Anglican clergy hoped to see a reconciliation with Rome along Gallican lines, and added that their apparent repugnance to popery was merely intended to mislead the public. Panzani was skeptical; how was it, he asked, that there were still so many bishops with Puritan sympathies?[40] Panzani prepared the way for Father George Con, a most agreeable and accomplished emissary accredited to Henrietta Maria's court. Leander Jones, head of the English Benedictines, was given an official reception by the university of Oxford, and he assured his hosts that the relations between the churches could be greatly improved. Franciscus a Santa Clara, a Franciscan chaplain to Henrietta Maria, argued that the articles of the Church of England could easily be reconciled with the doctrines of the Church of Rome, and he supported his contention with references to the works of Andrewes, Montagu, and Francis White.[41] Of this group of able and ingratiating men, Panzani was perhaps the most interesting; his letters provide a revealing glimpse of the world of frivolous unreality in which the queen lived. Even the servants of the king were often astonishingly unaware of the mood of the country, while Charles himself was cordial to the Catholics in a slightly remote but highly injudicious way.[42] These charming agents of the pope probably increased in court circles the popularity and the prestige of the Church of Rome; but it is doubtful whether they were an asset to the English Catholic community. Laud fumed to Wentworth about the damage the queen's entourage did the royal cause, but even he failed to appreciate the bitterness that was

[39] E.g., Weston, the lord treasurer, Cottingham, Windbank.

[40] Letter of Panzani to Cardinal Barberini, 11/21 May 1636, quoted by George Albion, *Charles I and the Court of Rome*, p. 185.

[41] Franciscus a Santa Clara, *Paraphrastica Expositio Articulorum Confessionis Anglicanae* (1634). Before his conversion to Rome, his name was Christopher Davenport; he was a brother to John Davenport, founder of New Haven, Connecticut.

[42] Cf. Albion, *op. cit., passim.*

building up among the king's Protestant subjects. The grievances, already reaching explosive proportions, were of many kinds; all of them acquired an added intensity when associated with what many people regarded as the Romanizing policies of the king and his court.

Actually Charles should have been forewarned. His favor to the court Catholics was most pronounced during his eleven years of nonparliamentary government. He chose to forget the long and bitter "Resolutions on Religion Drawn by a Sub-Committee of the House of Commons" (24 Feb. 1628/29), with their recurrent complaints about his leniency toward papists.[43] In his indignation at the "Protestation of the House of Commons" (passed while the Speaker was held in his chair to prevent him from adjourning the House), he may have overlooked the first grievance of the members: "Whosoever shall bring in innovation of religion, or by favour or countenance seek to extend or introduce Popery or Arminianism, . . . shall be reputed a capital enemy to this kingdom and commonwealth." [44] But Charles should not have been surprised by the tenor of John Pym's great speech when the king was finally compelled to summon parliament in April, 1640. Having detailed "the grievances against the privileges and liberties of Parliament," Pym turned to "those that concern matters of religion"; "wherein," he continued, "I will first observe the great encouragement which is given to them of the Popish religion by a universal suspension of all laws that are against them, and some of them admitted into public places of trust and power." [45] In the minds of his people, Charles had identified royal policy with favor toward the Catholics. In the coming months the Catholics responded by proving that the accusations of disloyalty formerly leveled against them were now wholly groundless; during the Civil War they were royalist to a man. As we have noted more than once, it might be argued that the identification of the king's interests with those of the Catholics proved of little benefit to either party. Because religious considerations so deeply colored all political judgments, Charles's leniency toward the Catholics deepened his subjects' suspicions about all the other aspects of his policy. As far as the Catholics were concerned, they had suffered in the early years of the century because of doubts about their genuine submission to royal authority; in the middle decades of the century they were penalized because they accepted it so fully.

II

The English Catholics were a minority. They were exposed to constant and often subtle pressures. This situation, one might have thought, would

[43] Gardiner (ed.), *Constitutional Documents of the Puritan Revolution*, pp. 77–82.
[44] *Ibid.*, pp. 82–83.
[45] Kenyon, *The Stuart Constitution, 1603–1688*, pp. 198–199.

have fostered unity and banished domestic feuds. The opposite was true. Seldom has a religious body been so riven by dissension, and most of the disputes concerned authority. No Catholic denied that in matters of faith ultimate authority resided in the pope, but there was much disagreement about its precise scope (as the Oath of Allegiance showed) and a great deal of fierce debate concerning the exercise of such authority in England. Many factors combined to explain this unhappy and contentious phase of Catholic life. The natural leaders of the community had fled abroad; with the passage of time they had lost touch with English life and were sometimes betrayed into lamentable lapses of judgment.[46] It was easy to become irritable and discouraged. Cardinal Allen, for so long the wisest and ablest leader of the English Catholics, once spoke of "this exile, which of itself breeds murmurings, complainings, contradictions and discontent." [47] Morale inevitably suffered. Conditions favored contention; a combination of circumstances produced it.

Natural allies were converted into bitter foes. The secular clergy and the members of the religious orders were drawn into a struggle that affected English Catholicism until the nineteenth century. Most of the disputes were aggravated by the peculiar bitterness that the activities of the Jesuits so often engendered. The Benedictines, usually on the fringe of the battle, were involved in an early and interesting example of this kind of struggle. A skirmish about the administration of the English college at Valladolid, Spain, spread to Douai and raised serious questions about the college that had done so much to man the English mission.[48] The college in Rome was also the center of prolonged and bitter controversy. The seculars claimed that the Jesuits had seized control of it by most perfidious machinations. England, however, was the battlefield on which the almost continuous struggle between the Jesuits and the seculars was chiefly fought. The feud first erupted in "the Wisbech stirs." The government had converted Wisbech Castle into a detention center for captured priests, and pointed with some pride to the honorable treatment accorded its prisoners. Father Parsons admitted that when Father Weston, the head of the Jesuit mission in England, was imprisoned at Wisbech, he "did more good than when he was free. . . . [He was] the most esteemed and consulted man in England." But even honorable detention became irksome. The morale of the prisoners declined. Father Weston concluded that they were suffering from too slack a regimen. Only a return to a disciplined corporate life would rectify matters. Accordingly, he refused to participate in any community activities unless a strict rule of life were adopted. Latent tensions immediately erupted into an open split. A majority of the prisoners sided with Weston. The remainder followed a

---

[46] Note how often a brilliant man like Fr. Parsons misjudged the English situation.
[47] Letter to Fr. Agazzani, S.J., *Letters and Memorials of Cardinal Allen* (ed. T. F. Knox), p. 136.
[48] *The Letters of Thomas Fitzherbert*, p. 26n.

distinguished secular priest named Dr. Christopher Bagshaw. His opponents dismissed him as a difficult and unreasonable man. Certainly he
showed himself an unflagging opponent of the Jesuits, and this doubtless
explains much that happened at Wisbech.[49] In Weston's proposed
reforms, the seculars detected an implied slur on their moral standards and
their way of life. It is true that when Father Garnet, a leading Jesuit,
wrote at length to Bagshaw, his letter in no way suggested that the
recipient was either living a careless life himself or was encouraging other
priests to do so.[50] Thanks to the intervention of respected leaders on both
sides, the differences were composed. But the scars left by these wounds
could not quickly be erased. Both then and since, the merits of the dispute
have been carefully canvassed. The ascertainable facts hardly explain the
peculiar venom that marked "the Wisbech stirs." Obviously other factors
were also involved.[51]

The bitterness of the struggle was due in part to the unrivaled ability of
the Jesuits to awaken hatred and distrust. The reaction that they aroused
was certainly not limited to England, and it was perhaps due as much to
their magnificent qualities and their unparalleled success as to certain less
admirable attributes or more questionable policies. The seculars claimed
that initially they had welcomed the Jesuits to England, and that their
hospitality had been grievously abused.[52] The Jesuits boasted, wrote
Father William Watson, that no one could "equal them in any degree of
perfection," whereas any dispassionate observer could see "what foul,
loathsome and fearful vices are amongst them." Their faults were simply
"pharisaically overshadowed with a pretence of religious zeal." [53] Consider, he added, how grievously the Jesuits had complicated the position of
the English Catholics. Their incursions into politics had had disastrous
consequences. Their doctrine of equivocation ("which you may term in
plain English lying and cogging") had made even the solemn oaths of
Catholics worthless. The Jesuits seemed to believe, he continued, that

[49] Cf. R. Persons [Parsons], *Notes concerning the English Mission* (Catholic Record Society, Vol.
IV), pp. 116–119. Cf. also the charge (*The Wisbech Stirs*, p. xv) that the aim of some of the
seculars was to exclude the Jesuits from the English mission.

[50] *The Wisbech Stirs*, Letter III, pp. 14–18. Garnet's letter is given in Dodd, *Church History of
England* (ed. Tierney), III, App. civ–cxiv. (This work will be referred to as Dodd-Tierney.)

[51] One of the earliest accounts was *The True Relation of the Faction begun in Wisbech* (1601). It
set forth the secular case and has strongly influenced all subsequent accounts.

[52] Early in the seventeenth century, Thomas James, writing from "the Public Library,
Oxford," issued an anthology of the accusations leveled by the seculars against the Jesuits.
Some of the charges (e.g., interference in politics, a dangerously flexible morality) are not
distinctive of the English struggle, but it was also claimed that the Jesuits suspended the
seculars from their faculties, debarred them from the altar, prevented them from preaching,
deflected from them the gifts of the faithful. Cf. T. James, *The Jesuits downefall*, Props. 43–50.
In Parr's *The Life of James Usher* there are interesting letters from James to Ussher about his
book and about the Roman Controversy, pp. 303–318.

[53] W. Watson, *A Sparing Discoverie*, Ep. to the Reader. Watson, it should be noticed, was
one of the most violent and relentless of the secular enemies of the Jesuits.

nothing was done well unless they did it; consequently, they thrust themselves into every situation and in the process aggravated all resentments. They wormed their way into the houses of the powerful. They entrapped the sons of the rich. They professed to seek only the good of the church, "yet their chiefest care is how to advance their own society." [54]

Even detached observers were drawn into the vortex of this unhappy quarrel. Humphrey Ely, a distinguished Catholic exile, protested that he had never been interested in this kind of controversy, nor was he involved with either side. But he had read Father Parsons' *A Briefe Apologie or Defence of the Catholicke Ecclesiastical Hierarchie,* and had been "much moved at that not only unchristianlike but uncivil and barbarous behaviour." [55] Both sides, he suggested, were at fault. The seculars might be excused for writing in their own defense, but they did not need to descend to the kind of abuse they had employed. The Jesuits had been meddling with matters that are no concern of theirs: "what have they to do with the affairs, associations and contentions of secular priests?" [56] In addition, observed Ely, certain specific grievances were involved. The Jesuits had attempted to arrogate to themselves the control of all the English colleges and seminaries abroad, and they had been none too nice in the methods they had used.[57] The seculars were clearly smarting under what they regarded as the arrogant pretensions of the Jesuits. They resented the Jesuits' claim that all conversions effected in England should be credited to their efforts. Parsons, when discussing the dissensions at the English College in Rome, had reputedly announced that "you know what you have best to do; but if you mean to do any good for our country you must unite with the Jesuits; for the common cause hereafter is like to lie altogether with them." [58] Fathers Garnet and Weston frankly said "that they saw no reason why the Jesuits in England should not as well rule us all here as the Jesuits in Rome did rule the English seminary in Rome." [59] The commonest charge brought against the Jesuits was their utter lack of charity. This, it was argued, must account for many of their actions; it could be the only explanation for the torrent of abuse that disfigured Parsons' polemical works.[60] To mitigate this spirit was the aim of the message that the archpriest Birkhead wrote to the Jesuits from his deathbed. If charity does not guide their efforts, their work will be fruitless. The seculars, he

[54] *Ibid.,* pp. 2–3, 5, 10, 12–13, 15–16, 21–27. Cf. also W. Watson, *Important Considerations,* a vehement attack on the treasonable and subversive political activities of the Jesuits.

[55] Humphrey Ely, *Certaine Briefe Notes upon a Briefe Apologie,* Preface.

[56] *Ibid.,* Ep. of the Author.

[57] *Ibid.,* pp. 72–80, 82–90, 208–212.

[58] Letter of J. Bennet to H. Griffin, Dodd-Tierney, III, lxxxi.

[59] Andreas Philathes, *An Answer made by one of our brethren a secular priest,* n.p.

[60] Ely, *op. cit.,* pp. 155–156, 189–201, 298. Cf. Parsons, *A Manifestation of the Great Folly and Bad Spirit of certayne . . . calling themselves secular priestes.*

believed, were ready to give the Jesuits the kind of cooperation demanded by a successful missionary effort. "They only desire that in their government you meddle no further than they do in yours. . . . This being done, there will be no occasion but that you will friendly and charitably set forward this great work you have undertaken." [61]

The tension between the Jesuits and the seculars had flared into open contention over the "Wisbech stirs." It was further aggravated by the archpriest controversy. The question at issue concerned the way in which ecclesiastical authority should be exercised in England. In 1585 the hierarchy of the English Catholic Church became extinct. Nine years later, the death of Cardinal Allen removed the most respected of the English leaders. By 1598 it became clear that disorders within English Catholicism demanded the presence of someone capable of speaking with authority. The problems that principally required solution all arose in some degree from the friction between Jesuits and seculars. It was not a good omen for peace, therefore, when Cardinal Cajetan, the protector of the English mission, appointed as archpriest George Blackwell, an admitted partisan of the Jesuits. The seculars had hoped for a bishop. They had not been consulted in any way. They detected the hand of Parsons both in Blackwell's nomination and in the stipulation that on all crucial issues he must consult the head of the Jesuits in England. The seculars challenged a major appointment announced by neither bull nor brief, and sent two of their respected leaders to Rome to present their grievances. The "appellants" were seized by Parsons and treated with a violence that boded ill for the future. Their trial before two cardinals was hardly a model of impartiality, and they were disgraced and forbidden to return to England.[62] At home, Father Lister, S.J., had published a vehement attack on the seculars, and when a brief reached England confirming the archpriest, Blackwell felt justified in attacking his opponents. He pronounced them guilty of schism, and demanded that they make suitable acknowledgment of and reparation for their sin. The seculars refused. Blackwell tried to increase his pressure. The seculars both defended their position and submitted it to the judgment of the university of Paris. The university ruled in their favor. The seculars addressed a further appeal to Rome, and sent a deputation of four to support it. In this enterprise every assistance was extended by the English authorities. Bishop Bancroft of London recognized the potentialities latent in this widening division among the Catholics; he mastered the details of the controversy and made certain that the government helped the seculars in every possible way.[63]

[61] Letter of George Birkhead, Dodd-Tierney, V, clxi.

[62] The secular version of this was set forth by Colleton, *A Just Defence of the slandered priestes,* pp. 32, 57, 85–86, 238, 292.

[63] In *The Archpriest Controversy,* I, 226–238, there is an excellent summary of the controversy, evidently by Bancroft. Among many Protestant references to the internecine Catholic feuds,

While a verdict was pending in Rome, the seculars continued both to justify their stand and to attack the Jesuits. The Jesuits replied in kind, and early in 1602 Parsons published his *Briefe Apologie,* a fierce attack on the seculars. Blackwell immediately released a papal Brief forbidding all further debate; but since he had withheld it for four months (to allow Parsons' book to appear, said his critics) it was ineffective from the outset.[64] At last Rome rendered judgment on the seculars' appeal. It did not meet their request that political writing be forbidden (this was attributed to the Spanish ambassador's intervention) and it forbade Catholics to communicate with heretics to the prejudice of Catholics. It refused to brand either side with heresy. It imposed silence on both parties to the controversy, but at certain important points it met the seculars' demands. "For the sake of peace" the archpriest was forbidden to consult the Jesuits either in England or in Rome, and he was instructed to select some of his assistants from among the appellants.

The archpriest occupied an uncomfortable position. He was expected to perform many of the functions of a bishop, but he was denied episcopal authority.[65] He was exposed to attack from within the Catholic community and to government pressure from without. We have seen that when the Oath of Allegiance was passed, Blackwell encouraged the English Catholics to take it. The authorities, however, intercepted his correspondence with Bellarmine. In trying to convince the cardinal that his ruling could be justified on Catholic principles, he left himself open to the charge of knowingly interpreting the oath in a sense very different from that intended by the government. For this, they reminded him, he had no excuse; they had carefully explained the scope of the oath to him before he had advised the faithful to take it. They could not accept the present situation; it was not clear what "the Roman Catholics in England would do if the pope should de facto proceed with his Majesty as some of his predecessors did with the late queen of worthy memory, which uncertainty the state may not endure." [66] Blackwell was ground between the upper and the lower millstones, between the demands of the pope and the cardinal on the one hand and the pressures of the government and the implications of his own previous statements on the other. The authorities subjected him to a grueling cross-examination. They pressed him without mercy, and finally extracted from him a further letter to his people, explaining in meticulous detail the nature and purpose of the oath.[67] His

---

see Sutcliffe, *The subversion of Robert Parsons, his . . . worke,* Ep. Ded.; Bell, *The Downefall of Poperie,* Ep. Ded., and *The Popes Funerall, passim;* L. O. [Owen], *Speculum Jesuiticum.*

[64] Cf. Ely, *op. cit.,* pp. 6, 9, 136, 150; [J. Bennet], *The Hope of Peace,* p. 14.

[65] Ely, *op. cit.,* p. 169.

[66] *A Large Examination taken at Lambeth . . . of Mr George Blackwell,* p. 13. At the beginning of the volume there is an affidavit, signed by Blackwell, that the record faithfully represents the examination.

[67] *Ibid.,* pp. 145–170.

ecclesiastical superiors had no pity on him either, and in 1608 he was deposed from his office.

Blackwell was succeeded by George Birkhead, and he in turn by William Harrison. The pattern of rule by archpriests seemed to be firmly established, but many English Catholics were dissatisfied with this solution of their problems. They felt it strange that a church which ostensibly set such store by the apostolic ministry should, year after year, be deprived of episcopal oversight. Did not this incongruity invalidate many of its claims? The question was incessantly debated.[68] The lack of unity, the legacy of the archpriest controversy, was cited both to prove the need of a bishop and to show that it was inopportune to appoint one. Dr. Bavant, one of the archpriest's assistants, opposed the appointment of a bishop. The English government, he claimed, would take offense and would intensify pressure on the Catholics; under existing circumstances the dignity of the office would inevitably suffer; by stimulating the ambition of some clerics, it would poison the atmosphere of the mission.[69] Father Parsons, however, supported the plan to give the English Catholics a bishop, but at the time he assumed that a Jesuit would be appointed. When it appeared that a secular might be chosen, the regulars united to oppose the idea. In 1623 the Holy See appointed William Bishop as vicar apostolic with the titular dignity of bishop of Chalcedon. Bishop was a secular, one of the appellants who had been so roughly treated by Parsons in Rome. He died the following year, and Richard Smith was chosen to fill the vacant position. This inaugurated a period of acute turmoil. The turbulence endemic for so long among the Catholics became even more pronounced. Bitter conflict raged through a series of appeals and pamphlets, sustained by ceaseless recrimination on both sides. Smith demanded that the regular clergy secure authorization from him before exercising a pastoral ministry in England. They refused. The controversy was envenomed; at times, and on both sides, it was unscrupulous. Typical of this internecine warfare was an exchange between Dr. Kellison, of the Douai College, and John Floyd, the Jesuit. Kellison appealed to the regulars to accept Smith, and to treat him with the respect a bishop should receive from his flock. In addition, he contrasted the benefits of episcopal oversight with the drawbacks of the archpriests' rule. He claimed that a Catholic church bereft of bishops was an intolerable anomaly, a continual violation of the divine law, a grievous departure from the pattern of the early church.[70] Floyd denounced Kellison for mounting an attack on "that form of government which the Holy See thought most fit for us during persecution." [71] It was outrageous of Kellison to urge English

[68] *Letters of Thomas Fitzherbert*, pp. 14–15.

[69] *Ibid.*, pp. 75–76.

[70] Kellison, *A treatise of ecclesiastical hierarchy, passim.*

[71] Floyd, *An Apology of the Holy See apostolicks Proceeding*, Preface; cf. pp. 262–263. For a work very similar to Floyd's both in outline and in arguments, see Nicholas Smith, *A Modest Briefe*

Catholics to accept the bishop of Chalcedon "as their bishop, their spiritual king and prince of pastors." This was not what the pope intended. A bishop was superfluous, since episcopal functions could well be reserved to the Holy See, "without any other particular bishop." [72] Kellison had argued that confirmation was a part of the Catholic system of nurture, and that Catholics should not indefinitely be deprived of it. But Floyd retorted that Kellison exaggerated its importance; the faithful could survive perfectly well without it.[73] A particular church could exist quite satisfactorily without a bishop, especially if it were adequately supplied with members of the religious orders. The apostles were regulars; therefore regulars surely participate in the apostolic character. Floyd didn't explicitly claim that regulars can deputize for bishops, but he clearly gave them a place in the hierarchy distinctly above the secular clergy.[74] Much of this controversy strikes the reader as bordering on civil war. There is the same bitterness and intolerance. There is the same tendency to forget that possibly there are other enemies and consequently other dangers. Richard Smith may not have been a perfect bishop or even a particularly wise man, but the Catholic Church surely suffered more than it gained when in 1631 a combination of hostile forces drove him from the country.

III

The Catholic community in England led a precarious and troubled life. It was threatened by persecution from without. Within it was torn by strife. It was denied the blessings of both unity and peace. But beneath the agitated surface there ran a persistent and refreshing strain of mysticism. The sixteenth century had witnessed a revival of a tradition that had been temporarily obscured in much of western Europe. In the fourteenth century there had been a vigorous school of mystics in England. A little later there was a comparable flowering of mysticism in the Low Countries and the Rhineland. Eventually it spread to Italy and Spain. But both the Reformation and the Counter-Reformation demanded a different kind of devotion, more closely related to doctrine, better adapted to teaching, more explicitly bound to moral achievement. In Catholic circles the Jesuit type of spiritual nurture eclipsed other traditions, and the

---

Discussion of some points taught by M. Doctour Kellison in his treatise of the Ecclesiasticall Hierarchy. The similarity is not surprising; "Nicholas Smith" was one of Floyd's pseudonyms.

[72] Floyd, *An Apology,* Preface.

[73] *Ibid.,* pp. 69–76.

[74] *Ibid.,* pp. 77 ff., 132 ff., 303 ff. The argument about the relative place of the regulars was continued in A. B., *A Defence of Nicholas Smith against a reply to his discussion of some pointes taught by Mr Doctour Kellison.* The Jesuits procured a Breve, *Britannia,* which declared that as the regulars had apostolic authority, the leave or approbation of the ordinary "neither was nor is hereafter needful unto them." Dodd-Tierney, III, 160.

forward surge of a reawakened Catholicism carried Ignatian patterns into many parts of Europe. But the mystical strain persisted. Spain witnessed a powerful renascence of the contemplative life, and many of the greatest names in devotional literature are associated with this amazing outburst of mysticism. From Spain its influence spread to France; eventually it reached the colonies of English exiles in the Low Countries. A type of devotion developed that had clear affinities with the fourteenth-century English school of mystics and yet was enriched by the influence of the great Spaniards. The monastic communities provided the context within which this devotional life could flourish. In the late sixteenth and early seventeenth centuries there was a significant revival of the religious orders in English Catholicism, and the houses that were established in the Low Countries fostered the efflorescence of mystical literature.

One of the earliest products of this renascence was Benet Canfield's *The Rule of Perfection*.[75] The pattern of the work was novel, but its sources were clearly traditional. The perfect life, Canfield believed, consists in achieving conformity with the will of God. This seems neither original nor impressive. Every theologian agrees that sin is the transgression of God's will, while submission to that will is the true goal of human life. Canfield was concerned to elaborate a subtle and sophisticated form of voluntarism. The problem, as he saw it, is how man is to achieve that identification of the two wills (the divine and the human) which religious writers so readily agree is necessary. He began by identifying three distinct aspects of the will of God. There is the external will, made known in revelation and operative in the hierarchy and in the discipline of the church. In his active life the Christian achieves conformity with this will. In the second place there is the interior will; we know it through the graces, motions, illumination with which God enriches the soul, and in embarking upon the life of contemplation the Christian submits to this will. Finally there is the essential will of God, indistinguishable from the divine essence, and consequently identical with God himself. To achieve perfect conformity with this will is to be united to God, to be transformed into him, and to become deiform in nature.[76] Canfield admitted that the distinctions that he draws are pedagogic, not essential; they assist the learner, they do not define the nature of God. In describing the stages of spiritual growth, Canfield also provided a means by which the growth of the soul could be studied. The first phase is mortification. It consists solely in inner conformity to the will of God, and without it there can be no progress in the spiritual life. This opens the way for the mystical experiences that lead the soul into more and more complete identification with the divine. The

---

[75] Published in Rouen in 1609, but written earlier. Canfield (William Fitch before his conversion) was a Capuchin.

[76] *The Rule of Perfection* is divided into three parts, each devoted to one aspect of the divine will and to our means of submitting to it.

supereminent life to which we aspire cannot be attained by the customary forms of human endeavor. Imaginative and discursive meditation are useful only as initial steps in a pilgrimage that carries us far beyond reliance on our own powers. Our goal is a kind of experience that cannot be achieved by dialectical reasoning or indeed by any rational means. We do not reach God by our understanding; God's will must transform our wills by absorbing them into itself. The seeker takes the first step, but the divine initiative accomplishes what the human will can never achieve. The soul loses its life to find it. The deiformity at which it finally arrives is a life marked by simplicity, continuity, fusion with the divine and therefore depersonalization of the self. At this point the mystic experiences complete freedom of action, because what he does is the act of God, who now entirely possesses him.

Canfield's work was popular and influential. In certain circles it was carefully studied, and it did much to foster a certain kind of mystical life. But a much more significant figure was Father Augustine Baker, O.S.B. He was converted to Catholicism in 1603. He died, when on the point of returning to the English Mission, in 1641. He served his novitiate as a Benedictine in Padua, then returned to England to act as a chaplain in country houses. At one time, when living in London, he practiced as a solicitor (though this was a profession barred by law to Catholics). Subsequently, while working on Benedictine origins, he was on familiar terms with Camden, Selden, and Cotton, the great antiquaries of the age. These facts indicate the extent to which the penal laws were often allowed to lapse. They also provide an illuminating insight into his own religious history. Baker spoke of three conversions that he had experienced. The first was his reconciliation to Rome. The second occurred five or six years later, and was followed by a period of pronounced aridity. He was oppressed with anxiety. Prayer seemed so devoid of meaning that he gave it up. At this time he returned to the practice of law. But during a chaplaincy in a remote part of Devon, he resumed a life of strict meditation and prayer—his third conversion. He spent his happiest and most fruitful period as an auxiliary confessor to an English Benedictine nunnery that had been recently founded at Cambrai. Much of his finest work was prepared for the nuns. He saturated himself in the English mystics of the fourteenth century and wrote a commentary on *The Cloud of the Unknowing,* one of the major works of that period.[77] Unfortunately, trouble developed. He differed sharply with one of his colleagues about methods of spiritual discipline and about his own doctrine of "inspirations." He was transferred to Douai, and again difficulties beset him. He quarreled with his prior, Father Barlow, who arranged to have Baker sent

---

[77] Augustine Baker, *Secretum sive mysticum.* This contains a spiritual biography which extends as far as 1629. Pt. I has been published by Dom J. McCann as *The Confessions of Venerable Father Augustine Baker, O.S.B.*

back to the English Mission. This had all the marks of a vindictive assignment. Baker was old and ill, and he died before he could take up his new position.[78] Baker was a very great man in many ways; possibly he was a difficult one as well. The closing years of his life illustrate only too clearly the strangely envenomed atmosphere that so often pervaded the English Catholic community.

Baker produced a vast collection of miscellaneous writings on a wide variety of religious subjects. Some of his material was prolix and formless, quite unfit for publication in the form in which he left it. From this rich but chaotic source, Father Serenus Cressy (before his conversion Lord Falkland's chaplain) edited *Sancta Sophia: or Holy Wisdom*. This is the most important devotional work produced by the English Catholics during this period. As Dom David Knowles has pointed out, it is the only work in English that gives magisterial guidance over a great part of the spiritual life. Baker's contribution suffers only when compared with that of the very greatest mystics.[79] The materials out of which *Holy Wisdom* was assembled were prepared as a guide for those engaged in what Baker calls the "monastical contemplative life." It is true that he had limited experience of that life. It is also true that he lacked specific theological training. His resources were the insights of others. He was deeply versed in the writings of various schools of religious life and thought. He borrowed widely and judiciously, but he never quite succeeded in fusing what he owed to others into a completely integrated system of his own. *Holy Wisdom* is partly a treatise on ascetic and mystical theology. As its subtitle announces, it also provides "directions for the prayer of contemplation."

The work consists of three "treatises." The first deals with "a contemplative life in general." Baker begins with the assumption that "continual union in spirit with God is the end of man's creation."[80] Devotion, a natural response on the part of man, may be active or contemplative. The latter is both more perfect and more simple; it leads to a higher type of life and issues in a more divine union with God. But a strong resolution is needed at the outset, and courage to persevere is required throughout our pilgrimage. For such a life a guide is necessary, and "divine inspirations . . . are to be our light in internal ways."[81] At the beginning, however, an external director is also required, and the book describes in detail the nature of his task and the methods he ought to use. For progress beyond the elementary stages "supernatural illumination" is necessary, and Baker indicates precisely how it can be appropriated. Only within the religious life (technically defined) may such graces be expected, and "the school of contemplation" is delineated with care.[82]

[78] Cf. *Memorials of Father Augustine Baker* (ed. J. McCann and H. Connolly), *passim*.
[79] D. Knowles, *The English Mystical Tradition*, p. 150.
[80] Baker, *Holy Wisdom*, p. 29.
[81] *Ibid.*, p. 71.
[82] *Ibid.*, pp. 134–192.

The second "treatise" deals with "the first instrument of perfection, viz. mortification." All the duties of the contemplative life can be reduced to two: mortification and prayer. Each promotes the other; of the two, prayer is the nobler. Some mortifications are necessary; others are voluntary. Some are general—solitude, silence, abstraction of life, and tranquillity of mind; some concern the senses, the mind, the affections.[83] The survey covers a wide range of experience and dwells with particular care on the problem of scrupulosity.[84]

The final "treatise" is devoted to prayer. There are a few preliminary comments on the value of prayer in general, followed by a discussion of "internal affective prayer" and the conditions governing its successful practice, but Baker is primarily concerned with mental prayer. He emphasizes its necessity and defines its stages. Meditation is the first and most elementary type of mental prayer, the place where the novice ought to begin.[85] From this he passes to "the second degree of internal prayer": "the exercises of immediate forced acts." By these Baker means "affections and aspirations," and he sharply distinguishes them from acts of the will.[86] The third stage is contemplation, and with his usual exactitude Baker distinguishes between the various aspects of the exercise and shows how the soul can advance step by step toward its goal. "The end of all the precedent exercises, and of all the changes in a spiritual life" is "a stable state of perfection and prayer." [87] The intensely practical nature of the treatise, apparent all along, emerges clearly at the end. Baker was not composing a theoretical dissertation on the inner life; he was writing a guide for people dedicated to a certain type of religious discipline. His book is clear and explicit as well as detailed. It is unusually comprehensive, but its emphasis clearly falls on inner prayer. Baker felt constrained to urge the need of the interior life and to open to those who embraced it the nature of mental and contemplative prayer. He believed that the monastic vocation found its fulfillment in the prayer of the heart and of the will. He began with certain presuppositions which his readers shared; he moved toward a goal that was their objective as well as his. Doubtless the quality of his work can fully be appreciated only by those who apply its teachings as he intended, though any sympathetic reader can discern something of its power and persuasiveness. Here is a kind of authority different from any of those about which so many controversialists raised such angry disputation; and to those who accepted that constraint Baker offered a kind of freedom that many neither sought nor understood.

The Catholic spirit found expression in other ways besides controversy and mystical devotion. It drew much of its sustenance and strength from

[83] *Ibid.,* pp. 206–243.
[84] *Ibid.,* pp. 278–309.
[85] *Ibid.,* pp. 406 ff.
[86] *Ibid.,* pp. 431–437.
[87] *Ibid.,* p. 541.

two types of literature: poetry and popular devotional works. Most English Catholic writers were exclusively engaged in supplying the demand for polemical material; occasionally an English book appeared that afforded a more palatable diet, but on the whole the need for something to sustain the spirit could be met only from abroad.[88] Throughout this period a steady stream of French, Italian, and Spanish devotional writings appeared in English translations. They were printed in one or another of the Continental cities where the exiles congregated, and apparently were smuggled into England in considerable numbers.[89] One example—by no means exceptional—may suffice to indicate the popularity of such works. In 1609 there was published at Rouen a translation from the Italian of Alfonso de Villegas' *Flos sanctorum: the lives of the saints.* The next year another edition appeared in the same city. It was reprinted at Douai in 1615 and 1621, at St. Omer in 1623, with three further editions at short intervals, and again at Rouen in 1636. This, of course, was not the final appearance of the book, but it is needless to pursue its publishing history beyond this period. The work was popular in character and appealed to a simple and unsophisticated piety.

Addressed to a different constituency and probing religious feeling at far greater depths was Robert Southwell's *An Epistle of Comfort.* The author had died for his faith before this period of study opens, but his message to the persecuted continued to circulate. With insight and care, Southwell identified the various sources of comfort and distilled from each the appropriate measure of spiritual reassurance. But more significant than the general pattern are the illustrative details. The work has an unmistakably baroque quality. It is intense in spirit and lush in expression. With great vividness he compares the plight of the heretic to the miseries of a man "that in a hot summer's day is walking in a dry and barren field, and being sore parched with the sun and extreme thirsty, . . . so they that walk in the fruitless field of heresy, in which it is impossible that either the fountain of grace should spring or the arbours of glory grow." [90] How different is the privilege of the true believer, persecuted though he be! "Happy therefore is he that drinketh in the way of the torrent of martyrdom, for he shall lift up his head to an unspeakable crown. Happy is he that is *quasi torris raptus ex incendio,* like a firebrand snatched out of the flames of persecution; because with a most fortunate violence is he carried bright with an enflamed charity to the presence of God." [91]

---

[88] There are exceptions of course: e.g., John Heigham, *A Devout Exposition of the Holie Masse* and *The Life of our Blessed Lord;* E. T. Hill, *A Plain Path-way to Heaven.*

[89] Interest in this kind of contemplative literature was not restricted to Catholics. Donne, we know, had an extensive collection of Spanish religious works, but he was limited, of course, to translations.

[90] Robert Southwell, *An Epistle of Comfort,* pp. 364–365.

[91] *Ibid.,* p. 413.

Southwell's poetry was even more influential than his prose. A relatively direct type of Catholic verse, simple in its structure, poignant in its mood, still persisted in England.

> Hierusalem, my happy home,
>   When shall I come to thee?
> When shall my sorrows have an end
>   Thy joys when shall I see? [92]

But this was not to be the note most characteristic of Jacobean Catholic literature. Like his prose, Southwell's verse has all the baroque exuberance so characteristic of the art and literature of the Counter-Reformation. *Magdalen's Tears* not only incorporated the flamboyant qualities that marked much of the Continental poetry of the day, but it transmitted the pattern to other poets. Southwell was not the only source of this exotic element. Spanish and Italian poets provided luxuriant models that invited imitation. William Crashaw, the ardent Puritan who was preacher at the Temple Church, was deeply shocked at the theology of the Jesuit poet Clarus Bonarscius—at his exaltation of Mary to a position of importance parallel to that of Christ, at his equating the effect of the Virgin's milk with the power of the Savior's blood—and he freely reproduced passages so erotic that it is impossible to quote them.[93]

William Crashaw, the author of one of the fiercest attacks on baroque imagery, was the father of Richard Crashaw, one of the greatest of English baroque poets. Sir Kenelm Digby, in speaking to the pope about Richard, described him as "the learned son of a famous heretic." [94] The younger Crashaw's Catholic sympathies are obviously more than merely a reaction against a Puritan upbringing. In contrast with Donne, he is a baroque poet of a peculiarly un-English character. Here he parts company with Donne and Herbert; they are definitely English, he is unmistakably Continental. He took Mariano as a model, and "Sospetto d'Herode" is basically a translation of one of the Italian's poems. The luxuriance of Mariano was a dangerous influence; it was fortified by the example of various Jesuit poets. Fortunately, the worst dangers of this strain were held in check by the powerful influence of the Spanish mystics. Crashaw's debt to St. John of the Cross was great; to St. Theresa he was drawn by an affinity even more profound. The great Spaniards intensified the mystical strain in his nature. They encouraged him in his ardent self-abandonment to the intensities of religious experience. They provided a model; they inspired a form of literature capable of plunging to emotional extremes in order to give tangible form to its intellectual insights and its spiritual visions. The intensity of Crashaw's feeling was matched by the luxuriance

[92] Anon., quoted in F. P. Wilson, *Elizabethan and Jacobean*, p. 73.
[93] W. Crashaw, *The Jesuites Gospel*, pp. 6–7, 37 ff., 56, 68, 89–90, 105–106.
[94] *The Poems of Richard Crashaw* (ed. L. C. Martin), p. xviii.

of his poetry. He fixed his attention on the physical manifestations of his faith—the wounds of the crucified Christ,[95] the blood and water, the tears of St. Mary Magdalene,[96] the heart of St. Theresa transfixed by love.[97] The erotic strain in Counter-Reformation devotion found a ready response in Crashaw. Self-imposed suffering seemed to him a natural way for the believer to identify himself with the self-offering of the saints. Florid form and ecstatic emotion went naturally together. Lush imagery conveyed the intensity of mystical experience.

> Amorous languishments, luminous trances,
>   Sights which are not seen with eyes,
> Spiritual and soul piercing glances
>   Whose pure and subtle lightning flies
> Home to the heart, and sets the house on fire;
> And melts it down in sweet desire.
>
> . . . .
> Delicious deaths, soft exhalations
> Of soul; dear, and divine annihilations.[98]

English poetry of the period was bold in its use of conceits; its imagery was vivid yet challenged thought. What separates Crashaw from his fellow countrymen is the extravagance with which he multiplies his metaphors, the unpruned luxuriance of his imaginative exploration of the realm of religious emotion. It is a strange irony that the greatest Catholic poet of the century wrote much of his finest material while still a Laudian fellow of Peterhouse, Cambridge. His conversion did not inspire his poetry, it merely confirmed the direction in which he had long been moving. Crashaw had traveled far from the Puritanism of his youth; he had left behind the sober Anglicanism of Andrewes and Laud. His legacy to his new church fortified the prevalent suspicion that much of the piety and devotion of English Catholicism was permeated by a foreign atmosphere. But it also struck with unique intensity the authoritative note that belongs to a certain type of religious experience.

> O thou undaunted daughter of desires!
> By all thy dow'r of lights and fires;
> By all thy lives and deaths of love;
> By thy large draughts of intellectual day,
> And by thy thirsts of love more large than they;
> By all thy brim-fill'd bowls of fierce desire;
> By the last morning's draught of liquid fire;

[95] Cf. "Lo! a mouth whose full bloomed lips / At too dear a rate are roses." From "On the Wounds of our crucified Lord," verse 2, *Steps to the Temple*.

[96] "The Weeper," *Steps to the Temple*.

[97] "A Flaming Heart," *Carmen Deo Nostro*.

[98] R. Crashaw, "On a Prayer Book sent to Mrs. M. R.," *Steps to the Temple*.

By the full kingdom of that final kiss
That seized thy parting soul and seal'd thee his;
By all the heavens thou hast in him
(Fair sister of the Seraphim!)
Leave nothing of myself in me.
Let me so read thy life, that I
Unto all life of mine may die.[99]

[99] R. Crashaw, "The Flaming Heart upon the book and picture of the seraphical Saint Teresa," in *Carmen Deo Nostro*.

VIII

"AFTER THE STRAITEST SECT": THE SEPARATISTS

THE PURITANS demanded further reformation in the church. "The reliques of Rome," they complained, "continue still among us to adulterate the sacred purity of our gospel of peace." [1] When resistance by the government made visible changes difficult to achieve, many of the Puritan leaders turned (as we have seen) to the task of inward reformation. But there were always some impatient spirits who found this method unsatisfactory and the progress that it achieved intolerably slow. In the latter part of Elizabeth's reign the voice of protest had been audibly raised. Robert Browne, who left the Church of England to seek a purer fellowship but returned to it to enjoy the security of its communion, bequeathed a twofold inheritance to the Separatist movement. His name provided a convenient designation; both friend and foe found that "Brownist" was a useful term. He also coined a memorable slogan. His best-known work was *A Treatise of Reformation Without Tarying for Anie* (1582), and impatience with needless delay became the distinguishing mark of the more radical groups. The Separatists proposed to withdraw from spiritual Babylon; they would erect forthwith a church that would correspond to the perfect pattern delineated in the Word of God.

The Separatists were relatively few in number. Many of them were people of humble origin. A contemptuous critic dismissed them as "masons, carpenters, bricklayers, coursers, weavers, stone gravers and what not." "In their persons," he added, "they were of worthless quality"; because of "their low condition and obscurity of living," they "escaped presentment and passed unregarded." [2] Bacon, writing when they seemed to be a spent force, claimed that "they were, at their height, a very small number of silly and base people, here and there in corners dispersed, and now by the good remedies suppressed and worn out so that there is scarce any news of them." [3] Bacon's verdict was much too sweeping. Occasion-

---

[1] Peter Studley, *The Looking-Glasse of Schisme,* p. 187.
[2] *Ibid.,* p. 185.
[3] Bacon, "Observations on a Libel," *Occasional Works,* I, 104–106.

ally the Separatists attracted men of substance. Thomas Helwys, William Brewster, William Bradford belonged to the minor gentry. Their leaders were often men of education. Francis Johnson and John Smyth had been fellows of Christ's. Others as well, had been trained at Cambridge— William Brewster at Peterhouse, Henry Ainsworth at Caius, John Robinson at Corpus. Thomas Helwys, like Bacon himself, was a member of Gray's Inn.

In the spectrum of English religious life one group shaded imperceptibly into the next. The devout conformist was often closely allied in sympathy with the Puritan, still a member of the established church but uneasy about the abuses that he detected in it. He in turn was next of kin to the Puritan who felt the logic of the Separatists' position, but shrank from joining them. After an agonizing assessment of the alternatives, he might draw back and refuse to cast in his lot with the seceders. He might, however, resign his preferment, make his way abroad, and become the minister of a congregation that allowed him greater liberty without committing him to separation. Then, too, he might be drawn to the fellowship of a small company seeking purer ways of worship in England, and, finding the pressures too relentless at home, he and his companions might purchase freedom at the price of exile in Holland. Arthur Hildersam, the highly respected incumbent of Ashby de la Zouch, is a notable example of the concerned Puritan who desired further reformation but was prepared to await it within the Church of England. In the early years of the seventeenth century, his counsel was eagerly sought by men who were troubled about the course of duty. There is little evidence that he ever thought of renouncing the church. Richard Bernard of Worksop agreed with Hildersam in most things, but he was more responsive to the lure of radical courses. He felt the appeal of a religious fellowship free to refashion its life in complete obedience to the precepts of Scripture. He trembled on the brink of separation, but he finally accepted a comfortable living in Somerset and became one of the most vocal critics of those who forsook the national church.

Among the Puritans who left the country but did not abjure the church were men like Richard Parker, William Bradshaw, William Ames, and (in his earlier phase) Henry Jacob.[4] These men were highly critical of the Church of England, but they did not dismiss it as beyond redemption. William Bradshaw was an Independent by conviction and a conformist in practice. He seemed to write on both sides of current disputes, but the explanation is simple. He and Henry Jacob were the pioneers of a Puritan Independency that was not free to refashion outward forms in England but that looked toward a time when the national establishment would be

---

[4] Henry Jacob can in part be classified with this group. From conformist Puritanism he passed to Puritan Independency, and many of his writings reflect this position. By Francis Johnson he was converted to Separatism, and he can be quoted in support of this view also.

purged and reformed in conformity with the pattern which they found in the Bible. Similarly William Ames withdrew to Holland, but he was not a Separatist. He was an exile from England but he debated strenuously with men like Robinson, and the line of cleavage between them was defined by their attitude to participation in the worship of the Church of England. William Ames profoundly affected the theology of the Puritan Independents. He gave to the doctrines first fashioned by John Calvin and subsequently modified by William Perkins the distinctive cast that marked the outlook of those who settled in the colony of Massachusetts Bay. One of the most celebrated statements of this general position—reforming in spirit, Calvinist in theology, Independent in polity, but not Separatist in program—is Francis Higginson's famous exposition of the aims of the departing colonists:

> We will not say, as the Separatists were wont to say at their leaving of England, "Farewell, Babylon!" . . . but . . . "Farewell, the Church of God in England!" . . . We do not go to New England as separatists from the Church of England though we cannot but separate from the corruptions in it. But we go to practise the positive part of church reformation and propagate the Gospel in America.[5]

Those who left the Church of England did not conform to any uniform pattern of belief or practice. Many of them discovered that separation did not fulfill their expectations. Browne returned to the Church of England and died as a rector in Northamptonshire. Henry Barrow's last words suggest that he felt that he had been misguided in the things that he had taught his followers. Peter Fairlambe, the author of *A Recantation of a Brownist*, gave a detailed account of why he returned to the Church of England. Henoch Clapham suffered imprisonment as a Separatist, but recanted and secured preferment in the church. Edmond Jessop explained that "he had gone from one form of religion unto another" till he became an Anabaptist. Even then he found that he was "wandering up and down among the dry hills and mountains, conceiving comfort, when alas I was far from it; and the farther I wandered up and down in that Egyptian darkness, the more intricate labyrinth of error and darkness my soul was plunged into." Of the Anabaptists he spoke, with contempt and yet with pity, as

> this little silly sect . . . , who (poor people) though [Satan] have much possessed their minds with error yet there is some hope that they will be reclaimed, because it appeareth plainly (with some of them) that they are carried [away] through zeal, being

[5] Cotton Mather, *Magnalia Christi Americana,* I, 362.

merely seduced by such as have been longest settled in the deceit.[6]

Among the abler leaders of the Separatists—Francis Johnson, Henry Ainsworth, John Smyth, and John Robinson—we find greater consistency as well as a measure of similarity in their experience. From increasing restlessness within the church they moved to a precarious insecurity outside it; then, after the crisis of flight, they settled down to the life of a small religious minority in a foreign land.

At first sight it might seem that there was much to unite them. They held the same basic beliefs; they had come through similar experiences. They provide convincing proof that nothing divides so bitterly as common convictions held with a difference. It is not surprising that Richard Bernard disputed with the Separatists; he knew the arguments against their position because he had weighed them against an appeal to which he had nearly succumbed. Ames and Bradshaw, too, for all the ties that bound them to the seceders, drew different inferences from the convictions that they shared. What you do not expect is the fierce contentions within and between the little groups that gathered around Johnson and Ainsworth, Robinson and Smyth. Controversy was incessant, "which malady," remarked Robinson, "is also so frequent and ordinary as may truly be said of many, that they then think themselves most acceptable unto God, when they can make their brethren, differing from them in some smaller matters, most odious unto men." [7] If they had not disagreed, of course, we would know comparatively little about their faith and practice. The constant contentions among the Separatists suggest that those who claimed religious freedom had not yet discovered how to reconcile it with any measure of corporate authority.

The congregations of Johnson, Smyth, and Robinson differed on a number of issues, and the letters that they exchanged make this abundantly clear. Johnson's followers were especially prone to internal dissensions. Early in the century, Francis Johnson's brother, George, published *A Discourse of some Troubles and Excommunications in the banished English Church at Amsterdam.* Much of the trouble, he felt, could be traced to the disruptive influence of the minister's wife. Mrs. Johnson dressed in a style that was considered ostentatious and extravagant. Her behavior shocked the congregation and aggravated all the causes of division. So George Johnson drew up a table of offenses: eleven points at which his sister-in-law offended in dress and four respects in which her conduct was unbecoming. Each item was enforced by texts from Scripture and by what George regarded as appropriate comments. What Mrs. Johnson wore or

[6] Edmond Jessop, *A Discovery of the Errors of the English Anabaptists,* Ep. Ded.

[7] Robinson, *Works,* III, 12. Cf. A. T., *A Christian Reprofe against Contention,* To the Christian Reader: "So we have at Amsterdam fought with men of a beastly condition. . . . Who is more ready to carp at the zeal of God's people than loose persons or lukewarm Christians?"

did was "contrary to the former rules of modesty and shamefastness,"
"contrary to modesty and sobriety," "contrary to the former rules in a
pastor's wife," "contrary to the rules of modest behaviour in the daughters
of Zion, and condemned, Isah. 3.16." [8] Friction was almost endemic in the
congregation. Johnson encouraged frank discussion of all important
problems, but the distinction between friendly debate and acrimonious
controversy was often obscured. In 1610 a group led by Henry Ainsworth,
the teacher in the congregation, seceded. This was not a precipitate step;
for at least a year the factions in the congregation had canvassed, in speech
and writing, the points at issue. Discipline and charity were the initial
questions; the ultimate one was the constitution of the church. Some of
the members, it was claimed, had been guilty of scandalous behavior, and
no steps had been taken to purge the congregation of this infection. But
Johnson suspected that malice had inspired the complaints; he believed
that such problems could seldom be wisely handled in a full meeting of the
congregation, and in the interests of a just verdict he had referred the
matter to the elders. Unfortunately, he justified his decision by insisting
that the elders, not the entire membership, constituted the church.
Ainsworth retorted that Johnson was violating the principles on which the
church had been founded, and the upshot was the formation of a new
congregation.

The internal problems of these Separatist groups are admirably
illustrated by the pamphlets of Christopher Lawne. As an aftermath of
the Ainsworth split, and possibly related to it, there arose further
contentions among the Johnsonians about discipline in the congregation.
Lawne and three companions began to have doubts about the principles of
Separatism. Johnson, they claimed, tried to deal with the matter
privately, between the minister and elders on the one hand and the
dissidents on the other. Lawne insisted on a public hearing before the
whole congregation. As soon as the dissenters had expressed their
reservations, Johnson responded with "a furious reply." His congregation,
he claimed, was the culmination of all movements of reform from John
Hus to John Calvin; "they were by the mercy of God the purest church
and the freest from corruptions and set in a more excellent order than any
church he knew this day in the world." [9] Lawne and his friends were
excommunicated; they returned to the Church of England, uttering shrill
denunciations as they went. The discipline in Johnson's church, they
insisted, was detestable. One of the elders was guilty of shocking lewdness,
another of cruelty in dealing with his employees. They boast of their
discipline, complained the critics, but it is distorted by favoritism, and its
result is perpetual disorder.[10] The Separatists pretend to be the elect, but

[8] George Johnson, *A Discourse of some Troubles and Excommunications in the banished English Church at Amsterdam*, pp. 135–137.

[9] Christopher Lawne, *The Prophane Schisme of Brownists or Separatists*, p. 4.

[10] *Ibid.*, p. 157; Lawne, *Brownisme turned the Inside Outward*, pp. 27–32.

their lives invalidate the claim. "But . . . as they are to be seen in this present world, in the city of Amsterdam, they consist of a company and fellowship of irreligious and profane people, gathered together in schism, abusing Christ and all his offices, profaning his worship and ordinances through their contention and bitter envying and wrangling." Their church is "led by the spirit of schism and confusion; . . . with a most frail and villainous pastor, a most simple and piteous teacher, most careless and unright governors, most negligent and untrusty deacons." [11] All this was only one facet of a much wider problem; Lawne pointed to the "mutual reproaches, dissensions and curses" which marked the feuds between Johnson, Ainsworth, and Robinson, and he might have shown, he added, "what bitings there be among the lesser factions and broken pieces of the Separation." [12]

A fragile unity bound together these seekers after freedom, and a single person of stubbornly independent spirit could cause untold trouble. The maneuvers of Sabine Staresmore amply demonstrate this regrettable fact. In London he had joined Henry Jacob's non-Separatist church; when he moved to Holland, he tried to become a member of Ainsworth's congregation on the strength of the covenant he had already taken. But the intent of that covenant was different from the one that united Ainsworth's people, so Staresmore and his sympathizers were ejected. But he was not a man who was easily rebuffed. He regularly attended worship and invariably created a disturbance. In due course he moved to Leyden, joined Robinson's congregation, and when he returned to Amsterdam proposed to transfer his membership to Ainsworth's church. This involved the two bodies in lengthy controversy.[13] Indeed, some of the bitterest disagreements among the Separatists were caused by problems related to the reception into membership of those who tried to move from one congregation to another.[14]

John Robinson was one of the ablest of the Separatist exiles. Like Francis Johnson, he was a man of some learning; like Johnson too, he had the grace to treat his opponents with magnanimity. But he was a much firmer guide than Johnson, and his congregation was never riven by the internal disputes so common among the Separatists. He and his people were engaged in controversy with the followers of Johnson, of Ainsworth, and of Smyth. He also debated theological issues with Bradshaw and Ames.

John Smyth and his followers came to Holland after experiences in England that were closely similar to those of Robinson and his people. When Smyth found Johnson's congregation already organized, it seemed

[11] *Ibid.,* pp. 3, 6.
[12] Lawne, *The Prophane Schisme,* pp. 70 ff., 88. Lawne also emphasized the disagreements within the Johnson family—between Francis and his father and brother, pp. 59–66.
[13] Cf. A. T., *A Christian Reprofe against Contention, passim.*
[14] John Paget, *An Arrow against the Separation of the Brownists,* pp. 1–7.

natural for his group to coalesce with the earlier arrivals. But differences in belief and emphasis soon emerged. Smyth became convinced that his baptism in the Church of England was invalid. He therefore rebaptized first himself, then his people. Characteristically he came to question the wisdom of this step. He should, he concluded, have turned to the Mennonites; their views were akin to his own, and they were a Christian body already in existence. Smyth's convictions were in process of almost continuous evolution.[15] He was a patient and persistent seeker after truth, and he was honest enough publicly to acknowledge both his new insights and his past errors. Few works of that contentious and dogmatic age breathe so conciliatory a spirit as Smyth's *Retractions*.

If it was characteristic of Smyth to change his views, it was typical of his Separatist congregation that it split. Thomas Helwys, Smyth's close friend and associate, concluded that his leader was wrong both in questioning his rebaptism and in seeking closer relations with the Mennonites. He also decided that their flight from England was an act of apostasy. They ought to be witnessing to their fellow countrymen; should the cost be high, they would have to accept suffering as part of their discipleship. So Helwys and his friends returned to London. His *Mistery of Iniquity*, presented to King James with a very outspoken inscription, caused his imprisonment, which apparently resulted in his death. Smyth may justly be considered the spiritual ancestor of modern Baptists, but it was Helwys who organized the first Baptist church on English soil.

During the early part of the seventeenth century the Separatists groups were always small and usually unstable. Helwys must have been beguiled by an excess of zeal when he spoke of "thousands being out of all doubt" concerning the justice of the Anabaptist claims.[16] Contemporaries were chiefly impressed by the differences that divided men who in essentials were so much alike. "Of the Brownists," wrote John Paget,

> there are sundry sects. Some separate from the Church of England for corruptions; and yet confess both it and Rome also to be a true church, as the followers of Mr. Johnson. Some renounce the Church of England as a false church; and yet allow private communion with the godly therein, as Mr. Robinson and his followers. Some renounce all religious communion both public and private with any member of that church whosoever,

---

[15] This could be (and sometimes was) misinterpreted. Cf. John Robinson's reference to Smyth's constant changes of opinion: ". . . his instability and wantonness of wit is his sin and our cross." Robinson, *Works*, II, 62. Ainsworth claimed that Smyth was "fickle," and that his three most recent books reflected three distinct religious positions, Henry Ainsworth, *A Defence of the Holy Scriptures, Worship and Ministrie*, To the Reader. Cf. also Bernard, *Plain Evidences: the Church of England is Apostolicall, the Separation Schismaticall*, pp. 17–22.

[16] Thomas Helwys, *A Short Declaration of the Mistery of Iniquity*, p. 72. In 1639, Robert Abbot claimed that there were "very few Anabaptists," *A Triall of our Church Forsakers*, p. 17.

as Mr. Ainsworth and such as hearken unto him, being deepest
and stiffest in their schism. The evil of this separation is great.[17]

The shifts of opinion among the leaders, together with the divisions among
the members, make it difficult to define the precise position of the
Separatists. But it is relatively simple to isolate the issues with which they
were chiefly concerned and to compare the convictions that prevailed
among them. And although at the time these beliefs attracted a comparatively modest following, their subsequent importance has been immense.[18]

Freedom to follow the truth wherever it might lead was of cardinal
importance to the Separatists. It affected the way in which they were
drawn into the fellowship of faith; it determined the steps by which that
community was constituted. Most Englishmen assumed that church and
state were coterminous. To toy with any alternative was irresponsible, and
the critics of the Separatists implored them to weigh the disastrous results
of any change. But the problem assumed a very different guise when
examined from a novel point of view. The power of bishops, instead of
appearing as a natural consequence of the constitution of society, seemed
to be an invasion of the office of Christ and a violation of the freedom of
the Christian man.[19] The church, said the Separatists, is the result of
God's gracious initiative in human history. The covenant was the
distinctive means by which he created a people for himself. A new
covenant replaced the first one, and this second covenant has never been
abrogated. It still represents the only proper means by which a church
can be constituted. This is a theme that constantly recurs in Separatist
literature. John Murton's account of the origins of John Robinson's
congregation emphasized the essential role of the covenant in the
emergence of a new company of God's people. "Do we not know the
beginnings of his church? that there was first one that stood up and made a
covenant, and then another, and these two joined together, and so a third,
and these became a church." [20] Similarly, when John Smyth defined the
church, he spoke of it as those who are "joined together by covenant with
God and themselves." [21] One of the first clear indications that Smyth was
moving toward Separatism was the covenant that he drew up for his
followers, and that we have in the words of William Bradford, who took it.

> They shook off this yoke of antichristian bondage, and as the
> Lord's free people joined themselves (by a covenant of the Lord)
> into a church estate, in the fellowship of the Gospel, to walk in
> all his ways, made known or to be made known unto them,

[17] Paget, *An Arrow,* To the Christian Reader.

[18] Note their contribution to the ferment of the Interregnum as well as their ancestry of the
chief tenets of some of the largest denominations in English-speaking Christianity.

[19] Robinson, *Works,* III, 172.

[20] Murton, *A Description of what God hath Predestinated,* To the Reader.

[21] Smyth, *Works,* I, 252.

according to their best endeavours, whatsoever it should cost them, the Lord assisting them.[22]

This was a principle that consistently guided the Separatists.[23] In discussing the nature of the true church with Richard Bernard, John Robinson declared

that we hold and affirm that a company, consisting though but of two or three, separated from the world, whether unchristian or antichristian, and gathered into the name of Christ by a covenant made to walk in all the ways of God known unto them, is a church, and so hath the whole power of Christ.[24]

Whereupon Robinson proceeded to support this claim with eight arguments, gleaned from the Scriptures and from Bernard's own works.

The gathered church was constituted by covenant. Its essential nature was determined by Scripture. "A true visible Church of Christ," said Johnson, "is a company of faithful people by the Word of God called out and separated from the world and the false ways thereof, gathered and joined together in fellowship of the Gospel, by a voluntary profession of the faith and obedience of Christ." [25] Robinson pointed out that the Greek word *ekklēsia* "denoteth an assembly of persons called out of the state of corrupt nature into that of supernatural grace, by the publishing of the Gospel." [26] Smyth's views on this question are clear, but his words, constantly interrupted by Scriptural references, are not always easy to quote. "The Catholic church," he said, "is the company of the elect and it is invisible." For all practical purposes we are therefore concerned with the "visible church"—"a visible communion of saints, . . . all which are to be accounted faithful and elect . . . till they by obstinacy in sin and apostasy declare the contrary." [27] To meet his requirements three qualities are necessary: true matter, true form, true properties. "The true matter of a true visible church are saints. . . . Saints are men separated from all known sin, practising the whole will of God known unto them, growing in grace and knowledge, continuing to the end." The true form is partly inward, partly outward. In the former respect, it consists of the Spirit, faith, and love; in the latter, it is "a vow, promise, oath or covenant betwixt God and the saints." The true properties of a true visible church "are two: 1. communion in all the holy things of God; 2. the power of our Lord Jesus Christ." [28]

[22] *Ibid.*, p. lxii; William Bradford, *The History of Plimouth Plantation*, p. 13.

[23] It may be noted that in the writings of Helwys and Murton the covenant falls into the background, because believer's baptism has become an ordinance of comparable significance.

[24] Robinson, *Works*, II, 132.

[25] F. Johnson, *An Answer to Maister H. Jacob, his defence*, p. 196. A similar definition is found in Ainsworth and F. Johnson, *An Apologie or Defence of such true Christians*, p. 36.

[26] Robinson, *Works*, III, 33.

[27] Smyth, *Works*, I, 251.

[28] *Ibid.*, I, 253–254.

In one form or another these points recur in the works of all the Separatists. A true church need not be large; it is more likely to be genuine if it is small. Here the testimony of Scripture left no room for doubt: "two or three gathered together must be a church which hath the whole power of Christ." [29] For Helwys the matter of primary importance was "the two or three gathered in the name of Christ"; from this, every significant inference about the church's nature could be deduced.[30] It was necessary, of course, that every member should participate in the life of the religious community. As a consequence, the congregation had to be restricted to a size that would permit each person to know the others and all to share fully in the responsibilities of the fellowship. Therefore, declared Robinson, "no particular church under the New Testament ought to consist of more members than can meet together in one place." [31]

The gathered company might be small, but it was assumed that it would be sanctified. A church member ought to conform to a certain standard of holiness. "A true visible church . . . is a communion of saints";[32] here again the example of "the apostolic constitution" ought to be decisive for all Christian societies. The wicked had no place in the congregation of the righteous.

> To conceive of a church, which is the body of Christ and household of God, not separated from the profane world which lieth in wickedness, is to confound heaven and earth, and to agree Christ with Belial; and in truth the most profane and dangerous error which this day prevails amongst them that fear God.

Nothing threatens the true life of the church so seriously as to admit those who have not been genuinely converted. To do so runs counter to the explicit injunctions of the church's Lord, and Robinson confidently concluded "that the church, in the right gathering of it . . . , must be and is constituted and compact of good only, and not of good and evil." [33] Because every true church consists of those who are called out of the world and separated from it, "no known atheist, unbeliever, heretic or wicked liver [may] be received or retained a member of the Church of Christ which is his body, God having in all ages appointed and made a separation of his people from the world, before the Law, under the Law, and now in the time of the Gospel." [34] A company of people gathered by the Word of God and cleansed by the Holy Spirit will necessarily witness

[29] Robinson, *Works,* II, 131.
[30] Helwys, *An Advertisement or Admonition unto the Congregations which men call the New Fryelers,* p. 44.
[31] Robinson, *Works,* III, 12–13.
[32] Smyth, *Works,* II, 350.
[33] Robinson, *Works,* III, 129; II, 126. Also III, 66, 126; II, 321–327, 486.
[34] Ainsworth and F. Johnson, *An Apologie,* p. 36.

to the truth. This, as Helwys realized, must be the church's primary task, and here he was clearly in advance of most of his associates.

All decisions concerning the outward and visible form of the church were governed by Scriptural precedents. The authority of the apostles could not be challenged. "It is unto me," said John Robinson, "a matter of great scruple and conscience to depart one hair-breadth (extraordinary accidents ever excepted) from their practice and institution in anything truly ecclesiastical, though never so small in itself, . . . touching the government of the church." [35] As Robinson saw, the membership of the church must always come before the organization of that membership. All ministrations are therefore vested in the faithful people.[36] This accounts for what he described as "the popular constitution of the church." [37] Observe, he said, how often the life of the early Christians was shaped by decisions taken by the whole company of believers; obviously they sought the assent of the entire fellowship.[38] But the ideal kind of organization, he believed, would incorporate the elements of strength present in all proven systems of government—"monarchical, aristocratic and democratical." "And all these three forms have their place in the Church of Christ. In respect of him the head, it is a monarchy; in respect of the eldership, an aristocracy; in respect of the body, a popular state." [39] It was clearly unjust, he pointed out, to insinuate that "we either exercise amongst ourselves or would thrust upon others any popular or democratical church government." "First," he added,

> we believe that the external church government under Christ, the only mediator and monarch thereof, is plainly aristocratical, and to be administered by some certain choice men, although the state, which many unskilfully confound with the government, be after a sort popular and democratical. By this it appertains to the people freely to vote in elections and judgments of the church; in respect of the other, we make account it behoves the elders to govern the people, even in their voting, in just liberty, given by Christ whatsoever.[40]

When officers are mentioned, the discussion of church organization shifts to a different area: can the freedom of the members be reconciled with the authority of the leaders? No one questioned the need for officers; everyone insisted that they must not usurp the rights of the people of God. Smyth contended that the full power of Christ resided in the membership

[35] Robinson, *Works*, III, 40–41; cf. Smyth, *Principles and Inferences concerning the visible Church, Works*, I, 252.
[36] Robinson, *Works*, II, 137–139; cf. Smyth, *Works*, I, 251–256.
[37] Robinson, *Works*, II, 139–142.
[38] *Ibid.*, III, 36–40.
[39] *Ibid.*, II, 140.
[40] *Ibid.*, III, 42–43.

as a whole; to appoint officers merely added order. The congregation was to administer the affairs of the church in obedience to God's will; in doing so, the elders were simply the agents of the people. "The eldership," he claimed, "hath . . . all their power from the church." [41] For Robinson the "popish clergy" was distinctively at fault because it "would exempt itself from the common condition of Christians, in the common Christian ordinances of the church, as though their office ate up their brotherhood, and their special calling of officers their general calling of Christians." [42] All authority in the church is derived from the members and is exercised exclusively for their benefit.[43]

Since officers are necessary, their functions must be defined. The Separatists believed

> that Christ the Lord hath by his last testament given to his Church and set therein sufficient ordinary offices, with the manner of calling or entrance, works and maintenance, for the administration of his holy things, and for the sufficient ordinary instruction, guidance and service of his Church unto the end of the world.[44]

Consequently, the church has power to choose suitable men for all the offices enumerated in Scripture—pastors, teachers, elders, deacons, helpers.[45] This catalog inspired the pattern adopted by "the Ancient Church" in Amsterdam (Johnson's congregation), but when John Smyth came to know it, he found it needlessly elaborate. It presupposed three classes of elders (pastors, teachers, rulers) when one was clearly enough. The only necessary distinction was between officers charged with the spiritual oversight of the congregation (elders) and those responsible for its temporal affairs (deacons). Elders did not form a consistory apart from the people, and the autonomy of each congregation precluded their meeting as a presbytery. The elder corresponded to the primitive bishop; he preached the Word, he taught and ruled the people, always with due regard for the congregation's will.[46] Smyth was clearly determined to safeguard the rights of the members against the encroachments of officialdom. Robinson, who conceded greater authority to the ministry, was careful both to limit that authority to the congregation that had called the minister and to define the qualities that entitle him to occupy his office. "We make," said he, "no dumb ministers, neither dare we admit of

---

[41] Smyth, *Works,* II, 326.
[42] Robinson, *Works,* II, 326.
[43] *Ibid.,* II, 237.
[44] Ainsworth and F. Johnson, *op. cit.,* p. 36.
[45] *Ibid.,* p. 37.
[46] Smyth, *Works,* I, 307–315; II, 325–326. According to Smyth, eldership is a ministerial office: "we hold that all elders of the Church are pastors, and that lay elders (so called) are antichristian." *Ibid.,* I, 273.

any man either for a teaching or a governing elder, of whose ability in prayer, prophesying and debating of church matters we have not had good experience before he be so much as nominated to the office of an elder amongst us." But he insisted that the church is prior to its officers; they remain its servants and never become its overlords.[47]

The church, once it is properly organized, must thereafter be adequately supported. Independency required that the congregation provide for its own maintenance, and in discharging this duty everyone must bear his proper share. "All the members of the church," said Smyth, "are to contribute something, because the alms or contribution is the manifestation of grace." The gifts would vary with the members' means. "They that have much are to give much; they that have but little are to contribute little by proportion." [48] The church, in fact, was to be maintained by voluntary contributions, "and not by popish lordships and livings, or Jewish tithes or offerings." [49]

Organization presupposes discipline; without the latter the former is of no avail. To the Separatists nothing so seriously vitiated the witness of the Church of England as its failure to enforce evangelical discipline. The church must be preserved from the infection of sin.[50] "The care of the whole church jointly must be to keep her power given her by Christ, and not to suffer any open known sin or any tyranny or usurpation over them." [51] As soon as a church becomes aware of the contagion of evil, it must act at once to purge away the stain. If it fails to do so, it becomes a partaker in the sin. "This I hold," wrote Robinson,

> that if iniquity be committed in the church, and complaint and proof accordingly made, and that the church will not reform or reject the party offending, but will on the contrary maintain presumptuously and abet such impiety, that then by abetting that party and his sin, she makes it her own by imputation and enwraps herself in the same guilt with the sinner.[52]

The Separatists believed that the proper method of applying discipline was clearly specified in the Bible. The first step was private admonition. If this proved insufficient, the rebuke was repeated in the presence of witnesses. Should the offender confess his fault and repent, his sin was to be buried in oblivion. If he continued obdurate, the matter was to be laid before the church. He could still turn from his evil ways; a change of heart would still ensure him his place in the fellowship and his standing as a

[47] Robinson, *Works*, III, 17; II, 131–132; 146–148.
[48] Smyth, *Works*, I, 316.
[49] Ainsworth and F. Johnson, *op. cit.*, 37.
[50] Hence the serious attention given to this subject. About a third of Smyth's *Principles and Inferences concerning the visible Church* is devoted to a discussion of discipline.
[51] Smyth, *Works*, I, 261.
[52] Robinson, *Works*, II, 259. Cf. Ainsworth and F. Johnson, *op. cit.*, p. 36.

232   FREEDOM AND AUTHORITY

brother in the family of God. "Thus the church and all the members
thereof shall be preserved and kept pure within, and their communion
shall be holy." [53] The obdurate sinner, however, could expect no further
respite. There was one sufficient cause of expulsion from the church: "sin
obstinately stood in without repentance and confession after due conviction." [54] Excommunication was a step of terrifying seriousness; "the
separating of the impenitent from the outward communion of the church
is a figure of the eternal rejection and reprobation of them that persist
impenitent in sin." [55] It was a drastic step, but not necessarily irrevocable:
"that persons separated from the communion of the church are to be
accounted as heathens and publicans, and that they are to be so far
shunned, as they may pollute: notwithstanding being ready to instruct
them and relieve them in their wants, seeking by all lawful means to win
them." [56]

Discipline was distinctively a corporate responsibility. John Robinson
laid down twelve reasons to prove that this duty ought to be discharged by
the whole congregation, and must not be delegated to its elders.[57] Still less
might any individual arrogate to himself a task that belonged to the entire
body. By the same token, every member, however great his gifts or
learning, had to be "subject to the censure and discipline of the
congregation." [58] Unfortunately, it was easier to propound the theory
than to enforce it. Many of the disputes that erupted in Separatist
congregations were connected with discipline. As we have already seen,
Christopher Lawne charged that favoritism distorted discipline into an
instrument of injustice. Thomas White claimed that in practice Johnson's
church did not exclude even notorious offenders. Dean Stanley, an officer
of the congregation, was accused of flagrant immorality, and Johnson (so
his critics charged) shielded him, even at the cost of violating the
principles on which the church was founded.[59]

The authority of the congregation was manifest in the way it enforced
discipline; its freedom appeared in the way it regulated worship. Two
principles governed the pattern of worship: simplicity and an appeal to the
example of the New Testament. Both presupposed a spontaneous and
unfettered approach to God. Consequently, the Separatists refused to
submit to a prescribed and written liturgy. "We cannot," said Robinson,
"but mislike that custom in use, by which the pastor is wont to repeat and
read out of a prayer-book certain forms, for his and the church's prayers."
"This external mien and manner of worshipping God in prayer," he

[53] Smyth, *Works*, I, 262–263.
[54] *Ibid.*, I, 264.
[55] *Ibid.*, II, 746.
[56] *Ibid.*, II, 747.
[57] Robinson, *Works*, II, 238–255; cf. III, 37–43, and Smyth, *Works*, II, 386.
[58] Ainsworth and F. Johnson, *op. cit.*, p. 30.
[59] Lawne, *Brownisme turned*, p. 27; Thomas White, *A Discoverie of Brownisme*, pp. 7, 8, 10.

added, "is nowhere found in the written Word, by the prescript whereof alone he is to be worshipped." [60] The Psalms could not be invoked in support of prescribed patterns, nor could the Lord's Prayer; since even the Evangelists recorded the latter with variations, we can be certain that it did not restrict the apostles to a fixed form of words.[61] True petition cannot be reconciled with the reading of prayers. "In prayer we do pour out matter, to wit, holy conceptions of the mind, from within to without; that is, from the heart to God; on the contrary, in reading we do receive and admit matter from without to within; that is, from the book into the heart." [62] Indeed, "the Spirit is quenched by set forms of worship, for therein the Spirit is not at liberty to utter itself, but is bounded in." [63]

The Separatists showed little disposition to challenge these principles. They favored a form of worship that included a few simple but essential elements. Richard Clyfton, a colleague of Johnson, described in detail the service at the Ancient Church in Amsterdam.

1. Prayer and giving of thanks by the pastor or teacher. 2. The Scriptures are read, two or three chapters, as time serves, with a brief explanation of their meaning. 3. The pastor or teacher then takes some passage of Scripture, and expounds and enforces it. 4. The Sacraments are administered. 5. Some of the Psalms of David are sung by the whole congregation, both before and after the exercise of the Word. 6. Collection is then made, as each one is able, for the support of the officers and the poor.[64]

Probably most of the Separatist congregations followed, with minor variations, a pattern similar to this. The service was unadorned in its simplicity, since this corresponded to what Johnson called "the plainness of the Word and ordinances of Christ." The reason was obvious: "God abhors in his worship the mixture of man's inventions with his Word and ordinances." [65]

John Smyth accepted these basic principles but applied them in a highly distinctive way. Since he was attempting to reconcile the freedom of the congregation with the authority of the Scriptures, it is impossible to ignore his practice. He believed that "prayer, prophesying and singing psalms [are] the true and only parts of the worship of the New Testament." [66] He could find no justification in Scripture for reading as a part of the service, so he rigidly excluded it. It was permissible, of course,

[60] Robinson, *Works,* III, 19.
[61] *Ibid.,* III, 20–24.
[62] *Ibid.,* III, 26.
[63] Smyth, *Works,* I, 277.
[64] Richard Clyfton, *An Advertisement Concerning a Book, &c.,* quoted by Robinson, *Works,* III, 485.
[65] F. Johnson, *An Answer to Maister H. Jacob his defence,* pp. 128, 61, 101, 209.
[66] Smyth, *Works,* II, 324.

to study the Bible before worship began, and evidently the congregation did so. But since "reading words out of a book is the ministration of the letter," [67] the Bible was laid aside when the service started. What happened next is described in a letter written by two members of the congregation.

> After a solemn prayer made by the first speaker [apparently Smyth] he propoundeth some text out of Scripture and prophes-ieth out of the same by the space of one hour. . . . After him standeth up a second speaker and prophesieth out of the same text the like time and place, sometime more, sometime less. After him the third, the fourth, and the fifth, &c., as the time will give leave. Then the first speaker concludeth with prayer as he began with prayer, with an exhortation to contribute to the poor, which collection being made is also concluded with prayer. This morning exercise begins at eight of the clock, the like course and exercise is observed in the afternoon from two of the clock unto five or six of the clock. Last of all the execution of the government of the church is handled.[68]

These people were earnest Sabbatarians; a program like this allowed them no alternative. Smyth's refusal to read even the Scriptures was a deviation from normal practice that caused some dismay among his fellow Separatists,[69] but this anomaly does not alter the fact that prayer and the exposition of the Bible were the essential ingredients in Separatist worship.

A people whose life was so exclusively governed by Scripture inevitably gave much thought to the nature and place of sacraments. All the congregations regularly celebrated the Lord's Supper, always as a part of the life of a fellowship in which discipline was duly exercised. Like true Protestants, they insisted that marriage was not a sacrament at all; they even denied that it was a ceremony which a minister should rightfully perform. When the Bible specifies that the man of God must be perfectly furnished to every good work, it does not mention marriage; therefore, the minister has no business to officiate at marriages.[70] They were sharply divided about baptism. To whom should it be administered? It ought to be equated with circumcision, said Robinson, and therefore the baptism of infants had ample Scriptural authority. On the contrary, replied Smyth, "the outward baptism of water is to be administered only upon such

---

[67] *Ibid.,* I, 282. Smyth devotes a good deal of space to showing why translations must not be used in worship, *ibid.,* pp. 282–292. Apparently he felt that it was permissible to bring the Greek and Hebrew texts and translate from them at sight!

[68] Letter of Hugh and Anne Bromhead to William Hamerton, B. M. Harleian MS. 360, ff. 70, 71. Quoted in Smyth, *Works,* I, lxxx–lxxxi.

[69] Cf. Ainsworth, *A Defence of the Holy Scriptures, Worship and Ministrie used in the Christian Churches separated from Antichrist,* pp. 1–2; Ainsworth and F. Johnson, *op. cit.,* pp. 4, 5, 23, 41 ff.

[70] Robinson, *Works,* III, 18–19.

penitent and faithful persons as are (aforesaid) and not upon innocent infants and wicked persons." [71]

All questions of order and worship were significant because they were related to certain fundamental theological beliefs. The Separatists were not unique in treating matters of faith with the utmost seriousness. Almost everyone was concerned about doctrinal issues, and among thoughtful people there was a surprising measure of agreement. The Separatists did not challenge the faith as traditionally interpreted. They accepted its authority; within its context they sought freedom of interpretation on certain points. On many of the articles of belief they agreed with their Puritan brethren. Initially, their theological views were similar to those of the great majority of their more earnest countrymen, and many of them never seriously deviated from this position. As we have seen, they exalted the Bible to a place of undisputed authority. "The original Scriptures," said Smyth, "are the image of the mind of God." [72] They accepted the Word; therefore they believed that their position must be sound: "the crime of heresy is not to be imputed to them whose faith doth wholly rely upon most sure grounds of the Scripture." [73]

What they deduced from the Bible corresponded in large measure to the Calvinism so prevalent among English Protestants. There is little that is distinctive about a document like "The Confession of Faith of certain English people living in exile in the Low Countries." Yet on certain of the characteristic doctrines of Calvinism the Separatists ultimately disagreed. When the English exiles reached Holland the Arminian controversy was agitating the Reformed Church. They could hardly ignore the issue. Original sin, universal redemption, predestination, and free will were highly topical subjects. Robinson believed that original sin was taught by Scripture and confirmed by experience.[74] Smyth disagreed. He was convinced "that original sin is an idle term and that there is no such thing as men intend by the word, because God threateneth death only to Adam, not to his posterity." Even if the guilt of man's first transgression could have been transmitted, its progress would have been arrested long ago: "Christ's death, which was effectual before Cain and Abel's birth (he being the lamb slain from the beginning of the world) stopped the issue and passage thereof." The conclusion seemed inescapable "that infants are conceived and born in innocency without sin and that so dying are undoubtedly saved." [75]

[71] Smyth, *Works*, II, 745. In I. P., *Anabaptismes Mysterie of Iniquity Unmasked,* the author reproduces a letter setting out in detail the "Anabaptist" position regarding baptism (pp. 1–8), and then refutes it at great length.
[72] Smyth, *Works*, II, 324.
[73] Robinson, *Works*, III, 246–253.
[74] *Ibid.*
[75] Smyth, *Works*, II, 735. Smyth's Anti-Calvinism may have been due more to the Mennonites than to the Arminians. It is clear, however, that Robinson was aware of the

Those who denied original sin challenged related doctrines. Smyth, Helwys, and Murton believed in universal redemption. To teach that all men can be saved was to deny that only some are elect, and so the favorite Puritan doctrine of predestination was challenged. Smyth felt that the whole concept was as implausible as it was hateful, and he boldly set forth the proposition "that as no man begetteth his child to the gallows, nor no potter maketh a pot to break it, so God doth not create or predestinate any man to destruction." [76] Helwys argued that what the Calvinists called "God's eternal decree" was inconsistent with what we know of his love and mercy; how, then, "can it be said that God hath decreed any man to sin or any man to condemnation"? [77] By the time John Murton took up the subject, the Synod of Dort had rendered its uncompromising verdict. But Dort, said Murton, was subject to error, and nowhere more clearly than in connection with election—"which doctrine, how it impeacheth not only the justice of God, the mercy of God in Christ and protestations of God to the contrary in the Scriptures, but also the sufficiency and meritoriousness of Christ's most precious death and sufferings and laying the imputation of man's damnation not only on his own sin and unbelief but also on God and Christ" he proposed to examine in detail in his book.[78] But Murton did not entirely reject the doctrine of election; he merely denied that the Calvinists accurately interpreted the Biblical evidence. Most of the Separatists, however, could not accept a view that took such liberties with their most cherished traditions. John Robinson wrote an elaborate vindication of the decrees of the Synod of Dort, and Henry Ainsworth published a short but sharp attack on the "Anabaptist" position.[79]

The implications of this particular debate demanded—and received—further attention. Predestination, it was argued, not only threatened God's mercy but destroyed man's freedom. In attacking the rigidities of Calvinist election, Smyth felt that he was defending the liberty with which God has endowed his children. "God created man with freedom of will," he wrote, "so that he had ability to choose the good and eschew the evil, or to choose the evil and refuse the good, and this freedom of will was a natural faculty or power, created by God in the soul of man." [80] Murton agreed. "I hold," he claimed, "that there is yet left in man the faculty of will to choose or refuse, which I will make plain, 1. By many Scriptures, 2. by many undeniable reasons." [81] But the key term was obviously

debates that culminated in the Synod of Dort, and it is reasonable to assume that the Separatists' differences were affected by the current controversy.

[76] Smyth, *Works,* II, 736.
[77] Helwys, *An Advertisement,* p. 87.
[78] Murton, *A Description of what God hath Predestinated,* To the Reader.
[79] Robinson, *A Defence of the Doctrine Propounded at the Synod of Dort (Works,* I, 260 ff.); Ainsworth, *A Seasonable Discourse or a Censure upon a Dialogue of the Anabaptists.*
[80] Smyth, *Works,* II, 734–735.
[81] Murton, *A Description,* pp. 95–96.

imprecise. Having denied predestination, Helwys was equally concerned to repudiate "free will." This phrase concealed a "damnable heresy"; it abolished universal redemption, because it presupposed in man "an absolute power . . . to work righteousness," and thus eliminated any need for Christ.[82] Here again John Robinson intervened to defend the doctrine that most Puritans accepted. No one, he pointed out, denied free will in ordinary matters; the issue was restricted to "spiritual things." His opponents erred through a simple confusion of thought: "they unskilfully confound necessity and compulsion, and conceive not how a thing both free and casual in itself may by the overruling hand of God's providence be determined necessarily this way or that." He could prove, he claimed, that "man's free will in choosing that which is evil and God's powerful hand in governing him in that his choice according to his wise counsel, to his holy ends, may well stand together." [83] It required some ingenuity to reconcile the rigidities of Calvinism with the freedom of man, but Robinson believed that the task could be accomplished.

Both the freedom of the congregation and the authority of the church were involved in the relations between various Christian bodies. Even those who shared the same interpretation of the true pattern of church organization found it difficult to agree among themselves; unfortunately, they too often allowed debate to degenerate into recrimination. Is it not better, asked a critic, to endure corruptions in a church "than to be turmoiled into such distractions and to be brought into such confusion, even a Babel of languages, of opinions, of assemblies, of governors, and what not"? [84]

These feuds among the Separatists were far less serious than the controversies between those who remained in the Church of England and those who felt obliged to leave it. Richard Bernard was the principal spokesman for the conformist Puritans, and to the Separatists it seemed a grave offense that he followed them so far yet shrank from the final step. Smyth described him as "changeable as the moon, mutable as Proteus, and variable as the chameleon." [85] Bernard opened his chief contribution to this debate (*Christian Advertisements and Counsels of Peace*) with a plea for unity. "Read (my friend) considerately; expound charitably; and judge, I pray thee, without partiality; do as thou wouldst be done unto." The attitude of the Separatists seemed to him both dangerous and unreasonable. It was dangerous because it encouraged the growth of popery. It was unreasonable; it was based on a novel and divisive doctrine, it issued in schism, it flourished because of unfounded attacks on other churches.

---

[82] Helwys, *An Advertisement*, p. 96.
[83] Robinson, *Works*, I, 393–394; cf. also 290–291.
[84] Bernard, *Plain Evidences: the Church of England is Apostolicall, the Separation Schismaticall*, p. 6.
[85] Smyth, *Works*, II, 336. Smyth's "Letter to Mr. Ric. Bernard," which forms the greater part of his *Parallels, Censures, Observations*, is a sustained attack on Bernard's "cowardice" as well as on his position.

Those who hold such views hinder the Word of God where they come; "they leave a curse and not a blessing." [86] As spokesman for "some godly ministers of the Gospel," Bernard defended the validity of the faith and order of the Church of England, and demolished the criticisms that the Separatists directed against it.[87] He enumerated seven probabilities why they were wrong, three principal reasons for not accepting their way, ten cardinal errors of which they were guilty, and added three brief but cogent arguments to prove that the worship of the Church of England satisfied all legitimate demands.[88]

The bitterest debates concerned the legitimacy of the Anglican Church. Bernard pointed out that to the Separatists "every of our assemblies be false Churches." [89] The gist of their complaints was clear: "1. They deny us to have a true Church. 2. They deny us to have a true ministry. 3. They deny us to have a true worship." [90] They regarded the constitution of the Anglican Church as false; they complained that its adherents treated it with superstitious reverence. Consider Bernard, said Smyth; he serves a false church, has a false standing in it, exercises a false ministry in a false parish, by a false service, under a false form of church government.[91] A ruthless analysis led to a harsh verdict. "Therefore I am bound to pronounce your false and idolatrous church constitution to be worse than your false ministry, worse than your false worship, worse than your false government, &c." [92] All the rites and ritual of the Church of England, all its organization and its activities bore the mark of Antichrist and were in enmity against the reign of Christ.[93] John Robinson was less sweeping in his condemnation. He saw the Church of England as an amalgam of truth and error.[94] The Separatists were not content with denunciation. They clearly implied that fellowship with the Church of England should be severely restricted, if not completely forbidden. Was it legitimate, they asked, to have any kind of communion with a church so vitiated by disorder? Smyth's answer was immediate and uncompromising. It was unlawful, he claimed, for any true Christian to listen to the preaching of the Anglican clergy, or to join with them in prayer, "because your ministers are false ministers and your people of false churches. . . . Now how can we who are the Church and Body of Christ have any spiritual communion with you, who are the ministers and subjects of

[86] Bernard, *Christian Advertisements*, p. 43. Smyth replied to this work; so did Robinson, in his longest work (*A Justification of Separation from the Church of England*, 1610). Ainsworth also answered it in *Counterpoyson* (1608).

[87] Bernard, *Christian Advertisements*, pp. 163–192.

[88] Bernard, *Plain Evidences*, pp. 38–80, 86–118, 123–325, 326–327.

[89] *Ibid.*, p. 240.

[90] R. Abbot, *A Triall of our Church Forsakers*, p. 28.

[91] Smyth, *Works*, II, 347. He attacks Bernard's *Christian Advertisements*, pp. 78–81.

[92] *Ibid.*, II, 352.

[93] F. Johnson, *An Answer*, pp. 38 ff., 61, 69, 72.

[94] Robinson, *Works*, II, 5, 6, 81, 360, 480.

Antichrist?"[95] Here again Robinson was more moderate than others. The impurities of the Church of England forbade any formal participation in its life, but this did not preclude fellowship, as individual Christians, between those who had forsaken the established Church and those who remained within it.[96] This rejection of Christian fellowship provoked a controversy that at least clarified the Separatists' position. William Ames and William Bradshaw took exception to the arrogance that dismissed as "the ministry of Antichrist's apostasy"[97] the service of conscientious conformists. Bradshaw carefully examined Johnson's arguments for severing all contact with the Anglican communion, and then set forth at length his conviction that "it is a sin to separate from the public ministry of the Church assemblies of England." Ames insisted that Robinson's attitude was illogical and inconsistent: it was impossible, he pointed out, to permit private fellowship without advancing step by step to a fuller measure of communion.[98] A church is a much more complex organism than the oversimplifications of the Separatists suggested. Did Robinson really believe, asked Ames, that so many men of knowledge, sincerity, and godliness live "in such continual practice of idolatry as he doth in words accuse them of"?[99] In particular he rebuked Robinson for ignoring the subtle ways in which the authority of the church is intertwined with the claims of the state; lawful jurisdictions are so intimately related that they cannot rashly be torn asunder.[100]

The Separatists, it is true, insisted that it was "antichristian and not to be submitted to" that a bishop should be "joined in commission with a civil magistrate in courts of justice established," and that their joint decisions should be enforced by the king's authority.[101] They were equally clear that their own claims to spiritual freedom in no way infringed upon the legitimate jurisdiction of the magistrate. It was totally unjust to accuse them of civil disaffection or disloyalty. "We do unfeignedly acknowledge the authority of earthly magistrates, God's blessed ordinance, and that all earthly authority and command pertains unto them; let them command

[95] Smyth, *Works*, II, 500.

[96] Robinson, *Works*, II, 12; III, 116 ff., 172. Paget (*An Arrow*, To the Reader) describes the shades of opinion current among the Separatists: "Some separate from the Church of England for corruption, and yet confess both it and Rome also to be a true Church, as the followers of Mr. Johnson. Some renounce the Church of England as a false Church, and yet allow private communion with the godly therein, as Mr. Robinson and his followers. Some renounce all religious communion both public and private with any member of that Church whosoever, as Mr. Ainsworth, and such as hearken unto him, being deepest and stiffest in their schism."

[97] Bradshaw, *The Unreasonablenesse of the Separation*, n.p.

[98] Ames, *A Manduction for Mr Robinson*, p. 35.

[99] Ames, *A Second Manduction for Mr Robinson*, p. 35.

[100] *Ibid.*, pp. 17–22. The protests of Ames and Bradshaw are illuminating because these men agreed at so many points with the Separatists. A more conventional Anglican attack on Smyth and Robinson can be found in Bishop Hall, *Works*, IX, 379 ff.

[101] I. P., *Anabaptismes Mysterie of Iniquity Unmasked*, Advertisements to the Reader.

what they will, we must obey, either to do or suffer upon pain of God's displeasure, besides their punishment. But all men must let God alone with his right, which is to be lord and lawgiver to the soul, and not command obedience for God where he commandeth none." [102] Here a number of characteristic emphases are combined. The magistrate is appointed by God, and is entrusted with the duty of seeing that just and righteous laws are obeyed. Rulers may legitimately constrain their subjects "to the outward acts of justice, honesty and the like," since "these serve properly and immediately to preserve civil societies, of which magistrates are properly kings and lords." [103] This coercive authority entitles them "to suppress and root out by their authority all false ministries, voluntary religious and counterfeit worship of God." [104] This was a sensitive area, and anyone attracted in any degree by the Separatist position perforce discussed it. Henry Jacob, who moved reluctantly from a typically Puritan position to Independency, exalted the authority of the ruler to such a degree that voluntary religious societies forfeited virtually all their autonomy. He believed that the Christian magistrate should "oversee and order his churches in spiritual matters"; he ought "to cherish and prefer the godly and religious and to punish (as truth and right shall require) the untractable and unreasonable." [105] Jacob even admitted that the magistrate might do what no "spiritual authority" should attempt: "impose on [the Christian people of a congregation] spiritual matters by civil power (yea, whether they like or dislike), if he see it good." [106] John Robinson was much more cautious. The Christian ruler, he conceded, might exercise a general care of the church. It was the prince's duty to check gross error; it was not his right to interfere in questions of religious truth.[107] On this point the Scriptures are explicit: the ruler "may alter, devise or establish nothing in religion otherwise than Christ hath appointed, but proves not that he may not use his lawful power lawfully for the furtherance of Christ's kingdom and laws." [108] The reasons for Robinson's hesitations are clear. He believed that some of his friends pressed the matter too far because they assumed that the magistrate would be a Christian. Actually, the Bible shows that the magistrate occupies a civil office; from it he derives his authority, and his prerogatives are in no way determined by his religious beliefs.[109]

[102] *Objections: Answered* (1615), in *Tracts on Liberty of Conscience* (Hanserd Knollys Society), p. 100.
[103] Robinson, *Works*, I, 41. Cf. Jacob, *An Attestation of Many Learned, Godly and Famous Divines*, pp. 313–314.
[104] Ainsworth and F. Johnson, *op. cit.*, p. 27. Cf. F. Johnson, *An Answer to H. Jacob*, p. 199.
[105] Jacob, *A Confession and Protestation of the faith of certain Christians in England*, Art. xxvii; *idem*, *The Divine Beginning and Institution of Christ's true visible or ministerial Church*, E5.
[106] Jacob, *An Attestation*, p. 115.
[107] Robinson, *Works*, III, 61.
[108] *Ibid.*, III, 277.
[109] *Ibid.*, III, 63.

If a ruler should seek to join a "gathered church," would the situation be modified in any way? The Separatists discovered that the Dutch Mennonites debarred magistrates from membership because coercive functions could not be reconciled with Christian discipleship. Helwys, however, was satisfied that a radical inconsistency lurked in this position; a church that successfully propagated such a view would gain converts at the price of creating anarchy.[110] This is clearly contrary to the express command of Scripture. We know that "magistracy is a holy ordinance of God"; we therefore believe that the man who holds the office may legitimately belong to the community of faith. But the position that he occupies in the state entitles him to no special authority in the church. Helwys thus pushed to its logical conclusion an important strain in Separatist thought. There is no necessary correlation between the office that the magistrate holds in the state and the prerogatives he can claim in the church. "The King," said Helwys, in inscribing his *Mistery of Iniquity* to James I, "is a mortal man and not God, therefore hath no power over the immortal souls of his subjects, to make laws and ordinances for them, and to set spiritual lords over them." [111]

By discussing the role of the magistrate, the Separatists helped to define the nature of religious toleration. Here they can claim the honor that belongs to pioneers. At the time, they faced the penalties reserved for dangerous innovators. John Smyth, who progressively modified his views of the magistrate's office, reached the conclusion that the ruler's authority is necessarily restricted by the just claims of his subjects to freedom of conscience. "The magistrate," he said, "is not by virtue of his office to meddle with religion or matters of conscience and to handle only civil transgressions." [112] This position was the natural result of a growing perception that his ideal of spiritual worship could not be reconciled with the prevailing theories about uniformity. Error cannot be eliminated by civil means. Persecution is therefore ineffectual as well as immoral. Instead of persisting in his customary policies, the magistrate must

> take up his Cross and follow Christ; he must love his enemies and not kill them; he must pray for them and not punish them; he must feed them and give them drink, not imprison them, banish them, dismember them, and spoil their goods; he must suffer persecution and affliction with Christ, and be slandered, reviled, blasphemed, scourged, buffeted, spit upon, imprisoned and killed with Christ; and that by the authority of magistrates, which

[110] Helwys, *An Advertisement*, pp. 56, 80.

[111] The inscription is on the flyleaf of the copy of *The Mistery of Iniquity* in the Bodleian Library, Oxford.

[112] Smyth, *Works*, II, 748. This is Article 84 of "A Confession of Faith." Articles 83–85 are devoted to the magistrate's office. Cf. Smyth's eight points on the magistracy, *ibid.*, II, 519–520.

things he cannot possibly do and retain the revenge of the sword.[113]

Smyth is the earliest English writer to state in unequivocal terms an uncompromising theory of toleration. Where he led, his associates followed, and the Baptists first developed a carefully defined position. Robinson reached an essentially similar view. At this point he is important not because his ideas are novel but because he advanced them in a reasonable and conciliatory spirit. Religious contentions, he insisted, "are sometimes necessary but always dangerous." If we must debate, we should earnestly pray that we may always "strive for God and according to God," and so avoid the passion and bitterness to which many disputants succumb. He noticed that

> men are for the most part minded for or against toleration of diversity of religions according to the conformity which they themselves hold or hold not with the country or kingdom where they live. Protestants living in the countries of Papists commonly plead for toleration of religion; so do Papists that live where Protestants bear sway: though few of either, specially of the clergy, as they are called, would have the other tolerated, where the world goes on their side.[114]

Robinson, a Calvinist by theological persuasion, forsook the Calvinist view of church order. Once he was released from the ecclesiastical orthodoxy of the Genevan system, he was able to exploit the strain of toleration that was actually latent in the doctrine of predestination.[115]

The disciples of Smyth were more adventurous in exploring the significance of toleration than were the followers of Robinson. Helwys, Murton, and their fellow Baptists returned to England, and their pleas for religious freedom were the product of a situation where the authorities were determined to deny them such liberty. As Robinson realized, these were the conditions under which seventeenth-century men were likely to be concerned about toleration; they awoke to the value of freedom when it was withheld. Helwys' long and often moving pamphlet, *Mistery of Iniquity*, contains an important section devoted to freedom of conscience. The king, he conceded, has received his power from God, and the citizen must accept the duty of obedience. The king's authority extends to the subject's goods, and all matters that concern the framework of man's material life can legitimately be controlled by the laws that the ruler enforces.[116] But royal authority cannot be extended to embrace the subject's conscience. Queen Mary was wrong to use the power of the sword to make her people papists;

[113] *Ibid.*, II, 748.
[114] *Ibid.*, I, 36, 40.
[115] Cf. W. K. Jordan, *The Development of Religious Toleration in England*, II, 243–244.
[116] Helwys, *The Mistery of Iniquity*, pp. 37–40.

King James would be just as wrong if he compelled his people to be Anglicans.[117] Ultimately, each man must answer for his loyalty to truth. "Is it not most equal," asked Helwys, "that men should choose their religion themselves, seeing they only must stand themselves before the judgment seat of God to answer for themselves?" [118] Actually, the king is merely a subject of Jesus Christ ("we are but dust and ashes, and our Lord the King is but dust and ashes as well as we"); therefore he dare not impose a pattern of church government that lacks Christ's authorization, that offends men's consciences, and that hinders free spiritual worship and obedience.[119] "Our Lord the King," he insisted,

> is but an earthly king, and he has no authority as a king but in earthly causes, and if the King's people be obedient and true subjects, obeying all human laws made by the King, our Lord the King can require no more. For men's religion to God is betwixt God and themselves; the King shall not answer for it, neither may the King be judge between God and man. Let them be heretics, Turks, Jews or whatsoever, it appertains not to the earthly power to punish them in the least measure.[120]

Helwys published his tract in 1612. In 1614, Leonard Busher took up the same theme, and his *Religion's Peace* was the first pamphlet entirely devoted to religious toleration. Truth, he said, can be established only by spiritual means, and it can be defended only by weapons of the same kind. Persecution is a defiance of Christ's law; by uprooting the tares before the time of harvest, it usurps Christ's prerogative of judgment. Moreover, repression is neither necessary nor effective, and it strikes at the stability and well-being of the community. The aim of the argument was to enforce an appeal. "May it please your majesty and parliament to understand that, by fire and sword, to constrain princes and people to receive that one true religion of the Gospel, is wholly against the mind and merciful law of Christ, dangerous both to king and state, a means to decrease the kingdom of Christ and a means to increase the kingdom of antichrist." [121] Busher considered the existing situation intolerable; his remedy was a resolute divorce of church and state. At the moment, they were so entangled that each inflicted serious injury on the other.

A year later, John Murton and his friends advanced essentially the same arguments and presented to the king a very similar petition. The title page of *Objections: Answered* provides a brief and reasonably exact epitome of the contents of the tract: "wherein is proved by the law of God, by the law of our land and by his Majesty's many testimonies that no man ought

---

[117] *Ibid.,* p. 43.
[118] *Ibid.,* p. 46.
[119] *Ibid.,* pp. 42, 49–50, 54–64.
[120] *Ibid.,* p. 46.
[121] Leonard Busher, *Religion's Peace; or a Plea for Liberty of Conscience* (Ep. Ded.), p. 17.

to be persecuted for his religion, so he testify his allegiance by the oath appointed by law." It had long been common practice to quote Scripture to support one's arguments; Murton was the first to exploit the possibilities latent in the works of James I. But apparently this was a use of his writings that the royal author did not appreciate, and the pleas of the Baptists passed unheeded.

In the years before the summoning of the Long Parliament, the history of the Separatist groups becomes indistinct and obscure. Their numbers remained small, their membership was fluid, their frontiers were often confused. The day of their effective influence seemed to be indefinitely deferred. But they had already accomplished a great deal. They had clearly defined their convictions concerning the true character of the church. They had claimed on behalf of the gathered company of believers the right to regulate its worship and to enforce its discipline. They had entered their plea for liberty to pursue the truth as they understood it, without interference from the authorities of either church or state. "This," they concluded,

> is the sum of our humble petition, that your Majesty would be pleased not to persecute your faithful subjects who are obedient to you in all civil worship and service, for walking in the practice of what God's word requireth of us, for his spiritual worship, as we have faith; knowing, as your Majesty truly writeth in your Meditations on Matthew xxvii these words, "We can use no spiritual worship nor prayer that can be available to us without faith." [122]

[122] *A Most Humble Supplication of Many of the King Majesty's Loyal Subjects,* p. 231.

IX

THE LIBERALS: THE CLAIMS
OF FREEDOM AND THE LIMITATIONS
OF AUTHORITY

IN THE EARLY seventeenth century the champions of authority
were legion. The defenders of freedom were relatively few. As a rule the
claims of intellectual liberty emerged hesitantly amid the contentions of
those who asserted the unique supremacy of one system or another. But
throughout the period there persisted a precarious but important witness
to the rightful place of a balanced freedom. Its advocates wielded an
influence out of all proportion to their number. Some of them were clerics,
some were laymen. One of the most famous coteries took its name from
Lord Falkland's estate at Great Tew in Oxfordshire. Probably all who
were interested in the problem of freedom met from time to time in the
relatively small circle of literary men in London.[1]

The liberal often became aware of his position because he found himself
in reaction against views that could no longer retain his loyalty. The
appropriation of a wider freedom was consequently the final stage of a
pilgrimage that was initially hesitant and even painful. Since Calvinism
was the position most widely held among English Protestants, it was likely
to be the point of departure. It has been plausibly assumed that Lord
Falkland was educated in circles where Calvinist influences were strong.[2]
Reflection convinced him that through a comparison of partial insights
"men may draw forth a whole and perfect body of truth." [3] Circumstances
gave him leisure for intensive study; inclination led him to a searching
examination of the problem of authority and of the place of reason in
Christian thought. He relied on "private sense" rather than on traditional
formulations, but this made him no less ardent in his search for a secure

---

[1] Note Clarendon's account of the circle that, as a young lawyer, he found most congenial.
Clarendon, *Life and Continuation*, I, 28–55.

[2] This seems to be true in spite of his mother's conversion to Roman Catholicism. Trinity
College, Dublin, where he was educated, was strongly Calvinist. K. Weber, *Lucius Cary,
Second Viscount Falkland*, p. 35.

[3] Falkland, quoted in B. H. G. Wormald, *Clarendon: Politics, Historiography and Religion*,
p. 259.

basis for faith. He steadily modified his earlier views. In discussing free will he acknowledged that he found Pelagianism preferable to Calvinism, "since the first doth not wholly overthrow God's grace (for whatever we have by nature his grace gives us), but the second wholly overthrows his justice." On election, also, he had clearly broken with the Calvinist position. "God may be said," he wrote, "to have mankind for his elect, if they shut not themselves out of the way to be so; and all men (especially Christians) I believe have, and always shall have, means enough to perform those conditions in such a measure . . . as shall by God be from them required." [4] Falkland was now prepared to devote the full vigor of his mind to three closely related causes: the advocacy of religious tolerance, the defense of the supremacy of reason, and the championship of intellectual freedom.

More clearly charted was the intellectual pilgrimage of "the ever memorable Mr. John Hales of Eton College." [5] As a young man he had been content with the theology in which he had been trained. When James I sent a delegation to join the representatives of other "Reformed" churches at the Synod of Dort, Hales was included in its membership. One of his duties was to keep Sir Dudley Carleton, ambassador at The Hague, informed of the progress of the debates, and initially his letters reflected no uneasiness about the Calvinist position. The synod had been convened to deal with the challenge to high Calvinism posed by the theology of Jacob Arminius, and the crucial point at issue was the doctrine of predestination. When the Remonstrants (the critics of Calvinist orthodoxy) were finally admitted to the synod, Hales's comments were conspicuously lacking in cordiality. He remarked on "the exorbitancy of the Remonstrants"; the chief problem of the moment, he believed, was how "to contain it." [6] Episcopius' great plea for a more generous definition of the scope of salvation failed to move the synod, but it must have converted Hales. As he subsequently reported, it was at Dort that he "bid John Calvin good night." [7] Clarendon quoted Hales's remark that "he would renounce the religion of the Church of England tomorrow if it obliged him to believe that any other Christians would be damned: and that no body would conclude another man to be damned, who did not wish him so." [8] Hales reached the conviction that "the will of God and his manner of proceeding in predestination is undiscernible and shall so

[4] Falkland, *A Reply*, pp. 126, 144. This work is an answer to a response to his *Discourse on Infallibility*. The three are often published together.

[5] This was the designation by which his immediate successors knew him. It appears on the title page of *The Golden Remains* (a very popular seventeenth-century selection of his writings), and of the collected edition of his works published in Glasgow in 1765.

[6] Hales, "Letters from the Synod of Dort," *Golden Remains*, pp. 410, 448. Cf. also pp. 434, 439.

[7] Hales, *Golden Remains*, Prefatory Letter of Mr. Faringdon.

[8] Clarendon, *Life and Continuation*, I, 50.

remain until that day wherein all knowledge shall be made perfect." [9] He could quote Calvin's opinions and criticize them severely.[10] But his reaction against his former beliefs was sane and balanced. Though increasingly opposed to Calvinism, he remained aware of the importance of the issues it raised, and he was quite prepared to give Calvin credit where he felt that such credit was due.[11]

In certain respects William Chillingworth was the most distinguished member of the group.[12] He reached essentially the same position as Falkland and Hales, but he came to it by a much more tortuous route. As a fellow of Trinity College, Oxford, he seemed assured of a brilliant career in the university and in the church. Then, to the dismay of his Anglican associates, he was reconciled to the Church of Rome. Subsequently he explained his motives with care: "I thought myself to have sufficient reason to believe that there was and must always be in the world some church that could not err; and consequently, seeing all other churches disclaimed this privilege of not being subject to error, the Church of Rome must be that church which cannot err." [13] The fragmented state of Christendom seemed tragic; the first step in restoring its lost unity, he felt, was to recognize a single center of authority, at once universal and supreme. Initially the Reformation had promised men a wider measure of liberty; it had ended by multiplying the tests and standards so destructive of freedom. He believed that Rome possessed the authority which he considered desirable, and that she would permit sufficient latitude of interpretation to enable him to enjoy the liberty that he deemed so necessary. He soon discovered that he had misconceived the temper of the post-Tridentine Roman church: doctrinally it was less comprehensive than he had expected, nor was it so ready to respect the intellectual integrity of its members as he had hoped. Still searching for an accommodation between freedom and authority, Chillingworth therefore began the return journey which ultimately brought him to preferment in the Church of England. The considerations that persuaded him to reject Roman claims made him suspicious of Calvinist dogmatism.[14] He was

[9] Hales, "Of Dealing with Erring Christians," *Golden Remains,* p. 65.

[10] Hales, "A Tract Concerning the Sin Against the Holy Ghost," *Tracts,* pp. 18, 24–35.

[11] Hales, *Golden Remains,* pp. 133, 282; *ibid.,* p. 26: one factor compelling Catholics to take more seriously the meaning of Scripture was "the great credit of Calvin's writings in that kind."

[12] R. R. Orr's study of Chillingworth, *Reason and Authority,* appeared after this chapter was written, but it was of great value in thoroughly revising my material.

[13] Chillingworth, "Additional Discourses, VIII, An Account of what moved the Author to turn Papist . . . ," *The Works of William Chillingworth* (12th ed.), p. 720.

[14] Cf. Chillingworth, *The Religion of Protestants,* Ch. VII, §4 (p. 480). Chillingworth's famous work is divided into chapters (answering those of his opponent Knott), and these into numbered paragraphs. References are therefore to chapter and paragraph in Chillingworth's (not Knott's) contribution; the page references are to the 12th edition of *The Works of William Chillingworth* (1736).

equally reluctant to submit to the demands of Laudian Anglicanism. Laud's letters had won him back from Rome; he was duly grateful, but he was not prepared to accept without careful scrutiny Laud's type of churchmanship.[15] The background of the liberals was authoritarianism— Catholic, Laudian, or Puritan. In reaction against it they sought an accommodation between faith and reason; once this was achieved, they believed it could be combined with a comprehensive tolerance and commended to others in the spirit of charity.

It has sometimes been suggested that the antecedents of these men should be sought, not in the Reformation but in the humanism of the Renaissance. Certainly they recognized in Erasmus a kindred spirit. They quoted him with approval. Like him, they were critical of dogmatism and impatient with ecclesiastical pretensions. They had something of the versatility and intellectual curiosity that had flourished in an earlier day. They combined a spirit of critical inquiry with a strong desire for peace. They wanted a resolution of religious strife that would safeguard both their intellectual integrity and their Christian charity. All this suggests a debt to Erasmus, but with certain strains of Renaissance humanism they had no sympathy at all. They sought to safeguard the dignity of man, but they looked for its fulfillment in complete dependence upon God. "Beloved," said Hales, "our case is like that of the men of Athens; Vulcan the devil hath made us fools and weak, and so we are indeed of ourselves. But the Son of God, the true Pallas, the Wisdom of the Father, hath given us this gift, that our weakness shall never hurt us. For look, what strength we lost in Adam, that with infinite advantage, is supplied in Christ."[16] Whereas man often forgets his actual need, he usually neglects his potential strength—which is not a natural endowment but a divine gift.[17] It might be fair to suggest that the liberals were the heirs of Erasmus in their distaste for dogma, their reverence for reason, their charitable spirit, and their commitment to the scholarly examination of the Scriptures. But they were children of the Reformation in their distrust of Rome, their denial of infallibility, and their conviction that the Bible supplies a sufficient basis for religious authority. They believed, indeed, that the upheaval of the sixteenth century had been a valid and necessary reformation but an imperfect and tentative one. To the task of appropriating the further gifts that they believed God would confer, they humbly dedicated their efforts.

In establishing a true concept of authority, the first step was to sweep away misconceptions. The controversies of the age made the liberals particularly sensitive to the problem of infallibility; Chillingworth's

[15] Laud, as Chillingworth's godfather, took a particular interest in his case; he was doubtless also concerned about the fate of a brilliant member of his university. Chillingworth attributed his reconversion to Laud's letters; unfortunately, they do not survive.
[16] Hales, "Christian Omnipotency," *Golden Remains,* p. 147.
[17] *Ibid.,* pp. 153–154.

experience as a Roman convert pushed it to the forefront of attention. Facts alone seemed to demolish any special claim to be exempt from error. Hales believed that "infallibility either in judgment or in interpretation or whatsoever" cannot automatically be attributed to any institution or to any individual within it. Councils cannot establish a claim. Neither can the fathers.[18] Chillingworth pointed out "that there are popes against popes, councils against councils, some Fathers against others, the same Fathers against themselves, a consent of Fathers of one age against the consent of the Fathers of another age, the church of one age against the church of another age. Traditive interpretations of Scripture are pretended, but these are few or none to be found." [19] Careful study convinced Hales that there is no guarantee that church decisions can appeal to more than human authority, and consequently there is no guarantee that churches will not err even in fundamental matters. Admittedly it would be reassuring if unassailable certainty could be found. Falkland acknowledged that he would have been relieved to accept what he had "rationally rejected, an infallible judge here on earth in all controversies in point of religion." [20] Since none could be found, there was no alternative, said Chillingworth, but to repudiate "the vain and arrogant pretence of infallibility." [21] When churches claimed the right to define the truth infallibly, they were merely attempting to establish an impregnable empire over the minds of men. "He that would usurp an absolute lordship and tyranny over any people," said Chillingworth,

> need not put himself to the trouble and difficulty of abrogating and disannuling the laws, made to maintain the common liberty; for he may frustrate their intent, and compass his own design as well, if he can get the power and authority to interpret them as he pleases, and to add to them what he pleases, and to have his interpretations and additions stand for laws; if he can rule his people by his laws, and his laws by his lawyers. So the Church of Rome, to establish her tyranny over men's consciences, need not either to abolish or corrupt the holy Scriptures, the pillars and supporters of Christian liberty; . . . but the more expedite way, and therefore more likely to be successful, was to gain the opinion and esteem of the public and authorized interpreter of them, and the authority of adding to them what doctrine she pleased, under the title of traditions or definitions.[22]

The case for infallibility was weak; the results of pressing it were bad. The corrupting effects of power were always present. Edward Knott,

---

[18] Hales, *Works,* I, 65–69. Cf. Chillingworth, *op. cit.,* II, §128, and Falkland, *A Reply,* p. 7.
[19] Chillingworth, *op. cit.,* VI, §56 (p. 465).
[20] Falkland, *Sir Lucius Cary, late Viscount of Falkland, his Discourse of Infallibility,* Ep. Ded.
[21] Chillingworth, *op. cit.,* II, §1 (p. 90).
[22] *Ibid.*

Chillingworth's antagonist, had argued that if the Scriptures had not been
entrusted to an infallible guardian, they would inevitably have been
corrupted. This, retorted Chillingworth, misconceives the danger; the
truth was "more likely to have been corrupted . . . for the advantage of
those men whose ambition it hath been a long time to bring all under their
authority." [23] Perils still more subtle and pernicious lurked within the
doctrine. It fostered the dangerous illusion that "the commandments of
men can be taught as the commandments of God," and this deprived men
of the responsibility of exercising their critical faculties. At this point we
touch one of the fundamental convictions of the liberals. They saw God
and man linked in a relationship that is profoundly moral in quality.
Consequently, man dare not evade his ethical responsibility, and this
obligation embraces the spheres both of action and of thought. We are
free moral agents and must behave accordingly. We are summoned to
obey the truth, with the sobering awareness that we must see for ourselves
its validity and accept its constraint by our own free choice. This emphasis
appears repeatedly in Chillingworth. We also meet it in Hales's belief that
there is only one infallible judge in controversies of faith: the reason and
conscience of each man as he confronts the ethical decisions in which his
daily life involves him.[24] Yet it was precisely this kind of moral sensitivity
that, in Chillingworth's opinion, had been steadily eroded by the claims of
an infallible church. Men had not been allowed to approach ethical
dilemmas with the alertness of morally free agents because casuistry had
applied to difficult questions a series of answers based on infallible
authority. But since Chillingworth had argued at considerable length that
infallibility was logically an indefensible concept, he believed that man's
ethical decisions demanded a more secure foundation than anything it
provided.

If infallibility endangers ethical alertness, it equally threatens intellectual endeavor. Man is summoned, by the character of his relationship
with God, to seek the truth. But the specter of infallibility discourages the
fainthearted and intimidates the sincere,[25] and as a result both abandon
the quest for truth even before they have begun. Moreover, the man who
regards his reason as a divine endowment and uses it in the pursuit of truth
too often finds that, if his conclusions diverge from authorized teachings,
the upholders of authority condemn him even for his quest. "Nay, grant
the church to be infallible," said Falkland, "yet methinks that he that
denies it and employs his reason to seek if it be true, should be in as good
case as he that believeth it and searcheth not at all the truth of the
proposition he receives." [26] If intellectual integrity is prized, the champi-

[23] *Ibid.,* §27 (p. 188).
[24] Hales, "Of Enquiry and Private Judgment in Religion," *Works,* III, 155.
[25] Chillingworth, *op. cit.,* VII, §17 (p. 490).
[26] Falkland, *Infallibility,* n.p.

ons of infallibility have accomplished very little. "Where there is fire for them that disagree, they need not brag of their uniformity who consent." [27]

A critique of infallibility presupposed a reassessment of authority itself. Chillingworth, of course, had condemned a view that he had once embraced but that he could no longer accept. In spite of the apparent vagaries of his intellectual pilgrimage, he had consistently pursued certain objectives, and his loyalty to these affected the kind of authority he ultimately recognized. As we have already noted, he sought a church that would be comprehensive in doctrine and sensitive to the intellectual integrity of its members. He left the Roman communion because he felt that these concerns were not respected. He hesitated to accept preferment in the Church of England because similar doubts were unresolved. As he wrote to his friend Gilbert Sheldon, he was satisfied that "the damning sentences in St. Athanasius' creed . . . are most false, and also in high degree presumptuous and schismatical. And therefore I can neither subscribe, that these things are agreeable to the word of God, seeing I believe they are certainly repugnant to it; nor that the whole Common Prayer is lawful to be used, seeing I believe these parts of it certainly unlawful." [28] Sheldon, in some alarm, pointed out that such an attitude was likely to "ruin you here and not advantage you at the last day," but Chillingworth was not suffering from an attack of spiritual quixotry. As always he was disturbed by the suggestion that a particular church could claim the final word in theological disputes, and he distrusted any view that further postponed the possibility of reuniting a divided Christendom. In this case Chillingworth believed that his private scruples illustrated a wider problem. The church was always prone to insist that matters which are essentially uncertain must be accorded the status of necessary truth, with the result that the church is rent by schism.

> This presumptuous imposing of the senses of men upon the word of God, the special senses of men upon the general words of God, and laying them upon men's consciences together, under the equal penalty of death and damnation; this vain conceit that we can speak of the things of God better than in the words of God; this deifying our own interpretations, and tyrannous enforcing them upon others; this restraining of the word of God from that latitude and generality, and the understandings of men from that liberty, wherein Christ and the apostles left them, is, and hath been, the only fountain of all the schisms of the church, and that which makes them immortal.[29]

The crux of the problem of authority lies precisely in the difference

---

[27] *Ibid.*
[28] Chillingworth, *op. cit.*, VII, §17 (p. 490).
[29] Chillingworth, *op. cit.*, IV, §16 (p. 253).

between things that are metaphysically certain and those that are morally
probable. It is tempting to believe that the truths that we profess belong in
the former category; actually they usually fall in the latter. But this is
quite sufficient for most purposes. Only within a very narrow range do our
beliefs possess coercive certainty. A man who has never been to
Constantinople may be reasonably satisfied that the city exists, even
though he must rely on the reports of others. It can be shown, moreover,
that we gain rather than lose from the fact that we must commit ourselves
to truths which fall short of absolute finality. There are advantages in
beliefs that are open to question: if our faith is validly founded, discussion
is more likely to enlarge our insight than to diminish our assurance.
Criticism strips away irrelevant or erroneous features; it may even
persuade us to abandon an indefensible belief in favor of one more firmly
based upon the truth. The circumstances that make humble inquiry an
advantage make most controversies a curse. Most of the debates that then
divided his contemporaries could only be resolved, Chillingworth believed,
if men had access to a measure of certainty which was actually denied
them. They anathematized one another for the sake of matters in which
finality cannot be achieved, and in the process they distorted Scripture—
the true source of spiritual illumination—to serve ends other than those for
which it was given. And all the while they forfeited the kind of assurance
that morally certain truths can convey.

In most things men ought to be content with assurance that is within
their reach rather than to strain after certainty that is beyond it.
Chillingworth returned repeatedly to the essential fact that it is only when
we forgo the pretense to certainty that we are free to seek and find the
truth for ourselves—and herein is the only dependable guarantee of our
intellectual integrity. More than our own moral nature is thus protected.
Our view of authority affects our understanding of God. If salvation
depends on the acceptance of truths that are not metaphysically certain,
all who hesitate to submit to such demands are damned, though their fault
may be caused by a conscientious reluctance to believe what cannot be
proved. This penalizes men for integrity, and it makes God guilty of
arbitrary and immoral judgments. On few points were the liberals so
emphatic as on the need to think of God in moral terms. Mercy is more
important than might; the attributes revealed by his dealings with men
are more significant than our definitions of what he must be in himself.
God's goodness, as Hales pointed out, is "not that metaphysical conceit
which we dispute of in our schools, and is nothing else but that perfection
which is inwardly due unto the being of every creature . . . but that which
the common sort of men do usually understand, when they call a man
good; by which is meant nothing else but . . . a soft, and sweet, and
flexible disposition." [30] One firm inference that we may draw from the

[30] Hales, "Of Dealing with Erring Christians," *Golden Remains*, p. 25.

moral goodness of God is that he will not lay upon us unreasonable demands. Unlike Pharaoh, he will not require bricks if he provides no straw.[31] "But this I am sure of," wrote Chillingworth, "as sure as that God is good, that he will require no impossibilities of us; not an infallible, nor a certainly unerring belief, unless he hath given us certain means to avoid error; and if we use those which we have, he will never require of us, that we use that which we have not." [32] This obviously holds true of what is demanded of us in terms of conduct, but it equally applies to what is expected of us in terms of belief. As Chillingworth remarked, "our obligation expressly to know any truth must arise from God's manifest revealing of it, and his revealing unto us that he hath revealed it, and that his will is we should believe it"; but since these conditions are not easily satisfied, we can be sure that it is part of God's gracious purpose to treat erring mortals with mercy: "neither doubt I, but God, who knows whereof we are made, and what passions we are subject unto, will compassionate such infirmities and not enter into judgment with us for those things, which, all things considered, were unavoidable." [33] His demands are adjusted to the resources at our disposal: "it is sufficient that he denies us nothing necessary to salvation." [34] Any church, therefore, that requires implicit acceptance of debatable points obscures the moral nature of God, threatens the intellectual integrity of man, and jeopardizes the relationship that ought to unite God and man. Cumulatively this is a severe indictment of ecclesiastical pretension. "For where the truth of God doth once suffer," wrote Hales, "there . . . authority is but tyranny." [35]

At certain points, one might expect, the lack of a precise definition of authority would have to yield to the demand for greater precision. Surely some doctrines must be accepted without question; the distinction between beliefs which are fundamental and those which are not (cited by many Protestants) must have some binding effect. Similarly must there not be some test by which faith can be distinguished from heresy? Here it is sufficient to remark that Chillingworth believed that there are certain fundamental articles of belief, but he was notably reluctant to enumerate them. In one passage he mentions a number of doctrines that he obviously regards as essential to the Christian faith, but the list is not exhaustive, and he insists that it is not decisive.[36] He is perfectly satisfied, moreover, that salvation is not dependent upon identifying the crucial doctrines and accepting them. Once more he falls back on his understanding of what God expects of men. Christianity is not a kind of intricate puzzle. God may intend to communicate certain truths in certain passages of Scripture,

[31] Chillingworth, *op. cit.*, II, §104 (p. 131).
[32] *Ibid.*, II, §152 (p. 150).
[33] *Ibid.*, III, §19 (p. 184).
[34] *Ibid.*, III, §88 (p. 230).
[35] Hales, "A Tract Concerning the Sacrament of the Lord's Supper," *Tracts*, p. 83.
[36] Chillingworth, *op. cit.*, II, §127 (p. 140).

"but to believe this or that to be the true sense of them, and to avoid the false, is not necessary either to faith or salvation. For if God would have had his meaning in these places certainly known, how could it stand with his wisdom, to be so wanting to his own will and end, as to speak obscurely?" [37] The exercise of reason is the condition of recognizing fundamental doctrines. Heresy also is not determined merely by definition. Its primary symptom is disloyalty to the truth. The clear sense of Scripture will reveal what must be rejected, and a heretic is not he who misses his way in the realms of abstract theology but he who denies "what is clearly manifest to be the truth." [38] "An heretic therefore I conceive him, that holds an error against faith with obstinacy. Obstinate I conceive him, who will not change his opinion, when his reasons for it are so answered, that he cannot reply; and when the reasons against it are so convincing that he cannot answer them." [39]

It does not rest with human institutions, declared Chillingworth, to determine the infallible truths that men must accept in order to escape damnation. Reflection convinced him that authority is a highly complex idea. He concluded that probability is as close to certainty as we can normally hope to come, and this modest view compelled him to examine a variety of related topics. The organ of authority, he believed, is reason. The locus of authority is the Bible. The agent of authority is the church. The transmission of authority is assisted by tradition. Salvation is the all-engrossing theme that warrants the whole debate. Freedom and moral responsibility are the values that must not be forfeited. Charity is the temper that should be inseparable from so serious a quest, and a generous tolerance of others ought to mark our attitude to all engaged in the same momentous enterprise.

It was safe to depreciate the authority of ecclesiastical institutions, provided some adequate substitute could be found. The liberals challenged the church's right to lift its pronouncements above controversy because they believed that man's moral autonomy compelled him to depend on more guides than one. In particular, they exalted reason and Scripture as the aids on which he could normally rely. This seemed appropriate enough: "natural reason" is "the only principle, beside Scripture, which is common to Christians." [40] Sometimes the two were treated as alternatives, sometimes as coordinates. "Every man," said Chillingworth, "is to judge and choose; and the rule whereby he has to guide his choice, if he be already a Christian, is Scripture; which, we say, is the rule to judge controversies by." [41] An optimistic view of human

[37] *Ibid.*

[38] *Ibid.* Cf. *The Religion of Protestants,* Ch. III (pp. 176–232).

[39] Chillingworth, "Additional Discourses: A Conference Betwixt Mr. Chillingworth and Mr. Lewgar," in *Works,* p. 675. Chillingworth's views on heresy are most fully developed in *The Religion of Protestants,* Ch. VI (pp. 412–471).

[40] Chillingworth, *op. cit.,* II, §3 (p. 91).

[41] *Ibid.,* II, §11 (p. 95).

nature involved a generous appreciation of man's faculties. "Oh, the strength of reason rightly managed!" cried Falkland. "Oh, the power of truth clearly declared." [42] Surely it betrayed "poverty of spirit and indiscretion" to belittle the gifts with which God has endowed his creatures, especially when reason is distinctively a human attribute. [43] This is what "gives us the prerogative above other creatures and wholly entitles us to future happiness"; is it convincing to suggest that it "should be laid aside and not used" in achieving our highest ends? [44] "And how then," asked Hales, "can it stand with reason, that a man should be the possessor of so goodly a piece of the Lord's pasture as is the light of understanding and reason, which he hath endowed us with in the day of our creation, if he suffer it to lie untilled or sow not in it the Lord's seed?" Hales believed that in our "course of integrity and sanctity," the "faculty of reason" is like "your eyes to direct you and your legs to support you"; "you may," he added, "no more refuse or neglect the use of it, and rest yourself upon the use of other men's reason, than neglect your own and call for the use of other men's eyes and legs." [45]

Reason, then, is a natural endowment that must not be neglected in the most important of all our human responsibilities. What exactly is the role of reason in religion? In the first place, it performs certain useful but essentially negative functions. It clears away "the rubbish and impertinent lumber" that have been permitted to obscure "the glorious simplicity" of Christianity. [46] In the second place, reason is the means by which we "discern between truth and falsehood"; when God endowed us with this faculty, he intended that we should use it for this purpose. [47] Furthermore, reason is necessary if we are to attain to any kind of valid faith. A man must not only know what he believes but why he believes it: there is no other way to God "but by thoroughly perceiving and understanding religion and discovering the uttermost grounds on which it subsists." [48] Finally, it seemed clear that reason is the means by which the essential truths contained in the Bible can be grasped. That such essential truths existed, Chillingworth did not doubt for a moment, but he also believed that the passive and negligent reader might not find them. Only "the reasonable man" will recognize and appropriate them, and he will need to be alert to criticism and ready to accept fresh evidence. This exercise of reason is our protection against the vagaries of erratic interpretations. "Neither do we follow any private men, but only the

[42] Falkland, *Infallibility*, Preface.
[43] Hales, "Of Enquiry and Private Judgment," *Works*, III, 155.
[44] Sir John Suckling, *An Account of Religion by Reason*, Ep. Ded.
[45] Hales, "Of Enquiry and Private Judgment," *Works*, III, 153-154.
[46] Chillingworth, "A Conference Betwixt Mr. Chillingworth and Mr. Lewgar," *Works*, p. 675.
[47] Chillingworth, *The Religion of Protestants*, II, §113 (p. 134).
[48] Hales, "Of Enquiry and Private Judgment," *Works*, III, 164.

Scripture, the Word of God, as our rule; and reason which is also the gift of God given to direct us in all our actions, in the use of this rule." [49]

It may be objected that Chillingworth and his friends did little to provide any clear understanding of reason itself. They were writing, of course, in the days before Locke defined with greater precision the terms crucial in the discussion. By reason they certainly meant the systematic use of our intelligence. They included the exact and logical examination of the subject under discussion. They had a strong confidence in the importance of using our mental powers, but they also recognized that there are limits that we ought to observe. Those who rely too heavily on reason, they noticed, were often involved in contention, but the risk had to be taken, since "that peace which ariseth out of ignorance is but a kind of sloth or moral lethargy, seeming quiet because it hath no power to move." [50] Beyond a certain point intellectual curiosity ceases to be a virtue and becomes a vice. "I have," wrote Hales, "I confess, the same disease that my first parents in Paradise had, a desire to know more than I need." [51] Consequently, the exercise of reason must be closely allied to the spirit of moderation. Through the association of these two we may hope to develop the critical objectivity that will save us from arrogance and pride, from the effects of passion or fanaticism, and from all other hazards to which human intelligence is peculiarly exposed. Here virtue is likely to be its own reward: as Falkland reminds us, "the truth in all likelihood is where her author God was, in the still small voice and not the loud wind." [52] Moderation will also preserve that humble quality which clever people so often overlook—common sense. In the early part of the seventeenth century there were still men who believed that a wound could be healed if the weapon that inflicted it were anointed with the appropriate salve. In Hales's letter on the subject, he combined a whimsical irony with a shrewd assessment of the medical advantages of cleanliness in order to reduce the medieval myth to its proper proportions. Only Sir Thomas Browne combined these ingredients to better effect. [53]

The liberals stressed the rightful place of reason in religion; they never suggested that it could be regarded as sufficient by itself. One of the conspicuous features of their thought is the intimate connection that they postulate between reason and revelation. The ideal that Hales invoked in all his inquiries was "Reason illuminated by revelation out of God's Word." [54] He believed that "right reason" was not as easily achieved as some overconfident rationalists implied, and the guidance of Scripture

[49] Chillingworth, *op. cit.,* VI, §55 (p. 464).

[50] Hales, "Of Enquiry and Private Judgment," *Works,* III, 156.

[51] Hales, "Abuses of Hard Places of Scripture," *Golden Remains,* p. 30.

[52] Falkland, *Infallibility,* n.p.

[53] Hales, "Miscellanies," *Golden Remains,* p. 360.

[54] Hales, "A Tract Concerning the Sacrament of the Lord's Supper," *Tracts,* p. 75. Hales used the identical words in "Of Dealing with Erring Christians."

became an extremely necessary supplement to what intelligence alone could provide. He was more concerned to insist on their complementary character than to determine their relative importance. This, indeed, was a matter on which he refused to be dogmatic. "I find it very hard to discover," wrote John Beale to Robert Boyle, "how much or how little of religion we have in the frame of our natures: and to distinguish that from all kinds of revelation or tradition. And Mr. Hales told me often, that he found himself utterly at a loss in that point." [55]

The proper use of reason will safeguard our intellectual integrity. The possession of holy Scripture will guarantee us access to the sources of revealed truth. The balance between these two elements is, as we have seen, important, but there is no doubt where the principal emphasis falls. Basically Christianity is not a form of rationalism, but a rational way of appropriating the truths of revelation. As Hales remarked, "it is most certain that the Scripture contains at least the fundamental parts of the Christian religion." [56] Chillingworth was quite aware of the temptation to erect the Bible into an infallible authority, but this seemed to him as serious a menace to the truth as any other authoritarian system. "The books of Scripture," he remarked, "are not so much the objects of our faith, as the instruments of conveying it to our understanding." [57] The instrument, of course, is of crucial importance. It not merely brings us the truth; it does so in such a way that our freedom is preserved, our essential unity maintained, and our ultimate salvation ensured. "There is no sufficient certainty but of Scripture only, for any considering man to build upon," said Chillingworth, but since this seems to imply a literalist view of Biblical authority, it is advisable to quote in full the passage that contains the most famous of all Chillingworth's phrases. The religious truths on which Protestants agree are not collected from the writings of any of the major reformers, nor from the confessional statements of the churches of the Reformation.

> But that wherein they all agree, and which they all subscribe with a greater harmony, as a perfect rule of their faith and actions: that is the Bible. The Bible, I say, the Bible only, is the religion of Protestants! Whatsoever else they believe besides it, and the plain, irrefragable, indubitable consequences of it, well may they hold it as a matter of opinion: but as matter of faith and religion, neither can they with coherence to their own grounds believe it themselves, nor require the belief of others, without most high and most schismatical presumption. I, for my part, after a long, and (as I verily believe and hope) impartial search of the true way to eternal happiness, do profess plainly

[55] John Beale to Robert Boyle, *The Works of Robert Boyle*, VI, 392.
[56] Hales, *Tracts*, p. 80.
[57] Chillingworth, *op. cit.*, II, §159 (p. 155).

that I cannot find any rest for the sole of my foot but upon this rock only.[58]

It is unjust, he claimed, to accuse Protestants of substituting the Bible for the pope, an infallible book for an infallible figure. The Bible coerces neither intellect nor conscience. In following Scripture, said Chillingworth,

> I shall believe many mysteries but no impossibilities; many things above reason but nothing against it; many things which, had they not been revealed, reason could never have discovered, but nothing which by true reason can be confuted; many things which reason cannot comprehend how they can be, but nothing which reason can comprehend that it cannot be. Nay, I shall believe nothing which reason will not convince me that I ought to believe it: for reason will convince any man, unless he be of a perverse mind, that the Scripture is the word of God: and then no reason can be greater than this, God says so, therefore it is true.[59]

The Bible plays a crucial role in the life of faith because of its intimate connection with salvation. "Believe the Scripture to be the word of God, use your endeavour to find the true sense of it, and to live according to it, and then you may rest securely that you are in the true way of eternal happiness." [60] Chillingworth believed that it was "sufficient for any man's salvation to believe that the Scripture is true, and contains all things necessary for salvation," and do his best to determine its exact meaning. But he added a qualification: this was sufficient but not necessary. "Men might be saved without believing the Scripture to be the word of God, much more without believing it to be a rule, and a perfect rule of faith." In other words, we must believe the substance of the good news; we need not commit ourselves to certain views about its source. We "should believe the matter of these books, not the authority of the books." [61]

The measure of authority that Chillingworth assigned to the Bible was the direct outcome of his doctrine of "sufficiency." He believed that by virtue of his moral nature God was obliged to make available to every man sufficient means to enable him to work out his own salvation. He was not required to provide enough for everyone to fashion a complete theological system. So the meaning of Scripture need not be "effectually and irresistibly" evident; it is enough for it to be "sufficiently clear." We can therefore expect a reasonable certainty concerning the truth of Scripture and the meaning of that truth. We cannot look for more. Since the Bible

[58] *Ibid.,* VI, §56 (pp. 464–465).
[59] *Ibid.,* VI, §62 (p. 466).
[60] *Ibid.,* IV, §53 (p. 277).
[61] *Ibid.,* II, §159 (p. 155).

is a long book and a very complex one, we should not be surprised if it contains many things that we do not understand. But are there any standards that we can apply in this seemingly indeterminate area? In reply, Chillingworth pointed to the distinction between "points fundamental and not fundamental." Some truths are set forth in the Bible so clearly that no one can miss their meaning. Such truths are embodied in doctrines that are essential to the faith, and all Christians, he felt, could be persuaded to accept these fundamental articles of belief. This interpretation both of Scripture and of doctrine was in keeping with Chillingworth's basic convictions. Man and his rational freedom in pursuit of truth, God and his moral purpose of revealing such a measure of truth that man's needs are satisfied and his liberty preserved—these are safeguarded by his view of the Bible as revelation. In "those places which are so plain and clear that they need no interpreters" God has disclosed "those particular doctrines which integrate Christianity." [62] We can safely assume, therefore, "that all things necessary to be believed are evidently contained in Scripture, and what is not there evidently contained, cannot be necessary to be believed." [63] His appeal is to the ability of the average person to recognize and appropriate what is true; he is convinced that there are parts of the Bible "so plain and evident that no man of ordinary sense can mistake the sense of them." [64] The purpose of revelation, we must assume, is to reveal; what God wants us to know, he will not declare in unintelligible terms.[65] Undoubtedly there are many passages in the Bible that are ambiguous, "capable of diverse senses." What are we to say of these? Surely we must conclude that they contain truths that may be interesting or even profitable, but that are certainly not essential to salvation. "And in such cases," added Chillingworth, "it is no marvel, and sure no sin, if several men go several ways." [66]

When the Bible was conceded such a measure of authority, the way it should be used became a crucial question. The problem of interpretation was a major preoccupation of the early seventeenth century, and the fact that the liberals did not treat the Bible as an infallible book made the issue more acute, not less so. Chillingworth believed that men are morally responsible for the way they use Scripture—even for the interpretations they advance. The seriousness of the task is related to its difficulties. Everyone, said Hales, can understand the Bible; but not everyone is qualified to expound it. "Scripture is given to all, to learn; but to teach,

---

[62] *Ibid.,* II, §150 (p. 149).

[63] *Ibid.,* II, §155 (p. 153).

[64] *Ibid.,* III, §24 (p. 186). Cf. Hales, "Abuses of Hard Places of Scripture," *Golden Remains,* p. 25.

[65] Cf. Chillingworth, *op. cit.,* II, §127 (p. 140): "How can it consist with his justice, to require of men to know certainly the meaning of those words, which he himself hath not revealed?"

[66] *Ibid.,* I, §13 (p. 70).

and to interpret, only to a few." [67] Because he shared Chillingworth's view
of plain and unintelligible parts of the Bible, he felt that skill and learning
were necessary qualifications for the exegete. Chillingworth agreed; the
interpretation of Scripture demanded the sustained use of all our
intellectual powers. Those undertaking so demanding a task will find that
"Scripture is a rule which will not fit itself to the obliquity of our conceits,
but our perverse and crooked discourse must fit itself to the straitness of
that rule." [68] Before Scripture can be wisely used, two preliminary
questions must be answered: What method of interpretation will enable us
to find in the Bible the source of religious truth? In view of the bitterness
caused by conflicting views, how can peace and charity be maintained?
Hales admitted that some parts of the Bible invited more than one
interpretation, but much of the contention created by differing explanations arose from human error. He detected three causes chiefly responsible
for "the wresting of Scripture": we are too prone to find in dark passages
"the image of our own conceits"; we bring to the task too much
"greenness" of scholarship; we entertain "too great presumption of the
subtlety of our own wits." We twist the meaning of the Bible, we wrangle
about it, we rely too largely on our own sufficiency, we prematurely jump
to indefensible interpretations.[69] The first step in avoiding this danger is to
discover what the Bible actually says—"the literal, plain, uncontroversa-
ble meaning of Scripture, without any addition or supply by way of
interpretation." [70] The next requirement is to resist the temptation to
impose upon the text "some pretended sense of Scripture," some personal
idiosyncrasy of exegesis. Actually there are "but two certain and infallible
interpreters of Scripture: either itself, or the Holy Ghost the author of
it." [71] As a corrective of the bitter spirit so often engendered by debate,
Hales recommended charity and moderation. We would all benefit from
"restraining ourselves from presumptive confidence in our own judgement." It would actually "befit our Christian modesty to participate
somewhat of the sceptic, and to use their withholding of judgement, till the
remainder of our knowledge be supplied by Christ." [72]

The unique authority of the Bible derives from its relation to the
paramount issue of salvation, but in other areas also it plays a vital part.
It is "a rule by which we judge controversies," indeed, "as perfect as a
written rule can be." [73] In this respect it takes the place assigned by
Chillingworth's opponent, Edward Knott, to the pope and to the church.
Knott assumed that faith would prove untenable if deprived of an

[67] Hales, *Tracts*, p. 12.
[68] *Ibid.*, p. 3.
[69] *Ibid.*, pp. 3–10.
[70] *Ibid.*, p. 24.
[71] *Ibid.*, pp. 18–19.
[72] *Ibid.*, p. 30.
[73] Chillingworth, *op. cit.*, II, §155 (p. 152).

infallible judge, qualified to resolve all disputes. Such a need might be asserted, said Chillingworth, but it could not be proved.[74] Some problems do not admit of assured and final answers, and this is a blessing in disguise. The margin of doubt that persists is a valuable concomitant of our freedom: uncertainty is sometimes a protection against the tyranny of authority. But most religious controversies can be resolved by Scripture, provided Scripture is used as reason and insight direct.[75] Furthermore, the authority of the Bible is evidenced by the fact that it provides the necessary foundation for Christian unity. In its clear and essential teaching, the Scripture sets forth the basic truths on which all Christians should—and can—agree. "For we want not unity, nor means to procure it in things necessary. Plain places of Scripture, and such as need no interpreter, are our means to obtain it." [76] Furthermore, the Bible provides the kind of latitude that freedom demands: it offers all that is necessary to those who "are willing to leave all men to their liberty, provided they will not improve it to a tyranny over others." [77] Allow men to read and interpret the Bible without external constraint, and they will soon isolate the essential truths of the gospel. "Let, I say, these most certain and divine truths be laid for foundations, and let our superstructions be consequent and coherent to them; and I am confident peace would be restored and truth maintained." [78] Nor were the liberals likely to forget that, though the Bible serves important intellectual ends, it ministers to the totality of man's life. It provides truth on which his mind must work and the commands that his will must obey. In the last resort, salvation is not the reward of brilliant speculation but of faithful discipleship.

Any pattern of thought, any type of institution, or any form of faith derives its authority from the ultimate concerns that it serves. All the issues that we have thus far examined were seen as closely related to the supremely important issue of salvation. The liberals were not greatly concerned to describe either the state to which it admitted the believer or the nature of the experience in which he participated. They were greatly interested, however, in the way by which men attained salvation; this touched in the most intimate way the issues of truth and freedom that were so central to their thought. The reigning theologies, whether Catholic or Protestant, seemed to distort both the kind of demand God could rightfully impose on man and the moral autonomy that ought to mark man's response to God. Chillingworth, for one, felt that the way salvation was usually conceived and pursued seriously obscured the true function of religion. The primary task of Christianity is not to provide certainty of salvation. Assured claims always left him unconvinced; this one in

[74] *Ibid.*, II, §85 (p. 122).
[75] *Ibid.*, II, §27 (p. 101).
[76] *Ibid.*, VI, §55 (p. 464).
[77] *Ibid.*, III, §81 (p. 227).
[78] *Ibid.*, IV, §84 (p. 291).

particular seemed to him to deflect men from the kind of quest that provides some reasonable assurance of personal fulfillment. More important than a preoccupation with salvation itself is an awareness of the conditions that ensure it. The first of these is an unceasing search for the truth. This is a moral obligation imposed on all men, since all enjoy the gifts of reason and freedom. God compels no man to accept the truth he has revealed. The Bible records innumerable instances of how God pointed the way to fuller truth or richer experience, but he "constraineth no man to follow . . . ; that was left to their liberty." [79] So the willingness to seek is even more important than success in finding. In this life the Christian is a pilgrim, on the way, not at the goal. The formidable obstacles to salvation are the negligence that does not search for the truth, the carelessness that neglects truths already found, and the disobedience that does not apply our understanding of the truth in daily life. The inquiring spirit finds its counterpart in the honest mind. Ambiguities and uncertainties are so numerous that errors are inevitable: "an honest man, whose heart is right to God, and one that is a true lover of God and of his truth, may, by reason of the conflict of contrary reasons on both sides, very easily and therefore excusably mistake and embrace error for truth, and reject truth for error." [80] Exact knowledge is consequently not a condition of salvation. A man's destiny does not depend on intellectual assent to the approved dogmatic formulas. On few points was Chillingworth so insistent as on the need to be generous in making allowances for error. He was acutely conscious of the ambiguities of Scripture, the uncertainties of knowledge, the imperfections of reason, the ill effects of prejudice and even of education. Under such circumstances to suggest that "God obliges men under pain of damnation not to mistake through error and human frailty is to make God a tyrant." [81] Such a view would turn religion into slavery. It was his understanding of God that made this view intolerable to Chillingworth. "Neither doubt I but God, who knows whereof we are made, and what passions we are subject unto, will compassionate such infirmities and not enter into judgement with us for those things which, all things considered, were unavoidable." [82] In other words, what can a moral being, though divine, expect from another moral being, admittedly imperfect? He can expect him to try to reach the truth. He can require "honest endeavour" in thought and conduct. "It cannot consist with the revealed goodness of God, to damn him for error, that desires and endeavours to find the truth." [83] In his account of the way man attains salvation, Chillingworth thus combined the elements that we have already encountered in a variety of other contexts: the moral nature of God, the

[79] *Ibid.*, II, §93 (p. 125).
[80] *Ibid.*, The Answer to the Preface, §26 (p. 48).
[81] *Ibid.*, II, §104 (p. 131).
[82] *Ibid.*, III, §19 (p. 184).
[83] *Ibid.*, III, §14 (p. 182).

duty of man to seek the truth, his freedom in doing so, and the reasonable consideration with which his mistakes and failures will be treated. God is not "lavish in superfluities; and therefore having given us means sufficient for our direction and power sufficient to make use of these means, he will not constrain or necessitate us to make use of these means: for that were to cross the end of our creation, which was to be glorified by our free obedience; whereas necessity and freedom cannot stand together: that were to reverse the law which he hath prescribed to himself in his dealings with man; and that is, to set life and death before him, and leave him in the hands of his own counsel." This view is further enforced by Chillingworth's account of what God expects man to give in return. "Now that which he desires of us on our part," he continued,

> is the obedience of faith, and love of the truth, and desire to find the true sense of it, and industry in searching it, and humility in following, and constancy in professing it; all which, if he should work in us by an absolute irresistable necessity, he could no more require of us as our duty, than he can of the sun to shine, of the sea to ebb and flow, and of all other creatures to do those things which by mere necessity they must do, and cannot choose.[84]

In the seventeenth century any debate about authority inevitably involved the church and its claims. This was an aspect of the subject that the liberals had no intention of evading. Extreme ecclesiastical pretensions, they believed, distorted authority and endangered freedom. Hales found himself in trouble with Laud about his views concerning the church, and Chillingworth's controversy with Knott was concerned with this problem as much as with any single subject. Knott insisted that the thoughtful man had to choose between two alternatives: on the one hand, he could reconcile himself to complete skepticism; on the other, he might admit "that all points defined by Christ's visible church belong to the foundation of faith in such sense that to deny any one cannot stand with salvation." [85] But Chillingworth repeatedly pointed out that to plead the necessity of an infallible source of truth does not establish its existence; Rome itself, he added, conceded that the true church can only be identified by rational inquiry.[86] Clearly the claims of a church that insists it is the final authority in matters of belief cannot be reconciled with the fact that we lack irrefutable certainty that we have attained the truth. It is quite possible for a church to lose its grasp of essential truth. He admitted that our definitions even of crucial terms might lack precision; for example, a true church is "a company of men that professed at least so

---

[84] *Ibid.*, II, §93 (p. 125).
[85] Knott, *Charity maintayned by Catholiques*, IV, §19 (p. 243 in Chillingworth's *Works*).
[86] Chillingworth, *op. cit.*, IV, §53 (pp. 276–277).

much truth as was absolutely necessary for their salvation." [87] It is
dangerous as well as presumptuous for the church to define the limits of
her own powers.[88] The perils of intellectual tyranny are very real and
never far away; the safeguard of a man's freedom lies in his right to
evaluate for himself the claims of the church in the light of the testimony
of Scripture and tradition. The pretensions of the institution are serious;
so are those of certain individuals within it. Hales disliked clericalism;
priests, he felt, are too apt "to impropriate the keys unto themselves." The
keys committed to Peter, and the command to feed Christ's sheep "import
no more than that common duty, laid upon all disciples, to teach all
nations." "To save a soul, every man is a priest." [89] The question of
authority has been complicated by the attempt to define too explicitly the
nature of the church. The characteristics to which controversialists usually
appealed are of little value. Visibility may cease; perpetuity is unnecessary.[90] "Marks and notes to know the church there are none. . . . And as
there are none, so it is not necessary there should be." [91] The church can
be known by its conformity with the gospel of Christ.[92] "So if the church
be divided," said Falkland, "I have no way to know the true church but by
seeking which agrees with Scripture and antiquity and so judge accordingly (but this is not to submit myself to her opinions, as my guide, which
they tell me is necessary)." [93] It is important, however, to take seriously
Christ's words that his kingdom is not of this world. "For I know no error
so common, so frequent, so hardly to be rooted out, so much hindering the
knowledge of the true nature of the church, as this that men do take the
church to be like unto the world." [94] Since false models had too readily
been accepted, it was important to clarify the ideals enshrined in the
institution itself. Because the liberals were deeply concerned about intellectual freedom, they stoutly maintained the need of a genuinely
comprehensive church. Charity would be its most conspicuous characteristic. Intellectual differences are never sufficient to justify separation. "If
the spiritual guides and fathers of the church would be a little sparing of
encumbering churches with superfluities, and not overrigid either in
reviving obsolete customs or imposing new, there were far less danger of
schism or superstition." [95] This degree of forbearance would, of course, be
joined to a humble awareness that all human doctrines are fallible. A
church prepared to admit this would open to its members the full range of

[87] *Ibid.*, The Answer to the Preface, §18 (p. 42).
[88] *Ibid.*, III, §62 (p. 215).
[89] Hales, "A Tract concerning the Power of the Keys," pp. 170, 173; "Miscellanies," *Tracts,*
p. 242.
[90] Chillingworth, *op. cit.*, V, §13 (pp. 332–333); VI, §13 (p. 420).
[91] Hales, *Tracts,* p. 235.
[92] Chillingworth, *op. cit.*, IV, §53 (p. 277).
[93] Falkland, *Infallibility,* n.p.
[94] Hales, "Christ's Kingdom not of this World," *Golden Remains,* p. 201.
[95] Hales, "A Tract concerning Schisme and Schismaticks," *Tracts,* pp. 217–218.

its resources without insisting that they sacrifice their intellectual freedom or surrender the right to criticize accepted doctrines.

In the seventeenth century a discussion of Scripture and the church also presupposed an examination of the authority of tradition. The issue was never far from mind. The unceasing controversy with Rome kept it in the forefront of attention. The Catholics insisted that it represented a deposit of truth always at the disposal of the church and always able to authenticate its claims. High churchmen like Andrewes, Montagu, and Laud disputed the Roman interpretation of tradition but insisted that their own view was sounder and more useful. Many of the Puritans dismissed tradition with sweeping disdain. The liberals regarded both extremes as wrong. A critical examination convinced them that reason would demolish any doctrine of tradition committed to the view that through the ages it had borne unvarying testimony to the truth. On the other hand, to repudiate all that the church has transmitted would impoverish our understanding both of the past and of the present. Chillingworth spoke with respect of "the testimony of the primitive Christians." "Universal tradition" (as he liked to call it) seemed to him "a thing credible of itself and therefore fit to be relied on." [96] He saw it, not as concentrated in a single institution, but as widely disseminated among Christians; "for this whole depositum was committed to every particular church, nay, to every particular man which the apostles converted." This, of course, left it exposed to the risk of distortion: "no man, I think, will say that there was any certainty that it should be kept whole and inviolate by every man and every church." [97] Reflection convinced him that the crucial difference in this matter lay between a critical and a supine attitude to the past. Tradition was an unreliable authority when it presupposed a docile submission to the wisdom of former times. It might prove a useful guide if inherited views could be subjected to careful scrutiny, and so accepted, amended, or rejected as might seem best. Traditional doctrines, he believed, stood in greater need of such discriminating examination than did ancient institutions. The latter benefited more fully from the safeguards afforded by historical continuity; doctrines were easily exposed to subtle change and modification. When sound beliefs have been obscured by time, "it might be great wisdom to forsake ancient errors for more ancient truths." [98] Scripture is the great safeguard of doctrine; tradition, which never supplants it, may usefully supplement it by assisting right interpretation. The testimony of the past cannot lightly be disregarded, and Chillingworth's emphasis on "universal tradition" was a protection against the vagaries of ephemeral fads or fancies. A doctrine

[96] Chillingworth, *op. cit.*, II, §25 (p. 100). Chillingworth contrasts the credibility of tradition, which he regards as "highly reasonable" (II, §24), with the "authority of your church."

[97] *Ibid.*, II, §148 (p. 148).

[98] *Ibid.*, VI, §53 (p. 462).

could safely be considered true if it were supported by "the joint tradition of all the apostolic churches, with one mouth and one voice teaching the same doctrine." [99] Tradition is judged by Scripture; it is tested by reason. Only careful thought can disclose the true meaning of beliefs transmitted by the past. We must "use our reason and rely upon it. Otherwise as light shows nothing to the blind, or to him that uses not his eyes; so reason cannot prove anything to him that either hath not or useth not his reason to judge them." [100]

Primitive Christianity provided the crucial test of the value of tradition. The Catholics, though they confidently appealed to the earliest age, found no incongruity in treating its evidence with a measure of freedom: a living church could authorize certain modifications. The school of Andrewes received the evidence provided by the primitive church with the greatest deference: it came from the period of the undivided church, from a time close enough to the apostolic age for its teaching to have escaped serious corruption.[101] At this point Chillingworth and his friends showed the consequences of their intermediate position. They refused to be intimidated by the past. Hales reminded Laud that the way the early church fixed the date of Easter hardly encouraged an uncritical submission to times past. [102] On occasion he spoke in bantering tones of the ancients ("by whom many are more affrighted than hurt") and found it necessary "to disabuse those who, reverencing antiquity more than needs, have suffered themselves to be scared with imputation, above due measure." [103] There are plenty of examples by which "we may plainly see the danger of our appeal to antiquity, for resolution in controverted points of faith, and how small relief we are to expect from thence." [104] Why should we rely upon past ages? "Antiquity, what is it else (God only expected) but man's authority born some ages before us? Now for the truth of things, time makes no alteration." [105] Chillingworth spoke with deference of doctrines that could claim general patristic support, but he refused to let even the greatest names dictate his views. "I am not," he said, "such an idolater of St. Augustine as to think a thing proved sufficiently because he says it, nor that all his sentences are oracles." [106]

The issues with which the liberals were preoccupied sometimes seem predominantly intellectual—even theoretical—in character. This ignores the extent to which the members of the Great Tew circle discussed religious problems in a basically moral context. They never suggested that

[99] *Ibid.*, VI, §40 (p. 450).
[100] *Ibid.*, II, §119 (p. 137).
[101] Cf. Andrewes, *Works,* IX, 91.
[102] Hales, "A Letter to Archbishop Laud," *Works,* I, 139.
[103] Hales, *A Tract concerning Schisme and Schismaticks,* p. 3.
[104] *Ibid.*, p. 5.
[105] Hales, "Of Private Judgment in Religion," *Works,* III, 163.
[106] Chillingworth, *op. cit.*, III, §44 (p. 200).

ethics embraced the whole of religion, but they assigned to it a vital role in the life of faith. With dismay they noted the extent to which controversies about religion deflected men from fulfilling their moral obligations. They denied that Christianity is primarily an exercise of man's intelligence. He must think hard and courageously about his faith, but anyone who wishes to discover the true nature of religious belief will find that sincerity is of more help than scholarship. It is entirely wrong to make justification before God depend on an intellectual grasp of certain creedal propositions, especially if this unbalanced approach involves the neglect of the moral obligations of daily life.[107] "Two parts there are," said Hales,

> that do completely make up a Christian man, a true faith and an honest conversation. The first, though it seem the worthier and therefore gives us the name of Christians, yet the second in the end will prove the surer. For true profession without honest conversation not only saves not, but increases our weight of punishment; but a good life without true profession, though it brings us not to Heaven, yet it lessens the measure of our judgement; so that a moral man, so called, is a Christian by the surer side.[108]

At the same time intellectual integrity obviously ranks very high among the moral qualities that distinguish the good life. If a man does not deal honestly with himself in his own quest for the truth, he is unlikely to be honest in any other context. The liberals believed that freedom affects and modifies every aspect of man's moral experience. An unfettered mind is the condition of genuine liberty of action. The quality both of behavior and of thought is determined by the autonomy without which man cannot be himself. The freedom to investigate, the possibility of obeying the mandate of truth when it is found, the significance of choice between the right and the wrong, or between the better and the best, all have profound moral implications. Most important of all is the freedom to follow wherever conscience leads. No abuse of authority is so sinister as the attempt to coerce men to do what they consider wrong or to accept as true what they believe is false. "It is a fearful thing," wrote Hales, "to trifle with conscience in all circumstances, for most assuredly according to it a man shall stand or fall at the last." [109] It is futile as well as wicked to try to manipulate men's consciences, for "all the power in the world is neither fit to convince nor able to compel a man's conscience to consent to anything." [110]

Respect for conscience easily merges into charity toward others. The

---

[107] Cf. Hales, "Of Dealing with Erring Christians," *Golden Remains*, pp. 44–46.
[108] *Ibid.*, p. 48.
[109] Hales, "A Letter to Archbishop Laud," *Works*, I, 142.
[110] Chillingworth, *op. cit.*, II, §18 (p. 97).

generous spirit of the liberals was partly a matter of temperament, but their candor, moderation, reservation of judgment, and their dispassionate view of theological controversy were all allied to fundamental intellectual concerns. There is a kind of agreement, argued Hales, that is more basic than "identity of conceit"; our hearts can be united though our tongues disagree on such speculative questions as predestination. Since Scripture is so often ambiguous, "it remains that we seek out a way, not so much to establish an unity of opinion in the minds of all, which I take to be a thing likewise impossible, as to provide that the multiplicity of conceit trouble not the church's peace." We would therefore be wise to remember that the inferences that we deduce with such confidence from Scripture "are at the best but our opinions. For this peremptory manner of setting down our conclusions under this high commanding form of 'necessary truths,' is generally one of the greatest causes that keeps the churches this day so far asunder; whenas a gracious receiving of each other, by mutual forbearance in this kind, might peradventure in time bring them nearer together." [111] To facilitate this, Hales urged the desirability of a simple liturgy, which, while providing the essentials of worship, would impose "nothing of private opinion, or of church pomp, of garments or prescribed gestures, . . . of many superfluities that creep into the church under the name of order and decency." He could see no reason, he said, why "men of different opinions in Christian religion may not hold communion *in sacris,* and both go to one church." [112] His ideal was a church that would be broadly comprehensive rather than strictly uniform. "Let it not offend any that I have made Christianity rather an inn to receive all than a private house to receive some few." [113]

Every one of the principal convictions emphasized by the liberals pointed to toleration as its inescapable consequence. A charitable spirit, sensitive to the claims of conscience, alert to the rights of reason, suspicious of imposing authority, inevitably leads to a generous consideration of the beliefs of others. A strong general case can be made against persecution. The spirit that condemns those who differ from us in religion corrupts everything else in religion.[114] Many of the truths of Christianity have been taught by other religions—a reassuring fact since common consent is an advantage, and one that ought to make us respectful of the faiths of others.[115] "God," said Chillingworth, "hath authorized no man to force all men to unity of opinion." [116] The inference to be drawn from this seemed obvious: "whatsoever man or church doth for any error of simple belief, deprive any man so qualified . . . either of his temporal life, or livelihood,

[111] Hales, "Of Dealing with Erring Christians," *Golden Remains,* pp. 65–66; cf. *ibid.,* p. 2.
[112] Hales, *A Tract concerning Schisme and Schismaticks,* p. 10.
[113] Hales, "Of Dealing with Erring Christians," *Golden Remains,* p. 44.
[114] Falkland, *Infallibility,* n.p.
[115] Suckling, *An Account of Religion by Reason,* p. 122.
[116] Chillingworth, *op. cit.,* II, §85 (p. 122).

or liberty, or of the church's communion and hope of salvation, is for the first unjust, cruel and tyranny; schismatical, presumptuous and uncharitable for the second." [117] Christian history affords too many examples of the repressive cruelty of one party to another, but the story is not wholly sad. In the early church, Christians and Arians met together, and difference of belief did not keep apart those willing to unite in worship. "Severity against separation from heretical companies took its beginning from the heretics themselves; and if we search the stories we shall find that the church did not at their first arising thrust them from her; themselves went out." [118] As the contemporaries of the liberals were aware, this was an attitude far more generous than most of the leaders of the early seventeenth century were prepared to accept. Edward Knott warned that Chillingworth advocated a kind of toleration very different from anything that Laud and the English bishops could sanction.[119] John Floyd, in an equally alarmist vein, argued that no one could set bounds to the kind of freedom Chillingworth proposed: one would even have to recognize the rights of "Puritans, Brownists, Anabaptists, Arians, Socinians" and others.[120] Knott and Floyd felt that this was the *reductio ad absurdum* of a foolish mental aberration. To Chillingworth and Hales toleration was the inescapable consequence of their whole understanding both of the nature of man and of his place in the purpose of God.

Chillingworth and his friends put forward a courageous interpretation of freedom and authority but it was obviously affected by its seventeenth-century context. These men anticipated the new age but they still belonged to the old. Consequently, they failed to see many of the consequences of their own position; only a later period fully recognized the implications of their thought. It is possible to find in Hales and Chillingworth specific anticipations of Locke, of the Latitudinarians and the Deists, even of Burke. But more important than their specific contributions was the spirit that they engendered. During their lifetime their stress on reason, freedom, and the moral autonomy of each man invited misunderstanding. They were widely accused of Socinianism, and the vague fear of this heresy was so pervasive that, in Suckling's words, it rendered "every man that offer[ed] to give an account of religion by reason suspected to have none at all." [121] Though their testimony was temporarily drowned by the din of civil war, they profoundly affected later Anglican thought. The appeal to reason and the vindication of toleration steadily gained ground as the seventeenth century moved to its close. The continuing influence of the liberals can be seen in the prevalence of a mentality little addicted to dogmatism, rational in tone but not doctrinal

---

[117] *Ibid.,* IV, §12 (p. 252).
[118] Hales, *Golden Remains,* p. 66.
[119] Knott, *Christianity Maintained,* Ch. VI.
[120] Floyd, *The Church conquerant over humane wit,* Ch. VI.
[121] Suckling, *op. cit.,* Ep. Ded.

in interest, suspicious of authoritarianism, ethical in its concerns, tolerant amid its disagreements. Unfortunately, the Erastianism in which Chillingworth and Hales had found a safeguard against clerical dominance became in time a state control that smothered ecclesiastical freedom. The dawn of the age of reason brought an even greater loss: the disappearance of a temper enlightened but not aridly rationalist, devout but not narrowly pietistic. Hales and Tillotson belong to different parts of the seventeenth century; in spirit and temper they belong to different worlds.

The close-knit coterie that gathered around Lord Falkland at Great Tew represented an attempt, inspired and sustained by profoundly religious motives, to achieve a stable accommodation between freedom and authority. Throughout this period there was also a tenuous but pesistent strain of liberality of outlook maintained by a group whose interests were largely lay and secular. Bacon and Selden were lawyers who combined a devotion to learning with active participation in public life. Military adventure and diplomacy made Lord Herbert of Cherbury entirely at home in the world of cosmopolitan society. Robert Burton was a scholarly recluse, clerical only in a marginal way. John Earle, George Wither, and Francis Quarles were minor literary figures.

As a rule, the witness of these men to freedom was genuine but restrained. It was inspired by common sense rather than by enthusiasm, and moderation was its distinctive mark. They disliked extremes; they were repelled by those who

> Suppose that no man's doctrine saves
> The soul of anyone, unless he raves
> And rears aloud, and flings, and hurleth so
> As if his arms he quite away would throw.[122]

Where there is little zeal there is often some skepticism. A quietly pessimistic strain runs through Quarles's *Emblemes:*

> Man's state implies a necessary curse;
> When not himself, he's mad; when most himself, he's worse.[123]

Burton regarded with quizzical detachment the absurdities and extravagances of his fellowmen: how can you defer to authorities who usually buttress their claims with folly and irrationality? [124] Skepticism sometimes bordered on cynicism. Selden remarked that when justification was invoked for fighting, religion provided the most effective pleas since it alone touched the interest of both the highest and the lowest.[125]

---

[122] George Wither, *Britains Remembrancer* (Spenser Society Pub.), p. 497.

[123] Quarles, *Emblemes* (Bk. 2, xiv), p. 118. This was one of the most popular books of poetry in the early seventeenth century. Cf. also Quarles's famous line in *Hieroglyphikes*, XV (pp. 90,10), verse 8: " 'Tis glorious misery to be born a man."

[124] R. Burton, *The Anatomy of Melancholy*, Democritus to the Reader.

[125] O. Chadwick, *The Reformation*, p. 366.

When dogmatism is dangerous, the study of the past can place contemporary claims in due perspective, and can often deliver us from the specious tyranny of an overconfident authority. Selden believed that history enables us to understand both our own nature and the proper working of our political society. He admitted that "the too studious affectation of base and sterile antiquity" was "nothing else but to be exceeding busy about nothing"; on the other hand he claimed that

> the neglect or only vulgar regard of the fruitful and precious part of it, which gives necessary light to the present in matter of state, law, history and the understanding of good authors, is but preferring that kind of ignorant infancy, which our short life alone allows us, before the ages of former experience and observation which may so accumulate years to us as if we had lived even from the beginning of time.[126]

In evaluating the lessons of history, as in restraining the ardors of dogmatism, reason plays an indispensable role. "Every man," said Quarles, "is a king in his own kingdom. If reason command and passion obey, his government speaks a good king." [127] One of the functions that reason discharges is the separation of the fundamental (which most of these men accepted as revealed) from the nonessential, and then the determination, in the latter category, of what is true and what is not. It is important, said Bacon, that "the points fundamental and of substance in religion" should be "truly discerned and distinguished from points not merely of faith, but of opinion, order, or good intention." [128] Lord Herbert of Cherbury was "very sure" that the common principles that form the essential core of all religions were few in number and firmly established, and beyond these it was reason's task to explore the frontiers of truth.[129] The lay liberals dismissed with impatience all ecclesiastical claims to offer an exclusive salvation. Submission to doctrinal systems is not the way in which men usually come to a fuller understanding of the truth. The clash of opinion is a more promising path. "The way to find out truth is by other's mistakings," said Selden.[130] Sir Thomas Browne believed that matters that are not numbered among the essentials of faith "may admit a free dispute," and may therefore be observed

> according to the rules of my private reason, or the humour and fashion of my devotion; neither believing this because Luther affirmed it, or disapproving that because Calvin hath dis-avouched it. I condemn not all things in the Council of Trent,

[126] Selden, *The Historie of tithes*, Ep. Ded.
[127] Quarles, *Enchiridion*, Cent. II, XXII.
[128] Bacon, "Of Unity in Religion," *Essays*.
[129] Herbert, *De Veritate*, pp. 120–121.
[130] Selden, *Table Talk*, p. 131.

nor approve all in the Synod of Dort. In brief, where the
Scripture is silent the church is my text; where that speaks, 'tis
but my comment; where there is a joint silence of both, I borrow
not the rules of my religion from Rome or Geneva, but the
dictates of my own reason.[131]

Men who rely heavily on reason are always apt to be suspicious of
external authority, especially that of the church. " 'Tis a great question,"
said Selden,

how we know Scripture to be Scripture, whether by the church
or by man's private spirit. Let me ask how I know anything?
How I know this carpet to be green? First, because somebody
told me it was green: that you call the church in your way. And
then after I have been told it is green, when I see that colour
again, I know it to be green, my own eyes tell me it is green; that
you call private spirit.[132]

This might imply that the church guides and man's experience confirms.
But Selden felt that experience called into question the practical wisdom
of the church's guidance. The English bishops had acted foolishly and
damaged their own cause. Even their virtues often disqualified them for
their duties, and they had not improved matters by laying claim to
authority *jure divino,* though "the practice of the kingdom [had] ever been
otherwise." [133] In any case, the bishops had seriously harmed their cause
by asserting too high an authority. "That which is thought to have done
the bishops hurt is, their going about to bring men to a blind obedience,
imposing things upon them, though perhaps small and well-enough,
without preparing them and first insinuating into their reason and
fancies." [134]

Much more is involved here than a feeling that the leaders of the church
have been ill-advised. In Selden, particularly, there is a strong anticlerical
strain. "The clergy," he said, "would have us believe them against our
own reason." [135] He would not trust a synod of clergy to their own devices:
"there must be some laymen . . . to overlook the clergy, lest they spoil the
civil work." [136] Political problems were always aggravated by clerical
interference, and his remedy was simple: "chain up the clergy on both
sides." [137] Bacon believed that ministers were too apt to let their own

[131] T. Browne, *Religio Medici,* Pt. I, §5.
[132] Selden, *Table Talk,* p. 10.
[133] *Ibid.,* pp. 18–20.
[134] *Ibid.,* p. 14.
[135] *Ibid.,* p. 31.
[136] *Ibid.,* p. 126. In the last two comments, Selden drives home his point with homely
illustrations that have a distinctly sharp edge.
[137] *Ibid.,* p. 32. For Selden's tactics at the Westminster Assembly of Divines, see Fuller's
famous account in his *Church History,* Bk. XI, Sec. ix, §54.

interests affect the policies they pursued, especially when they coerced others to believe or act as the church demanded: "those which held and persuaded pressure of consciences were commonly interested therein themselves for their own ends." [138] Unfortunately the theological activities of the clergy did little to atone for their practical ineptitude.

> God never yet did bid us take in hand
> To publish that which none can understand.[139]

The way to control the clergy is to keep the church in its proper place. A diffused anticlericalism issued in a strong Erastianism, and this is particularly evident in Selden. Even the church benefits from being controlled with a resolute hand. "It has ever been the gain of the church when the king will let the church have no power to cry down the king and cry up the church." [140] "It is very requisite," said Quarles, "for a prince to keep the church always in proportion to the state. . . . Durable is that state where Aaron commands the people and where Moses commands Aaron." [141] So Selden found it reasonable as well as necessary to permit divines to function only within the boundaries that the state defined.[142] Behind this view lay a theoretical justification as well as a practical assessment of the situation. The power to direct institutions and control events can never be conceded to the church, because there is "no such thing as spiritual jurisdiction, all is civil." [143] The government decided what form of religion to admit to a country and how long to allow it to function there, for "the state still makes religion." In the early seventeenth century so naked an assertion of the authority of the temporal ruler needed some justification, and Selden appealed to the example of Jesus Christ, who, as "a great observer of the civil power, did many things only justifiable because the state required it." [144] So in the contemporary situation, he argued, the proper "judge of religion" was neither the church nor the Scriptures, but the state.[145] Few issues exercised contemporary clerics so much as the question whether episcopacy or presbytery could claim divine approval. The controversy was irrelevant, said Selden; no pattern of church government exists *jure divino,* and whether we have bishops or not depends on the decision of the state.[146] As the Scots Presbyterian Robert Baillie indignantly reported, "Selden and others . . . will have no discipline at all in any church *jure divino,* but settled only upon

---

[138] Bacon, "Of Unity in Religion," *Essays.*
[139] Wither, *op. cit.,* p. 503.
[140] Selden, *op. cit.,* p. 29.
[141] Quarles, *Enchiridion,* Cent. I, §lxxxix.
[142] Selden, *op. cit.,* p. 101.
[143] *Ibid.,* p. 60.
[144] *Ibid.,* p. 100.
[145] *Ibid.,* p. 117.
[146] *Ibid.,* p. 20.

the free will and pleasure of the parliament." [147] To the Catholic gibe that the Church of England was merely a parliamentary creation, Selden replied that of course it was. What was more, the same situation prevailed in countries obedient to papal authority. "The church is not only subject to the civil power with us that are Protestants, but also in Spain; if the church does excommunicate a man for what it should not, the civil power will take him out of their hands. So in France . . ." [148]

Erastianism is the theme that gives Selden's *Table Talk* such unity as a collection of conversational comments can possess. Since the book records the informal *obiter dicta* of a vigorous mind, they are frank and pungent. A less candid work but one with much greater contemporary impact was Selden's *The Historie of tithes*. In the Preface he pointed out that his aim was to approach in a wholly objective spirit a subject that had been treated as the preserve of divines. Since he was dealing publicly with a sensitive topic, he carefully guarded his flank against attack. He did not write the book, he said, "to prove that tithes are not due by the law of God" or "that the laity may detain them"—"in sum, not at all against the maintenance of the clergy." [149] But the subject had been sadly distorted by the assumption of canonists and divines that by arguing from precept to fact you can establish the truth. Selden proposed to rectify persistent errors by a sober scrutiny of the historical record. He wrote his treatise for the benefit of those who "enquire about this ecclesiastical revenue, and preferring truth before what dulling custom hath too deeply rooted in them, are not unwilling to change their old acorns for better meat." [150] He claimed that he simply collected the historical evidence and drew from it certain inescapable inferences. He had no ulterior motives; he had merely assembled the relevant facts.

Selden disclaimed any ulterior motives in his handling of the history of tithes. The clergy did not believe him. Foulke Robartes argued that it is unwarranted and unfounded popish doctrine to argue that tithes are not due by the moral law. Scripture and all the evidence of church history prove that by God's will and the custom of many centuries tithes "are due to those who are God's ministers in holy things." [151] William Sclater, discussing at great length both the Biblical evidence and the arguments advanced by opponents, posed a challenge: "Think seriously, you that put us to plead our *jus*, whether it lie not on your consciences to prove repeal of that divine law given for tithing." [152] Richard Perrot, concerned at the

---

[147] Robert Baillie, *Letters and Journals*, II, 31. Cf. also Fuller's comment on Selden's attack on *Jure divino* pretensions, *Church History*, Bk. XI, Sec. ix, §54.

[148] Selden, *Table Talk*, p. 101.

[149] Selden, *The Historie of tithes*, Preface, p. i.

[150] *Ibid.*, Preface, p. vi.

[151] Foulke Robartes, *The Revenue of the Gospel is Tythes, passim*, esp. Ch. IV. Cf. Sir Thomas Ryves, *The Poore Vicars Plea*, pp. 20 ff., 144.

[152] William Sclater, *The Quaestion of Tythes Revised*, Introduction; also p. 224.

growing belief that Selden's thesis was unanswerable, offered a digest of the major critiques of *The Historie*, plus two instances from his own experience to show that the facts to which Selden appealed were inaccurate.[153] But though even the minute scrutiny of Selden's case offered by scholars such as Dr. Tilesley did not seriously shake his arguments, the clergy were probably right to be suspicious of his disclaimer of any malign intention. If *The Historie* implied that tithes were payable only as the state happened to command, this certainly corresponded to his convictions. He believed that moral principles are created by authority. The basic moral law rests on divine commandment (transmitted by the Bible), and everyday morality on the laws of the land. Legal precedents are therefore more than interesting historical data; they provide the only basis on which subsequent decisions can be made. He could not be entirely dispassionate about the evidence he amassed; it afforded the only reliable guidance on a very important issue—how civil power should control church revenue.

The authority that Selden acknowledged was therefore of the kind to which the common lawyers appealed. Like Coke and his parliamentary associates, he turned to the custom and constitution of the land. His Erastianism was based on law. In his *De Synedriis*, he amassed case after case to show that the civil power has always controlled even the seemingly ecclesiastical weapon of excommunication. This approach also affected his interpretation both of freedom and of toleration. On the flyleaf of the books in his library he inscribed in Greek the motto, "liberty above all things," but this does not in any way suggest an unfettered freedom. The latitude that a citizen can claim is determined by the law. The ideals that reformers can pursue are limited by precedent. Selden's parliamentary career clearly illustrated his fundamental convictions. Law, he believed, is the technical definition of certain established remedial procedures. In 1629, Speaker Finch created an uproar by trying to adjourn the House of Commons on the King's instructions, and Selden protested that if this procedure were permitted, it would establish a precedent. In the same year, certain printers presented a petition to the House complaining of their treatment by Laud and the High Commission. Laud's chaplain, while licensing books "holding opinions of Arminianism and Popery," had banned certain works of unquestioned orthodoxy, and when the printers had defied the prohibition, Laud had punished them. The case might have been treated as one that involved religious liberty and the freedom of the press. Characteristically enough, Selden upheld the petition on purely legal grounds: the common law supported the printers, and Laud had abused the powers of the prerogative courts. "There is no law," said Selden, "to prevent the printing of any book in England but only a decree in the Star Chamber. Therefore that a man should be fined, imprisoned

---

[153] Richard Perrot, *Iacobs Vowe*, Ep. Ded., *passim* and Appendix.

and his goods taken from him, is a great invasion of the liberty of the subject." [154]

Selden and those who agreed with him can hardly be regarded as crusaders for the abstract principle of religious toleration. Selden was deeply interested in a technical legal liberty. He was vigilant in detecting and resisting any infringement of parliamentary privilege. He accounted freedom of conscience an asset insofar as it promoted the peace and security of the state. If it provided a means of settling disputes that might disrupt the community, it should be promoted. Robert Burton, while rejecting complete toleration as a quixotic ideal, believed that a certain measure of freedom was a practical advantage. Admittedly it would provide no certain cure for religious melancholy, but it had limited uses. Most men are "so refractory, self-conceited, obstinate, so firmly addicted to that religion in which they have been bred and brought up, that no persuasion, no terror, no persecution, can divert them. The consideration of which hath induced many commonwealths to suffer them to enjoy their consciences as they will themselves." [155] Lord Herbert did not explicitly examine either toleration or the conditions that govern it, but the purpose of his treatise disposed him to a comprehensive generosity of outlook. "The whole aim of the work," he said, "is the common nature of the search for truth which exists in every normal human being." [156] If we may judge by the results, the quest is difficult and perplexing. We must therefore expect agreement on a very few essentials, and treat errors with forbearance and compassion. [157] Persecution is therefore unreasonable and indeed immoral. It is a last resort under desperate circumstances. We have no right, said Bacon, "to propagate religion by wars, or by sanguinary persecutions to force consciences; except it be in cases of overt scandal, blasphemy, or intermixture of practice against the state; much less to nourish seditions; to authorize conspiracies and rebellions; to put the sword into the people's hands; and the like; tending to the subversion of all government, which is the ordinance of God." [158]

These comments suggest a cautious approach to religious toleration. The lay liberals advanced a rather subdued plea on behalf of freedom. They recognized that any progress was dependent on the increase of a spirit of forbearance. Charity would chasten the tendency to persecute. If, said Bacon, the contending parties would behave reasonably one to the other, some advance might be possible, and since general exhortations are usually ineffective, Bacon specified five areas in which Puritans and bishops had been at fault and where both should manifest a different

[154] Gardiner, *History of England,* VII, 51.
[155] R. Burton, *The Anatomy of Melancholy,* Pt. III, Sec. IV, Mem. I, Subsec. v.
[156] Herbert, *op. cit.,* Preface.
[157] *Ibid.,* pp. 289 ff., pp. 302 ff.
[158] Bacon, "Of Unity in Religion," *Essays.*

spirit.[159] Few of the liberals doubted that charity would be greatly enhanced if the spirit of controversy could be controlled. Disputation often gave free rein to the most discreditable impulses of the most disreputable adherents of both sides.[160] Some men are qualified to participate in controversy, others are not. Selden felt that religious debate would be a little less unprofitable if it were restricted to the learned instead of being open to the clergy at large.

The lay liberals were willing to advocate modest adjustments in church and state, but they did not approve of sweeping changes. They were cautiously progressive; they were certainly not revolutionaries. In political life they reverenced precedents and set freedom firmly in a context of ancient law and custom. In the church they redefined the locus of authority, but they wanted to see the process of change rigorously controlled. As Selden pointed out: "Alteration of religion is dangerous, because we know not where it will stay. 'Tis like a millstone that lies upon the top of a pair of stairs." [161] Before long a different breed of liberals would arise, ready to challenge old authorities on behalf of new concepts of freedom and quite prepared to see the millstone plunge to the bottom of the stairs.

[159] Bacon, "An Advertisement touching the controversies of the Church of England," *Works*, II, 489.
[160] Cf. Selden, *Table Talk*, p. 118.
[161] *Ibid.*, p. 117.

X

PREMONITIONS OF CRISIS:
THE STRIDENT VOICES OF DISSENT

As THE FOURTH DECADE of the seventeenth century drew to
a close, England seemed to be a fortunate and happy land. While the
Thirty Years' War, unleashing the peculiar bitterness of religious strife,
was ravaging the continent, England remained at peace. Ardent Protestants might complain that the timid expedients which served King Charles
as a foreign policy were betraying the cause of the Reformation, but at
least English blood was not spilled, nor were English cities sacked. For
over ten years the king had avoided the distasteful necessity of confronting
parliament. His people grumbled about impositions and forced loans, but
their protests had been wholly ineffective. By exercising reasonable
economy, Charles had been able to govern as he pleased. Strafford was
reducing Irish affairs to order. Laud was suppressing dissent at home.
The king seemed well on the way to proving that a ruler who could appeal
to the royal prerogative need take account of no other kind of authority.
Meanwhile, he had leisure for the chase and sufficient money to patronize
the arts. He was, he told his nephew in 1637, the happiest king in
Christendom.[1] Others confirmed his judgment. During the years of
personal government, said Clarendon, "this kingdom . . . enjoyed the
greatest calm and the fullest measure of felicity that any people in any age,
for so long time together, have been blessed with; to the wonder and envy
of all the other parts of Christendom." [2] There seemed to be no reason
why this happy interlude should end.

But premonitions of approaching trouble had begun to multiply. For
the moment, the king's council and the courts of law had silenced most of
the protests against his policies, but it was clear that discontent was rising.
What was more, it was rising precisely among the classes that would
finally resist with the most telling effect. For the moment, they bided their
time and waited for the day when parliament would reassemble. But

[1] Cf. C. V. Wedgwood, *The King's Peace*, p. 21.
[2] Clarendon, *The History of the Rebellion*, I, 115.

there were other critics who refused to be silenced, and their protests were becoming increasingly strident. Those who defied the system of "thorough" and risked its most savage punishments may indeed have belonged to the lunatic fringe of society, but they were clearly awakening an ominous kind of response. Laud was aware of this. Though harsh to his critics, he was apprehensive when attacked. In his diary he noted every inauspicious omen. To Strafford he anxiously repeated his premonitions of approaching troubles.

Ironically enough, he himself was largely responsible for inspiring precisely the kind of protest he was most eager to suppress. Laud did not realize that society could no longer be treated as though it were a certain type of ecclesiastical polity. He ignored the fact that an increasing number of Englishmen wanted the freedom to organize their religious life in obedience to the dictates of their own consciences. This was a kind of liberty with which Laud (and indeed many of his contemporaries) had little patience. But when he denied it to his fellow countrymen it became a matter of immense importance to some of them to claim it as a right. Laud's insistence on uniformity built up pressures that finally made the recognition of diversity inevitable. In other ways also, Laud endangered his own ideals. He was suspicious of preaching. He and his friends were determined to impose strict limitations on the things that might or might not be said in the pulpit. This placed restrictions on the sober Puritans; it gave a powerful incentive to those who felt that the truth could be proclaimed through other than its traditional and duly accredited spokesmen. The "mechanic preacher" began to appear. The authorities dismissed with contempt these unlettered pretenders, but in 1631, Thomas Heywood was attacking certain weavers, "infamous upstart prophets," as he called them.[3] Ten years earlier such deluded impostors had already merited attention in a sermon at St. Paul's Cross.[4] Ten years later, the dikes were on the point of bursting; as a preacher, the despised tradesman was about to come into his own.

In their own way Laud's great opponents, the Puritans, had also unwittingly fostered the spirit of protest. Queen Elizabeth, it will be recalled, had smothered the clamor for further reform. The "classical movement" was checked; the Church of England would not immediately be remodeled according to the pure Genevan pattern. Reform in the rites and ceremonies might still be desirable, but its achievement seemed remote. So the Puritans devoted their energies to achieving a different kind of change—the creation of the new man (cf. Chapter VI). The doctrines they preached seemed abstract enough, but they had powerful implications. The elect man was called to a certain way of life. The Puritan moral code, when reinforced by the great Puritan doctrines,

[3] Thomas Heywood, *A True Discourse of two infamous upstart prophets.*
[4] Cf. Stephen Denison, *The White Wolfe,* pp. 38–56, 65 ff., 71 ff.

challenged not only existing manners and conventions but the very organization of church and state. The sober preachers were no revolutionaries, but they proclaimed their doctrines to all who would hear. While the respectable listened with complacency, the people—the common people—heard them gladly. The latent discontent, aggravated by the political incompetence of the early Stuarts, began to stir. In particular, a new mentality was being shaped. For too long society had forgotten the ordinary person, but his needs could not indefinitely be ignored. God, said the preachers, speaks to every man. So if the forms and the ceremonies of the church muffled that voice, men would seek it elsewhere. The mounting ferment was creating a new and revolutionary mentality. The preachers had proclaimed that all superiority not of the spirit had been leveled. But if all men are equal before God, why should they not be a little more equal one to another? The preachers may not have recognized all the implications of their message, but what they said certainly fostered the revolutionary spirit that would find such varied expression in the sects of the Interregnum. The little groups that would spring up as soon as the traditional pressures were removed were not the product of spontaneous generation. The way had been prepared. The Puritans had created a new kind of individualism. This individualism found its outlet in the sects. But before the sects, there came the heralds of discontent.

The heralds, too, were the beneficiaries of the Puritans. The preachers made their followers a reading people. They created an appetite, and then provided the material to satisfy it. The printing press poured forth a flood of sermons. The godly bought and read them. So the press grew strong. It ceased to be a client of the pulpit and became a power in its own right. In its new vigor it proved to be increasingly difficult to control. What was more, the heralds of protest discovered that this formidable new instrument could powerfully promote their ends.

Thomas Scott is a good example of a man who early recognized the potentialities of the political pamphlet. He was unusually skillful in exploiting them. He was a Cambridge man, a moderate Anglican, and for many years a rector in Norwich. For a time he was apparently a chaplain to James I. This may have aroused his interest in political problems; it certainly did not prevent him from discussing them. In the early part of James's reign neither preachers nor pamphleteers showed much disposition to touch on matters of state; religious questions seemed more interesting and more urgent. But after the outbreak of the Thirty Years' War there was a marked increase in the references to national policy. King James was annoyed. He issued a proclamation warning all persons "to take heed how they intermeddle, by pen or speech, with causes of state or secrets of empire, either at home or abroad." [5] As pressure mounted, Scott found it expedient to flee. He went to Holland and became preacher

[5] Thomas Rymer, *Foedera,* XVII, 279.

to the English merchant colony in Utrecht. When leaving church one Sunday in 1625, he was murdered.

Scott was an effective writer. His style was clear and vigorous. He avoided the common fault of the seventeenth-century pamphleteer; he never smothered his material in references and quotations. Both in his readability and in his approach to the problems of the day he anticipated Daniel Defoe. Like Defoe, he was a great political pamphleteer; unlike Defoe, he was a pioneer in a field that few had yet exploited. Like many others, he wrote tracts against the papists. He was unique in pushing ahead to the political problems that the Catholic controversy raised. He believed that Spain was a present menace as well as a traditional foe. He disliked the popularity of Count Gondomar, the Spanish ambassador in London, and he was apprehensive of the pro-Spanish foreign policy which James was pursuing. In 1620, Scott published a daring piece of anti-Spanish propaganda. His *Vox Populi, or Newes from Spayne* was ostensibly a translation of the minutes of a meeting of the Spanish royal council, to which Gondomar reported on the progress of his mission to England. At the time the English public accepted it as authentic. It was an impudent but highly ingenious fabrication. In it Gondomar explained his scheme for reducing England to subservience to Spain. He described his success in bribing the leading courtiers at Westminster. He told of the vast crowds that thronged his chapel for mass. He recounted his triumph in securing the execution of that popular Elizabethan hero, Sir Walter Ralegh. With great skill Scott emphasized precisely the points in James's policy most likely to antagonize the English public. The particularly damaging details in the report were often elicited by questions asked by figures like the Grand Inquisitor—the symbols of everything that Englishmen feared and hated in Spanish policy. The public bought the pamphlet and read it with delight, so Scott produced a second installment. The machinations of the Spanish king, he pointed out, were a serious menace; if detected in time, they need not prove fatal. "But I trust Almighty God (as he hath already begun) will open the eyes of all Christian kings and princes in time not only to pry into but effectually to oppose these his immense and ambitious designs, which else in time will fall heavy upon our children and posterity." [6]

Spanish policy was a threat to England; it was a disaster for the Palatinate. James's son-in-law, the elector palatine, had rashly precipitated the Thirty Years' War. By accepting the throne of Bohemia he had challenged the Catholic powers; in the upshot he forfeited both his new kingdom and his hereditary principality. James had no intention of plunging into war to salvage the rash escapade of his son-in-law. But the English public saw the matter in a different light. The Princess Elizabeth, James's only daughter, was a much more popular figure than her father.

<hr />

[6] [Thomas Scott], *The Second Part of Vox Populi*, Ep. Ded.

Moreover, the Protestant cause was being overwhelmed while England, in the leading strings of Spain, remained a passive observer. So Scott published his *Votivae Angliae* to show the "many strong reasons and true and solid motives" why James should intervene. The whole Christian world, he declared, was watching "to see whether Great Britain (in this just and famous quarrel) will courageously resolve to redeem her lost honour, or else cowardly consent to lose it without any other sense or hope of redemption." [7]

James could hardly be expected to applaud such publications. Nor was he likely to relish the account of a conversation in heaven among the Tudor monarchs. In describing what had been happening in English political life, Scott kept returning to the issues concerning which public opinion was specially sensitive. Subservience to Spain had encouraged arrogance among English Catholics: "they became passionately and insultingly confident of the free toleration of their religion and, in the sky-reaching mountains of their ambitious and superstitious hopes, were already preparing to erect their groves and altars, to set up their idols and images, and consequently to introduce their pope and his mass in the temples of our God." [8] Scott was too popular and too effective to be ignored, but he was too elusive to be suppressed. He illustrated the problem of the government in coping with this inconvenient new instrument, the press. Theoretically, the authorities had ample powers. The stationers company had certain responsibilities. The requirement that new books should be licensed imposed a degree of censorship. But such limitations, though effective enough to be a nuisance, were not stringent enough to be a deterrent. Authors grumbled about the inequities under which they suffered, but they could usually get a proscribed manuscript published by an unlicensed press, or, failing that, it could be printed in Holland and smuggled back into England.

Scott was a pioneer, not in pamphleteering but in its use for specifically political ends. It seemed at first that Alexander Leighton might follow a similar course; his first work was an intemperate exhortation to England to declare war on Spain.[9] Leighton's career, no less than his writings, suggests an able mind but an ill-adjusted personality. He was a graduate of St. Andrew's and was ordained in Scotland. In due course we find him ministering in the diocese of Durham. Then he moved to London, from there to Leyden (where he graduated in medicine), and so back to London, to find that the College of Physicians blocked his attempts to practice his new profession. In his ministerial capacity he gathered a group of disciples. He and they were alarmed at the course of events in England. Leighton traced the mischief to the increasing influence of the

[7] [*Idem*], *Votivae angliae,* Ep. Ded.
[8] [*Idem*], *Vox Coeli,* Ep. Ded.
[9] Leighton, *Speculum Belli Sacri* (1624).

new school of bishops. He collected signatures to a petition addressed to the House of Commons, went to Holland to get it printed, and ended with a lengthy treatise on the iniquities of episcopacy. The work circulated secretly, but when a copy fell into Laud's hands he decided to make an example of the offender.

Leighton's blast against the bishops[10] was doubtless inspired by personal conviction and embittered by private grievances, but it was not original. Late in Queen Elizabeth's reign it was apparent that a radical difference concerning episcopacy was developing in the Church of England. Bancroft traced the office of bishops to apostolic times; Bilson believed it to be "immediate from Christ, not from men or by men." [11] But there were others who insisted that bishops received their office from the queen; episcopal authority was a reflection of the royal supremacy, and to locate it elsewhere was to challenge the whole basis of the Elizabethan settlement. To claim that "the superiority of bishops is God's own institution," said Sir Francis Knollys, "doth impugn her Majesty's supreme government directly." Knollys urged that the bishops be compelled to admit that they had "no authority but such as is to be derived unto them from her Majesty's supreme authority and government." [12]

The Stuart kings were sympathetically disposed to an episcopacy of divine origin: it suitably complemented a monarchy of divine right. But the Erastian view, so widely held under Elizabeth, did not disappear simply because it had forfeited royal favor. It merely sought new allies, and it found them among the Puritans. The Puritans had plenty of sympathizers in parliament, and the "Arminian" advocacy of *jure divino* episcopacy clearly had political implications. Here was an issue on which royal policy could be attacked while professing submission to the king himself. Leighton insisted that when he began to collect signatures to his protest against episcopal abuses he was warmly supported by numerous members of the House of Commons.

Leighton's *Appeal* was addressed to "the right honourable and high court of Parliament," though the dissolution of 1629 meant that his work was never presented to those for whom it was ostensibly intended. It was not enough, he told the members, to protest. They must act. "Make way then for religion and righteousness by removal of all ungodliness and unright-eousness, and God will be with you." [13] Significantly enough, he dated the beginning of corruption from the death of Queen Elizabeth. Most Englishmen, he believed, were opposed to the current innovations. God

[10] Leighton, *An Appeal to the Parliament; or Syons Plea against the Prelacie* (1628).

[11] Richard Bancroft, *A Sermon Preached at Paules Crosse*, p. 99; Thomas Bilson, *The Perpetual Government of Christ his Church*, Pref. Ep. The same view was expressed by Hooker.

[12] Sir Francis Knollys to Burghley, quoted by Allen, *A History of Political Thought in the Sixteenth Century*, p. 192.

[13] Leighton, *Appeal*, Ep. Ded.

himself detests them. The bishops "are a terror to all and loved by none, except by such as stand too nigh them in a contiguity of profit, popery and profaneness." [14] To remain silent was to be a coward; "when a body politic is run all into one festered sore of sin and one benumbing bruise of judgment," honest men must protest.[15]

Leighton therefore analyzed in detail the evils entailed in episcopacy. Under ten headings he showed how contrary it was to all good laws and to all sound government. The present hierarchy, he pointed out, "are not ashamed to bear the multitude in hand, that their calling is *jure divino*. But they dare not but confess when they are put to it that their calling is a part of the king's prerogative. So they put upon God what he abhorreth, and will hold of the king when they can do no other." [16] Actually, Leighton insisted that the bishops were demanding a measure of obedience that could not be reconciled with the king's claim upon his subjects. For the space of six hundred years episcopacy had been at the root of all the disasters that had overtaken the country. All the evils currently impending could be traced to the same source. In a remarkably comprehensive survey, Leighton proved that "the prelacy is the mother of all sin"; remove prelacy, therefore, and "you stay the course of sin." [17] What is more, "the lord-like means" by which bishops have been transformed "from religious priests to temporal princes . . . might serve his Majesty for many good uses." [18] Leighton was careful throughout to insist that the king himself was in no way responsible for the evils that had developed. Actually, the bishops had cut him off from effective contact with his devoted people. "Put the case," he said, "that the good harmless king be a captivated Joash, by Ataliah's Arminianized and Jesuited crew." [19] Leighton did not restrict himself to analysis and denunciation. He enumerated six "means of removal" by which the nation could be cleansed of "this leprosy of the prelates." [20] The responsibility lay with the members of parliament: if they would remove that "Asteroth or grand idol, and erect the purity of Christ's ordinances," Leighton confidently predicted

> a ceasing from exorbitant sins, a removal of judgment, a recovery of God's favour, a repairing of the breaches of the church and commonwealth, a redeeming of the honour of the state, a dashing of "Babel's brats against the stones." Yea, this shall remove "the wicked from the throne," strike a terror and astonishment to the hearts of all foreign and domestic foes. In a

[14] *Ibid.*, To the Reader.
[15] *Ibid.*, p. 2.
[16] *Ibid.*, p. 4. In the first six pages, Leighton listed the heads of his analysis; then, for the space of two hundred pages, he amplified each in turn.
[17] *Ibid.*, p. 24.
[18] *Ibid.*, p. 264.
[19] *Ibid.*, p. 208.
[20] *Ibid.*, p. 332.

word, God will go forth with us and smite our enemies. Yea, a glorious prosperity shall rest upon Zion, king, state, and commonwealth.[21]

Leighton was probably a difficult and irascible person. This is the obvious explanation of the trouble he consistently created for himself. But he had a clear mind and considerable ability as a pamphleteer. He stated his case with great cogency, and the vigor of his style arrests the reader and carries him effortlessly to the end. His book anticipated much that was to come later. The tone, the arguments, and the program would all reappear in the Long Parliament, and Charles and the bishops would have done well to ponder this symptom of unrest. Laud, however, was determined to allow no quarter to the kind of views Leighton expressed. The confident appeal to parliament merely aggravated the offender's fault. So the authorities proceeded to punish him severely. The High Commission stripped him of his clerical privileges; and the Court of Star Chamber imposed a fine of £10,000 and sentenced him to stand in the pillory, there to be whipped, and then to "have one of his ears cut off and his nose slit, and to be branded in the face with SS, for a sower of sedition." This was the kind of savage sentence usually reserved for rogues and vagabonds. It was novel to have a cleric (even a defrocked one) exposed to such indignities. It was unusual for the sufferer to turn his humiliation to such good account. "All the arguments brought against me," he said to the bystanders at the pillory, "are prison, fire, brands, knife and whip." [22] Leighton was not a popular hero to the same extent as those who soon followed him in the same place, but the king's ministers had embarked on a policy certain to arouse sympathy for their victims and to awaken hostility against themselves. Moreover, anyone could see that the judges who imposed the sentence were parties to the dispute. As Leighton pointed out in his *Epitomie*, Bishop Neile helped to launch the case against him. Laud spoke for two hours against him. When sentence had been pronounced, Laud raised his cap, lifted his hands, and "gave thanks to God who had given him the victory over his enemies." [23]

Where Leighton led, others promptly followed. It was clearly possible to attack the new trends in politics while merely criticizing the pattern of church polity. It was soon apparent that it was also possible to invoke the same punishment that Leighton suffered. The celebrated trio of Prynne, Burton, and Bastwick were certainly critics of authority, though it was not immediately clear how far they were advocates of freedom. "These were three persons," said Clarendon, "most notorious for their declared malice

[21] *Ibid.*, p. 6.
[22] Leighton described his sufferings in detail in his *Epitomie or Briefe Discoverie* (1646). Prynne also protested against having the bishops sit as members of the court when they were parties to the case, *A Briefe Relation of certain speciall and most materiall passages*, pp. 4, 9.
[23] Leighton, *Epitomie or Briefe Discoverie*, p. 78.

against the government of the church by bishops, in their several books and writings, which they published to corrupt the people, with circumstances very scandalous, and in language very scurrilous and impudent; which all men thought deserved very exemplary punishment." [24]

By his personal idiosyncrasies and by his extravagance of utterance, Prynne probably attracted more attention than either of his two associates. It has sometimes been assumed that a man so extreme in his statements must have been equally extreme in his views. A contemporary critic dismissed him as a "furious novelist." [25] Prynne was undoubtedly a fanatic; for the greater part of his long career he was certainly not a revolutionary.[26] For a short time, from 1641 to 1645, he advocated radical policies, but for most of his life he was more preoccupied with the past than with the future. In his later years he was a constitutional historian of distinctly conservative bent. Most of his works show him as a blend of the antiquarian scholar and the common lawyer. In the former area he was in the select company of men like Selden; in the latter he could challenge comparison with Coke. His works are usually marred by the masses of recondite learning with which he burdened his pages. His attack on the drama, the *Histrio-mastix*, ran to over a thousand pages, and into it he poured the miscellaneous materials that his tireless energy had accumulated and that his phenomenal memory had retained. In an age easily overawed by erudition, it was assumed that a man who knew so much could not be wrong. Fortunately for his cause, Prynne's dedicatory epistles were straightforward and effective. He stated his case simply; in subsequent pages he conveyed the impression that weight of learning made it irrefutable.

In the period when he was causing greatest consternation to the authorities, Prynne was actually advocating a return to customary ways. He was the consistent enemy of innovation. His earliest book, *The Perpetuitie of a regenerate man's estate*, was a defense of Calvinist theology, and Calvinism had been the mark of the Elizabethan church. In these latter days of apostasy, he argued, the true doctrine was being submerged by the foul tide of Arminian novelties. So in due course he underlined the contrast in *The Church of England's old antithesis to the new Arminianisme*. When he turned to contemporary manners he showed himself the defender of the old and critic of the new. In *The Unloveliness of lovelockes* he exposed the vanity of long hair. In *Healthes Sicknesse* he attacked the custom of drinking toasts without number—and so without point or purpose. Above all, he showed in *Histrio-mastix* that the theater was dragging morality through the mire. Prynne, however, was not simply an undiscriminating defender of

---

[24] Clarendon, *The History of the Rebellion*, I, 146–147.

[25] Page, *A Treatise of Justification of bowing at the name of Jesus*, Ep. Ded.

[26] Cf. W. M. Lamont, *Marginal Prynne, 1600–1669*. I find his interpretation of Prynne as a moderate entirely convincing.

past times. His point of view had been deeply colored by John Foxe and John Jewel. Foxe provided him with a view of history. From the *Acts and Monuments* he learned to see Elizabeth as the English Constantine and her bishops as the successors of the Marian martyrs. These great and godly men transmitted a certain view of the church and of their proper place in it. They recognized the right of the queen to govern the church; from her they received their office, and by her authority they exercised it. But now, claimed Prynne, there has arisen a new breed of churchman, intent on subverting all the ancient ways. They hold views "point blank against the established doctrine of the church of England." These "unpreaching, domineering secular prelates" countenance "Arminianism, popery and popish ceremonies." They themselves do not preach, but they silence godly ministers who are willing to do so but who now stand mute and idle. But worst of all, they so exalt their office that they claim for it a divine institution.[27] To Prynne the Laudian position was a veiled attack on the royal supremacy. Though he had some very harsh things to say about "certain late detestable practices of some domineering lordly prelates," as yet he was not advocating the overthrow of episcopacy. He vehemently objected to what Laud and his friends were making of the office, but he still held to his ideal of the Elizabethan church. The new breed were cryptopapists, scheming to reduce the nation "to popish idolatry." So he lashed out against "those bloody prelates,"

> disguising themselves with strange vestments, disguises, vizors, and play-like apparel, as rochets, copes, stoles, abbeys and other massing trinkets to difference them from all other men, and dancing, cringing and playing the mummers, with divers new antique gestures, piping organs, and minstrelsy, before their new-erected altars, hopping, limping and dancing before them like the ancient pagan priests before their idolatrous altars.[28]

Laud, of all men, was not likely to submit meekly to such fulminations. A wiser and more patient man might have seen that naked fanaticism engenders its own reaction. But such perception was not in the tradition of seventeenth-century justice. So Prynne was called to account. He suffered severely, but he did not suffer alone.

Prynne would have been unique in any age. Henry Burton was merely an exceptional example of a common type. His zeal, like Prynne's, had been fostered on tales of the Marian martyrs. One of his mother's treasures was a New Testament which "had been my grandfather's in Queen Mary's days." From its pages Burton learned to read, and it was

[27] [Prynne], *Newes from Ipswich*, n.p.

[28] [Prynne], *XVI New Quaeries Proposed to our Lord Praelates*, pp. 14–15. Cf. *A Lookinge Glasse for all Lordly Prelates*, passim; *Lord Bishops none of the Lords Bishops*; *Breviate of the Prelates Intollerable usurpations upon the kings prerogative and the subjects liberties.*

given to him as a reward. At Cambridge his piety was nurtured by
Chaderton and Perkins; he had no sooner left the university than he began
to show his antipathy to the prevailing drift in church affairs. An
observant woman, he tells us, "took such notice of my spirit then, and
chiefly of my zeal against the prelates' pride and practices that she said
then to some . . . of me, This young man (said she) will one day be the
overthrow of the bishops." [29] Temporarily forgetful of this prediction, he
tried a career at court, and in retrospect thanked God that he was saved
from the temptations of success—though he continued his efforts for
fourteen years.[30] As rector of St. Matthew's, Friday Street, he soon found
scope both as a preacher and as a pamphleteer. He had difficulties getting
his attacks on the Laudians licensed; for evading the regulations he was
soon in difficulties with the High Commission. His reply to Montagu's
Appello Caesarem was offensive to the authorities; his *The Baiting of the Pope's
Bull* was doubly so. With considerable relish he described how Neile and
Laud harried him for hours at a time, and how, by ingenuity and with the
help of friendly lawyers, he consistently frustrated their stratagems.[31] But
the cleavage between him and his opponents was deep and impassable.
"For I more and more disliked their usurpations and tyrannical government, with their attempts to set up popery." The nature of the new
episcopacy became increasingly apparent to him,

> because I saw how every day they got ground in the hearts of
> simple and credulous people, apt to believe their plausible
> pretences and pompous shows of piety, as if all they did were to
> maintain the Protestant religion, when under that specious
> colour the withered whore of Babylon came in masked at the
> first, till at length she began to shew her painted face in her
> superstitious altar-service, and other garbs. And as they la-
> boured to undermine and overthrow the true Protestant religion,
> and instead thereof to set up popery, so they did no less seek to
> overthrow the civil state, with the good laws thereof and just
> liberties of the subject, and to introduce an arbitrary govern-
> ment, otherwise called tyranny, which taketh away every man's
> property in his own goods and estate, as plainly sheweth by all
> their practices, as in exacting ship money . . . and other
> impositions, with a thousand monopolies.[32]

As Burton pondered these iniquities, the situation crystallized in his mind
as a struggle between good and evil, darkness and light. On the one side
he saw the godly ministers who faithfully preached the Word; on the

---

[29] H. Burton, *A Narration of the Life of Mr Henry Burton*, p. 1.
[30] *Ibid.*, pp. 3–4.
[31] H. Burton, *A Plea to an appeale*, Ep. Ded.
[32] H. Burton, *A Narration of the Life of Mr Henry Burton*, pp. 8–9.

other, the "blind watchmen, dumb dogs, plagues of souls, false prophets, ravening wolves, thieves and robbers of souls." [33] On 5 November 1639—the anniversary of frustrated popish stratagems—he preached two sermons, in which he poured out the bitterness of his soul. The bishops' pursuivants were at his heels at once, but he barricaded himself inside his house and, while the pursuivants raged outside the door, he wrote out his sermons, and dispatched the manuscript, sheet by sheet, to the printer. That finished, he opened the door and was dragged off to prison to await trial with Prynne.

Bastwick, the third member of this celebrated trio, had been at Emmanuel College, Cambridge, had seen service abroad as a soldier, and had qualified as a physician. Neither his background nor his secular contacts predisposed him to accept the high-flying clericalism of the Laudian school. He published a couple of Latin tracts against the bishops' claims, and for his pains he found himself a prisoner in the Gatehouse. Visitors flocked to see him. They pressed on him a single question: Why not state his case against the bishops in English, so that the common people could read it? He responded with *The Letany of John Bastwick, doctor of Physicke*, "printed by the special procurement and for the especial use of our English prelates." Bastwick argued that the bishops' authority depends upon the king's appointment; they have insisted that "they hold directly from Christ." Ultimately, however, this was a practical issue, not a theoretical one. The bishops' claims are "injurious to God, the king, the whole nobility, and all the subjects." [34] Study history, he urged: it will show "how many flourishing kingdoms have been made desolate by bishops, but none established by them." [35] The bishops, living in arrogance and luxury, do not themselves preach, yet they silence those who are eager to do so. The king, Bastwick assumed, was not involved in the malpractices of the bishops; he, no less than his people, had been despoiled by them. In Bastwick there was a more pronounced strain of anticlericalism than in either Prynne or Burton. "Of all creatures," he declared, "bishops, priests and deacons are the worst, most dangerous and most to be prayed against; for they are not only evil in themselves, but they corrupt all others like a contagion." [36] Still, an unholy preeminence belongs to the bishops: "for as many prelates in England, so many vipers in the bowels of church and state." [37] Yet this is more than mere vituperation. In *The Letany* and in its sequel Bastwick explicitly raised the question of authority. Who conferred it? To what ends should it be used? What results have followed from its exercise?

In theory Bastwick agreed with Prynne and Burton. He objected to the

[33] H. Burton, *For God, and the King*, pp. 39–40.
[34] Bastwick, *The Letany*, p. 2b.
[35] *Ibid.*, p. 3a.
[36] *Ibid.*, p. 9a.
[37] *Ibid.*, p. 20a.

principle of *jure divino* episcopacy; it was a corruption, in the interests of
Romanism, of the Church of England, and it was a threat to the
constitutional rights of the king. But Bastwick promptly lost sight of the
theoretical distortion of episcopacy as he denounced its practical abuses.
"I pray you see a little more," he said, "the horrible cruelty and arrogancy
of the prelates in the execution of their pontifician offices." [38] The
distinction between legitimate episcopacy and its Laudian corruption (by
which Prynne initially set such store) had dropped from sight; Bastwick
had been caught up in the excitement of a fight in which no quarter was
given on either side. Others promptly caught the same infection. Here we
see a real distinction between Bastwick and his associates. Prynne, peering
from under his peaked nightcap at his ponderous folios, lifting his head
only to gnaw at his crust of bread or take a draught from his flagon of ale,
was always a kind of caricature of a scholar—inexhaustibly erudite,
fanatically opinionated, venomously embittered. Burton had a good
command of prose, and, by the standards of the time, a vigorous
controversial style. But Bastwick's prose is a new phenomenon. An old
gentleman who had urged him to write *The Letany* could hardly contain
himself for mirth when he read the manuscript. The modern reader finds
it less irresistibly amusing, but he recognizes at once a new idiom. A style
has emerged which holds the promise that the press will become a medium
of mass communication.

Bastwick was well aware that a program of reform would never succeed
unless it reached the common people. They would ignore ponderous
erudition. They might respond to humor. So in "The Second Part of the
Letany of John Bastwick," [39] he defended his sardonic approach to serious
questions. "And now to speak something to the matter in hand and for my
own particular. You cannot be ignorant that for these threescore years
and upward there have been thousands that have writ with all manner of
gravity and humble lowliness, calling for reformation, and yet nothing
hath been listened unto, but for their pains they have been severely
punished and for their pains undone by the prelates." [40] Why should
people object if he resorts to the methods that the bishops themselves
countenance? He has used comedy; they applaud comedies, especially
those that revile the Puritans. He has resorted to ridicule; they employ it
even in their sermons. They have made the pulpit a place of contention;
why may not he refute their charges in a pamphlet? [41] And what about
the objects of the prelates' wrath? He himself, said Bastwick, had been
brought up with a strong antipathy to Puritans: they were generally
reviled, and there were only a couple of them in the entire county where

[38] *Ibid.*, p. 18a.
[39] This is the subtitle of *The Answer of John Bastwick, doctor of Physicke, to the exceptions made against his Letany.*
[40] *Ibid.*, p. 2.
[41] *Ibid.*, pp. 2–4.

he was born. But experience and observation had brought him to a better mind. "And I then well perceived, looking into the lives and manners of men, that those that were commonly branded with the name of Puritans were the happiest, and that if any were eternally blessed, they were such of them as squared their lives in sincerity according to their profession." He had seriously pondered the lives of other people too. "And for my own particular, to speak now my conscience, I had rather go the way of the meanest Puritans that live and die according to their profession than of the greatest prelate that ever lived upon the earth." [42] Bastwick was now thoroughly aroused. His sufferings had converted him from a critic into a revolutionary—and one with a very dangerous weapon to hand. "Now I pray," he said, "take notice of the prelate of Canterbury's arrogancy." [43]

The prelate of Canterbury had decided that it was high time to take further notice of the arrogancy of Bastwick and his kind. One result of the development of popular polemics is that we know in remarkable detail exactly what happened to Prynne, Burton, and Bastwick. They were not men content to suffer in a corner. We can follow step by step the charges laid against them and their replies. We can see how angry Laud got at Prynne's maneuvers, which were always designed to put the archbishop legally in the wrong. We can watch the accused appealing over the heads of their judges to that much more formidable court which they had discovered how to convene; they were summoning their opponents to the bar of public opinion. "If you condemn me for this," said Prynne, "I hope all the world will acquit me." [44]

The Court of Star Chamber found the prisoners guilty and imposed one of those brutal sentences intended to deter others from committing similar offenses. Each man was fined £5,000; he was to stand in the pillory, was there to lose his ears, and was to be imprisoned for the rest of his life in a distant castle. Prynne, who had had his ears cropped on a previous occasion, was also to be branded on the cheeks with S.L.—Seditious Libeller. To conclude the proceedings, Laud delivered a lengthy speech to justify his policy.[45] It was argumentative and involved. It must have been tedious when spoken. It was ineffective journalism when published.

But Laud did not have the last word in this controversy. His victims were duly led out to suffer, and they turned the occasion into a popular triumph. The government had provided its most vocal critics with something between a platform and a stage. The immense crowd had come, not to watch, but to sympathize and applaud. Even Clarendon mentioned the coincidence that was widely noted at the time: "they were of the three several professions which had the most influence on the

[42] *Ibid.*, pp. 4–5.
[43] *Ibid.*, p. 8.
[44] *A Briefe Relation of certain speciall and most materiall passages*, p. 21.
[45] Laud, *A Speech delivered in the Starr-chamber.*

people, a divine, a common lawyer and a doctor of physic." [46] Each of the
sufferers addressed the crowd. They reaffirmed what they had previously
said in their pamphlets; the circumstances gave to their witness and to
their criticism of the prelates an overwhelming emotional impact. The
wives of Burton and Bastwick were present to support and comfort their
husbands. Burton wore new gloves and carried a nosegay, because, he
said, this was in truth his wedding day. They faced their ordeal with
courage. Bastwick calmly instructed the executioner how to cut off his
ears. The huge crowd "wept and grieved for Mr. Burton, and at the
cutting of each ear there was such a roaring as if every one had at the same
instant lost an ear." [47] Prynne was horribly hacked about. The branding
was clumsily done, and was therefore repeated, but the indomitable man
refused to be intimidated. "The more I am beat down," he cried, "the
more I am lift up." On his way back to prison he coined a pun: S.L., he
said, really stood for "Stigmata Laudi." [48]

Then after the briefest possible interval there appeared on the streets *A
Briefe Relation of certain speciall and most materiall passages . . . at the censure of
. . . Dr Bastwicke, Mr Burton and Mr Prynne,* recounting in graphic and
spirited terms the entire story. Each detail was described, each comment
repeated, each speech recorded in the very words the protagonist had
used—or should we say the words he might have used? Whether this is
exact reporting or highly imaginative reconstruction hardly matters. Here
were men with a grievance against the authorities, and they had found the
means of setting their case before the widest possible audience. The
problem of the authorities was genuine enough. They believed that they
were confronted not with a plea for freedom but with the threat of sedition.
To Strafford, Prynne's case provided an alarming example of

> the humour of the time to cry up and magnify such as the
> humour and justice of the king and state have marked out and
> adjudged mutinous to the government and offensive to the belief
> and reverence the people ought to have in the wisdom and
> integrity of the magistrate. Nor am I now to say it anew . . .
> that a prince loseth the force and example of his punishments,
> loseth withal the greatest part of his dominion; and yet still,
> methinks, we are not got through the disease—nay, I fear, do not
> yet sufficiently apprehend the malignity of it. In the meantime a
> liberty thus assumed, thus abused, is very insufferable; but how
> to help it I know not. [49]

The government was paralyzed by honest perplexity. In addition, it was

[46] Clarendon, *The History of the Rebellion*, I, 147. Cf. *A Briefe Relation*, p. 21.
[47] Gardiner (ed.), *Documents Relating to the Proceedings against William Prynne*, p. 87.
[48] *A Briefe Relation of certain speciall and most materiall passages . . . at the censure of . . . Dr
Bastwicke, Mr Burton and Mr Prynne*, p. 22.
[49] Strafford, *Letters*, II, 119.

handicapped by psychological obtuseness. Laud and his colleagues seemed unaware of the simple fact that it is usually wisest to ignore fanatics. With strange ineptitude, Chief Justice Richardson remarked, during the 1634 proceedings against Prynne, that if the accused wished to read in prison, he should be given Foxe: "Let him have the *Book of Martyrs,* for the Puritans do account him a martyr." [50] He may be pardoned for not knowing that Foxe had originally kindled Prynne's zeal and would certainly sustain it. He should have realized that if Prynne was becoming a popular hero, further punishment was hardly the way to discourage the cult. The adulation that surrounded the sufferers became steadily more apparent. In 1637, when Prynne, Burton, and Bastwick set out from London for their remote places of imprisonment, they were escorted on the first stage of their journey by crowds that would have gratified a conquering hero. For this self-defeating policy of persecution the heaviest responsibility lies at Laud's door. Doubtless he succeeded in intimidating the fainthearted; in the process he raised up an apostolic succession of eager sufferers. Leighton called forth Prynne. Prynne's initial punishment in 1634 was merely a curtain raiser to the great drama of the three martyrs of 1637. They in turn were directly responsible for the emergence of John Lilburne.

Lilburne, an impressionable young man from the country, had come to London to make his way. He felt that his progress had somehow been barred by the bishops, and consequently he nursed a private grievance. He met Bastwick, already in prison, and was attracted by his religious witness and by his protest against ecclesiastical oppression. For complicity in printing and circulating Bastwick's works, Lilburne found himself in trouble. He was seized, examined before the Court of Star Chamber, and sentenced to be whipped at the cart's tail from the Fleet Prison to Palace Yard, Westminster, and there to stand in the pillory. True to the tradition already established, he published an account of his trial even before he suffered the punishment.[51] Far more disturbing to the authorities and far more inflammatory to the public was his next work. Long before Lilburne's back had healed, there appeared on the streets of London *The Worke of the Beast, or A Relation of a most unchristian censure executed upon John Lilburne.* He wrote it, he tells us, both to expose the barbarous cruelty of the bishops and to encourage, by the record of his own witness against oppression, others who might be willing to resist. He recounted his sufferings as a triumph of Christian patience over the dark forces of cruelty and hate. On the day of his ordeal he had little time for preparation. He could only fortify his spirit by dwelling on some of the wonderful promises of Scripture; then he was led out to be stripped to the waist and tied to the tail of the cart. He was acutely aware that he was a gentleman's son,

[50] Gardiner, *History,* VIII, 334.
[51] John Lilburne, *The Christian Mans Triall.*

exposed to the treatment reserved for vagabonds; others knew it, too. "I
have whipped many a rogue," remarked the executioner, "but now I shall
whip an honest man." [52]

Every step of the way to Westminster he was sustained by "an inward
joy and consolation that carrie(d him) high above all pains and torments."
"Oh my brethren," he cried, "there is such sweetness and contentedness in
enjoying the Lord Jesus alone, that it is able, where it is felt, to make a
man go through all difficulties, and endure all hardships that may possibly
come upon him." [53] Even the spectators offered reassurance and support.
As he set out, a young man "bid me put on a courageous resolution to
suffer cheerfully and not to dishonour my cause, for you suffer (said he) for
a good cause." "I know," replied Lilburne, "that the cause is good, for it is
God's cause, and for my own part I am cheerful and merry in the Lord,
and am contented with this my present position as if I were to receive my
present liberty. For I know that my God that hath gone along with me
hitherto will carry me through to the end." [54] As he came down the
Strand, a friend called out to him to speak with boldness, "to whom I
replied, when the time comes, I will."

No sooner was he placed in the pillory than he began to harangue the
crowd. With the flair for the dramatic that came so naturally to his
contemporaries he turned to account everything that befell him—the
emissaries from the High Commission who tried to silence him with a
promise of pardon, the fat lawyer who tried to browbeat him into holding
his tongue, even the joint threats of this same lawyer and the warden of the
Fleet, who ended his speech by gagging him. This exasperated gesture of
frustration followed one of the unexpected features of Lilburne's speech.
He had managed to hide in his pockets three of Bastwick's pamphlets.
Having quoted the author and praised his stand, Lilburne produced the
books and tossed them into the crowd.[55] The gagging may have cut short
his speech, but when he came to recount his sufferings it improved his
story. To the crowd it was a visible proof of the eagerness of the authorities
to silence his protest.

If Lilburne spoke as effectively as he wrote, his speech from the pillory
must have been a singularly telling utterance. He made no great claims
on his own behalf. He acknowledged that he was but a young man, and
no scholar; "yet," he added, "I have obtained mercy of the Lord to be
faithful." [56] He protested against the illegality of his trial, which was
against the law of the land, the Petition of Right, the Law of God, and the
practice of Christ. He touched on the indignity of treating a gentleman
like a rogue. At the same time, he emphasized the spiritual equality which

[52] *Ibid.*, pp. 21–22.
[53] *Ibid.*
[54] *Ibid.*, p. 5.
[55] *Ibid.*, p. 20.
[56] *Ibid.*, p. 19.

Christ's summons creates: "whatever by place or calling thy rank or degree be, be it higher or lower," if Christ calls you, obey, for in obeying you learn the equality created by suffering.[57] Both in the pillory and subsequently in his various pamphlets, Lilburne reserved his most scathing attacks for the bishops. These men "challenge their callings to be *jure divino*," but Prynne, Burton, and Bastwick ("which men I love and honour") have convincingly proved that "bishops originally derived their jurisdiction, callings and power from the king." [58] They are insinuating popery into the church, which is perhaps natural since "their calling is of the devil." [59] In subsequent pamphlets Lilburne returned repeatedly to the cruelty he experienced at the hands of the bishops. They were directly responsible for depriving him in prison of human society, of amenities of every kind, even of food itself. "I verily believe," he wrote, "that if Beelzebub the prince of devils had sat in personal presence at the inner Star Chamber instead of the Pope of Lambeth his dutiful son, he could not have made a more merciless inhuman order against me." [60] How fortunate the apostle Paul was! He only had to deal with pagans, not with the Christian bishops of England. "Oh! all you Christian ears that hear these things, stand amazed and wonder at the bloodthirsty unparalleled cruelty and tyranny of the bishops." [61] In the pillory, Lilburne publicly challenged the bishops to debate with him in the presence of the king and council. As he pointed out, he was forthwith gagged. He repeated the challenge again and again in his pamphlets. The bishops, he claimed, were too cowardly to face him.[62]

The bishops were disturbed.[63] No one could tell how far this kind of agitation might reach. Lilburne began by attacking the abuses of episcopacy, went on to attack episcopacy itself, and was already advocating "the way of total separation (commonly but falsely called Brownism)." Sectarianism, so long quiescent, was stirring once more. And the attacks launched by the agitators were not likely to be confined to ecclesiastical matters. For the moment, as Laud reminded the king, the critics ostensibly struck at the bishops, "but through our sides your majesty, your honour, your safety, your religion is impeached." [64] In Prynne, Burton, Bastwick, and perhaps most of all in Lilburne there was clearly a premonition of things to come. Here was the unmistakable proof that prison walls could not silence a man who was determined to be heard. Here was a clear demonstration of the formidable power of the press and

[57] *Ibid.*, p. 23.
[58] *Ibid.*, p. 14.
[59] *Ibid.*, p. 25.
[60] Lilburne, *A Coppy of a letter*, p. 4.
[61] Lilburne, *Come out of her*, pp. 31–32.
[62] *Ibid.*, pp. 25, 32, 33.
[63] Cf. Laud, *The History of the Troubles*, p. 59.
[64] Laud, *A Speech delivered in the Starr-chamber*, Ep. Ded.

of the impossibility of muzzling it. Here was a foretaste of the powers soon to be let loose in the approaching revolution. What Bastwick and Lilburne said about the bishops today would be repeated tomorrow by noblemen like Lord Falkland and Lord Brooke.[65] The freedom of speech, so shrilly demanded by Lilburne, would be claimed with memorable eloquence by Milton. In Lilburne, the more extreme consequences of a generation of Puritan preaching became clear. His fondness for apocalyptic imagery showed that the common man was learning to clothe his dreams in Biblical language. He claimed the freedom to speak the truth as he saw it and to join with others in such associations as might commend themselves "to every man's conscience in the sight of God." Having been in the pillory once, Lilburne expected soon to be there again; then, "by the might and strength of my God I will, come life, come death, speak my mind freely and courageously." [66] Here was a confidence that was willing to face any danger and to accept any suffering. "And for my part," he said, "the Lord himself hath by his enlightening spirit so firmly convinced me and settled my soul so unmovably in his truth that I assuredly know that all the power in earth, yea and the gates of Hell itself, shall never be able to move me or prevail against me, for the Lord is the worker of all my works in me and for me." [67]

[65] Falkland, *A Speech made to the House of Commons concerning Episcopacy;* Robert Greville, Lord Brooke, *A Discourse opening the nature of that Episcopacie which is exercised in England.*
[66] Lilburne, *Come out of her*, p. 4.
[67] *Ibid.*, p. 5.

XI

CONCLUSION

THE EARLY PART of the seventeenth century raised more questions than it was able to answer. It shares this characteristic, of course, with many other periods. It was exceptional in isolating the issues that were not only of immediate interest but would continue to be of engrossing concern for generations to come. It asked the important questions; its answers did not always solve the problems, but they often clarified them.

The political developments of the time demanded serious thought and concentrated it on the structure and functioning of the state. The nature of authority and its location became questions of urgent importance. The experience of other countries, particularly of France, pointed to certain possible solutions. Ancient theories, hammered out during the struggle between the empire and the papacy, proved to have more relevance to the debates than might have been expected. The divine right of kings invested monarchy with religious sanctions, though originally it had reference to the freedom from ecclesiastical interference which the emerging national states claimed. In the early seventeenth century there was little disposition to deny that kingship was the ideal form of government or that it was invested by God with indisputable authority. But there were other elements in the body politic that also had ancient traditions and undoubted (though sometimes unspecified) rights. The champions of the common law insisted that its proper place must be recognized; its demands not only clashed with other legal systems but raised important questions about the relation of the king's will to the king's law. Parliamentary institutions presupposed that the people and their representatives had certain rights and powers. The prerogatives of the king might easily clash with the privileges of the people, and the lack of clear definition on both sides made the danger all the more acute. The tension between royal sovereignty and popular rights was aggravated both by the theoretical claims advanced by the Stuarts and by the administrative methods that they employed. Experience showed that the king could not dispense with

parliament, but when the personal rule of Charles ended in failure, it
proved an impossible task to reconcile the freedom that the people claimed
with the authority that the king insisted on exercising. The issues had
been sharpened. Debate failed to provide an answer. Civil war was no
more successful in resolving the problem.

The questions raised by the problem of authority were urgent. This is
proved by the variety of answers that proliferated during the next few
years. A whole literature sprang up devoted to the issue. Thomas Hobbes
believed that the existing confusion pointed to the need for a strong central
authority to exercise power. However, the overthrow of monarchy
inspired a host of writers who located the source of authority in the people.
Theories might vary as to the kind of compact by which the citizens
delegated power to the rulers. The proper form and pattern of government stimulated a vast amount of debate. On the rights of the people and
the inalienable character of their liberties there was much agreement.
The literature devoted to freedom is one of the exciting features of the
middle years of the seventeenth century. If the indecisive results of the
constitutional struggle prompted Hobbes to advocate absolutism, they
encouraged Milton and Lilburne, Overton and Walwyn to champion the
freedom of the people. It was far from clear exactly how that freedom
should be defined. The Army Debates reflected high hopes and strong
convictions but little unanimity. The constitutional problems became
increasingly insoluble. The passage of time proved that it was easier to
complain of grievances than to apply solutions. In due course the
parliament and the army, the protectoralists and the republicans all
attempted to resolve the impasse. All failed. When the turmoil was over,
a Stuart king once more occupied the English throne. Admittedly the
Interregnum destroyed any possibility of reverting to Stuart absolutism, but the problem of authority was as confused and ill defined as
ever.

The struggles of the seventeenth century showed that tradition was a
power which could not be ignored. In the early part of the period it had
frequently been invoked. Its authority had been claimed on behalf of
bishops and their right to govern the church, of the common law and its
precedence over competing legal systems, of parliamentary privilege and
the rights of the people. In the aftermath of the civil war, many of the
ancient institutions were destroyed. The king was beheaded and the
monarchy suppressed. The House of Lords was abolished. Episcopacy
was swept away. The radicals demanded a comprehensive revision of the
legal system. The Restoration proved that old institutions are very
persistent and have amazing powers of recuperation. Nothing (except
perhaps episcopacy) was restored in exactly the same form as before. The
patterns might be similar; the spirit had subtly changed. In 1640 the
authority of tradition seemed particularly vulnerable to attack. Twenty
years later it had shown a unique power to rally the support of a people

who had grown weary of experiment and longed for a return to familiar ways.

One of the earliest casualties of the assault on authority was uniformity in the church. Laud's system collapsed. Episcopacy, in the form in which he had maintained it, proved to have many enemies and few friends. Those who had groaned under the demands of uniformity believed that conscience would now be free. The ideal of toleration proved much more difficult to apply than its advocates had anticipated. "New presbyter" had disconcerting resemblances to "old priest"; certainly he was quite as determined that the right way—his way—should triumph and that dissent should be suppressed. Those who advocated freedom soon discovered that it became entangled with those problems of political loyalty which had so complicated Queen Elizabeth's treatment of the Catholic recusants. The Independents were more generous than the Presbyterians, but they were faced with the problem of proliferating sects. What basic rights belong to moral anarchists or to social revolutionaries? Does a plea for freedom entitle some people to disrupt the worship of others? Cromwell had genuine convictions about religious liberty. Milton, a harsh critic of the performance of others, admitted that in the early stages of the Interregnum Cromwell sincerely tried to translate his principles into practice. Subsequently, Milton turned fiercely upon his former hero; Cromwell's dilemma and Milton's response merely emphasize the problems inseparable from applying toleration. When the Restoration brought back the traditional system, the evidence of an attempt to revive the old ways was the passing of the Act of Uniformity. But even the disciples of Laud could not really revive his system, and in less than a generation the Act of Toleration symbolized the triumph of a different approach. Freedom might still be restricted, but the attempt to organize the religious life of the nation according to a single pattern was abandoned.

Experience showed that it was not easy to achieve freedom of worship. It seemed all the more important to establish "liberty for printing and speaking." Few subjects stirred Milton so deeply; none moved him to more sustained eloquence. Other men, after their own manner, also pleaded for the same kind of freedom. "Let there be liberty of the press for printing, to those that are not allowed pulpits for preaching. Let that light come in at the window which cannot come in at the door, that all may speak and write one way that cannot another." [1] As a corollary to this, John Saltmarsh saw a society in which "free debates and open conferences" would encourage the unhindered pursuit of truth. But freedom of this kind was also difficult to control. It had been so before 1640; it was to be the same after 1660. The great eruption of pamphleteering during the Interregnum made the prospect of a regulated press increasingly remote, but the attempt to secure it was abandoned with reluctance.

[1] John Saltmarsh, *The Smoke in the Temple*, p. 3.

The Puritans believed that religious experience must be granted a place in any adequate doctrine of authority. But it is difficult to concede it a necessary role and then refuse its claim to a certain degree of latitude. Until 1640 the appeal to experience was kept within the decorous limits sanctioned by Laud's interpretation of decency and order. With the collapse of the old order there was a dramatic efflorescence of religious sects. Many of them were small. Most were short-lived. All emphasized the role of experience. Few of these groups endured long enough to make any significant contribution to English religious life. The Quakers were a conspicuous exception. George Fox constantly appealed to the demonstration of the Spirit's power in the life of the believer. "Then thou wilt feel the power of God," he wrote to Elizabeth Cromwell ("the Lady Claypole"), "that will bring nature into his course, and to see the glory of the first body. And there the wisdom of God will be received, which is Christ, by which all things were made and created, in wisdom to be preserved and ordered to God's glory. There thou wilt come to receive and feel the physician of value, which clothes people in their right mind, whereby they may serve God and do his will." [2] The exalted tone of this passage is characteristic of Fox; so is the expectation that his message will produce visible results in the life of his correspondent. The Quaker method of combining a strong but flexible doctrine of spiritual authority with a responsible concept of freedom made the sect notable at the time and is one of the secrets of its enduring influence.

The Quakers appealed to an inner light that illuminated a man's heart. It gave him assurance and was the source of power. This was a very different approach from the reliance on argument which had been the staple of most religious debate. Fox touched a principle of spiritual vitality: "the power of the Lord was over all." His appeal to an unpredictable, seemingly irrational force alarmed his contemporaries. Many Englishmen felt that "enthusiasm" was the essence of sectarianism. The appeal to experience, so full of promise as a means of revitalizing religion, was dismissed as the symptom of blind fanaticism. A reaction was natural, and it took a predictable form. There must be some intermediate position, men argued, between the dry Scholasticism of much theological controversy and the vagaries of sectarian inspiration. The group which met at Wadham College, Oxford, during the Interregnum sought intellectual fellowship "without the wild distractions of that passionate age." They were weary of dogmatism and self-confident inspiration. They believed they had found an effective answer to both, "for such spiritual frenzies, which did then bear rule, can never stand long before a clear and deep skill in nature." [3] The Cambridge Platonists represent a parallel but distinguishable reaction against the kinds of authority on

---

[2] George Fox, *The Journal of George Fox* (ed. J. L. Nickalls), p. 347.
[3] T. Sprat, *History of the Royal Society* (ed. of 1702), pp. 53–54.

which men had too frequently relied. "The more false any one is in his religion, the more fierce and furious in maintaining it; the more mistaken, the more imposing." [4] Consequently, Whichcote and his disciples appealed for an approach to religious problems that would avoid superstition by recognizing the true role of reason. "To go against reason is to go against God; it is the selfsame thing to do that which the reason of the case doth require and that which God himself doth appoint. Reason is the divine governor of man's life; it is the very voice of God." [5] The Cambridge Platonists exalted reason without succumbing to an arid rationalism. They saw reason as a part—but only one part—of the comprehensive unity of man's mental and spiritual life, and therefore they related it closely to insight and imagination. Out of the interaction of all of these they believed that true wisdom might develop. But the trend of the times encouraged men to accept a clearer, colder, harder interpretation of reason. The new tendency found its high priest in John Locke, while the Latitudinarian clerics of the late seventeenth century showed that the tension between faith and reason could be resolved in a manner wholly different from that which had satisfied their predecessors. On the eve of the new century, Jonathan Swift's *Tale of a Tub* dissected with biting irony most of the types of authority to which the seventeenth century had submitted. One of the greatest masters of sarcasm thus provided a mordant epilogue to the recent search for acceptable ways of controlling thought and action.

The search for freedom also passed from the intense excitement of the earlier phase of the revolutionary era to a decorous contentment with traditional liberties. In the first flush of enthusiasm, Milton saw "in [his] mind a noble and puissant nation rousing herself like a strong man after sleep and shaking her invincible locks." He believed that England was "destined to become great and honourable in these latter ages," and its glory would be fulfilled in every kind of liberty.[6] Experience showed that it is easier to praise freedom than to achieve it. The pursuit of great ideals was a frustrating experience. Dreams often proved to be mirages. After two decades of resounding slogans, men were willing to settle for humbler expectations. During the election of 1656, Edmund Chillenden was warned against voting for a certain candidate on the grounds that he was not a godly man. Chillenden had been a captain in Whalley's regiment of horse; he had been sympathetic to the ideals of the New Model Army and the Levellers. "Pish," he answered, "let religion alone; give me my small liberty." [7]

The early part of the seventeenth century attempted to define the basis

[4] Whichcote, *Moral and Religious Aphorisms*, No. 499.

[5] *Ibid.*, No. 76.

[6] Milton, *Areopagitica*, in *Works* (Columbia ed.), IV, 344.

[7] *A Collection of State Papers of John Thurloe*, V, 287; quoted by G. Davies, *The Restoration of Charles II*, p. 360.

of freedom and its legitimate extent, but found that preoccupation with authority restricted the claims that could usefully be advanced. During the Interregnum men struggled to achieve the fullest measure of freedom in as many areas as possible. They discovered that the existing confusion about authority reduced even their most promising schemes to disarray. In the Restoration era, weariness with experiments and perhaps a greater realism about the bounds of probable achievement encouraged more modest expectations. The "small liberty" of the ordinary man was buttressed by the reassertion of traditional forms of outward authority, and the debate gradually shifted to areas where intellectual freedom could be discussed in predominantly abstract terms.

BIBLIOGRAPHY

THIS is not a bibliography of the subject; it is a list of works quoted in the text or referred to in the notes. In "I. Primary Works," the place of publication is London unless otherwise specified.

I. Primary Works

A., C. [J. Sweet]. *Monsigr. fate voi, or a discovery of the Dalmatian apostate.* [St. Omer,] 1617.

A., O. *The uncasing of heresie.* [Douai,] 1623.

A., T. [Thomas Owen]. *A Letter to a Catholicke Man beyond the seas.* St. Omer, 1610.

Abbot, George. *The Reasons which Doctour Hill hath brought for the Upholding of Papistry Unmasked.* Oxford, 1604.

——— *A Treatise of the perpetuall visibilitie and succession of the true church in all ages.* 1624.

Abbot, Robert [bp]. *A defence of the Reformed Catholicke of M. W. Perkins against the bastard Counter-Catholicke of D. Bishop.* 1606.

——— *The true ancient Roman catholike.* 1611.

Abbot, Robert. *The danger of Popery detected.* 1625.

——— *A Triall of our Church Forsakers.* 1639.

Adams, Thomas. *The Sermons of Thomas Adams.* Ed. John Brown. Cambridge, 1909.

——— *The Works of Thomas Adams.* 3 vols. Edinburgh, 1861–1862.

Ailesbury [Aylesbury], Thomas. *Paganisme and Papisme.* 1624.

Ainsworth, Henry. *Counterpoyson.* [Amsterdam?] 1608.

——— *A Defence of the Holy Scriptures, Worship and Ministrie used in the Christian Churches separated from Antichrist.* Amsterdam, 1609.

——— *A Reply to a Pretended Christian Church of Rome.* 1618.

——— *A Seasonable Discourse or a Censure upon a Dialogue of the Anabaptists.* 1623.

303

Ainsworth, Henry, and Johnson, Francis. *An Apologie or Defence of such true Christians.* Amsterdam, 1604.

Alembert, J. Le R. d', and Diderot, D. *Encyclopédie.* Paris, 1751.

Ames, William. *Conscience with the power and cases thereof.* 1639.

———— *A Fresh Suit against human ceremonies in God's worship.* 1633.

———— *A Manduction for Mr Robinson.* Dort, 1614.

———— *The Marrow of Sacred Divinity.* 1642.

———— *A Reply to Dr Mortons general defence of three nocent ceremonies.* 1622.

———— *A Reply to Dr Mortons particular defence of three nocent ceremonies.* 1623.

———— *A Second Manduction for Mr Robinson.* 1615.

Anderton, Lawrence. *The Non-entity of Protestancy.* [St. Omer,] 1633.

———— *One God, One Faith.* [St. Omer,] 1625.

Andrewes, Lancelot. *Of Episcopacy.* 1647.

———— *A Pattern of Catechisticall Doctrine.* Revised ed. 1641.

———— *Sacrilege a Snare.* 1646.

———— *The Collected Works of Lancelot Andrewes.* Ed. J. Bliss. 11 vols. Oxford, 1841–1854.

An Answere to a Sermon preached . . . by George Downame. 1609.

Aphorismes or certaine selected points of the doctrine of the Jesuits. 1609.

An Appeal of the orthodox ministers of the Church of England. New ed. Edinburgh, 1641.

The Archpriest Controversy. Ed. T. G. Law (Camden Society). 2 vols. 1896, 1898.

The Arminian Nunnery, or a briefe description and relation of the late erected monasticall place called the Arminian Nunnery at Little Gidding. 1641.

The Articles or Charge exhibited in Parliament against D. Cozens of Durham. 1641.

Askew, Egeon. *Brotherly Reconcilement.* 1605.

Atkins, John. *The Christian Race.* 1624.

Aubrey, John. *Brief Lives, Chiefly of Contemporaries.* Ed. Andrew Clark. 2 vols. Oxford, 1898.

B., A. *A Defence of Nicholas Smith against a reply to his discussion of some pointes taught by Mr Doctour Kellison.* Rouen, 1630.

B., T. *A Preservative to keep a Protestant from becoming a Papist.* Oxford, 1629.

B., W. [Lawrence Anderton]. *One God, One Faith.* St. Omer, 1625.

Bacon, Francis. *Letters and Life of Sir Francis Bacon.* Ed. J. Spedding. 7 vols. 1861–1874.

———— *The Works of Sir Francis Bacon.* 10 vols. 1826.

Baker, Augustine. *The Confessions of Venerable Father Augustine Baker, O.S.B.* Ed. Justin McCann. 1922.

———— *Holy Wisdom.* Ed. Serenus Cressy. [1875].

———— *Memorials of Father Augustine Baker and other Documents Relating to the English Benedictines.* Ed. J. McCann and H. Connolly (Catholic Record Society, XXXIII). 1933.

Balcanquall, Walter. *The Honour of Christian Churches.* 1633.

Bancroft, Richard. *A Sermon Preached at Paules Crosse.* 1588.

Barclay, William. *Of the Authoritie of the Pope.* 1611.
———— *De Regno et Regali Potestate.* Paris, 1600.
Barlow, William. *An Answer to a Catholike Englishman.* 1609.
———— *Concerning the antiquitie and superiority of bishops.* 1606.
———— *The Sermon preached at Paules Crosse.* 1606.
———— *The Summe and Substance of the Conference . . . at Hampton Court.* 1604.
Bastwick, John. *The Answer of John Bastwick, doctor of Physicke, to the exceptions made against his Letany.* 1637.
———— *The Letany of John Bastwick, doctor of Physicke.* 1637.
Baxter, Richard. *A Christian Directory.* 1673.
———— *Reliquiae Baxterianae.* 1696.
Bayly, Lewis. *The Practise of Pietie.* 3d ed. 1612.
Bayne[s], Paul. *Briefe Directions unto a godly life.* 2d ed. 1637.
———— *Christian Letters.* 2d ed. 1637.
———— *The diocesans tryall.* 1621.
———— *The trial of a christians estate.* 2d ed. 1637.
Beard, Thomas. *Antichrist the Pope of Rome.* 1625.
———— *A Retractive from the Romish Religion.* 1616.
———— *The Theatre of God's judgements.* 1612.
Becanus, Martin. *A defence of the Roman Church.* St. Omer, 1621.
———— *The English Iarre.* St. Omer, 1612.
———— *The New Man.* Trans. William Crashaw. 1622.
Bédé, Jean. *The Masse Displayed.* Oxford, 1619.
———— *The Right and Prerogative of Kings.* 1612.
Bedell, William. *An examination of certaine motives to recusancie.* Cambridge, 1628.
Bedell, William, and Wadsworth, James. *The Copies of Certain Letters which have passed between Spain and England in the matter of Religion.* 1624.
Bedford, Thomas. *Luthers Predecessours.* 1624.
Bell, Thomas. *The Catholique Triumph.* 1610.
———— *The Downefall of Poperie.* 1604.
———— *The Jesuits Antepast.* 1608.
———— *Motives concerning Romish Faith and Religion.* 1605.
———— *The Popes Funerall.* 1605.
———— *The Woeful Crie of Rome.* 1605.
Bellarmine, R. *Apologia Roberti S.R.E. Cardinalis Bellarmini pro responsione sua ad librum Jacobi.* Rome, 1610.
Belloy, Pierre de. *De l'Authorité du roi.* Paris, 1587.
[Bennet, John]. *The Hope of Peace.* Frankford, 1601.
Bernard, Richard. *The Bible-Battells.* 1629.
———— *Christian Advertisements and Counsels of Peace.* 1608.
———— *The Fabulous Foundation of the Popedom.* Oxford, 1619.
———— *The Faithful Shepheard.* 1607.
———— *A Guide to Grand Jury Men.* 1627.

—— *The Isle of Man.* 12th ed. 1648.

—— *Looke beyond Luther.* 1623.

—— *Plain Evidences: the Church of England is Apostolicall, the Separation Schismaticall.* 1610.

—— *Rhemes against Rome.* 1626.

Bilson, Thomas. *The Perpetual Government of Christ his Church.* 1593.

Bishop, William. *Maister Perkins Reformed Catholique.* Douai, 1625.

Blackwell, George. *A Large Examination taken at Lambeth . . . of Mr George Blackwell.* 1607.

Bodin, Jean. *De la république.* Paris, 1576.

Bolton, Robert. *A Discourse about the state of true happinesse.* 1636.

—— *Some General Directions for a comfortable walking with God.* 1634.

—— *On Usury.* 1637.

Boughen, Edward. *An Account of the Church Catholic.* 1653.

—— *A Sermon Concerning decencie and order in the Church.* 1638.

—— *Unanimity in Judgment and Affection necessary to Unity of Doctrine and Uniformity in Discipline.* New ed. 1714.

Boyle, Robert. *The Works of the Hon. Robert Boyle.* 6 vols. 1772.

Bradford, William. *The History of Plimouth Plantation.* Boston, 1898.

Bradshaw, William. *A Consideration of certain positions archiepiscopal.* New ed. 1660.

—— *Divine Worship.* Amsterdam, 1604.

—— *English Puritanisme.* Amsterdam, 1605.

—— *A Shorte Treatise of the crosse in baptisme.* Amsterdam, 1604.

—— *A Treatise of the nature and use of things indifferent.* Amsterdam, 1605.

—— *Twelve General Arguments proving that the ceremonies . . . are unlawful.* Amsterdam, 1605.

—— *The Unreasonablenesse of the Separation.* Dort, 1614.

Brereley, John [Lawrence Anderton?]. *The Apologie for the Romane Church.* Douai, 1604.

Brigges, Anne. *The Disclosing of a late counterfeyted possession by the devyl.* 1574.

Brightman, Thomas. *Brightman Redivivus (Posthumous Sermons).* 1647.

—— *A Revelation of the Revelation.* Amsterdam, 1615.

Brinsley, John. *The Glorie of the Latter Temple.* 1613.

—— *The Preachers Charge and the Peoples Duty.* 1631.

Brooke, Robert Greville, Lord. *A Discourse opening the nature of that Episcopacie which is exercised in England.* 1641.

—— *The Nature of Truth.* 1641.

[Broughton, Richard]. *A Defence of Catholikes persecuted in England.* Douai, 1630.

—— *A Demonstration by English Protestant pretended Bishops and Ministers.* Douai, 1616.

—— *Protestant Demonstration for Catholicks Recusancie.* Douai, 1615.

Browne, Robert. *A Treatise of Reformation Without Tarying for Anie.* Middleburg, 1582.

Browne, Thomas. *The Works of Sir Thomas Browne*. Ed. Charles Sayle. 3 vols. Edinburgh, 1927.

Buckeridge, John. *A Sermon preached at Hampton Court*. 1606.

Burton, Henry. *An Apology of an appeale*. 1636.

————— *Babel no Bethel*. 1629.

————— *The Baiting of the Pope's Bull*. 1627.

————— *A Narration of the life of Mr Henry Burton*. 1643.

————— *A Plea to an appeale*. 1626.

————— *A Tryall of Private Devotions*. 1628.

Burton, Robert. *The Anatomy of Melancholy*. 4th ed. 1632.

Busher, Leonard. *Religion's Peace; or a Plea for Liberty of Conscience*, in *Tracts on Liberty of Conscience* (Hanserd Knollys Society). 1846.

Butterfield, Robert. *Maschil*. 1629.

C., B. *Puritanism the mother, sinne the daughter*. (St. Omer,] 1633.

Cade, Anthony. *A Justification of the Church of England*. 1630.

————— *A Sermon necessary for these Times*. Cambridge, 1636.

Canfield, Benet [William Fitch]. *The Rule of Perfection*. Rouen, 1609.

Carleton, George. *Directions to know the true church*. 1615.

————— *An Examination of those things wherein the author of the late Appeale holdeth the doctrines* . . . 1626.

————— *Jurisdiction, regall, episcopall, papall*. 1610.

Case, John. *Lapsis Philosophicum*. 1599.

Chamber, John. *A Treatise against Judicial Astrologie*. 1601.

Chapman, Alexander. *Jesuitisme described*. 1610.

Chillingworth, William. *The Works of William Chillingworth*. 12th ed. 1736.

Clarendon, Edward Hyde, Earl of. *The History of the Rebellion and Civil Wars in England*. New ed. 6 vols. Oxford, 1806.

————— *Life and Continuation*. 2 vols. Oxford, 1847.

Closse, G. *The Parricide Papist or cut-throate Catholicke*. 1606.

Clyfton, Richard. *An Advertisement Concerning a Book, &c*. Amsterdam, 1612.

Coke, Sir Edward. *The First Part of the Institutes of the Laws of England*. 1628.

————— *The Reports of Sir Edward Coke*. Ed. J. H. Thomas and J. F. Frazer. 6 vols. 1826.

————— *The Second Part of the Institutes of the Laws of England*. 1642.

————— *The Third Part of the Institutes of the Laws of England*. 1644.

Colleton, John. *A Just Defence of the slandered priestes*. 1602.

Cooke, Alexander. *The Weather-cocke of Romes Religion*. 1625.

————— *Worke, More Worke and a little More Worke for a Masse Priest*. 1628.

A Coppy of a letter sent from France by Mr Walter Mountagu.

Cosin, John. *A Collection of Private Devotions*. 6th ed. 1672.

Cosin, R. *An Apologie for Sundrie Proceedings by Jurisdiction Ecclesiasticall*. 1593.

Cowell, John. *The Interpreter*. Cambridge, 1607.

Cowley, Abraham. *The Works of Mr. Abraham Cowley*. 2 vols. 11th ed. 1710.

Crakanthorpe, Richard. *A Sermon of predestination.* 1620.

———— *A Sermon at the solemnization of the happy inauguration of our most gracious and religious sovereign King James.* 1609.

Crashaw, Richard. *The Poems of Richard Crashaw.* Ed. L. C. Martin. Oxford, 1927.

Crashaw, William. *The Fatall Vesper in the Black-Friers.* 1623.

———— *The Jesuites Gospel.* 1610.

D., P. [Matthew Patterson]. *The Image of Bothe Churches.* Tournai, 1623.

Davies, Sir John. *Nosce Teipsum.* 1602.

Dekker, Thomas. *Greevous Grones for the Poore.* 1621.

Dent, Daniel. *A Sermon against Drunkennes.* Cambridge, 1628.

Dillingham, F. *A goodly and learned sermon concerning the magistrates dutie and death.* 1605.

A Discoverie of the most secret and subtile practices of the Jesuits. 1610.

Dod, John, and Cleaver, Robert. *A plaine and familiar exposition of the Ten Commandments.* 1604.

Dodd, Charles [pseud.]. *Church History of England.* Ed. M. A. Tierney. 5 vols. 1839–1843.

Donne, John. *Biathanatos.* 2d ed. 1648.

———— *Devotions upon emergent occasions.* 1624.

———— *Essays in Divinity.* Ed. Evelyn M. Simpson. Oxford, 1952.

———— *Ignatius his Conclave.* 1611.

———— *The Poems of John Donne.* Ed. H. J. C. Grierson. Oxford, 1929.

———— *Pseudo-martyr.* 1610.

———— *The Sermons of John Donne.* Ed. George R. Potter and Evelyn M. Simpson. 10 vols. Berkeley and Los Angeles, 1953–1962.

Dove, John. *An Advertisement to the English Seminaries and Jesuites.* 1610.

———— *A Perswasion to the English Recusants.* 1603.

Dow, Christopher. *Innovations unjustly charged unto the present church and state.* 1637.

Downame, George. *An aposticall injunction for unity and peace.* 1639.

———— *A Treatise concerning Antichrist.* 1603.

Downame, John. *The Christian Warfare.* 3d ed. 1612.

———— *A Guide to Godlinesse.* 1622.

———— *A Treatise of Security.* 1622.

E., O. See Sutcliffe, Matthew. *A new challenge to N.D.* 1600.

Earle, John. *Micro-cosmographie.* 1628.

Ely, Humphrey. *Certaine Briefe Notes upon a Briefe Apologie.* Paris, 1603.

Fairlambe, Peter. *A Recantation of a Brownist.* 1606.

Falkland, Lucius Cary, Viscount. *Sir Lucius Cary, late Viscount of Falkland, his Discourse of Infallibility.* 1651.

———— *The Lord Falkland his learned speech in Parliament . . . touching the Judges.* 1641.

———— *A Speech made to the House of Commons concerning Episcopacy.* 1641.

Favour, John. *Antiquitie Triumphing over Noveltie.* 1619.

Featley, Daniel. *Clavis Mystica.* 1636.
——— *The Fisher Catched in his owne net.* 1623.
——— *Pelagius Redivivus.* 1636.
——— *The Practice of Extraordinary Devotion* (2d ed. of *Ancilla Pietatis,* 1626). 1630.
——— *A Second Parallel.* 1626.
Fenton, Roger. *A Treatise against the necessary dependance upon that one head.* 1619.
The Ferrar Papers. Ed. B. Blackstone. Cambridge, 1938.
Field, Richard. *Of the Church.* 1609.
The First Part of the Protestants Proofes. Paris, 1607.
Fisher, John. *The Answere unto the nine points of controversy.* St. Omer, 1625.
Fitzherbert, Thomas. *The First Part of a Treatise concerning Policy and Religion.* Douai, 1606.
——— *Letters of Thomas Fitzherbert,* 1608–1610. Ed. L. Hicks (Catholic Record Society). 1948.
Floyd, John. *An Apology of the Holy See apostolicks Proceeding.* Rouen, 1630.
——— *The Church conquerant over humane wit.* St. Omer, 1638.
——— *The overthrow of the protestants pulpit-babels.* St. Omer, 1612.
——— *A Plea for the Reall-presence.* St. Omer, 1624.
——— *The totall summe; or, No danger of damnation.* St. Omer, 1639.
——— *A word of comfort.* St. Omer, 1623.
Fox, George. *The Journal of George Fox.* Ed. J. L. Nickalls. Cambridge, 1952.
Franciscus a Santa Clara. *Paraphrastica Expositio Articulorum Confessionis Anglicanae.* 1634.
Freake, William. *The Doctrines and Practices of the Societie of Jesuites.* 1630.
Fuller, Thomas. *The Church-History of Britain.* 1648.
——— *The History of the Worthies of England.* Ed. P. A. Nuttall. 1840.
A Gagge for the Pope and the Jesuits. 1624.
Gee, J. *The Foot out of the snare.* 1624.
Gibson, Abraham. *The Lands mourning for vain swearing.* 1613.
Gifford, George. *A Dialogue concerning Witches and Witchcraftes.* 2d ed. 1603.
Gilbert, William. *De Magnete.* Gilbert Club Translation. 1900.
Goad, T. *The Dolefull Evensong.* 1623.
Goodman, Godfrey. *The Court of King James the First.* Ed. J. S. Brewer. 2 vols. 1839.
——— *The Fall of Man.* 1616.
Goodwin, Thomas. *The Works of Thomas Goodwin.* Ed. J. C. Miller. 12 vols. Edinburgh, 1861–1866.
Gordon-Huntley, James. *A Summary of Controversies.* 2d ed. Douai, 1618.
Gore, John. *The Way to Prosper.* 3d ed. 1636.
Gosselin, Pierre. *The State Mysteries of the Jesuits.* 1623.
Gouge, William. πανοπλια του θεου: *The Whole-armour of God.* 1616.
——— *God's Three Arrowes: Plague, Famine, Sword.* 1631.

——— *A Guide to go to God.* 1626.

——— *The Sabbaths Sanctification.* 1641.

Goulart, S. (ed.). *Mémoires de l'estat de France sous Charles Neufiesme.* Paris, 1576.

Grahame, Simion. *The Passionate Sparke of a Relenting Minde.* 1604.

Greenham, Richard. *The Works of the reverend and faithful servant of Jesus Christ, Mr Richard Greenham.* 4th ed. 1605.

Greville, Fulke. *Certaine learned and eloquent workes.* 1633.

Griffith, Matthew. *Bethel, or a forme for families.* 1634.

Gurnay, Edmund. *The Demonstration of Antichrist.* 1631.

H., I. *Christianity Maintained.* 1638.

H., L. [Hutten, Leonard]. *An Answere to a Certaine Treatise of the Cross in Baptisme.* Oxford, 1625.

Hacket, John. *Scrinia Reserata.* 1693.

Hakewill, George. *An Apologie or Declaration of the power and providence of God in the government of the world.* 1630.

Hales, John. *Golden Remains of the ever memorable Mr. John Hales of Eaton College.* 3d impression. 1688.

——— *A Tract concerning Schisme and Schismaticks.* 1642.

——— *Tracts.* 1677.

——— *The Works of John Hales.* 3 vols. Glasgow, 1765.

Hall, John. *An Humble Motion to the Parliament of England concerning the Advancement of Learning.* 1649.

Hall, Joseph. *The Works of Joseph Hall.* 12 vols. Oxford, 1837.

Harrice, Robert. *Samuels Funerall.* 1622.

Harris, Robert. *A Treatise of the new covenant.* 1634.

Harsnet, Samuel. *A Declaration of egregious popish impostures.* 1603.

——— *A Discoverie of the fraudulent practises of John Darrel.* 1599.

[Hayward, Sir John]. *A Reporte of a discourse concerning supreme power in affaires of religion.* 1606.

Heigham, John. *A Devout Exposition of the Holie Masse.* Douai, 1614.

——— *The Life of our Blessed Lord.* Douai, 1622.

Helwys, Thomas. *An Advertisement or Admonition unto the Congregations which men call the New Fryelers.* Amsterdam, 1611.

——— *A Short Declaration of the Mistery of Iniquity.* 1612.

Herbert, Edward, Lord Herbert of Cherbury. *De Veritate.* Trans. M. H. Carré. Bristol, 1937.

Herbert, George. *The Poems of George Herbert.* Ed. F. E. Hutchison. Oxford, 1941.

——— *A Priest to the Temple: or the Country Parson.* 2d ed. 1671.

Heylyn, Peter. *Antidotum Lincolniense.* 1637.

——— *Cyprianus Anglicus.* 1668.

Hieron, S. *A defence of the ministers reasons for refusall of subscription.* 1607.

——— *A dispute upon the question of kneeling.* 1608.

——— *The second part of the defence of the ministers reasons.* 1608.

———— *Three Sermons: the good fight; the worth of the water of life; Davids longing and Davids love.* Cambridge, 1607.

———— *Three Sermons: a remedie for securitie; the ruine of Gods enemies; the worldlings downfall.* Cambridge, 1609.

Higgons, Theophilus. *A Sermon preached at Pauls Crosse.* 1611.

Hildersam, Arthur. *The Doctrine of Fasting and Praier.* 1633.

———— *Lectures upon the Fourth of John.* 1629.

Hill, E. T. *A Plain Path-way to Heaven.* St. Omer, 1637.

Hoard, S. *The Churchs Authority Asserted.* 1637.

———— *Gods Love to Mankind.* 1633.

Hobbes, Thomas. *Leviathan.* Everyman edition.

Hoby, Sir Edward. *A Letter to Mr T. H., the late minister.* 1609.

Holmes, Nathanael. *Usuary is Injury.* 1640.

Holyoke, Francis. *A Sermon of Obedience.* Oxford, 1610.

Homilies. *Certain Sermons or Homilies, appointed to be read in churches.* S.P.C.K. ed. 1899.

Hooker, Richard. *The Works of Mr. Richard Hooker.* Ed. John Keble. 3 vols. Oxford, 1836.

Horn, Andrew. *A Mirror for justices.* 1624.

Horn, Robert. *The Christian governour.* 1614.

Hoskins, Anthony. See I., H.

Hotman, R. *Franco-Gallia.* Paris, 1573.

Howard, William. *A Patterne of Christian Loyaltie.* 1634.

Hughes, Lewis. *Certaine Grievances or the popish errors and ungodliness of the service book.* 5th ed. 1642.

An Humble Supplication to the King's Majesty (1620), in *Tracts on Liberty of Conscience* (Hanserd Knollys Society). 1846.

Hunt, John. *An Humble Appeale to the Kings Most Excellent Majestie.* 1620.

Hurst, Thomas. *The descent of authoritie.* 1637.

Hutton, Matthew. *The Correspondence of Matthew Hutton* (Surtees Society, XVII). 1843.

Hutton, Thomas. *Reasons for Refusal of Subscription to the Booke of Common Praier, with an Answere* . . . Oxford, 1605.

I., H. [Anthony Hoskins]. *A Briefe and Cleare Declaration of sundry pointes absolutely dislyked in the lately enacted Oath of Allegiance.* [St. Omer,] 1611.

Ireland, Thomas. *The Oath of Allegiance defended.* 1610.

Jackson, Thomas. *The Works of Thomas Jackson.* 12 vols. Oxford, 1844.

Jacob, Henry. *An Attestation of Many Learned, Godly and Famous Divines.* Middleburg, 1613.

———— *A Collection of sundry matters.* Amsterdam, 1616.

———— *A Confession and Protestation of the faith of certain Christians in England.* Middleburg, 1616.

———— *The Divine Beginning and Institution of Christs true visible or ministerial Church.* Leyden, 1610.

———— *Reasons taken out of Gods Word and the best humane testimonies proving a necessitie of reforming our churches in England.* Middleburg, 1604.

———— *To the right high and mightie prince, James.* [Middleburg,] 1609.

James I. *The Correspondence of King James VI of Scotland with Sir Robert Cecil* (Camden Society). 1861.

———— *The Political Works of James I.* Ed. C. H. McIlwain. Cambridge, Mass., 1918.

———— *The Workes of the Most High and Mightie Prince, James, King of Great Britaine,* &c. 1616.

James, Thomas. *The Jesuits downefall threatened by the secular priests.* 1612.

Jeanes, Henry. *A Treatise concerning a Christians carefull abstinence from all appearance of evill.* Oxford, 1640.

Jenney, George. *A Catholike Conference between a Protestant and a Papist.* 1626.

Jessop, Edmond. *A Discovery of the Errors of the English Anabaptists.* 1623.

Johnson, Francis. *An Answer to Maister H. Jacob his defence.* Middleburg, 1600.

Johnson, George. *A Discourse of some Troubles and Excommunications in the banished English Church at Amsterdam.* Amsterdam, 1603.

Jorden, Edward. *A brief discourse of a disease called the suffocation of the mother.* 1603.

A joynt attestation . . . , avowing that the discipline of the Church of England was not impeached by the Synod of Dort. 1626.

Kellison, Matthew. *A Survey of the new Religion.* Douai, 1605.

———— *The Touchstone of the Reformed Gospel.* The last edition, more correct, 1687. (Originally, *The Gagge of the Reformed Gospell.* Douai, 1623.)

———— *A treatise of ecclesiastical hierarchy.* Douai, 1629.

King, Henry. *A Sermon preached at Pauls Crosse.* 1621.

———— *A Sermon preached at St Pauls.* 1640.

King, John. *David's Strait.* 1604.

Knott, Edward [Matthew Wilson; Nicholas Smith]. *Charity Mistaken.* 1630.

———— *Christianity Maintained.* [St. Omer,] 1638.

———— *Mercy and Truth, or Charity maintayned by Catholiques.* [St. Omer,] 1634.

Laud, William. *The Archbishop of Canterbury's Speech: or his Funerall Sermon, preached by himself.* 1645.

———— *The History of the Troubles and Tryal of . . . William Laud, Wrote by Himself.* 2 vols. 1695, 1700.

———— *A Relation of the Conference between William Laud . . . and Mr Fisher the Jesuit.* 3d ed. 1673.

———— *A Speech delivered in the Starr-chamber.* 1637.

———— *The Works of William Laud.* Ed. W. Scott and J. Bliss. 7 vols. Oxford, 1847–1860.

Lawne, Christopher. *Brownisme turned the Inside Outward.* 1613.

Lawne, Christopher *et al.* *The Prophane Schisme of Brownists or Separatists.* 1612.

Lawrence, John. *A golden trumpet to rouse up a drowsie magistrate.* 1624.

Lay Catholics. See *A petition apologeticall.*

Lechmere, Edmund [V.M.C.F.E.]. *A Disputation of the Church.* Douai, 1629.

Leighton, Alexander. *An Appeal to the Parliament; or Syons Plea against the Prelacie.* [Holland?] 1628.

——— *Epitomie or Briefe Discoverie.* 1646.

Leslie, Henry. *A Treatise of the Authoritie of the Church.* 2d ed. Dublin, 1639.

——— *A Treatise tending to Unitie.* Dublin, 1623.

Ley, John. *A Discourse concerning Puritans.* 1641.

Lilburne, John. *The Christian Mans Triall.* 2d ed. 1641.

——— *Come out of her my people.* 1639.

——— *A Coppy of a letter written by John Lilburne* [1640?].

——— *The Poor Mans Cry.* 1639.

——— *The Worke of the Beast, or A Relation of a most unchristian censure executed upon John Lilburne.* 1638.

Linaker, Robert. *A Short Catechism.* 1610.

Lloyd, David. *State Worthies.* 1670.

Loe, William. *The kings shoe.* 1623.

Luther, Martin. *A Commentary on . . . Galatians.* Ed. P. S. Watson. 1953.

M., P. D. See Patterson, Matthew.

[Maihew, Edward]. *A Treatise of the Groundes of the old and newe Religion.* 1608.

Mainwaring [Maynwaring], Roger. *Religion and Alegiance.* 1627.

Mason, Francis. *The Authoritie of the Church in making Canons and Constitutions.* 1607.

Mason, Henry. *The epicures fast.* 1635.

——— *The New Art of Lying.* 1624.

——— *The tribunall of the conscience.* 1626.

Mather, Cotton. *Magnalia Christi Americana.* 2 vols. Hartford, Conn., 1853.

Maxey, D. *Five Sermons preached before the King.* 5th ed. 1623.

Maxwell, James. *A New Eightfold Probation.* 1617.

May, Thomas. *History of the Long Parliament.* 1647.

Mayer, John. *The Englishe Catechisme.* 1623.

Mico, John. *A Pill to Purge out Poperie.* 1623.

Milton, John. *The Works of John Milton.* Columbia ed. 18 vols. New York, 1931–1938.

[Mocket, Richard]. *Deus et Rex: God and the King.* 1615.

Montagu, Richard. *Appello Caesarem.* 1624.

——— *A New Gagg for an Old Goose.* 1624.

More, Henry. *Antidote Against Atheism.* 2d ed. 1655.

Morton, Thomas. *Christus Dei, the Lords anointed, or a theological discourse wherein is proved that regall or monarchicall power is not of humane but of divine right.* Oxford, 1642.

———— *A Defence of the innocencie of the three ceremonies of the Church of England.* 1618.

———— *An Exact Discoverie of Romish Doctrine.* 1605.

———— *A Full Satisfaction concerning a double Romish iniquitie.* 1606.

———— *The Grand imposture of the (now) Church of Rome.* 1626.

———— *A Preamble unto an Incounter with P. R.* 1608.

———— *A Sermon preached before the King's Most Excellent Majesty.* Newcastle-upon-Tyne, 1639.

A Most Humble Supplication of Many of the King Majesty's Loyal Subjects, in *Tracts on Liberty of Conscience* (Hanserd Knollys Society). 1846.

Muriell, Christopher. *An Answer unto the Catholiques Supplication.* 1603.

Murton, John. *A Description of what God hath Predestinated.* 1620.

———— *Objections: Answered,* reprinted under the later title, *Persecution for Religion Judged and Condemned,* in *Tracts on Liberty of Conscience* (Hanserd Knollys Society). 1846.

N., I. [John Norden]. *A godlie man's guide to happiness.* 1624.

N., O. *An Apology of English Arminianisme.* 1634.

Nashe, Thomas. *The Works of Thomas Nashe.* Ed. R. B. McKerrow. 5 vols. 1904–1910.

Nichols, Josias. *The Plea of the Innocent.* 1602.

Norden, John. *The labyrinth of mans life.* 1614.

———— *A load-starre to spirituall life.* 1614.

O., L. See Owen, Lewis.

Objections: Answered. See Murton, John.

Omerod, Oliver. *The Picture of a Puritane.* 1605.

Overall, John. *Bishop Overall's Convocation Book* (1606). 1690.

Overbury, Thomas. *The Miscellaneous Works of Sir Thomas Overbury, Knt.* Ed. E. F. Rimbault. 1856.

Owen, David. *Herod and Pilate Reconciled.* Cambridge, 1610.

Owen, Lewis [O., L.]. *Speculum Jesuiticum, or the Jesuites looking-glasse.* 1629.

———— *The unmasking of all popish monks, friers, and Jesuits.* 1628.

Owen, Thomas. See A., T.

Oxford, *The answere of the vice-chancellor, the doctors . . . to the humble petition of the ministers.* Oxford, 1603.

P., I. *Anabaptismes Mysterie of Iniquity Unmasked.* 1623.

P., J. *Romes Ruin.* 1629.

P., M. C. [Michael Walpole]. *A Briefe Admonition to all English Catholikes.* St. Omer, 1610.

Page, William. *A Treatise of Justification of bowing at the name of Jesus.* Oxford, 1631.

Paget, John. *An Arrow against the Separation of the Brownists.* Amsterdam, 1618.

Panke, John. *The Fal of Babel.* Oxford, 1608.

Parker, Henry. *A Discourse concerning Puritans.* 2d ed. 1641.
———— *Jus Populi.* 1644.
Parr, Elnathan. *The Grounds of Divinitie.* 8th ed. 1636.
Parr, Richard. *The Life of James Usher.* 1686.
———— (ed.). *A Collection of Three Hundred Letters.* 1686.
Parsons, Bartholomew. *The Magistrates charter examined.* 1616.
Parsons [Persons], Robert. *An Answere to the Fifth Part of Reports lately set forth by Syr Edward Cooke, Kt.* St. Omer, 1607.
———— *A Briefe Apologie or Defence of the Catholicke Ecclesiastical Hierarchie.* [London?, 1602?]
———— *A Conference about the next succession to the crown of England* [pseud. N. Doleman]. [Antwerp?] 1594.
———— *The Judgment of a Catholicke English-man.* St. Omer, 1608.
———— *A Manifestation of the Great Folly and Bad Spirit of certayne . . . calling themselves secular priests.* (n.p.) 1602.
———— *Notes concerning the English Mission* (Catholic Record Society, Vol. IV). 1907.
———— *A Treatise tending to mitigation towardes Catholicke subjects in England.* St. Omer, 1607.
Patterson, Matthew. *The Image of bothe churches.* Tournai, 1623.
Pemberton, William. *The charge of God and the king to judges and magistrates.* 1619.
Perkins, William. *The Arte of Prophecying, or, A Treatise concerning the sacred and onely true manner and methode of preaching.* (Trans. Thomas Tuke). 1606.
———— *A faithful and plaine exposition upon the first two verses of the second chapter of Zephaniah.* Cambridge, 1606.
———— *The Works of . . . William Perkins.* 3 vols. Cambridge, 1609.
Perrin, I. Paul [I.P.P.L.]. *Luthers Forerunners.* 1624.
Perron, Cardinal Jacques du. *The Catholike Moderator.* Trans. 1624.
———— *A Letter written from Paris by the Lord Cardinal of Peron to Monsr. Casaubon in England.* St. Omer, 1612.
Perrot, Richard. *Iacobs Vowe.* Cambridge, 1627.
A petition apologeticall. Douai. 1604.
The Petition and Articles or Several Charges exhibited in Parliament against John Pocklington. 1641.
Philathes, Andreas. *An Answer made by one of our brethren a secular priest to Mr George Blackwell.* 1602.
Pocklington, John. *Altare Christianum.* 1637.
Powel, Gabriel. *A Consideration of the deprived and silenced ministers arguments.* 1606.
———— *A Consideration of the Papists reasons for toleration of Poperie in England.* Oxford, 1604.
Preston, John. *The Breast-Plate of faith and love.* 1630.
———— *The Golden Scepter held forth to the humble.* 1638.

———— *A Heavenly Treatise of the divine love of Christ.* 1640.
———— *Life Eternall.* 1631.
———— *The New Covenant, or the saints portion.* 1629.
———— *Plenitudo Fontis: of Christs fulness and mans emptinesse.* 1644.
———— *The Saints Qualification.* 2d ed. 1634.
———— *Summe of Divinity.* Emmanuel College MS.
———— *Two Treatises: viz. The Christian Freedom and The Deformed Forme of a formall profession.* 1641.
Preston, Thomas. See Widdrington, Roger.
Price, Sampson. *Londons Warning by Laodiceas Lukewarmness.* 1613.
Pricke, Robert. *The Doctrine of superioritie and of subjection.* 1609.
The Proceedings of the Lords and Commons in the year 1628 against Robert Mainwaring. New ed. 1709.
[Proctor, Thomas]. *The Right of kings.* 1621.
———— *The Righteous mans way.* 1621.
Prynne, William (concerning). *A Briefe Relation of certain speciall and most materiall passages . . . at the censure of . . . Dr Bastwicke, Mr Burton and Mr Prynne.* 1637.
Prynne, William. *Anti-arminianisme.* 1630.
———— *A Breviate of the life of William Laud.* 1644.
———— *A Breviate of the prelates intollerable usurpations upon the kings prerogative and the subjects liberties.* 1635.
———— *Certain Quaeres propounded to the bowers at the name of Jesus.* 4th ed. 1636.
———— *Histrio-mastix.* 1633.
———— *Lame Giles his haultings.* 1630.
———— *Lords Bishops none of the Lords Bishops.* 1640.
———— *A New Discovery of the Prelates Tyranny.* 1641.
———— *Newes from Ipswich.* [Ipswich?] 1636.
———— *XVI New Quaeries proposed to our Lord Praelates.* 1637.
Purchas, Samuel. *Purchas his Pilgrim.* 1619.
———— *Purchas his Pilgrimage.* 1613.
Quarles, Francis. *Emblemes.* 1635.
———— *Hieroglyphikes of the life of man.* 1638.
———— *Enchiridion.* 1856.
Quelch, William. *Church Customes Vindicated.* 1636.
R., I. *The Spy.* [Strasburgh?] 1628.
Rainolds, John. *The Discoverie of the Man of Sinne.* Oxford, 1614.
———— *The Overthrow of Stage-playes.* 2d ed. Oxford, 1629.
Ralegh [Raleigh], Sir Walter. *The History of the World.* 1614.
———— *The Prerogative of Parliaments in England.* Middleburg, 1628.
———— *The Works of Sir Walter Raleigh.* 8 vols. Oxford, 1829.
Randall, John. *The Description of Fleshly Lusts.* 1622.
———— *The Mysterie of Godlinesse.* 1630.
———— *The Necessitie of Righteousness.* 1622.

Randol, John. *A Sermon preacht at St Maries in Oxford concerning the Kingdoms Peace.* Oxford, 1624.

Reeve, Thomas. *The Churches Hazard.* 1632.

Reynolds, Edward. *A Sermon touching the peace and edification of the Church.* 1638.

Ridley, Sir Thomas. *A View of the civile and ecclesiastical law.* 2d ed. Oxford, 1634.

Robartes, Foulke. *The Revenue of the Gospel is Tythes.* Cambridge, 1613.

Robinson, John. *The Works of John Robinson.* 3 vols. 1851.

Rogers, Henry. *An Answer to Mr Fisher the Jesuite.* 1623.

Rogers, Timothy. *Good News from Heaven.* 1628.

———— *The righteous mans evidence for Heaven.* 1629.

———— *The Roman Catharist or the Papist is a Puritan.* 1621.

Rous, Francis. *Testis Veritatis.* 1626.

Ryves, Sir Thomas. *The Poore Vicars Plea.* 1620.

S., A. C. [Anthony Champney]. *A Manual of Controversies.* Paris, 1614.

S.R.N.T. See Scott, Thomas.

Saltmarsh, John. *The Smoke in the Temple.* 1646.

Sanderson, Thomas. *Of Romanising Recusants and Dissembling Catholicks.* 1611.

Sandys, Sir Edwin. *A Relation of the State of Religion.* 1605.

Santa Clara. See Franciscus a Santa Clara.

Sclater, William. *The Quaestion of Tythes Revised.* 1623.

Scott, Thomas. *The Second Part of Vox Populi.* 1621.

———— *Votivae Angliae, or the Desires and Wishes of England.* Utrecht, 1624.

———— *Vox Coeli, or Newes from Heaven.* Utrecht, 1624.

———— *Vox Populi, or Newes from Spayne.* [Gorcum?] 1620.

The Secret Policy of the English Society of Jesuits. 1715.

Sedgwicke, Obadiah. *Military Discipline for the Christian Souldier.* 1639.

Selden, John. *The Historie of tithes.* 1618.

———— *De Synedriis.* Amsterdam, 1679.

———— *Table Talk.* Ed. Sir F. Pollock. Selden Society ed. 1927.

Sharpe, Lionel. *A Sermon preached at Cambridge.* Cambridge, 1603.

Sheldon, Richard. *Certain General Reasons proving the Lawfulnesse of the Oath of Allegiance.* 1611.

———— *The Motives of Richard Sheldon Pr. for his just and voluntary and free renunciation of communion with the Bishop of Rome.* 1612.

Sibbes, R. *The Complete Works of Richard Sibbes.* Ed. A. B. Grossart. 7 vols. Edinburgh, 1862–1864.

Sibthorpe [Sybthorpe], Robert. *Apostolike Obedience.* 1627.

Smart, Peter. *A Catalogue of Superstitious Innovations.* 1642.

———— *The Vanitie and Downe-fall of Superstitious Popish Ceremonies.* Edinburgh, 1628.

Smith, Nicholas. *An Ecclesiastical Protestant Historie of . . . the Popes of Rome.* 1624.

———— *A Modest Briefe Discussion of some points taught by M. Doctour Kellison in his treatise of the Ecclesiasticall Hierarchy.* 2d ed. Rouen, 1630.

Smith, Sir Thomas. *The Commonwealth of England, newly corrected.* 1609.

Smyth, John. *The Works of John Smyth.* Ed. W. T. Whitley. 2 vols. Cambridge, 1915.

Something written by occasion of that fatal and memorable accident in the Blackfriars. 1623.

Southwell, Robert. *An Epistle of Comfort.* [Douai?] 1605.

Sparke, E. *The Christians Map of the World.* 1637.

Sparke, Thomas. *A Brotherly Perswasion to Unitie and Uniformitie in judgement and practise.* 1607.

Spotswood [Spottiswood], J. *The History of the Church and State of Scotland.* 4th ed. 1677.

Sprint, John. *Cassander Anglicanus.* 1618.

———— *Propositions tending to prove the necessarie use of the Christian Sabbaoth.* 1607.

Stock, Richard. *The Churches Lamentation for the losse of the godly.* 1614.

Stoughton, John. *The Magistrates Commission.* 1640.

[Stoughton, William]. *An Assertion for true and Christian Church-policie.* 1604.

Strafford. *The Earl of Strafford's Letters and Despatches.* 2 vols. 1739.

Strype, J. *The Life and Acts of John Whitgift.* 3 vols. Oxford, 1822.

Studley, Peter. *The Looking-Glasse of Schisme.* 2d ed. 1635.

Suckling, Sir John. *An Account of Religion by Reason.* Ed. of 1658.

Sutcliffe, Matthew. *A briefe replie to a certaine odious and slanderous libel lately published by a seditious Jesuit.* 1600.

———— *The Examination and confutation of a certain scurrilous treatise.* 1606.

———— [O.E.]. *A new challenge to N.D.* 1600.

———— *The subversion of Robert Parsons, his . . . worke.* 1606.

Sutton, Christopher. *Disce Vivere; Disce Mori.* 1629.

Swan, John. *A Sermon, Pointing out the chief Causes and Cures of such unruly Stirres as are not seldom to be found in the Church of God.* 1639.

———— *Speculum Mundi.* Cambridge, 1635.

T., A. *A Christian Reprofe against Contention.* Amsterdam, 1631.

T., W. [Travers, Walter]. *Vindiciae Ecclesiae Anglicanae.* 1630.

[Texeda, F.]. *Texeda Retextus.* 1623.

Tillesley, Richard. *An Animadversion upon Mr Seldens History of Tythes.* 2d ed. 1621.

Tooker, William. *Of the Fabrique of the Church.* 1604.

Torshell, Samuel. *The Three Questions of Free Justification, Christian Liberty, the Use of the Law.* 1632.

Tozer, H. *A Christian Amendment.* Oxford, 1633.

The True Relation of the Faction begun in Wisbech. 1601.

Tuke, Thomas. *A discourse of death.* 1613.

———— *The Highway to Heaven.* 1609.

———— *The Picture of a true Protestant.* 1609.

—— *A Treatise against Painting and Tincturing of Men and Women.* 1616.

Turner, Roger. *The Usurers Plea Answered.* 1634.

Twisse, William. *The Doctrine of the Synod of Dort.* n.p., n.d.

Ussher [Usher], James. *An Answer to a Challenge made by a Jesuite in Ireland.* Dublin, 1624.

—— *A Briefe Declaration of the Universalitie of the Church of Christ.* 1624.

—— *The soveraignes power and the subjects duty.* Oxford, 1644.

V.M.C.F.E. See Lechmere, Edmund.

Valentine, Henry. *God save the king.* 1639.

Vaughan, William. *Natural and artificial directions for health.* 1600.

—— *Approved directions for health.* 4th ed. 1612.

Venner, Tobias. *A brief and accurate treatise concerning the taking of the fume of Tobacco.* 1621.

Villegas, Alfonso de. *Flos sanctorum: the lives of the saints.* Rouen, 1609.

Vindiciae Contra Tyrannos. Paris, 1578.

Wakeman, R. *The Poore-mans Preacher.* 1607.

Walker, George. *Fishers Folly Unfolded.* 1624.

—— *The Summe of a Disputation.* 1624.

Walpole, Michael. See P., M. C.

Walsingham, Francis. *A Search made into matters of Religion.* [St. Omer,] 1609.

Ward, Samuel. *A Collection of such sermons as have been written by Samuel Ward.* 1628.

Warmington, William. *A Moderate Defence of the Oath of Allegiance.* 1612.

Watson, William. *Important Considerations which ought to move all true Catholikes.* [Frankfort?] 1661.

—— *A Sparing Discoverie of our English Jesuits.* [St. Omer,] 1601.

Webster, John. *Academiarum Examen.* 1653.

Welwood, James. *Memoirs of the Most Material Transactions in England.* 1700.

Whetenhall, Thomas. *A Discourse of the abuses now in question.* 1606.

White, Francis. *London's Warning by Jerusalem.* 1619.

—— *The orthodox faith and the way to the church.* 2d ed. 1624.

—— *A Replie to Jesuit Fishers Answere.* 1624.

—— *A Treatise of the Sabbath-day.* 1635.

White, John. *A Defence of the Way to the True Church.* 2d ed. 1624.

—— *The Way to the True Church.* 1624.

White, Thomas. *A Discoverie of Brownisme.* 1605.

Widdowes, Giles. *The lawlesse, kneelesse schismaticall Puritan.* Oxford, 1631.

—— *The schismaticall Puritan.* Oxford, 1631.

Widdrington, Roger [Thomas Preston]. *A New Years Gift for English Catholics.* 1620.

—— *A Theological Disputation concerning the Oath of Allegiance.* 1613.

Wilkes, William. *Obedience or ecclesiasticall union.* 1605.

Wilkins, John. *A Discourse concerning a new World.* 3d impression. 1640.

Willet, Andrew. *An Antilogie or counter plea to an apologeticall epistle.* 1603.

Williams, John. *Great Britains Salomon.* 1625.
—— *The Holy Table, Name and Thing.* 1637.
The Wisbech Stirs. Ed. P. Renold (Catholic Record Society). 1958.
Wither, George. *Britains Remembrancer* (Spenser Society Pub.). 1880.
—— *Hallelujah, or Britains Second Remembrancer.* 1857.
Wood, John. *Practicae Medicinae Liber.* 1596.
[Wotton, Anthony]. *A dangerous plot discovered.* 1626.
Yates, John. *Ibis ad Caesarem.* 1626.
Yaxlee, Henry. *Morbus et Antidotus, the Disease with the Antidote.* 1630.
Yonge, Walter. *The Diary of Walter Yonge* (Camden Society). 1848.

II. Collections of Documents

Calendar of State Papers, Domestic, James I (Cal. S. P. Dom.).
Calendar of State Papers, Scottish, 1589–93 (Cal. S. P. Scottish).
Cardwell, E. *A History of Conferences . . . connected with the Book of Common Prayer.* 3d ed. Oxford, 1849.
[*Commons' Journals*] *The Journals of the House of Commons,* Vols. I and II.
Elton, G. R. *The Tudor Constitution.* Cambridge: the University Press, 1960.
Frere, W. H., and Douglas, C. E. (eds.). *Puritan Manifestoes.* 2d ed. London: S.P.C.K., 1954.
Gardiner, S. R. (ed.). *The Constitutional Documents of the Puritan Revolution, 1625–1660.* 3d ed. Oxford: the Clarendon Press, 1962.
—— *Documents Relating to the Proceedings against William Prynne.* Camden Society. 1877.
—— *Parliamentary Debates in 1610.* Camden Society. 1862.
Historical Manuscripts Commission Reports (Hist. MSS. Com. Reports):
—— Cecil MSS.
—— Lord Montagu of Beaulieu MSS.
Kenyon, J. P. *The Stuart Constitution, 1603–1688.* Cambridge: the University Press, 1966.
[*Lords' Journals*] *The Journals of the House of Lords,* Vols. II and III.
Notestein, W., and Relf, F. H. (eds.) *Commons' Debates for 1629.* Minneapolis, 1921.
Prothero, G. W. (ed.). *Select Statutes and Other Constitutional Documents, 1558–1625.* 3d ed. Oxford, 1906.
Rushworth, John. *Historical Collections.* 1682.
Rymer, Thomas. *Foedera.* 20 vols. 1704–1732.
State Trials. Ed. Cobbett, W., and Howell, T. B. Vol. III. 1809.
Tanner, J. R. (ed.). *Constitutional Documents of the Reign of James I.* Cambridge: the University Press, 1930.
Tracts on Liberty of Conscience. Ed. E. B. Underhill for the Hanserd Knollys Society. 1846. (See under Busher, Leonard, and Murton, John.)
Wilkins, David. *Concilia Magnae Britanniae et Hiberniae.* 4 vols. 1737.

III. Secondary Works

Albion, George. *Charles I and the Court of Rome*. London: Oates & Co., 1935.

Allen, J. W. *English Political Thought, 1603–1644*. London: Methuen & Co., 1938.

———— *A History of Political Thought in the Sixteenth Century*. New ed. London: Methuen & Co., 1960.

Anderson, F. H. *The Philosophy of Francis Bacon*. Chicago: The University of Chicago Press, 1948.

Babbage, S. B. *Puritanism and Richard Bancroft*. London: S.P.C.K., 1962.

Baker, Herschel. *The Wars of Truth*. Cambridge, Mass.: Harvard University Press, 1952.

Bennett, H. S. *English Books and Readers, 1558–1603*. Cambridge: the University Press, 1965.

Bradbrook, M. C. *The School of Night*. Cambridge: the University Press, 1936.

Bredvold, Louis I. "The Religious Thought of Donne in Relation to Medieval and Later Tradition," in *Studies in Shakespeare, Milton and Donne*, by members of the English Department of the University of Michigan. New York, 1925.

Broad, C. D. *Ethics and the History of Philosophy*. London: Routledge & Kegan Paul, 1952.

Burrage, Champlin. *The Early English Dissenters*. 2 vols. Cambridge, 1912.

Butterfield, H. *The Origins of Modern Science, 1300–1800*. New York: The Macmillan Co., 1951.

Calder, I. M. *Activities of the Puritan Faction of the Church of England, 1625–1633*. London: S.P.C.K., 1957.

Carré, M. H. *Phases of Thought in England*. Oxford: the Clarendon Press, 1949.

Clark, G. N. *The Seventeenth Century*. Oxford: the Clarendon Press, 1947.

Davies, H. S., and Watson, Geo. (eds). *The English Mind*. Cambridge: the University Press, 1964.

Eusden, J. D. *Puritans, Lawyers, and Politics in Early Seventeenth Century England*. New Haven: Yale University Press, 1958.

Forster, John. *Sir John Eliot*. 2 vols. 1864.

Gardiner, S. R. *History of England, 1603–1642*. New ed. 10 vols. 1895.

———— *History of the Great Civil War, 1642–1649*. New ed. 4 vols. 1897.

Hall, A. R. *The Scientific Revolution, 1500–1800*. Boston: Beacon Press, 1956.

Hill, Christopher. *Economic Problems of the Church*. Oxford: the Clarendon Press, 1956.

———— *Intellectual Origins of the English Revolution*. Oxford: the Clarendon Press, 1965.

———— *Society and Puritanism in Pre-Revolutionary England*. London: Martin Secker & Warburg, 1964.

Holdsworth, Sir William. *A History of English Law.* Vol. V and Vol. VI (1924).

Hughes, P. *Rome and the Counter-Reformation in England.* London: Burns Oates, 1942.

James, D. G. *The Dream of Learning.* Oxford: the Clarendon Press, 1951.

Jones, R. F. *Ancients and Moderns.* 2d ed. Berkeley: University of California Press, 1965.

Jordan, W. K. *The Development of Religious Toleration in England,* Vol. II. Cambridge, Mass.: Harvard University Press, 1936.

———— *Philanthropy in England 1480–1660.* London: Allen & Unwin, 1959.

Knowles, David. *The English Mystical Tradition.* New York: Harper & Brothers, 1961.

Lamont, W. M. *Marginal Prynne, 1600–1669.* London: Routledge & Kegan Paul, 1963.

Lafrance, Pierre. *Sir Walter Raleigh Ecrivain.* Quebec: Presses de l'université Laval, 1968.

Mathew, David. *Catholicism in England.* London: Eyre & Spottiswood, 1936.

Merton, Robert K. *Science, Technology and Society in Seventeenth Century England* (*Osiris*, Vol. IV, Pt. 2). Bruges: Saint Catherine Press, 1938.

Murdock, K. B. *The Sun at Noon.* New York: The Macmillan Co., 1939.

Neale, Sir J. E. *Elizabeth I and her Parliaments.* 2 vols. London: Jonathan Cape, 1953, 1957.

Nicolson, Marjorie H. *The Breaking of the Circle.* Evanston: Northwestern University Press, 1950.

Nuttall, G. F. *The Holy Spirit in Puritan Faith and Experience.* Oxford: Blackwell, 1946.

Orr, R. R. *Reason and Authority.* Oxford: the Clarendon Press, 1968.

Pattison, Mark. *Essays.* 2 vols. Oxford, 1889.

Pocock, J. G. A. *The Ancient Constitution and the Feudal Law.* Cambridge: the University Press, 1958.

Porter, H. C. *Reformation and Reaction in Tudor Cambridge.* Cambridge: the University Press, 1958.

Raven, C. E. *Natural Religion and Christian Theology.* Vol. I, *Science and Religion.* Cambridge: the University Press, 1953.

———— *Science, Religion and the Future.* Cambridge: the University Press, 1943.

Rhys, H. H. (ed.). *Seventeenth Century Science and the Arts.* Princeton: Princeton University Press, 1961.

Rowse, A. L. *The England of Elizabeth.* London: Macmillan & Co., 1953.

Salmon, J. H. M. *The French Religious Wars in English Political Thought.* Oxford: the Clarendon Press, 1959.

Seventeenth Century Studies Presented to Sir Herbert Grierson. Oxford: the Clarendon Press, 1938.

Spedding, J. *Letters and Life of Sir Francis Bacon.* 7 vols. 1861–1874.

Stone, L. *The Crisis of the Aristocracy, 1558-1641.* Oxford: the Clarendon Press, 1965.

Taunton, E. L. *The History of the Jesuits in England.* 1901.

Taylor, A. E. *Philosophical Studies.* London: Macmillan & Co., 1934.

Tillyard, E. M. W. *The Elizabethan World Picture.* London: Chatto & Windus, 1943.

Thorne, S. E. *Sir Edward Coke, 1552-1952.* London: Quaritch, 1957.

Trevor-Roper, H. R. *Archbishop Laud.* 2d ed. London: Macmillan & Co., 1962.

———— *Historical Essays.* London: Macmillan & Co., 1957.

Usher, R. G. *The Reconstruction of the English Church.* 2 vols. 1910.

Watkin, E. I. *Roman Catholicism in England from the Reformation to 1950.* London: Oxford University Press, 1957.

Weber, Kurt. *Lucius Cary, Second Viscount Falkland.* New York: Columbia University Press, 1940.

Wedgwood, C. V. *The King's Peace, 1637-1641.* London: Collins, 1955.

Welsby, P. A. *Lancelot Andrewes, 1555-1626.* London: S.P.C.K., 1958.

Whitley, W. T. *A History of British Baptists.* 1923.

Willey, Basil. *The English Moralists.* New York: Norton, 1964.

Willson, D. H. *King James VI and I.* New York: Oxford University Press, 1956.

Wilson, F. P. *Elizabethan and Jacobean.* 2d imp. Oxford: the Clarendon Press, 1956.

Woodhouse, A. S. P. (ed.). *Puritanism and Liberty.* London: J. M. Dent & Sons, 1938.

Wormald, B. H. G. *Clarendon: Politics, Historiography and Religion.* 2d ed. Cambridge: the University Press, 1964.

INDEX